THE GLOBAL MIGRATION CRISIS

Challenge to States and to Human Rights

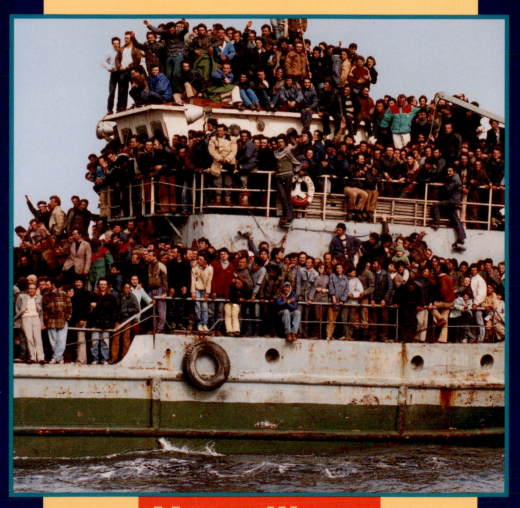

MYRON WEINER

THE GLOBAL MIGRATION CRISIS

The HarperCollins Series in Comparative Politics

Series Editors
Gabriel A. Almond
Lucian W. Pye

Almond/Powell	*Comparative Politics Today: A World View,* Fifth Edition
Almond/Powell/Mundt	*Comparative Politics: A Theoretical Framework*

Country Studies

Barghoorn/Remington	*Politics in the USSR,* Third Edition
Bill/Springborg	*Politics in the Middle East,* Fourth Edition
Dalton	*Politics in Germany,* Second Edition
Ehrmann/Schain	*Politics in France,* Fifth Edition
Pye	*China: An Introduction,* Fourth Edition
Richardson/Flanagan	*Politics in Japan*
Rose	*Politics in England,* Fifth Edition
Wiarda	*Politics in Iberia*

Analytic Studies

Monroe	*The Economic Approach to Politics*
Rustow/Erickson	*Comparative Political Dynamics*
Weiner/Huntington	*Understanding Political Development*

THE GLOBAL MIGRATION CRISIS

Challenge to States and to Human Rights

Myron Weiner
Massachusetts Institute of Technology

HarperCollinsCollegePublishers

Acquisitions Editor: Leo A. W. Wiegman
Project Editor: Susan Goldfarb
Text and Cover Designer: Alice Fernandes-Brown
Cover Photo: Reuters/Bettman
Electronic Production Manager: Alexandra Odulak
Manufacturing Manager: Alexandra Odulak
Electronic Page Makeup: Alice Fernandes-Brown
Table Makeup: Paul Lacy
Printer and Binder: RR Donnelley & Sons, Inc.
Cover Printer: RR Donnelley & Sons, Inc.

Portions of Chapter 6 reprinted from *International Migration and Security*, edited by Myron Weiner (Boulder, Colo.: Westview Press, 1993) by permission of Westview Press, Boulder, Colorado.

**The Global Migration Crisis: Challenge to States
and to Human Rights**

Library of Congress Cataloging-in-Publication Data

Weiner, Myron.
    The global migration crisis : challenge to states and to human rights / Myron Weiner.
      p.   cm.
    Includes bibliographical references and index.
    ISBN 0-06-500232-6
    1. Emigration and immigration—Government policy. 2. Immigrants—Government policy. 3. Refugees—Government policy. 4. Human rights. I. Title.
JV6271.W45   1995
325'.09'049—dc20
                                       94-38941
                                            CIP

95 96 97 9 8 7 6 5 4 3 2 1

CONTENTS

TABLES

PREFACE

This book examines the crises that have arisen as a result of the worldwide increase in migration across national boundaries. Every year millions of people leave their countries, fleeing violence, discrimination, or repressive regimes; searching for employment; or eager to join their families. These flows are truly global as people move from south to north, from east to west, and from one developing country to another. Some countries welcome immigrants; others merely permit them to enter; still others do what they can to seal their borders. Some governments see migrants taking jobs that others do not want, adding cultural diversity, and often invigorating the economy through their enterprise. They particularly welcome newcomers with whom they have a special cultural kinship. But more often, governments fear that migration will mean a loss of jobs for their citizens, cultural swamping, ethnic conflict, and higher welfare costs. They regard migrants as a threat to their political stability and national security and as a source of conflict with other states. These concerns are by no means confined to the rich industrial countries, for much of the burden of refugees and unwanted migrants is also felt by countries in the Third World. Indeed, almost everywhere, governments and their citizens in population-receiving countries have become concerned with the problems posed by international migration rather than with the benefits they provide and the needs they serve.

How these problems are defined varies greatly from one country to another. Countries that already have large numbers of migrants have either to determine how best to incorporate them, whether through assimilation or multiculturalism, or to induce or force the migrants to return home. Countries also have to decide how best to respond to pressures of people who seek admission—as legal migrants, as refugees, or as illegals. Should anyone be admitted? If so, how many, and how should they be chosen? Should migrants be admitted on the basis of a country's need for labor and its desire to admit people of the same culture, or should admission be based on the needs of the people who seek to enter, especially those who are fleeing persecution and violence? Is it, in any event, possible for governments to control who enters their countries, or are the forces of the global economy and worldwide political disorders so great as to overwhelm the capacity of states to control their borders? Alternatively, can and should governments attempt to change the conditions within states that produce refugee flows and illegal migrants? Does the worldwide flow of people mean an end to sovereignty, that is, the capacity of states to control their territory and define their membership? And if there are limits to what individual states can do, what role can be played by regional and international institutions? To deal with these issues, it is essential that we first consider how they are presently viewed by governments and international institutions attempting to cope with the international global migration crisis.

This book is guided by one methodological assumption, (at least) one normative assumption, and a particular policy perspective. The methodological assumption is that one should take perceptions and fears seriously and not dismiss them as irrational, xenophobic, or paranoid. Throughout this book, therefore, I am concerned with how governments and their citizens define the problems. If there is a single lodestar to this study, it is therefore to see global migration in a political context by considering the reactions to international migration within countries, the conflicts that these movements generate within and between states, and the difficult political choices that then confront governments and international institutions.

The normative assumption is that there is often a conflict between the moral obligations of governments to ensure the safety and well-being of their own populations and a more universal ethic that values the well-being of all humankind, irrespective of where people live. Even governments with the most liberal entry policies are not able to provide asylum to all people in the world whose human rights are violated and who live in the shadow of violence and poverty. It serves no purpose to assume that all moral claims can be equally served.

The policy perspective is that the problems created by international population movements differ greatly from one country to another. Some countries are in a position to accept and integrate large numbers of immigrants and refugees, while others are not. Some have the military, administrative, and political capacity to limit, if not control, who can enter; others do not. Some can intervene in the politics and economies of countries that produce emigrants and refugees; others cannot. Nor for that matter are states autonomous in the choices they make. Governments are constrained by the choices of other governments. And so it is necessary to understand how governments influence one another's exit and entry rules. Above all, one should not assume that global problems necessarily require or are amenable to global solutions. Solutions to the problems posed by unwanted international migration cannot easily be formulated into sound bites like increasing global trade or international aid or population policy or closed borders. Indeed, no general policy framework and no analytical model can encompass the diversity of state capacities or intentions. I am reminded of the economist who presented to his audience a formal model, internally consistent, elegant in its formulation, and brilliantly articulated. During the question period, a member of the audience provided an empirical example that contradicted the model. "Ah," said the economist, "reality is a special case."

This book tries to fill some wide chasms in the study of international migration. Economists and demographers have largely been concerned with individual or family migrant decision making and have paid rather less attention to how the exit and entry policies of states constrain individual and family decision making. Experts on refugees have primarily been concerned with human rights and protection, not with the concerns of host populations or their governments. Scholars of international relations have generally paid little attention to refugee flows, seeing them principally as consequences of international conflict, hardly ever as a determinant of conflict. Similarly, scholars of nationalism and ethnic conflict look on refugees as victims, rarely as actors who themselves play a role in generating conflicts. Political philosophers and ethicists have focused on issues of global justice, but their concerns are often far removed from the realm of political realities. And international lawyers pay more attention to international norms than to the capacities of international institutions.

I have tried to build a few bridges across these divides, but the bridges are made of rope rather than of steel girders, and they may wobble in the wind. Still, I will be content if readers will feel that I have identified problems that they have not seen before or that they will now see them in a somewhat different light.

PLAN OF THE BOOK

Each chapter of this book examines one or more dimensions of the global migration crisis. Chapter 1 amplifies what I mean by a global migration crisis. What are its various manifestations, and under what circumstances and for whom does migration become a crisis? Chapter 2 considers why there has been such a massive increase in the number of people who want to leave their home country. To what extent is it the result of the globalization of trade, communication, and transportation and to what extent the result of the politics and policies of sending countries?

Chapter 3 explores the migration crisis for Western Europe, Japan, and Australia, focusing on the political debate over admission and absorption. The central issues confronting Western Europe include the cultural and political difficulties of absorbing migrant populations, illegal entries, and the massive influx of asylum seekers. For Japan, a country that from time immemorial has been closed to outsiders, the increasing number of illegal migrants has raised the question of whether to have an immigration policy and whether it is possible to absorb people who are not racially Japanese. By way of contrast, Australia provides us with an example of a country that has chosen to diversify itself through migration and is consequently in the process of redefining its national identity.

Chapter 4 examines the process and the conflicts that arise over the absorption of immigrants in both developed and developing countries. What are the conditions for successful absorption? What can states demand of their migrants? And what changes need to take place within countries to accommodate to a migrant population? The chapter first considers the various efforts by governments to avoid the need to absorb immigrants, particularly the attempts of Western European and Persian Gulf countries to prevent permanent settlement. Opposition to migrants is examined in the United States, Western Europe, and several developing countries. The chapter then considers some of the factors that facilitate absorption, including the attitudes of the host population, citizenship legislation, the preferences of the immigrants themselves, and the structure of the labor market.

Chapter 5 considers how migration policies influence and are influenced by relations among states. The starting point is an examination of how different rules of emigration and immigration affect the relations that countries have with one another. Today, exit and entry rules, like import and export rules, are no longer purely sovereign decisions that states can make without regard for the views and rules of others. The compatibility or incompatibility of exit and entry rules therefore plays a central role in whether or not population movements between countries create international political conflict. An analysis of the political role played by the migrants themselves in shaping relations between their country of origin and their host society follows. Finally, we show that as migration policies have become issues in international relations rather than a purely domestic matter, the policy processes of states are changing.

Chapter 6 examines the perceived threats of unwanted population movements to the national security and internal political stability of states. It categorizes the various types of threats and reviews how states have reacted to them.

Chapter 7 looks at the crisis from the point of view of the international institutions dealing with international migration. It examines the challenges confronting international agencies faced with millions of refugees and internally displaced persons and how the United Nations High Commissioner for Refugees has been transformed from an agency principally concerned with the protection of refugees within host societies into one focused on humanitarian in-country assistance aimed at enabling people to stay. A major concern of this chapter is with the tensions between European governments overwhelmed with the population influx and fearful of its political consequences, on the one hand, and the United Nations agencies' concern with human rights and the protection of refugees, on the other.

Chapter 8 addresses the moral crisis posed by international population movements, focusing on the debate over the obligations of states toward migrants and refugees. In whose interests should migration and refugee policies be formulated? What are the moral claims of refugees? Is it morally acceptable for states to create a system of humane deterrence to separate out immigrants whose claims are unwarranted? Should asylum seekers be granted citizenship or given temporary resident status, and in the latter case, under what conditions is repatriation warranted? Do indigenous peoples have greater rights than settlers? Finally, how should democratic governments respond to the preferences of their citizens, who may be xenophobic, antimigrant, and antirefugee? A major aim of this chapter is to determine when moral considerations, as distinct from national self-interests and national values, should enter into policies.

The concluding chapter considers three ways in which states might meet the global crisis of migration: accommodation, control, and intervention. Are international population movements so inevitable and uncontrollable that states should accommodate these flows and focus not on how to stop them but on how best to absorb who comes? Alternatively, should they seek to control their borders even if it means establishing a system of *internal* controls? Or should they intervene in the countries producing unwanted migrants and refugees? Do states, individually or collective, have a morally justifiable right—or even a moral obligation—to intervene in states that create refugee flows? What interventions are desirable and feasible, with what costs and consequences?

We conclude with a discussion of whether the global migration crisis can be met by any principles that will satisfy both what states regard as their national interests and the concerns of human rights advocates for moral justice.

* * *

Many institutions and individuals made this study possible. I am especially grateful to the John D. and Catherine T. MacArthur Foundation for funding my research and writing in 1992–1993. Earlier, support from the Ford Foundation enabled me to conduct research on migration in South Asia, and a grant from the Social Science Research Council and the American Council of Learned Societies allowed me to conduct research in the Persian Gulf. The Alfred Sloan Foundation provided support to the MIT Inter-University Seminar on International Migration for a workshop on international migration and security. MIT, through its exchange program with Balliol College, provided me with an opportunity to spend a semester at Balliol, where I had access to the extraordinary library facilities of Oxford University, including the materials at the Refugee Studies Programme of Queen Elizabeth House.

I should like to thank a number of institutions whose materials were made available to me and/or whose officials I interviewed: the United Nations High Commissioner for Refugees, the International Organization for Migration, the International Labour Organization, and the Office of Intergovernmental Consultations, all in Geneva; the Ministry of Migration and Ethnic Affairs in Canberra, Australia; Amnesty International and the Minority Rights Group in London; the Refugee Policy Group and the Immigration Policy Project of the Carnegie Endowment for International Peace, both in Washington, D.C.; the Commission of the European Community and the UNHCR liaison office to the commission, both in Brussels; and government officials and others in New Delhi, Dhaka, Colombo, Kathmandu, Islamabad, Kuwait, Abu Dhabi, Manama, Ruwi, Muscat, and Bahrain.

My grateful thanks to those who commented on drafts of chapters and on articles on which these chapters were subsequently based: Hayward Alker, William Alonso, Rogers Brubaker, Joseph Carens, Nazli Choucri, Ethel P. Churchill, Paul Demeny, Lawrence Fuchs, James Hollifield, Donald Horowitz, Robert Jervis, Peter Katzenstein, Steven Krasner, Robert Lucas, Rosemarie Rogers, Sharon Russell, Andrew Shacknove, Eugene Skolnikoff, Oded Stark, Michael Teitelbaum, Robert W. Tucker, Nicholas Van Hear, and Aristide Zolberg. I have profited from the dissertations and research papers of current and past political science students at MIT: Clifford Bob, Ellie Glazel Brown, Karen Jacobsen, Elizabeth Leeds, Colin MacAndrews, Nithya Nagarajan, Elizabeth N. Offen, and Steven Ian Wilkinson. I received a great deal of efficient administrative and editorial help from Lois Malone. My research assistant, Cathy Scholz, deserves special thanks for her careful editing of the manuscript.

I was able to test out some of my ideas by giving lectures and seminar presentations at a number of institutions, including the Refugee Studies Programme at Oxford University; the Demographic Institute of the University of Indonesia in Jakarta; the Urban Studies Programme of Technion University in Haifa; the MIT Center for International Studies; the Woodrow Wilson School at Princeton University; the Center for Population Studies at Harvard University; the Population Council in New York; the American Academy of Arts and Sciences in Cambridge, Massachusetts; the International Studies Center of the University of Göttingen; the National Defense College in Washington, D.C.; the Special Program for Urban and Regional Studies at MIT; and the Center of Asian Studies of the University of Hong Kong.

Portions of several chapters have appeared in various journals and books. Sections of Chapter 2 appeared in "International Emigration and the Third World," in William Alonso, ed., *Population in an Interacting World* (Cambridge, Mass.: Harvard University Press, 1987). Materials in Chapter 4 appeared in "Citizenship and Migration: Implications for Liberal Democracies," in Edward Banfield, ed., *Civility and Citizenship* (New York: Paragon House, 1992); in "Immigration: Perspectives from Receiving Countries," *Third World Quarterly,* January 1990, pp. 140–165; and in "International Migration and Development: Indians in the Persian Gulf," *Population and Development Review,* March 1982, pp. 1–36. Portions of Chapter 5 appeared in "International Migration and International Relations," *Population and Development Review,* September 1985, pp. 441–456; in "International Population Movements: Implications for Foreign Policies and Migration Policies," in Donald Horowitz, ed., *Immigration and Integration: American and French Experience* (New York: New York University Press, 1992); and in "Asian Immigrants and U.S. Foreign Policy," in Robert W. Tucker, Charles B. Keely, and Linda Wrigley, eds., *Immigration and U.S. Foreign Policy* (Boulder: Westview Press, 1990). Portions of Chapter 6 appeared in "Security, Stability and International Migration," *International Security,* Winter 1992–1993, pp. 91–126, and in Myron Weiner, ed., *International Migration and Security* (Boulder: Westview Press, 1993). Some of the ideas in Chapter 8 were initially put forth in "The Moral Implications of International Population Movements," in *Bulletin of the American Academy of Arts and Sciences,* December 1992, pp. 7–16.

Myron Weiner

chapter 1

THE CRISIS DEFINED

In virtually every world capital, the flow of people is regarded with alarm. In Bonn, Paris, Bern, Vienna, Brussels, and other European centers, the major concerns are how to deal with a large-scale refugee influx from the Balkans, Eastern Europe, and the Third World; how to integrate millions of guest workers and their locally born children; what to do about illegal migration; and how to cope with the growth of antiforeign political parties. In the early 1990s, Germany became alarmed by the growing number of asylum seekers who were fleeing not political persecution or violence but simply economic deprivation. Paris is now concerned about the potential flight of refugees from an Algeria threatened by Islamic fundamentalism. In Washington, D.C., the key concerns are over Haitian, Cuban, and Chinese boat people; illegal migrants from Mexico and elsewhere; the burgeoning number of requests for asylum at U.S. airports; and the widespread violation of laws banning the employment of undocumented aliens. In Moscow, there is anxiety over the fate of Russian settlers in the Baltic states, the governments of which have established language and citizenship policies that may lead to a Russian exodus. In Japan, the primary concerns are the illegal population influx from China and Southeast Asia, the prospects of further refugee flows from Asia, and whether to formulate a guest worker policy.

Concern is not confined to advanced industrial countries. In the Pakistani capital, Islamabad, the issues are how to induce Afghan refugees to return home and whether to respond to the demands of Urdu-speaking residents of Bangladesh who want to migrate to Pakistan. In Johannesburg, hawkers complain of competition from illegal migrant traders from Mozambique, Zimbabwe, and China, while the new government debates whether to pursue a policy of Africanization or indigenization in high-skilled employment. In India, Bangladeshis flow illegally into Assam and into Delhi, and Dhaka worries that India may expel them. The Thai government is concerned over the growing illegal influx of hundreds of thousands of Burmese in search of employment. In Egypt, the government fears that UN sanctions against Libya will lead to the expulsion of thousands of Egyptian migrant workers from Libya to Egypt, adding to the country's unemployment and strengthening Islamic fundamentalist groups. Jordan remains concerned over the presence of large numbers of Palestinians who were forced to leave Kuwait after the Gulf War. And in Africa, country after country has been overwhelmed with the influx of refugees from Rwanda, Angola, Liberia, Ethiopia, Somalia, and Sudan.

The number of people fleeing to escape violence or persecution, to find employment, or to improve their own lives and those of their family members is

1

greater than it has ever been. Owing to the end of the cold war, the barriers to emigration have been removed from the successor states to the Soviet Union and from Eastern Europe, and pressure for entry has consequently grown throughout Western Europe. Large numbers of migrants from Eastern Europe, North Africa, and Asia have obtained legal entry as permanent residents or guest workers in North America, Western Europe, and the Persian Gulf. Other migrants languish in refugee camps in Africa, the Middle East, South Asia, and Hong Kong and along Cambodia's borders, victims of ethnic conflict, repressive and rapacious regimes, and civil wars. Many have fled their homes for other regions of their country. Still others have illegally crossed borders at night, crowded ramshackle ships, or landed at airports without papers, hoping to win legal asylum or quietly and illegally slip into the labor market to find employment in small businesses, shops, restaurants, households, and agriculture.

According to the United Nations Population Fund, in 1993 there were 100 million migrants worldwide—including 15.5 million migrants in Western Europe; 20 million in the United States; 8 million in Australia and Canada; and several million in the Gulf states, where they make up a majority of the workforce—and 19 million refugees.[1] These figures do not include the growing number of illegal migrants who fail to appear in official census statistics: an estimated 280,000 in Japan in 1992, a million illegal migrants to Malaysia from Indonesia and Thailand,[2] several million Bangladeshis in India's northeastern state of Assam, over 3 million in the United States, and significant numbers in Spain, Portugal, and Italy. Nor do these numbers include the many people who migrated within their own country—say, from Russia to Kazakhstan, Latvia, Estonia, and Ukraine or across republic boundaries within Yugoslavia—who became international migrants when their country disintegrated.

The number of refugees worldwide has been growing at an alarming pace, from 2.8 million in 1976 to 8.2 million in 1980, 11.6 million in 1985, 17.2 million in 1990, 18.2 million in 1992, and 18.9 million in 1993.[3] In the 1970s, Indochina produced 2 million refugees; in the 1980s, Afghanistan produced 6 million refugees; and in the early 1990s, there was a large outpouring of refugees from the former Yugoslav republics. Another 24 to 25 million are displaced persons within the borders of their own countries, often looking for opportunities to leave.

In many countries, citizens have become fearful that they are now being invaded not by armies and tanks but by migrants who speak other languages, worship other gods, belong to other cultures, and, they fear, will take their jobs, occupy their land, live off the welfare system, and threaten their way of life, their environment, and even their polity. A recent survey in New York City, the world's quintessential immigrant city, with a foreign-born population of 2.1 million, or 28 percent, found that most residents believed that the number of recent immigrants was too high, a

1. United Nations Population Fund, *The 1993 State of the World Population Report* (New York: United Nations, 1993).

2. Malaysia government officials have expressed concern over the security implications of a growing Indonesian population within the country. "It is a question of sovereignty," said Senator Mohamed Nasri Abdul Aziz, a member of the ruling United Malays National Organisation. "We cannot simply become an extension of another country by allowing people to walk in" (*Far Eastern Economic Review*, August 6, 1992, p. 21).

3. United Nations High Commissioner for Refugees, *The State of the World's Refugees* (New York: Penguin, 1994), p. 3.

majority saw illegal immigrants as a serious terrorist threat, and an overwhelming number believed that the bombing of the World Trade Center in February 1993 would not have occurred if controls over immigrant had been tighter.[4] Similar surveys in Western Europe found growing hostility to foreigners and support for proposals to restrict further entry. Virtually every country in Western Europe now has a right-wing antiforeign political party or movement—the British National Party in the United Kingdom, the Lega Nord in Italy, Jean-Marie Le Pen's National Front in France, the Liberal Party in Austria, the Republican Party in Germany, and the Vlaams Blok in Belgium. Many citizens feel that their governments have lost control of their borders, and governments are in turn alarmed by the growing hostility of their citizens to the foreigners living and working in their midst. A public opinion survey conducted by the European Community released in July 1993 reported that 52 percent of respondents said that there were too many immigrants.[5] A *New York Times*/CBS News poll reported growing anti-immigrant sentiment in the United States.[6] The survey reported that 61 percent of the people answering a national telephone survey wanted a decrease in the number of immigrants, compared with 42 percent in a 1977 Gallup poll. One reason for the increase is the popular belief that a large percentage of the immigrants are in the country illegally. Fully 68 percent of respondents agreed that "most people who have moved to the United States in the last few years are here illegally." In 1986, only 49 percent expressed this view. Interestingly, the 1993 survey reported that only 36 percent believed that most immigrants "take jobs away from American citizens," whereas 55 percent said that immigrants "mostly take jobs Americans don't want," not very different from the 1986 survey, in which the figures were 34 percent and 52 percent, respectively. Concern over illegals appears to be a more important element in the growth of antimigrant sentiment than a concern over immigrants taking jobs, even in a recession. The global recession has, however, been an important factor in the growth of hostility toward migrants. Migrant entrepreneurs may establish businesses that produce jobs; migrants may expand consumer demand for goods; migrants may take jobs that local people do not want; nonetheless, in the midst of a recession, there is a widespread concern, often felt most by low-skilled natives, that jobs are being taken by illegals. Moreover, many state and local governments in the United States regard migrants, especially illegal migrants, as a short-term drain on the welfare system, health services, and education.

The sense of crisis is not confined to advanced industrial societies.[7] The bulk of the world's refugees and immigrants are moving from one developing country to another. In portions of Pakistan, India, Bangladesh, Thailand, Mauritania, Senegal, Congo, Nigeria, and Libya, local citizens or their governments have turned against foreigners. In many countries, the burden of feeding and housing large numbers of

4. *New York Times,* October 19, 1993, p. B4.

5. *New York Times,* August 10, 1993, p. A8.

6. *New York Times,* June 26, 1993, p. 16.

7. Some people in the West do, however, see the migration crisis primarily in terms of the movement from south to north or, in racial terms, from nonwhite to white countries. For many Western countries, the central feature of the global migration crisis is that migration no longer flows from the core to the periphery but from the periphery to the core, resulting in changes in the racial, religious, and ethnic composition of advanced industrial societies.

refugees has placed acute strains on society. The flow of illegal migrants in search of land or employment has often led to violence, with local people fearful that they will lose their land and their jobs to people who are prepared to accept work at lower wages. International institutions, particularly the United Nations High Commissioner for Refugees (UNHCR) and the International Red Cross, are overwhelmed with the costs of handling refugees and internally displaced people fleeing violence and repression. And no one has a clear vision as to how to change the conditions within countries that induce people to leave their homes.

BENIGN PHENOMENON OR GROWING THREAT?

Not too many years ago, worldwide population movements were not regarded as particularly threatening. In the 1950s and 1960s, Western European countries imported several million migrant guest workers from Turkey, North Africa, and Southern Europe to meet the labor demands of their rapidly growing economies. The United States expanded its intake too, drawing migrants from Asia and Latin America. Australia ended its "white Australia" policy and opened its borders to immigrants from Asia and the Middle East. In the mid-1970s, the oil-producing countries of the Persian Gulf recruited migrant workers from other Arab countries and from Asia—so many, in fact, that in several countries there were more foreigners than natives in the labor force.

So long as economies were growing, both industrial and oil-producing countries were willing and often eager to welcome migrants. Governments and economists regarded migration as beneficial to both sending and receiving countries; for sending countries, it provided a way to reduce unemployment and earn remittances, and for receiving countries, it provided a way to satisfy labor shortages. Such positive views of migration were mitigated only by concerns with a "brain drain" of European scientists to the United States and of highly educated people from the Third World to the West.

In contrast, refugee flows were regarded as a problem. At the end of the Second World War, 7 million displaced persons in Allied occupied zones were in need of repatriation. This task was assumed by several new international institutions, such as the United Nations Relief and Rehabilitation Agency and the International Organization for Migration. Some 12 million Germans were moved from Eastern Europe when Germany's eastern borders were redrawn. Starting in the late 1940s, with the establishment of new states in Africa, the Middle East, and South and Southeast Asia, the number of refugees again increased, primarily as people fled from one newly independent country to another. Many observers believed that the turmoil that led large numbers of people to become refugees was temporary, the result of revolutionary upheavals in some states (Cuba, China, Iran), violent rivalries or ethnic clashes among newly independent states, and conflicts exacerbated by superpower rivalries. Although some of the flows were enormous— some 14 million people moved between India and Pakistan in 1947 and 1948—they were also perceived as short-lived. Both sending and receiving countries often regarded migration as a necessary concomitant of the redrawing of boundaries, an "exchange" of populations, as it were, and of what was then euphemistically called "nation building."

Many observers also regarded some of the refugee flows as the result of great power interventions—in Cambodia, Laos, Vietnam, Angola, Mozambique, the Horn of Africa, Central America, and Afghanistan. If only the great powers would remove themselves from these internal conflicts, it was said, in time the violence and the refugee flows would subside.

Starting in the early 1970s, many countries developed a less benign view of international migration. The countries of Western Europe no longer needed imported labor. They also had large numbers of foreign guest workers who did not wish to return home and to whom governments were unwilling or reluctant to grant citizenship. As many observers have noted, governments had hoped to import migrants as labor but soon found that the migrants were people with a will of their own. Though foreign workers were no longer recruited, the wives and children of workers soon migrated into the country. Despite a worldwide recession, the flow of migrants in search of employment continued. As governments became more restrictive on legal migration, illegal migration and claims for asylum increased.

The movement of people across borders has become less acceptable to developing countries as well. Already overburdened with large-scale rural-to-urban migration, many governments have become concerned with an influx of foreigners into their already congested urban centers. Local ethnic groups, increasingly self-conscious and organized, want to halt the flow of ethnic strangers, for both economic and cultural reasons. Nativist movements have begun to flourish in the Third World as they have in advanced industrial countries.

Worldwide refugee flows show no sign of abating. To the contrary, there has been an increase in the numbers of people from the Third World fleeing across borders. Within Africa alone, the number of refugees increased from 2.7 million in 1981 to 5.4 million in 1992, and in Asia, it went from 4.6 million in 1981 to 7.2 million in 1992. Wars in Yugoslavia and in the former Soviet Union have also resulted in a massive increase in refugees in Europe, from 600,000 in 1981 to 3.6 million in 1992. Growing numbers of refugees have sought asylum in the United States and in Western Europe, over 400,000 alone in Germany in 1992.[8] Though many are genuine refugees, others are economically motivated migrants using the asylum claim as a way of getting into countries that they cannot enter under migration laws. Furthermore, the war in the Persian Gulf generated still more new flows of refugees and displaced persons (most of whom were not classified as refugees because they were returning home) from Saudi Arabia to Yemen and from Kuwait and Iraq to South and Southeast Asia. The list of countries now producing refugees is long: Afghanistan, former Yugoslavia, Rwanda, Mozambique, Somalia, Ethiopia, Eritrea, Liberia, Angola, Azerbaijan, Tajikistan, Burma, Haiti, Sudan, Sierra Leone, Burundi, Sri Lanka, and Armenia. Many of these countries also had large numbers of internally displaced persons. Since 1980, the number of refugees has been increasing by nearly 1 million a year. According to the World Refugee Survey, there was a decline in the number of refugees in 1993, but the number of internally displaced persons has grown, reflecting perhaps the growing capacity of governments and international agencies to confine people in flight within their own country. There are no signs that the end of the cold war had reduced violent conflicts within states and decreased the numbers of people in flight. Many of the conflicts were

8. UNHCR, *State of the World's Refugees.*

Table I PRINCIPAL SOURCES OF THE WORLD'S REFUGEES
(end of 1992)

Region, Country, or Ethnic Group of Origin	Number of Refugees (thousands)	Region, Country, or Ethnic Group of Origin	Number of Refugees (thousands)
Afghanistan	4,286	Iraq	125
Palestinians	2,658	Georgia	130
Former Yugoslavia	1,767	China (Tibet)	128
Mozambique	1,725	Bhutan	95
Somalia	864	Vietnam	89
Ethiopia/Eritrea	834	Mali	81
Liberia	599	Moldova	80
Angola	404	Zaire	66
Azerbaijan	350	Iran	65
Burma	333	Mauritania	65
Sudan	263	Tajikistan	52
Armenia	202	Bangladesh	50
Rwanda	201	Guatemala	45
Sierra Leone	200	Laos	43
Burundi	184	Nicaragua	30
Sri Lanka	181	Chad	24
Western Sahara	165	El Salvador	22
Cambodia	148	Senegal	15

Source: U.S. Committee for Refugees.

no doubt greatly exacerbated by great power interventions—for example, in Afghanistan, Angola, Mozambique, and the Horn of Africa—but these conflicts have taken on a life of their own and are sustained by the ready availability of weapons. Moreover, many of the conflicts, as in Rwanda, Sudan, and Liberia, are unrelated to direct great power interventions, and there is a high potential for conflict in several other African states. The end of the cold war has not diminished (and has perhaps increased) the global flow of arms, now financially sustained by the drug traffic.

The breakup of the Soviet bloc has led to internal conflicts and massive flights similar to the crumbling of the Ottoman and Hapsburg empires at the end of the First World War and the colonial empires at the end of the Second World War. The disintegration of empires has been accompanied by the emergence of new ethnic identities, ethnic conflicts within states, and movements for autonomy and self-determination. As minorities feel threatened by an ethnic majority in control of the state, they look outside for support or, alternatively, for a place to flee. Three regions

Table 2   INTERNALLY DISPLACED PERSONS
(end of 1992)

Country	Number of Persons (thousands)	Country	Number of Persons (thousands)
Sudan	5,000	Rwanda	350
South Africa	4,100	Croatia	340
Mozambique	3,500	Colombia	300
Somalia	2,000	India	280
Philippines	1,000	Cyprus	265
Angola	900	Azerbaijan	216
Bosnia-Herzegovina	740	Sierra Leone	200
Ethiopia/Eritrea	600	Cambodia	199
Liberia	600	El Salvador	154
Sri Lanka	600	Guatemala	150
Afghanistan	530	Zaire	100
Burma	500–1,000	Kenya	45
Peru	500	Turkey	30
Iraq	400	Moldova	20
Lebanon	400	Georgia	15
Tajikistan	400		

Note: Information on internal displacement is fragmentary. This table therefore presents only reported estimates.

Source: U.S. Committee for Refugees.

hitherto relatively stable until the disintegration of the Soviet Union are now rife with conflict and refugee flows: the Balkans, the Caucasus, and Central Asia.

Civil conflicts are also producing an increase in the number of internally displaced persons as well—an estimated 25 million worldwide in 1993. Sudan, with 5 million, had the largest number, but there were also large numbers inside South Africa, Mozambique, Somalia, Angola, Bosnia-Herzegovina, Ethiopia, Eritrea, Liberia, Sri Lanka, Zaire, Afghanistan, Burma, Peru, Iraq, Lebanon, Tajikistan, Rwanda, Croatia, Colombia, India, Cyprus, and Azerbaijan.

Most troublesome to receiving countries was the increase in the number of illegal migrants. In the United States, a one-time amnesty program put in place in 1986 led 3.1 million people to come forth to regularize their status. The actual number of remaining illegals in the country is probably higher. Despite a policy of penalizing employers for hiring illegals, various studies reported that the flows across the U.S.-Mexican border continue to be large, adding perhaps 200,000 to 300,000 (some say more) to the stock of illegals each year.[9] Europe also experi-

9. The U.S. Census Bureau has estimated that there are about 1.3 million illegal immigrants in California, most of them from Mexico. *New York Times,* February 6, 1994, p. 22.

enced a significant rise in the number of illegals in the early 1990s. The total number of illegals in Western Europe is estimated at about 3 million, many from Eastern Europe and from Africa to Spain and Italy.[10] Japan, too, has reported an increase in illegals from the Philippines, mainland China, and continental Southeast Asia. Nor are the flows of illegals confined to the advanced industrial countries. In Africa, there have been substantial unauthorized or illegal flows into Côte d'Ivoire, South Africa, and Nigeria. Similarly, in Asia, illegal labor flows from Indonesia to Malaysia, from Bangladesh to India, from Nepal to Bhutan, and from the People's Republic of China to Hong Kong and Taiwan.

There are a number of reasons for these increased flows. Three are particularly noteworthy: the growth in global markets, which then give rise to migration networks; the removal of many of the political obstacles to emigration as a result of the breakdown of authoritarian and totalitarian regimes; and the emergence of a migration "mafia" or labor recruiters who extract fees from would-be migrants (sometimes turning illegal migrants into bonded laborers) to arrange their transportation and employment abroad.

Should we regard these population flows of workers and refugees with alarm? Is global labor migration, in combination with the flows of capital, technology, and trade, part of a developing global world community unfettered by national boundaries? "There is no intrinsic reason why migration should stir up concern," writes Johannes Pronk, the Netherlands' minister for development cooperation. "This holds equally true for international migration, which is only international by virtue of the existence of manmade national boundaries."[11] If this is the case, is international migration an economic burden and a threat to national identity and political stability, as some people assert, or is the problem the result of the xenophobic reaction of some citizens and politicians and exaggerated fears of being overwhelmed by foreigners? If citizens were not xenophobic and governments not so obsessed with control, couldn't countries live comfortably with open borders? In a more just world, shouldn't people freely choose where they want to live? Despite such reasoning, many governments and their citizens do believe that there is a crisis—although they do not always agree what the crisis is. It remains unclear as to whether the crisis is a matter of perceptions, exaggerated fears, and xenophobic reactions linked to economic recession or whether the global movement of peoples is a long-term threat to the security and the cultural and economic well-being of countries.

In the following pages, we shall attempt to disaggregate the various dimensions of the crisis to ascertain what aspects of these flows have created anxieties among political leaders and their citizens. We shall examine five dimensions of the global migration crisis: (1) control over entry, (2) absorption of migrants and refugees, (3) international relations, (4) international norms and institutions, and (5) moral considerations.

10. Sharon Stanton Russell, *International Migration in North America, Europe, Central Asia, the Middle East and North Africa* (Geneva: Economic Commission for Europe, 1993).

11. Johannes P. Pronk, "Migration: The Nomad in Each of Us," *Population and Development Review,* June 1993, p. 323.

FIVE DIMENSIONS OF THE GLOBAL MIGRATION CRISIS

Control over Entry

Since the development of the modern state from the fifteenth century onward, governments have regarded control over their borders as the core of sovereignty. It is axiomatic that states decide which people to admit, how many, and from where. But today many contemporary governments, and their citizens, fear that they can no longer control entry. Advanced industrial countries can protect their borders from invading armies but not from hordes of individuals who slip into harbors, crawl under barbed-wire fences, and wade across rivers. Tourists and students with visas stay on and disappear into the labor market. Airplanes bring in people with missing or false papers who then claim asylum. Asylum officers responsible for adjudicating claims are overwhelmed by the numbers. People whose asylum claims are pending may never appear in court, and those whose asylum requests have been rejected slip into the underground labor market to avoid repatriation.

The smuggling of migrants across boundaries has become an organized international business. "Businessmen," reports the *New York Times,* "arrange each stage of a smuggling operation: finding passengers, arranging their travel documents, guiding them across borders, and extracting payment after arrival. Most immigrants borrow from relatives or loan sharks to pay the full amount almost immediately after they arrive, working for years to pay off the debt."[12] When the United States halted ships at sea, smugglers moved larger numbers of immigrants by plane, providing passengers with forged passports and visas for check-in. The passports are then returned to the smugglers prior to departure so that upon arrival the passenger can request political asylum. Many illegal immigrants arrive with fake documents that are not readily detected by airport inspectors, who often spend less than a minute looking at the documents of each person entering the country. A task force at the U.S. Immigration and Naturalization Service (INS) has uncovered increasingly sophisticated ways in which smugglers get their clients into the country. One practice is to provide forged passports to individual members of genuine tour groups from Hong Kong and Thailand. The forged passports are then submitted to an airport inspector in a stack of real ones.

Many of the smugglers are Taiwanese businessmen moving illegal immigrants from Fujian province in China to airports in Los Angeles, Miami, and Seattle. Most of the illegals then join the Fujianese community in New York City. The migrant smuggling business has apparently become very lucrative. "No longer the 'mom and pop' operations that charged only a few thousand dollars in the 1980s," reports the *Far Eastern Economic Review,* "they are now multinational, billion-dollar businesses that stretch from China to Hong Kong, Taiwan, Singapore, Thailand, Central America and the U.S."[13]

Illegal migrants coming by sea are only infrequently caught. As ships near U.S. territorial waters, passengers are off-loaded into small boats, then landed on the

12. *New York Times,* August 23, 1993, p. B2.
13. *Far Eastern Economic Review,* April 8, 1993, p. 17.

Table 3   WORLD POPULATION FOR SELECTED YEARS, 1950–2025

Region	Population (millions)			
	1950	1990	1995 (est.)	2025 (est.)
Africa	221.98	642.11	746.82	1,596.86
North and Central America	220.36	427.23	452.25	595.62
South America	111.59	296.72	325.67	493.73
Asia	1,377.26	3,112.70	3,413.34	4,912.48
Europe	392.52	498.37	504.25	515.21
Former Soviet republics	180.08	288.60	298.62	352.12
Oceania	12.65	26.48	28.34	38.21
World	2,516.44	5,292.20	5,770.29	8,504.23

Source: United Nations Population Division.

U.S. coastline. The immigrants are then indentured to Chinese businessmen in New York until they pay off their debt for the voyage, ranging from $20,000 to $50,000. "Even with all the manpower available at our disposal," explained an INS official, "the U.S. remains totally vulnerable" to the smuggling operations unless they are stopped at their point of origin.[14]

The smuggling business has become worldwide. Professional smugglers, working closely with shipping companies, are able to arrange the illegal movement of people from almost anyplace on the globe. For a fee, asylum seekers can be smuggled into Germany or Canada or the United States and briefed as to what answers to give to officials to enable them to qualify under asylum laws. If the U.S. Coast Guard is particularly vigilant in interdicting boats from China, smugglers can divert the ships to Japan's west coast.

Almost every effort to control entry has run afoul of major obstacles. How can entry at borders be controlled when governments are trying to facilitate the flow of trade? Can every truck crossing an international border be inspected? Should all ships at sea be interdicted to ensure that no illegal immigrants are on board? Should travelers who arrive at airports without passports or visas be summarily repatriated without a hearing? How can employer sanctions be made to work when numerous small businesses and households find it advantageous to employ low-wage labor?

In the West, fears of uncontrollable entry are further fueled by anxieties that rapid population growth in developing countries will produce such vast numbers of unemployed young people in search of a livelihood that borders will not contain them. The world population has increased rapidly, from 2.5 billion in 1950 to 4.4 billion in 1980 and 5.3 billion in 1990. It is expected to reach 6.3 billion in the year 2000 and 8.5 billion by 2025. An estimated 100 million people are added to the world's population each year, mostly in low-income countries where the average annual population growth is 1.8 percent, compared to 0.5 percent in high-income countries. Is the West, then, experiencing a population overflow from the Third World, as North and South America and Australia experienced an overflow from Europe in the nineteenth century during its period of rapid population growth?

To put the world's population growth in perspective, it should be noted that world migration (including refugee flows) amounts to perhaps 4 million persons a year, or 4 percent of the world's annual population increase.[15] About half is to developed countries. Population growth in the Third World has declined from 2.5 percent annually in the early 1960s to 1.8 percent in the 1990s, but emigration has increased. Moreover, some of the largest flows of migrant workers came from countries with low or modest population growth rates—Yugoslavia and Greece into Western Europe, for example. The outflow from mainland China is growing in spite of declining birthrates.

The relationship between rapid population growth and emigration is a complicated one, not easily encompassed by the simple notion that one necessarily leads to the other. Population growth is clearly an intervening variable, in itself rarely a cause, but in combination with other factors, it can be a force for emigration. Where the number of young adults is increasing and incomes and employment are rising, many young people may acquire the financial means to act on the motivation to emigrate. Hence the emigration pressures in China's Fujian province notwithstanding its high rate of economic growth. After all, the great exodus from Europe in the nineteenth century—some 50 million people left for the United States—took place during a time of rapid economic and population growth. A similar combination has existed in Korea, Taiwan, Italy, Turkey, Algeria, Mexico, and Puerto Rico, all of which have experienced high emigration rates, high economic growth rates, and high population growth rates simultaneously.

Nor does a long-term decline in population growth rates necessarily foreshadow a decline in emigration rates. The sharp decline in fertility rates throughout Eastern Europe and the former Soviet Union has not led to a decline in emigration pressures—a situation attributable to increased unemployment, declining wages, and deteriorating economic conditions.

There is no evidence of a direct relationship between rapid population growth rates or even population density and high emigration rates. Global migration appears to be more closely associated with rising expectations in many developing countries, differentials in wages and employment opportunities, knowledge about opportunities elsewhere, access to low-cost transportation, high levels of violence in countries, violations of human rights, persecution of minorities, and, above all, growing knowledge about the ease of entering and remaining in another country.

---

15. These figures do not include return migration, which in some years can be quite substantial. According to the World Refugee Survey, an estimated 1,830,000 refugees returned home in 1993. During the Gulf War, 5.5 million people were displaced within a single year; most of them returned to their home country and are therefore not classified as either refugees or immigrants. From most countries of migration, there is also a significant return flow of former immigrants (about 200,000 yearly from the United States). Annual flows from one Third World country to another are not well reported, nor, of course, are worldwide statistics on illegal migration. The actual movement of individuals across international boundaries each year is thus highly variable and difficult to estimate accurately.

Nonetheless, fears that high population growth generates illegal migration, though unsupported by empirical evidence, has become an element in Western nations' anxieties about their inability to control their borders.

One explanation for these fears is not the high fertility rate of developing countries but the low fertility rate in industrial countries that receive migrants.[16] In countries with low population growth rates, migrants account for a very large proportion of the annual population increase. Though migrants add less than 0.5 percent to the U.S. population each year, immigrants and their offspring are expected to be responsible for almost two-thirds of the net population growth over the next 50 years.[17] Similarly, as the countries of Central Europe move toward zero population growth, virtually all of the annual population increase is the result of immigration. Moreover, migrants tend to be in the high-fertility age group, 20 to 35, and fertility rates among migrants from the Third World tend to be higher than those of natives in developed countries. The children of migrants are therefore particularly visible in classrooms, especially in the large urban centers where migrants tend to concentrate. For countries with a low rate of natural population increase, the demographic impact of migration on population growth and on school attendance is highly visible even though rapid population growth in the Third World is not in itself a decisive element in international population movements.

Concern that political turmoil and violence within Third World countries or among the states of the former Soviet bloc will lead to population movements is, however, far more realistic. European governments have a legitimate reason to believe that conflicts over Islamic movements in North Africa and the Middle East could lead to an exodus or that ethnic conflicts in the successor states of the former Soviet Union might create large refugee flows. Similarly, the United States has had a legitimate concern that domestic conflicts in Cuba, Haiti, or elsewhere in the Caribbean or Latin America could lead to population flight.

Though most Western governments are prepared to accept limited numbers of individual refugees who are persecuted and whose lives are at risk, their humanitarian sentiments are much reduced when the volume of asylum seekers is large, imposing a heavy burden on housing, employment, and the entitlement system. Governments are also reluctant to maintain a generous asylum system when so many asylum seekers are would-be migrants, not individuals fearing persecution.

Governments want to be able to choose which people to admit, how many, for what purpose, and for how long. They do not want these decisions to be made by employers, other governments, or would-be migrants. So long as conditions in the Third World and in the former Soviet bloc continue to encourage the exodus of large numbers of people, anxiety will increase among governments and citizens that they are unable to control entry.

---

16. I owe this point to Michael Teitelbaum of the Sloan Foundation.

17. Michael Fix and Jeffrey S. Passel, *Immigration and Immigrants* (Washington, D.C.: Urban Institute, 1994), p. 4. According to their estimates, the U.S. population is projected to increase from 249 million in 1990 to 355 million by 2040. Under current law, about 70 million immigrants and their offspring will be added to the U.S. population in the next 50 years.

Absorption

International migration changes the ethnic composition of states. In the case of multiethnic states, migration can change the ethnic balance and thereby precipitate a change in the balance of political power. For homogeneous countries, a large influx of migrants raises the question of what the country should demand of its immigrants. Should the goal be total assimilation into the culture of the host society so that migrants and their children are no longer distinguishable? Or should migrants be allowed to retain their language, their religion, an attachment to their country of origin, and their distinctive identity? Among the nation-states of Western Europe, there is the question of whether ethnic nationalism should give way to civic nationalism, that is, whether citizenship implies a uniform cultural identity, or whether cultural pluralism is compatible with citizenship. This is a particularly vexing question for European countries that are coming to realize that their guest workers will remain. In advanced industrial societies, much of the debate centers on educational policies—whether the educational system should be explicitly assimilationist or multicultural, whether children born of migrant parents should be permitted or encouraged to retain the language of their parents, and whether their religion has a place in the schools. Can and should traditional nation-states that have welcomed *political* pluralism come to accept and even welcome *cultural* pluralism? Should these differences be tolerated, respected, or even encouraged through government support, or should they be rooted out and eradicated? Almost every Western country is uncertain as to how to incorporate migrants and their children—whether to induce them to assimilate or to pursue a policy of multiculturalism.

What, in short, constitutes membership in the community, and how should the community in turn define itself? Given the varied conceptions of community and citizenship prevailing in the Western world (from political definitions of citizenship to cultural norms to notions of kinship and blood ties), it should not be surprising that countries vary in their responses to the issue of migrant absorption or to the contentious question of whether the locally born children of migrants should be granted automatic citizenship or not.

The issue of absorption, integration, or assimilation—the terms themselves are contentious—is as much a problem in the Third World as it is among the developed countries. The majority of the world's refugees and migrants move not from developed to developing countries but from one Third World country to another. Developing countries not only produce the largest number of migrants and refugees but are also the primary receivers. Third World governments and their citizens have often had a remarkable tolerance toward migrants and refugees from neighboring countries and a special generosity toward those with whom they share a common language, religion, or tribal identity. But many governments have been concerned that if the migrants and refugees belong to an alien ethnic group or add to the numbers of a minority community, the political, economic, social, and cultural dominance of the majority might be eroded. An influx of Indians to Fiji, Chinese or Vietnamese to Malaysia, Nepalis to Bhutan, Bangladeshis to India's northeast, or Palestinians to Lebanon could jeopardize the precarious political balance among ethnic groups. Moreover, most countries in the Third World—indeed, most countries in the world (168 of the 180 members countries of the United Nations)—are ethnically heterogeneous. How, many government officials ask, can a country possibly manage ethnic conflicts when the country is subjected to a continuous and substantial population influx?

Debates over cultural absorption are further complicated by the question of the absorption of migrants into the labor force. Some citizens want migrants to do the jobs that locals do not want. Members of the middle class want to hire domestics from abroad, owners of small businesses want low-wage foreign workers, and farmers want hardworking nonunion foreign laborers. But citizens also worry that migrants may be taking jobs from others, particularly that the country's own unskilled labor force may find it difficult to compete against foreign workers and that wages will be pushed down if the immigrant influx is substantial. Among economists, the question of whether migrants depress wages and exacerbate unemployment among the native population is contentious, but whatever the reality, large numbers of citizens are fearful of their jobs when unemployment levels are high and economic growth is sluggish.

In much of the Third World, the fear of economic losses from migration often have a solid basis in reality. In the Third World, there are few jobs that migrants take that locals do not want. Migrants from Central America to the Chiapas region in southern Mexico, from Bangladesh to the Indian state of Assam, from Haiti to the Bahamas compete against locals for jobs. Moreover, there are additional concerns when migrants and a rapidly growing local population compete for land and for dwindling forests.

The growth of antiforeign, antimigration political parties not only in Western Europe but in Third World countries as well has further complicated the task of absorbing foreigners. Governments are concerned that they will be weakened by right-wing xenophobic parties appealing to the visceral anxieties of their citizens. The issues of absorption and border controls thus become linked as governments see a continued unwanted influx as fueling citizen anxieties, thereby making community acceptance of existing migrants and their children more difficult.

International Relations

Scholars of international relations have said that wars create refugees but refugees do not create wars. Though that is generally true (India did, however, invade Pakistan in 1971 in large part because it was flooded with refugees from East Pakistan), refugee flows have increasingly become the basis for conflict between sending and receiving countries.

Governments are concerned when the government of another country creates conditions that cause its citizens to flee. A government that violates the human rights of its citizens, persecutes its minorities, or is unable to halt a civil conflict creates a burden for others when its people flee across borders. If a country creates refugees, receiving countries generally believe that they have thereby acquired a right of "intervention"—a concept that encompasses a spectrum of actions including conditionality in development assistance, restrictions on trade, sanctions, embargoes, and the threat and use of force.

How countries treat their own populations—once regarded as primarily an internal affair—has become an issue of international relations not simply because human rights are now a global matter but because governments may create refugee burdens for others. Thus the Russian government has been concerned over the citizenship rights in the Baltic states of Russians who migrated into the region when it was occupied by the Soviet Union, the Indian government has been concerned over ethnic conflicts in neighboring Sri Lanka, and the government of Turkey has been fearful that Iraq's Kurds might cross its borders. Russian policies toward many of the successor states to the Soviet Union will be greatly influenced by how the "near abroad" states treat Russians. The government of Turkey was influential in pressing the United Nations to protect the Kurdish population in Iraq by indicating that it would use force if necessary to prevent Kurds from crossing into Turkey.

In September 1994 the United States declared its intention to invade Haiti unless President Raoul Cedras and his colleagues stepped down. President Clinton offered as his reasons that there was a threat to democracy in the western hemisphere since General Cedras had overthrown Haiti's elected president, Jean-Bertrand Aristide, in September 1991; the Cedras government was committing atrocities against its citizens; and there was a flow of refugees. The president spoke of the need "to secure our borders." A last-minute mission by former president Jimmy Carter, backed by U.S. warships waiting outside Haiti's capital, successfully persuaded Haiti's dictators to step down and to accept the occupation of the country by U.S. and coalition forces.

Government strategies of deterrence and prevention may put countries on a collision course with one another, especially when states impose sanctions or threaten military intervention to change the internal behavior of another government (or to change the government) that is inducing people to leave.

Moreover, migration policies themselves have become a matter for international negotiations and conflict between sending and receiving countries and among receiving countries. When several thousand Cubans left their country on rafts and flimsy boats for Florida in August 1994, the United States negotiated an agreement with Cuba under which the United States would admit 20,000 Cuban immigrants yearly in return for a Cuban government policy of preventing unauthorized people from leaving. When the Soviet Union prevented the exodus of Jews to Israel and to the United States, emigration policy became an issue in U.S.-Soviet relations. Subsequently, Israel's policy of settling Russian immigrants in the West Bank was an issue in U.S.-Israeli relations. The British government's decision to forcibly repatriate Vietnamese refugees from Hong Kong was an issue in U.S.-British relations. Countries that border on states producing refugees call for a system of "burden sharing" with other countries, while distant countries often insist that the country of first asylum take responsibility. These two positions are particularly contentious in Europe.

The traditional obligations of states toward their own citizens living abroad have also become more complex not only as the numbers have increased but also as the migrant communities have become diasporas, communities whose members have citizenship in one country and ties of affection with another. Some 25 million people of Russian origin now live in the republics of the former Soviet Union; an estimated 30 million people of Chinese ancestry live outside of China, Hong Kong, and Taiwan; and millions of people of Indian, Turkish, and Arab origin live outside the country of their birth. The relationship of diasporas to their host country and their country of origin has often become the basis for international and domestic conflict.[18]

Refugee and migrant flows have moved to the top of the foreign policy agenda. When a boatload of Chinese immigrants was spotted off the coast of California, the United States asked Mexico to intercept them. When Arab governments protested that Israelis were encouraging Russian immigrants to settle in occupied territories, the United States threatened to withhold loan guarantees from Israel as a means of getting Israel to change its settlement policies. When civil war in Pakistan led to a large-scale flight of East Pakistanis into India, India responded by going to war against Pakistan, declaring that the security of India's northeast region was threatened by the influx. When British authorities in Hong Kong forcibly repatriated Vietnamese, the United States formally protested to the British government. And when several countries of Western Europe declared that they would no longer accept refugees and asylum seekers from countries of first asylum, there were protests from those European states that had previously accepted refugees on the understanding that they would provide transit to other countries. The migration and refugee decisions that countries make clearly have implications for others.

For these reasons, migration and refugee issues have become a matter of high international politics, engaging the attention of heads of state, cabinets, and key ministries involved in defense, internal security, and external relations.

International Regimes and Institutions

This issue has two closely related dimensions: the crisis for international regimes and the crisis for international institutions.

The international refugee regime is based on the 1951 United Nations Convention on Refugees. Under this convention, the definition of refugees is limited to individuals with a well-founded fear of persecution for reasons of race, religion, nationality, membership in a particular social group, or political opinion. In recent years, this definition has come under attack, both by advocates of extending the definition to include people fleeing from violence and by activists who seek to establish all violations of human rights as grounds for obtaining asylum. Some theorists argue that the new conceptions of persecution, such as gender-based oppression or coercive family planning, should be incorporated into asylum policies. However, many governments fear that such broader redefinitions would open their borders wide because only a minority of the world's peoples live in countries that respect human rights and are not torn by violence. Moreover, the international refugee regime is already threatened by large numbers of putative migrants who

---

18. Governments with large or influential diaspora populations may be politically responsive to their demands even when it results in conflicts with allies. In February 1994, the Clinton administration granted a visa to Gerry Adams, the political chief of the Irish Republican Army, over the strong objections of the British government, notwithstanding the "special relationship" between the two countries. President Clinton evidently responded to pressures from two Irish-American senators, Patrick Moynihan (New York) and Edward Kennedy (Massachusetts), both of whom were critical to the president's health and welfare reform proposals.

seek to use the asylum system to gain entry. As these numbers increase, governments have become less willing to follow the procedures put forth by the United Nations High Commissioner for Refugees. Instead of onshore adjudication procedures and rights of appeal, many governments have halted asylum claimants at the borders, interdicted them at sea, prevented them from flying on international flights without visas, or engaged in summary expulsions. The international refugee regime is thus under siege, both from those who would expand the definition of refugees to meet the burgeoning claims of people who live in repressive and violent societies and from those who find even the existing norms too difficult to enforce within UNHCR procedures in the face of growing claims for asylum.

International norms for the protection of migrant workers are no more satisfactory. Efforts by the International Labor Organization (ILO) to generate global norms concerning the freedom of guest workers to change jobs, join unions, have access to the benefits of the welfare state, bring in families, and acquire the right to remain and become citizens of their host societies have received little support outside of Europe. Labor-importing Arab countries keep far tighter controls on migrant workers than European states by restricting their rights to change jobs or remain. During and shortly after the Gulf War, large numbers of noncitizens were summarily repatriated, especially from Kuwait and Saudi Arabia. Neither Third World countries nor international institutions have been in a position to protect the several million migrants residing in the oil-producing states.

International institutions are also in crisis as a result of the massive increase in migration and refugee flows. The UNHCR, the ILO, the International Organization for Migration, the International Committee of the Red Cross, and a host of other international agencies concerned with migrant workers and refugees no longer see their mission primarily as responding to the requests of receiving countries. According to the United Nations Development Programme, of the world's 82 armed conflicts from 1989 to 1992 in which more than 1,000 people were killed, 79 took place within national borders.[19] Most refugee flows are the result of internal violence, not wars between states. Now international agencies ponder how to "intervene" over the objections of states from which people are fleeing. Officials of international agencies increasingly regard conceptions of sovereignty as impediments to their tasks. Yet even as the budgets of these international institutions expand, professional staffs enlarge, and responsibilities grow, they are unable legally to intervene unless authorized by the state or by the UN Security Council. Furthermore, even when the Security Council gives international agencies responsibilities for providing humanitarian assistance to stem the exodus propelled by violence, this expanded role is generally not accompanied by the military support and collective sanctions against transgressors often required to make such efforts successful. Moreover, many international organizations do not have sufficient financial resources or adequate administrative capacity to take on these responsibilities worldwide. A crisis thus emerges as states that are unwilling or unable unilaterally to address the conditions inside countries that lead people to flee have turned to international institutions. Most of these institutions in turn lack adequate legal

19. United Nations Development Programme, *Human Development Report, 1994* (New York: Oxford University Press, 1994), p. 47.

authority, military power, financial resources, and administrative capacity to take on such responsibilities.

Moral Considerations

Global migration creates a moral crisis in receiving countries in that more people want to leave their country than other countries are willing to accept. Because not everyone can be admitted, countries prepared to admit migrants or refugees must establish criteria for choosing among a large pool of candidates. Whenever policy-makers engage in rationing, there is a moral crisis over who should get the benefits and who should pay the costs. One dimension of the moral crisis in public policy, therefore, is the question of who should be admitted. Are some criteria for admission more moral than others? Should admissions be based on the needs and desires of the receiving country (which leads to a preference for migrants who are educated, know the local language, have ties to the local population, or are kinfolk of citizens—what some wags have called "designer migrants"), or should entry be based on the needs of the admission seekers?

The debate over who should be admitted is often muddled because of the ambiguity associated with the words used to refer to immigrants. The terms *migrant, expatriate, exile, guest worker, illegal, undocumented, refugee, and asylum seeker* have nuanced differences; they imply in some instances impermanence and high status (*exile*), permanence and high status (*expatriate*), permanence and low status (*immigrant*), impermanence and low status (*guest worker*), law breaking (*illegal*), individuals awaiting regularization of status (*undocumented*), and individuals forced to leave (*exile, refugee, asylum claimant,* and sometimes *expatriate*).

The choice of terms by journalists, scholars, activists, and government officials is often indicative of a normative preference. Illegal migrants presumably should be prevented from entering; undocumented aliens presumably should be regularized. Migrant workers, it may be implied, take jobs from natives while skilled migrants presumably contribute to national productivity. Boatloads of people seeking entry are called refugees, whether or not they have legitimate claims for asylum under international or national law.

The moral crisis has become a conflict between people who emphasize global human rights and those who would give priority to the national interests of states and their current residents. In one industrial country after another, this moral debate has become intensely political. At one pole are right-wing political parties in virtually every European country that call for a halt to all immigration. These groups would bar asylum seekers, deny citizenship to migrants and their children, and attempt to make life so unpleasant that migrants would be forced to return to their country of origin. At the other pole are human rights activists concerned that all who seek asylum be freely admitted and given a full hearing and that illegals be provided the entitlements of the welfare state and subsequently admitted into citizenship. They also argue that anyone in the world whose human rights are violated is entitled to asylum. Between these two poles are governments enmeshed in a moral quandary over how best to respond to people in other societies who want to migrate for jobs, decent incomes, and freedom from persecution and discrimination without imposing unacceptable costs on their own citizens.

To some observers, refugees' claims evoke sympathy, moral concerns, and the image of a just and humane global order in which people whose human rights are violated can move to wherever it is safe and free. To others, refugee flows are a form of population dumping in which states cruelly relieve themselves of unwanted minorities, political dissidents, and the poor. Hence refugees generate in some people feelings of compassion and in others anger against the states that produce them.

A further moral quandary arises over the relationship between indigenous populations, on the one hand, and immigrants and their descendants, on the other—a relationship made complex by uncertainty over what constitutes indigenous status. Some analysts restrict such status to nondominant sectors of society with ancestral links to a precolonial past; that can be construed to include both the indigenous peoples of Canada, New Zealand, Australia, the United States, and Latin America and the titular peoples of Lithuania, Latvia, Estonia, Kazakhstan, and other newly independent republics recently freed from Soviet rule and Russian occupation. In these latter nations, an alien people was imposed by imperial colonizers in territories that have now become sovereign states. Migrants and their descendants have committed no injustice, although an injustice may have been committed by the imperial powers that once forced or induced individuals to migrate. Some observers have therefore argued that the Russians settlers are illegitimate and must either return "home" or be given lesser rights than residents who have ancestral roots in the country. Similar arguments over the rights of settlers have shaped policies toward the Chinese in Malaysia and elsewhere in Southeast Asia and toward Indian settlers in East Africa. Contesting claims over group rights are increasingly being fought out in the political arena as each side asserts its own moral claims in a situation that is morally ambiguous.

As ethnic minorities come under siege, as failed states prove unable to protect their own citizens at home, as civil conflicts rage within many societies, and as authoritarian regimes continue to be oppressive, countries receiving people in flight face still another morally perplexing set of alternatives: Should they intervene to change the conditions that lead people to exit? Should they open their borders to people in distress? Or should they create a wall around themselves to keep out most of the outsiders who wish to enter?

Intervention in any form is rarely cost-free for either side. Intervention, even when morally justifiable, can be expensive. To cut off trade to an offending country and impose sanctions may do damage to workers and farmers producing goods for export and inflict pain on the poor living under an autocratic regime rather than on the government, a dilemma made sharply clear when the United States imposed sanctions on Haiti. Military intervention may result in a loss of life for members of the armed forces of the attacking country and for innocent civilians in the country under attack. If anticipated costs are low, states may act out of moral concerns. But if the anticipated costs are high, states will intervene only if they believe that their national interests are at stake. When states are unable or unwilling to intervene to remedy conditions in source countries, the moral pressures increase for more generous entry policies, but if the number of asylum seekers is high, governments may also conclude that domestic concerns require them to restrict entry. Governments may believe that there are conditions under which they are morally *justified* in intervening in the affairs of a sovereign state, but rarely do governments believe that they are morally *obligated* to do so. Even the moral willingness to accommodate people in flight is ultimately constrained by what governments believe is in their national or political interests.

It is conceivable that by the beginning of the twenty-first century, the global migration crisis will have subsided. Perhaps there will be fewer failed states in the Third World, fewer civil conflicts, fewer acts of ethnic violence, and fewer autocratic regimes. Perhaps minorities will feel more secure, employment and income levels will have significantly risen, and land pressures will have subsided. Perhaps migration-receiving countries will want a larger labor force than they can provide themselves through domestic population growth. Perhaps, with the end of the recession, their tolerance for foreigners will have grown. But few of these developments are likely. On the contrary, as the pressure for emigration increases, states are more rather than less likely to become restrictive. What is uncertain is whether states will be effective at halting unwanted entries. As the pressures for international population movements increase, we can expect to live in a world in which the great global collisions are not only among states but among peoples, when the world outside a country's borders intrudes, and when global forces continue to erode states and the communities that live in them.

2

GLOBAL EMIGRATION

The migration of people is as old as recorded history. Moses led his persecuted people from Egypt across the Sinai to Canaan. The seafaring Greeks established colonies in Sicily and elsewhere in the Mediterranean. Jews in Palestine were dispersed into Mesopotamia, Persia, Greece, North Africa, and Europe following the Roman destruction of the second temple in A.D. 70. From Central Asia, the Turkish people migrated into Anatolia, where they founded the Turkish state. In China, the Han people colonized non-Han regions to the south and the west. The Vikings colonized Normandy and in 1066 invaded and settled in Britain.

MIGRATION WAVES

In the modern era, there have been five distinctive waves of migration. The first wave began in the seventeenth century with the emergence of European states as imperial powers and continued through the end of World War I. Britain, Spain, Portugal, the Netherlands, and France established colonies that provided outlets for their expanding populations. For three centuries, Europe shaped much of the world's international population movements. From Spain, Portugal, and Britain came shiploads of migrants to settle North and South America, and the French moved to Quebec and later to northern Africa. Between 1846 and 1932, approximately 18 million people from the British Isles migrated to North America, Australia, New Zealand, southern Africa, and the Caribbean. Ten million Italians and nearly 5 million Germans also left the Continent, as did millions of Europeans from Central, Southern, and Eastern Europe. These groups settled primarily in the United States in the last half of the nineteenth century and the early part of the twentieth, populating agricultural lands in the Midwest and providing manpower for rapidly expanding industries. In total, an estimated 55 million Europeans migrated overseas between 1821 and 1924, fully 34 million of them to the United States. In 1925, the combined population of North and South America was 225 million, the overwhelming majority migrants or the descendants of migrants who had arrived over the previous three centuries.[1]

A second migration wave took place during this same period when the European powers shaped the flows of non-European people. In the seventeenth

---

1. Not all of this population, obviously, was of European origin, as it included, in addition to the indigenous population, a substantial number of people from Africa. In 1925, the population of Europe, including the USSR, was 505 million. *Encyclopaedia Britannica*, 1963 edition, vol. 18, p. 231.

and eighteenth centuries, European traders transported slaves from West Africa to the American South, the Caribbean islands, Brazil, and Guyana. In the nineteenth century, after slavery ended, the British recruited indentured workers from South Asia for employment in East Africa, Malaya, Fiji, Guyana, Jamaica, Suriname, and Trinidad. Chinese were also recruited for employment in Southeast Asia, especially Indonesia, Thailand, Malaya, and Indochina.

These three centuries of international migration transformed the world. European settlers created "fragments of Europe," in the words of Louis Hartz,[2] in Canada, the United States, Latin America, Australia, and New Zealand—fragments that were to become new states. Many indigenous populations were reduced to a minority, and political systems in the "New World" were totally transformed. Colonization under the European aegis did not always turn the indigenous people into a minority. In South Africa, the migration of Dutch (Boer) and subsequently British settlers was too small to make the Europeans a demographic majority but did result in the establishment of European political hegemony. South Africa's Zulu and Xhosa populations (themselves migrants from other parts of Africa) were made subordinate through the separatist system of apartheid, even while they constituted a majority of the population. The European-controlled flow of slaves and indentured servants from one colony to another also created migrant-majority countries in Suriname, Trinidad, and Jamaica and ethnically divided societies in Malaya, Ceylon (Sri Lanka), Fiji, Uganda, and Kenya.

A third wave of international migration took place with the dissolution of empires after the First World War. The breakup of the Hapsburg and Ottoman empires led to the formation of new states in Central, Eastern, and Southern Europe with boundaries that did not always coincide with existing ethnic settlements. The modern era of large-scale refugee flows began when these new states sought to create homogeneous populations through forced emigration. Greeks, Jews, Poles, Romanians, Hungarians, Bulgarians, Turks, Serbs, Macedonians, Armenians, and other minorities were put to flight. The 1920s witnessed substantial exchanges of populations throughout the Balkans as minorities moved to countries in which their ethnic group constituted a majority. Additional streams of refugees were produced by the Russian Revolution and the resulting civil war and, in the 1930s, by the rise of Hitler and the extension of Nazi military power throughout Europe.

After World War II, a fourth migration wave began with the disintegration of the colonial empires and the creation of dozens of newly independent states in Asia, the Middle East, and Africa. These new states were often ethnically divided countries, characterized by repressive authoritarian regimes and weak civil societies. Almost inevitably, violent conflicts erupted, and millions of people fled for their lives. Many of these population movements also reflected the new governments' view that the migrations that took place during colonial rule were illegitimate and that the descendants of the foreign settlers should now return home.

The world's largest refugee flow took place in South Asia, following the partition of India in 1947, when an estimated 14 million Hindus and Muslims migrated between India and Pakistan. However, minorities were on the move almost every-

---

2. Louis Hartz, ed. *The Founding of New Societies* (New York: Harcourt, Brace & World, 1964).

where in the newly emerging states: Arabs from the new state of Israel, Jews from North Africa, Chinese from Indonesia, and South Asians from East Africa, Burma, and Ceylon. Civil conflicts also produced refugee flows from Mozambique, Ethiopia, Sudan, Somalia, East Pakistan (Bangladesh), Angola, Nicaragua, El Salvador, Cambodia, Rhodesia (Zimbabwe), Laos, Vietnam, Cuba, Afghanistan, and Lebanon. The numbers of refugees during the postwar period were staggering: 10 million from Bangladesh, over a million from Vietnam, nearly 6 million from Afghanistan. In 1993, there were an estimated 18.9 million refugees worldwide, and 25 million internally displaced persons in their own countries in refugeelike situations.

Just as the flows during the colonial era sometimes led to the formation of new states, so did some of the flows after World War II. Pakistan was founded in 1947 primarily by Muslims who lived in the Muslim-minority areas of preindependence India. India's Muslim League, led by Mohammed Ali Jinnah, called for the partition of India so as to create a homeland for the subcontinent's Muslims. Pakistan was then formed out of the territories in the northeastern and northwestern parts of the subcontinent. An estimated 6 million Muslims from India, including many of the leaders of the Muslim League, then migrated into Pakistan (East Pakistan subsequently became the independent country of Bangladesh in 1971).

The political system of the Republic of China, as Taiwan called itself, was also created by a migrant population when the Chinese Communists took control of China. The Kuomintang (Nationalist) military and political leaders, their army, and their families fled the mainland for the island of Taiwan, where they established a base that they hoped to use for the eventual recapture of the mainland. They established political control over the local population, most of whom were themselves of migrant origin from China's Fujian province. Although both the Kuomintang and the Chinese Communists regarded Taiwan as a province of China, the Nationalists effectively created a new and independent Taiwanese state.

The state of Israel was created by European Jews who sought to establish a home in the land in which their ancestors originated. Jews from Europe began to migrate to Palestine toward the end of the nineteenth century in a succession of *aliyahs,* or returns. In 1948, Palestine was partitioned to create the state of Israel, which then admitted large numbers of migrants, including Holocaust survivors and, in even larger numbers, Jews from Arab countries.

Colonial rule left a legacy of major cleavages between the native peoples and the populations of migrant origin. Sometimes, as we have noted, the migrant community consisted of people who came from the imperial country: the British in Zimbabwe, Hong Kong, and South Africa; the Russians in Lithuania, Estonia, Latvia, Kazakhstan, Georgia, and Ukraine; the French in New Caledonia and Quebec; the Dutch in South Africa. In other instances, the migrants came from other colonies. In Fiji, there is a division between the native Melanesians and the immigrant Indians; in Malaysia, between the Malays and the Chinese and Indians; and in Guyana, between two migrant communities, Indians and Africans.

With independence, many newly established regimes sought to decolonize themselves by calling for the exodus of populations they regarded as imposed by the imperial power. With few exceptions, white settlers were pressed to return home. French settlers vacated Algeria; most Portuguese left Angola and

Mozambique; many British left Zimbabwe. The new regimes often forced the repatriation of the descendants of people who had been brought in by the imperial rulers as indentured servants, though they were now free laborers and many had become prosperous business owners and members of the middle class. Uganda forced South Asians to leave. Sri Lanka withdrew citizenship from Tamil tea estate workers and pressed for their "return" to India. The Fijian military overthrew an elected government dominated by Indian descendants of estate workers, and native Melanesian Fijians rioted against Indians in an apparent effort to force them to leave the island.[3] A similar process of rejection may soon be at work in the former Soviet republics, where 25 million Russians are widely regarded as illegitimate settlers imposed by the Soviet regime. In all, there are 65 million ex-Soviet citizens, Russians and non-Russians, who live outside their own ethnic polity. Migration is already under way from Kazakhstan, Ukraine, Uzbekistan, Armenia, and Azerbaijan.

The political consequences for the home country of these return migrations should be noted. The repatriation of French *pieds-noirs* from Algeria led to the growth of anti-Arab sentiment that contributed to the emergence of Jean-Marie Le Pen's National Front, which continues to be in the forefront of attacks against Algerians in France. The exodus of Greeks from Turkish Anatolia in the 1920s to northern Greece sparked the development of an antimonarchist movement because migrants held the monarchy responsible for Greece's aborted attack against Turkey, which resulted in the forced exodus. The subsequent overthrow of the monarchy and the growth of the Communist Party in Greek Macedonia was in some measure the result of a population influx. In Pakistan, the migrants from India (the *muhajirs*) lost their dominant political position after 1956 when the military assumed power, but they continued to operate as an ethnic lobby, especially in the province of Sind, where they frequently clash with the local population. The *muhajir*-Sindhi ethnic cleavage has been the centerpiece of politics in the province.

In India, the refugee population from Pakistan assumed importance in the politics of northern India. Hindu refugees from Pakistan provided the core support for India's Hindu nationalist political party, the Bharatiya Jana Sangh. Subsequently restructured into the Bharatiya Janata Party, the BJP emerged in the 1990s as India's leading opposition party. A regional party in the state of Punjab, the Akali Dal, derives its strength from Sikh refugees from Pakistan, many of whom have been in the forefront of the agitation for the secession of the state from India.

A fifth wave of international migration, overlapping with the fourth, emerged in the 1950s and 1960s in response to the rising demand for imported labor in Western Europe, the United States, and the oil-producing countries of the Middle East. Migrants from Turkey, North Africa, and Yugoslavia were recruited as temporary workers for industrial employment in Western Europe. The United States recruited temporary farmworkers from Mexico and the Caribbean. Saudi Arabia,

---

3. Colonel Sitveni Rabuka, a Melanesian, took over the government and arrested all cabinet members. The coup was endorsed by the Great Council of Chiefs and was quickly followed by race riots and attacks on Indian property. For an account of the 1987 coup, see *Far Eastern Economic Review,* June 4, 1987, p. 38. It is estimated that in 1987, Fiji's population of 714,000 was 48.6 percent of Indian origin and 46.2 percent of Melanesian origin. For an account of subsequent emigration by many Indians from Fiji, see *Far Eastern Economic Review,* June 28, 1990, p. 15.

Libya, Iraq, and the smaller states of the Persian Gulf recruited migrant workers from Egypt, Yemen, and South and Southeast Asia. Britain admitted migrants from its former colonies in South Asia and the Caribbean.

Though worker flows were intended by recruiting countries to be temporary, many guest workers have become permanent additions to the population of their host countries, thereby changing the ethnic and religious characteristics of the host societies. Islam has emerged as a new force in Europe; Asians have become the dominant non-Arab element in the labor force in the Middle East and in some countries are more numerous than the Arab immigrant population; and Latinos are rapidly supplanting blacks as the largest minority group in the United States.

The most distinctive feature of all five waves of migrations is that they changed the social structures, and especially the ethnic compositions, of both sending and receiving countries, sometimes in the direction of greater ethnic homogeneity, sometimes in the direction of greater heterogeneity. State formations have resulted in forced emigrations, which have in turn shaped the politics and social structure of the receiving country. Population movements across international boundaries have also led to the formation of new states. In short, migrants create states, and states create migrants.

GLOBALIZATION AND THE DEMOGRAPHICS OF EMIGRATION

Why has there been such a massive increase in the number of people who want to leave their countries? The global changes that induce international flows are by now well known. The emergence of a global system of communication provides individuals with knowledge of opportunities elsewhere and information about the entry rules of countries to which they might wish to go. Thanks to the ease and low cost of transportation, distances are no longer a significant barrier to global migration. Differentials in income and employment opportunities among countries are now known to populations throughout the world. High population growth rates have made it difficult for developing countries to provide employment for new entrants into the labor force. Low population growth rates in developed countries, combined with rapid rates of economic growth, have periodically generated employment demands. The structure of labor markets in advanced industrial countries has changed to produce an increased demand for low-wage labor in selected service sectors of the economy.

In sum, worldwide migration is to a large extent the result of the globalization of world trade, communications, and transportation. But not entirely. A considerable part of international migration is also the result of state policies to encourage or force emigration in pursuit of various political, economic, and foreign policy objectives. Indeed, much of the world's migration today is the result of the policies and actions of states that directly or indirectly encourage, induce, or force their citizens to leave. But before we examine these policies, let us first briefly review some of the demographic consequences of international migration.

The demographic impact of migration is generally felt more by the receiving than the sending country, but for a few source countries, emigration has made a noticeable demographic difference.[4] As much as one-third of the population of Suriname and Puerto Rico has emigrated. The exodus from other Caribbean states has also been proportionately large. About 1.7 million people emigrated from the independent Caribbean states to the United States between 1960 and 1983, out of a total population of 28 million.[5] Similarly, in North African countries, the proportion of emigrants to the total national labor force in the mid-1970s was considerable: 19.5 percent for Algeria, 12.3 percent for Morocco, 10.6 percent for Tunisia. For the countries of Southern Europe, the proportions were also high, at 8.8 percent for Yugoslavia, 6.8 percent for Greece, 5.2 percent for Turkey, and 6 percent for Italy.[6]

For most of the Third World, however, emigration has been of minor demographic importance. The population of today's low-income economies increased from 2.246 billion in 1980 to 2.948 billion in 1989, while that of middle-income economies increased from 872 million to 1.105 billion.[7] The population increase in the Third World thus averaged approximately 90 million per year, while the total flow of emigrants from the Third World has been about 3 to 4 million a year (with substantial fluctuations related to refugee flows), or no more than around 4 percent of the annual population growth in the Third World. According to UN estimates, 100 million people are resident outside their nations of citizenship—only slightly more than the entire annual increase in the population of the Third World. Thus no conceivable increase in emigration could provide significant relief from the burden of high population growth.

In this respect, the experience of the contemporary Third World differs from that of the countries of Western Europe during their periods of high population growth. In the nineteenth century, emigration provided Europe with an important outlet for its rapidly growing labor force. Significant portions of Europe's rural population, forced off the land by a declining demand for agricultural labor, migrated not to Europe's urban centers but to the United States, Canada, Latin America, and Australia. The proportion of annual entrants into the labor force who became emigrants was therefore demographically significant. In some decades, emigration drew off nearly 40 percent of Europe's natural increase.[8]

Some writers have argued, on the basis of the European experience, that there is a link—a necessary link—between high population growth and the need for emi-

---

4. For a statistical review of global migration trends, see Sharon Stanton Russell, *International Migration in North America, Europe, Central Asia, the Middle East and North Africa* (Geneva: Economic Commission for Europe, 1993), and Sharon Stanton Russell, *Migration Between Developing Countries in Sub-Saharan Africa and Latin America* (New York: United Nations Population Division, 1993).

5. Robert A. Pastor (ed.), *Migration and Development in the Caribbean* (Boulder, Colo.: Westview Press, 1985), p. 8.

6. S. Sassen-Koob, "The International Circulation of Resources and Development: The Case of Migrant Labor," *Development and Change,* 1978, p. 525.

7. For detailed data on population growth by geographic regions, income groups, and individual countries, see Rodolfo A. Bulatao, Eduard Bos, Patience W. Stephens, and My T. Vu, *World Population Projections 1989–90 Edition* (Baltimore: The Johns Hopkins University Press, published for the World Bank, 1990).

8. Frank Thistlethwaite, "Migration, Ethnicity, and the Rise of an Atlantic Economy," in *A Century of European Migrations: 1830–1930*, ed. Rudolph J. Vecoli and Suzanne M. Sinke (Urbana: University of Illinois Press, 1991).

gration. Historian Paul Kennedy asserts that the United Kingdom's population explosion in the nineteenth century (Britain's population rose fourfold, from less than 10 million in 1800 to 41 million in 1900) was eased by the export of more than 18 million people from the British Isles. He further argues that the contemporary refugee and illegal migration phenomena are the result of the vast "surplus" population presently arising in developing countries.[9]

Despite the widespread fear in advanced industrial countries that rapid population growth in the Third World will lead to large-scale emigration, or a kind of population dumping on the part of overcrowded countries, there is no evidence that emigration rates and population growth rates are related. It is true that some population-exporting countries have had high population growth rates—among them Algeria (3.0 percent in the 1980s), Morocco (2.6 percent), Tunisia (2.5 percent), and Mexico (2.1 percent)—but other major population-exporting countries such as Greece, Yugoslavia, and Portugal have had population growth rates below 1 percent per year since 1965. It should also be noted that populations often move from one high-population-growth country to another—from Bangladesh to India, from Columbia to Venezuela, from South Asia to the Persian Gulf States. There are also substantial population movements among low-population-growth-rate countries, as from Eastern Europe to Central Europe.

Nor do countries with high population growth rates and heavily populated regions with large numbers of young educated unemployed—the nightmare case for people who fear a population influx from the Third World—necessarily produce a massive exodus. If such conditions were sufficient, the island of Java ought to be one of the world's largest producer of emigrants. Java's population of 107 million people is crowded onto an island at a density of 798 persons per square kilometer. The population has literally exploded from 3 million in 1800. Furthermore, Java has a young age pyramid, meaning that 1.6 million young people enter the labor force each year. Educational levels are high because Indonesia has six years of compulsory schooling. Whereas 70 percent of the working-age population had not completed primary school in 1971, by 1984 the figure had dropped to 41 percent. Furthermore, young people in Java have at least as much access to global television as young people in countries of large-scale emigration. Yet few Javanese migrate to the Middle East, to peninsular Malaysia (Indonesian migrants to Malaysia are from Sumatra and the other "outer islands"), to Japan, or to nearby Australia, as other peoples in South and Southeast Asia do. Javanese students abroad generally return home, even those given opportunities to seek employment abroad. Nor have the Javanese been responsive to the government– and World Bank–sponsored program to encourage transmigration from crowded Java to the less populated islands of Indonesia. Clearly, rapid population growth, unemployment, high levels of education, exposure to global media, and ease of access to other countries are not necessarily determinants of migration. A single case, of course, does not refute all arguments that population growth or high population density will induce large-scale emigration, but it does suggest the need for extreme caution in suggesting that

9. Paul Kennedy, *Preparing for the Twenty-first Century* (New York: Random House, 1993), pp. 44–45. Kennedy writes: "In view of the imbalances in demographic trends between 'have' and 'have-not' societies, it seems unlikely that there will not be a great wave of migration in the twenty-first century. . . . Enhanced efforts to control migration, therefore, are unlikely to succeed in the face of the momentous tilt in the global demographic balance."

movements from low- to high-income states are the result of rapid population growth and that international migration can therefore by reduced by more effective population policies.[10]

Nor is there evidence that the low economic growth rates in developing countries necessarily induce emigration or, the reverse, that high economic growth rates will slow emigration. The average per capita annual economic growth rates of many countries with high emigration rates are no less, and in several instances are higher, than those of countries to which migrants go. Mexico's per capita growth rate between 1960 and 1980 was actually higher than that of the United States. Similarly, Colombia's economy grew faster than Venezuela's, and Turkey, Greece, and Yugoslavia did better economically than Germany when their emigration rates were high. More strikingly, Puerto Rico experienced rapid industrial growth and an expansion in the demand for labor at the very time that it was the source of the largest single migration from the Caribbean to the U.S. mainland.

Economic theory suggests that migration and trade are substitutes. Free trade, it is argued, "eventually" reduces migration as trade in labor-intensive goods is substituted for labor migration. In the short run, however, trade can induce flows by providing would-be immigrants with the financial resources, information, and greater opportunities to migrate; and in some instances, free trade can lead to job losses in selected industries in the population-sending country that cannot compete with its trading partner (for example, the corn industry in Mexico). Most economic analysts argue that when employment levels and wage rates between population-sending and population-receiving countries become nearly equal, the movement of peoples is likely to subside—neglecting to note that there are high internal migration rates within developed countries, reflecting the unequal growth in employment and wages that characterize modern economies.

Neither population growth rates in the sending countries nor short-term changes in the unemployment rate in the sending countries seem to be related to changes in emigration rates. Rather, the ebb and flow of international labor migration to the United States, Western Europe, and the oil-producing countries of the Persian Gulf, Nigeria, and Venezuela have largely reflected the changing demands for labor in these regions. Economic migration has been induced at least as much by demand as by supply. Once the flows begin, however, they can continue even after the demand for labor has ended. If there is a single "law" in migration, it is that a migration flow, once begun, induces its own flow. Migrants enable their friends and relatives back home to migrate by providing them with information about how to migrate, resources to facilitate movement, and assistance in finding jobs and housing.

---

10. Javanese attribute their unwillingness to emigrate to their deep cultural attachment to one another and to their intimate familial ties. "Eating or not, it is better to be together" is a Javanese aphorism. "We have a kind of mystical, almost cosmological feeling about Java," a Javanese demographer explained to me, "that makes us reluctant to be anyplace else." One foreign observer attributed the low outmigration rate to the Javanese sense of insecurity and anxiety about the unknown. Whatever the explanation, the contrast between Java and the Chinese province of Fujian, with its substantial emigration rate, could not be greater. The two cases demonstrate that international networks, historic flows outward, the ties of kinfolk and community, levels of aspiration, and willingness to take risks can influence the volume of emigration independent of demographic and economic considerations.

Conditions in sending countries obviously matter a great deal in increasing emigration flows. Internal political upheavals and mass expulsions have led to large-scale migration. Indeed, in many areas of the world, there are more refugees than there are people who migrated in response to employment opportunities. As we have already noted, worldwide refugee flows increased by a million or more a year in the past decade, and in some years crises in particular countries have led to large outpourings. A million or more fled Indochina after the Communist victories, and another 700,000 left Cuba between 1960 and 1983. The Communist coup and Soviet invasion of Afghanistan led 5 to 6 million Afghans to flee to Pakistan and Iran, the largest single exodus from any country in the 1980s. There have also been large-scale refugee movements within Africa and government-sponsored expulsions from Burma, Uganda, Sri Lanka, and Vietnam. Supply-push factors are as likely (if not more likely) to be political than economic.

FORCED EMIGRATION

Most of the world's population flows since World War II did not merely happen; they were made to happen. For the governments of sending countries, emigration may serve a variety of political objectives. Emigration can be a solution to the problems of cultural heterogeneity. It can be a device for dealing with political dissidents, including class enemies. And it can be a mechanism for affecting the domestic and foreign policies of other states.

Cultural Homogeneity or Ethnic Dominance

Emigration can serve as a means of achieving cultural homogeneity or of asserting the dominance of one ethnic community over another. Such flows have a long and sordid history. The rise of nationalism in Europe was accompanied by state actions to eject religious communities that did not subscribe to the established religion and ethnic minorities that did not belong to the dominant ethnic community. In the fifteenth century, the Spanish crown expelled the Jews. In the sixteenth century, the (Catholic) French expelled the (Protestant) Huguenots. In the seventeenth and eighteenth centuries, the British crown induced Protestant dissenters to settle in the colonies. And in the nineteenth and early twentieth centuries, Greek, Bulgarian, Turkish, and Romanian minorities throughout Eastern and Southeastern Europe were put to flight.[11]

Many of the population movements in postindependence Africa, the Middle East, and South and Southeast Asia were similarly linked to the rise of nationalism and the emergence of new states. The boundaries of the new postcolonial regimes often divided linguistic, religious, and tribal communities. Minorities in these situations, fearful of the future and often facing discrimination and violence, frequently migrated to join their ethnic brethren in a neighboring country. Many Third World countries also expelled their ethnic minorities, especially if they constituted

---

11. Eugene M. Kulischer, *Europe on the Move* (New York: Columbia University Press, 1948), pp. 248–249.

an industrious class of migrant origin competing with a middle-class ethnic major-ity.[12] Governments facing unemployment within the majority community and con-flicts among ethnic groups over language and educational opportunities often regarded the expulsion of a prosperous, well-placed minority as a politically popu-lar policy. Sometimes, more subtle tactics were used to induce migration. Minorities were threatened by the state's antagonistic policies toward their religion, language, and culture, as the state sought to impose a hegemonic ethnic or religious identity on its citizens.[13] Economically successful minorities were often told that others would be given preferences in employment, in effect making it difficult for minorities to compete on the basis of merit.[14]

Other governments were less covert about their goal of cultural homogeneity and simply expelled their minorities or created conditions so extreme that minori-ties had to leave. The list of minorities encountering such treatment is long: Chinese in Vietnam; Indians and Pakistanis in East Africa; Vietnamese in Cambodia; Chinese in Indonesia; Tamils in Sri Lanka; Baha'is in Iran, Kurds in Turkey, Iran, and Iraq; Ahmediyas in Pakistan; Chakmas in Bangladesh; and com-munities in Rwanda, Ethiopia, and Sudan.[15] To this list from the Third World we must now add the minorities in each of the successor states of Yugoslavia and in several of the successor states of the Soviet Union.[16]

The largest contemporary flow from successor states is from former Yugoslavia. When Yugoslavia was a single state, there was considerable migration within the country: Serbs and Croatians moved to Vojvodina and Slovenia, and all groups moved to multiethnic Bosnia. The disintegration of Yugoslavia led to a war in which the principal actors regarded the forced exodus of minorities as part of the process by which they created homogeneous ethnic states. The result was a massive exodus among the successor states. Croatia bears the burden of 600,000 refugees in a pop-ulation of 4.5 million, but an estimated 425,000 refugees had also fled to other countries by mid-1992. The largest group (200,000) went to Germany, where there was already a large Yugoslav population (mainly Croatians).

12. In 1969, for example, Kenya announced that 80,000 noncitizen Asians must leave, and in 1972, Uganda expelled its Indian population, most of which was part of the country's middle class. See Aristide R. Zolberg, Astri Suhrke, and Sergio Aguayo, *Escape from Violence* (Oxford: Oxford University Press, 1989), pp. 65–66.

13. Sri Lanka is an example. See Stanley J. Tambiah's books *Sri Lanka* (Chicago: University of Chicago Press, 1986) and *Buddhism Betrayed?* (Chicago: University of Chicago Press, 1992).

14. Two examples are Malaysia, where the government adopted a policy of giving preferences in employment and education to Malays over Chinese, and Sri Lanka, where government gave preference to Sinhalese over Tamils. For these and other examples, see Donald L. Horowitz, *Ethnic Groups in Conflict* (Berkeley: University of California Press, 1985), pp. 185–228.

15. Ibid., pp. 198–209.

16. The war for "ethnic cleansing" in Yugoslavia is a glaring example of governments seeking to force populations to move in an effort to establish ethnic hegemony over a territory; in this particular instance, it was combined with an effort to force a change in the borders by establishing Serbian demographic and military preponderance in areas of Croatia and Bosnia-Herzegovina that could then be incorporat-ed into Serbia. Misha Glenny, in "Yugoslavia: The Revenger's Tragedy," *New York Review of Books*, August 13, 1992, pp. 37–43, warns that majority-minority conflicts in Kosovo and Macedonia, accom-panied by similar refugee flights, could lead to military action by Albania, Bulgaria, Greece, or Turkey.

Political Dissidents and Class Enemies

The ancient Greeks were among the earliest to strip dissidents of citizenship and cast them into exile. Socrates himself was offered the option of going into exile rather than being executed. (He chose to drink poisonous hemlock rather than become a refugee!) Contemporary authoritarian governments have both expelled dissidents (Solzhenitsyn from the Soviet Union) and allowed them to go into exile as an alternative to imprisonment (Benigno Aquino from the Philippines).[17]

Governments have expelled not simply handfuls of dissidents but substantial portions of the population hostile to the regime. Revolutionary regimes have often regarded the large-scale emigration of a social class as a way of transforming the country's social and political structure. The exodus of 700,000 people from Cuba, a large proportion of the Cuban middle class, was regarded by the Castro regime as a way of disposing of a segment of society hostile to socialism. Similarly, in 1971, the Pakistani government sought to weaken the insurgency in East Pakistan by forcing large numbers of Bengali Hindus out of the country. The Vietnamese government used expulsions to eliminate a bourgeois class opposed to the regime. The Cambodian government forced into exile or killed citizens "tainted" with French and other Western influences in an effort to reduce its cultural and economic ties with the West. And in Afghanistan, the Soviet and Afghan military forced populations hostile to the Communist regime to flee to Pakistan and Iran.[18]

Foreign Policy Objectives

Governments force emigration to exert pressure on neighboring states or to establish political influence abroad, although they usually deny having any such intent. Implicit in some instances is the promise that these flows can be halted if the receiving country yields to one or more policy demands made by the sending country. The United States government believed that this was the case in Haiti in the late 1970s. The Haitian government was thought to be encouraging its citizens to flee by boat to Florida in order to press the United States to increase its economic aid.[19] (In mid-1994, opponents of the Haitian government urged Haitians to flee by boat in an effort to press the United States to take steps to remove the government

17. Contemporary political exiles are now primarily from the Third World. On exile politics, see the special issue *Third World Quarterly,* January 1987, and Yossi Shain, *The Frontier of Loyalty* (Middletown, Conn.: Wesleyan University Press, 1989).

18. For accounts of forced migration as an instrument of both domestic and foreign policy, see Michael S. Teitelbaum, "Forced Migration: The Tragedy of Mass Expulsions," in *Clamor at the Gates,* ed. Nathan Glazer (San Francisco: Institute for Contemporary Studies, 1985), and Peter H. Koehn, *Refugees from Revolution* (Boulder, Colo.: Westview Press, 1991).

19. This outcome was achieved. As part of its effort to halt Haitian migration to the United States, the Reagan administration promised increased amounts of foreign aid to improve the conditions that purportedly promoted the flow. For an account of how the United States used its aid program to persuade the Haitian government to prosecute traffickers in illegal migrants and to pledge not to mistreat return migrants, see Jorge I. Dominguez, "Immigration as Foreign Policy in U.S.–Latin American Relations," in *Immigration and U.S. Foreign Policy,* ed. Robert W. Tucker, Charles B. Keely, and Linda Wrigley (Boulder, Colo.: Westview Press, 1990); also see Gil Loescher and John A. Scanlan, *Calculated Kindness* (New York: Free Press, 1986).

of Haiti.) Similarly, in the 1980s, Pakistani officials believed that Soviet pressure on Afghans to flee was in part intended to force Pakistan to seek a settlement with the Afghan regime and withdraw military aid to the insurgents.[20]

In some cases, sending countries appeared to be after more than just a foreign policy change. In the 1970s, the Malaysian government thought that Chinese refugees were being sent by Vietnam to destabilize its already ethnically divided society.[21] And many observers believed that the East Germans permitted Tamil refugees to enter West Germany through Berlin in an attempt to force the Federal Republic to establish new rules of entry that would tacitly recognize the East German state or to gain additional financial credit. (In point of fact, the west subsequently granted credit in return for the east's halting the flow.)

In the eighteenth and nineteenth centuries, colonization was also an instrument of European and American foreign policy, a strategy for extending control over a territory. The British, as we have noted, settled colonies in the western hemisphere, in southern and eastern Africa, and in the Pacific; the French settled in North Africa; the Portuguese settled in Angola, Mozambique, and Brazil; the Russians moved into Ukraine, Moldova, the Baltic states, and portions of Muslim-populated Central Asia;[22] the Germans moved eastward into Poland and Russia; and the Americans moved westward into Mexican and Indian territories.[23]

Even when migration is not used by sending governments to gain explicit foreign policy objectives or to establish political control, emigration has been regarded as a means of extending political and cultural influence. For example, in the nineteenth century, the German economist Frederick List advocated emigration as a form of cultural colonization of the Turkish Empire by Germans. Other German leaders and nationalist intellectuals advocated emigration to extend Germany's political and cultural influence in Greece, which had a Bavarian king. German intellectuals, who initially advocated emigration to the United States, subsequently turned critical when it became apparent that there was a high rate of assimilation. Instead, they advocated emigration to Latin America, where migrants might retain German culture.[24]

Like the German government in the nineteenth century, the governments of a number of contemporary developing countries, including Turkey, Greece, India, Algeria, and pre-1991 Yugoslavia, have actively promoted the language and culture

20. U.S. Department of State, *Afghanistan* (Washington, D.C.: Government Printing Office, 1987).

21. For an account of Malaysia and Thai government responses to refugees from Vietnam, see Loescher and Scanlan, *Calculated Kindness,* p. 135; also see Lesleyanne Hawthorne, *Refugee* (London: Oxford University Press, 1982).

22. Alexandre A. Bennigsen and S. Enders Wimbush, "Migration and Political Control: Soviet Europeans in Soviet Central Asia," in *Human Migration,* ed. William H. McNeill and Ruth S. Adams (Bloomington: Indiana University Press, 1978).

23. There are also closely related economic motives to colonization. John Stuart Mill, among others, suggested that a country could overcome the tendency to diminishing returns from land by sending people overseas to cultivate open spaces. For an analysis of the economic dimensions of colonization, see Brinley Thomas, *Migration and Economic Growth* (Cambridge: Cambridge University Press, 1973).

24. Mack Walker, *Germany and the Emigration, 1816–1885* (Cambridge, Mass.: Harvard University Press, 1964), p. 118.

of their country among emigrants and their children. Koranic schools have been organized in Germany by the Islamic Cultural Center, a private Turkish group in Cologne. The Bharatiya Vidya Bhavan, an organization supported by the Indian government, promotes Indian culture in the United States. Hundreds of similar cultural institutions from other nationalities can be found throughout the United States and Western Europe. How effective they are in promoting the foreign policy interests of the country of emigration, in addition to promoting language and culture, is a matter that bears study. In the United States, Greek migrants and their descendants have clearly played an influential role in U.S.-Greek and U.S.-Turkish relations, and Jews, Poles, Cubans, and other groups of migrant origin have influenced U.S. foreign policy. If Algerians, Turks, Greeks, and other migrant groups acquire citizenship and voting rights in European countries, they may play a similar role there.

In the nineteenth century, the imperial powers also moved populations from one territory to another in pursuit of their own economic and political interests. Slaves were transported from Africa to the Caribbean and to North and South America. With the abolition of slavery, the British established a system of indentured labor that enabled them to satisfy the labor needs in their colonies (especially on British-owned plantations) by moving Indians to East Africa, Mauritius, the Caribbean, and Fiji.[25] The colonial powers also encouraged the migration of entrepreneurial communities, traders, and moneylenders, whom they regarded as politically pliable: Indians to the Persian Gulf states, Lebanese to West Africa, and Chinese to Southeast Asia.

Internal colonization can also have international repercussions if the native people of an internally colonized region flee across international borders, though the policy may not have been adopted with the intention of affecting other states. There are numerous instances of governments inducing their own settled agricultural populations to move from densely populated to less densely populated regions. In such cases, hostile and often violent reactions from the local population may lead to prolonged civil conflict and an exodus of local people across the international border. This was the case when an influx of Burmans into the Muslim areas of southwestern Burma led to the flight of Arakanese Bengali-speaking Muslims from Burma to Bangladesh. Similarly, the Chakma tribals, a Buddhist community in the Chittagong Hill Tracts of Bangladesh, fled to India when their lands were occupied by Bangladeshi Muslim agriculturalists.

In summary, then, induced or forced emigration can be and has often been a foreign policy tool. States have used this instrument to destabilize another, force recognition, stop a neighboring state from interfering in its internal affairs, prod a neighboring state to provide aid or credit in return for stopping the flow, or extend their own political, cultural, and economic interests or those of a dominant ethnic group through internal or external colonization or decolonization.

---

25. For accounts of how the British settled South Asians in their colonies in Burma, Uganda, Kenya, Malawi, Mauritius, Guyana, Malaysia, South Africa, Fiji, and the Caribbean, see two books by Hugh Tinker, *A New System of Slavery* (London: Oxford University Press, 1974) and *The Banyan Tree* (Oxford: Oxford University Press, 1977).

An examination of both historical and contemporary population movements thus demonstrates that countries of emigration have more control over international population flows than is widely believed and that apparently spontaneous emigration and refugee movements may actually represent deliberate policies on the part of sending countries. It is simplistic, if not naive, to view refugee flows simply as the unintended consequences of internal upheavals or economic crises. To do so is to ignore the eagerness of some governments to reduce or eliminate selected social classes and ethnic groups and to affect the politics and policies of other states.[26]

RESTRICTED EMIGRATION

Not only may states induce emigration, but they may also prevent or restrict the emigration of their citizens. Paradoxically, some countries that compel emigration also restrict emigration. These "complementary techniques of control," to use Aristide Zolberg's morally neutral phrase,[27] are essential policies for regimes that rely heavily on coercion. By foreclosing the option of emigration, authoritarian regimes seek to force their dissidents to come to terms with the prevailing political and social order. At the same time, expulsion is a mechanism that these same regimes employ against people that they do not want to assimilate culturally or integrate politically.[28]

Most of the countries that have had tight or partial restrictions on emigration were at the time members of the Communist bloc.[29] The list includes Angola, Ethiopia, Mozambique, Afghanistan, Cambodia, Laos, Mongolia, North Korea, Vietnam, Albania, Bulgaria, Czechoslovakia, East Germany, Romania, the Soviet Union, South Yemen, Cuba, Nicaragua, Poland, Hungary, and China. The Soviet Union and other Eastern bloc countries regarded emigration as a disloyal act, a rejection of their regimes, that undermined their policies to mobilize human resources for production. A large-scale exodus was, moreover, regarded as an unacceptable blow to Soviet self-esteem.[30] Hence fears that an open border could lead to a substantial outflow contributed directly to the East German and Soviet decision to erect the Berlin Wall to halt a hemorrhage to the West. Other countries that have forbidden or restricted emigration include Iraq, Namibia, Rwanda, South Africa, Tanzania, Cameroon, Togo, Iran, Somalia, Burma, Libya, Sudan, and Syria.

Authoritarian regimes that restrict emigration may at times allow exit, but only in pursuit of government objectives rather than as a matter of individual rights.

26. A useful bibliographic guide to the vast literature on refugees is Julian Davies (compiler), *Displaced Peoples and Refugee Studies* (London: Zell, 1990).

27. Aristide R. Zolberg, "International Migrants in Political Perspective," in *Global Trends in Migration,* ed. Mary M. Kritz, Charles B. Keely, and Silvano M. Tomasi (New York: Center for Migration Studies, 1981), p. 23.

28. Alan Dowty, *Closed Borders* (New Haven, Conn.: Yale University Press, 1987), pp. 60–61.

29. Ibid., p. 198.

30. Ibid., p. 73.

Thus the Bulgarian Communist regime sometimes permitted ethnic Turks to leave to ensure greater ethnic homogeneity. The Soviet Union permitted a limited number of Jews, Germans, and Armenians—groups with international ties—to emigrate. Foreign policy considerations were a factor, as the United States put considerable pressure on the Soviet Union to permit Jews to emigrate. For some time, the government of Romania permitted Jews to leave, but only if they repaid the government for the cost of their education. This policy—defined as compensation for educational expenditures by the Romanian government and as selling Jews for hard currency by its critics—ended after the U.S. government threatened to cancel its favored-nation tariff policy toward Romania.[31]

The dismantling of the Berlin Wall and the concomitant opening of Eastern European and Soviet borders ended the era of closed borders within Europe, but the right to exit continues to be denied in several remaining Communist states, notably China, Cuba, and North Korea. Western European refugee and immigration policies had been implicitly predicated on the assumption that the Communist countries of Eastern Europe prohibited exit; anyone who fled a country that barred exit was automatically assumed to have a well-founded fear of persecution and was therefore entitled to asylum. Moreover, few people actually succeeded in fleeing (except for onetime substantial flows from Poland, Hungary, and Czechoslovakia), so in most years the number of refugees was generally small and manageable. Finally, anyone who fled a country that prohibited emigration could plausibly argue that repatriation would result in imprisonment or some other form of punishment. Paradoxically, the removal of exit barriers made it more difficult for individuals from Eastern Europe to obtain asylum in the West because they no longer met the definition of refugees and because, as the number of asylum seekers increased, the European states made their refugee and asylum policies more restrictive. The removal of exit barriers did, however, make a difference for Jews in the former Soviet Union and in Eastern Europe, who were now free to migrate to Israel. From 1990 to 1993, more than 400,000 Jews from the Soviet Union and Eastern Europe migrated to Israel, increasing Israel's population by nearly 10 percent.

China remains the largest closed country in the world, its citizens denied the freedom to emigrate. Nonetheless, small numbers of Chinese, particularly from the southern coastal province of Fujian, have sought asylum in the United States. In June 1993, the freighter *Golden Venture* ran aground off New York City with a boatload of 300 Chinese immigrants seeking political asylum. Thousands of other mainland Chinese have reportedly been smuggled into California. Some request asylum, but most find employment in a growing underground economy. Should the Chinese government ever freely allow its citizens to emigrate, it is not clear how many Chinese will attempt to leave or where they will seek entry.

Would an exodus from China be driven by poverty, unemployment, and large-scale population growth? In a report from China following the arrival of the *Golden Venture, New York Times* correspondent Nicholas Kristof reported on sentiment in

31. For a brief account of Soviet and Eastern European emigration policies, see United Nations, *International Migration, Policies and Programmes* (New York: United Nations, 1982), pp. 17–18.

Fujian province toward emigration. "The United States—what a place!" said Mr. R. T. Liang, a Fujian farmer. "It's so rich! If there weren't restrictions, everybody would leave here."[32] The 32 million people who live in Fujian province, noted Kristof, are among the most prosperous in China. Why, then, do Fujianese want to go abroad? A history teacher he interviewed explained: "We're on the coast, and so we know more about what life is like abroad. So while we're better off, we also know more than people in other parts of China what we are missing." Fujian province has had an economic growth rate of more than 15 percent a year, and its prospects for further growth are great, given the rate at which Taiwanese companies are moving their assembly lines to Fujian. Bicycles, radios, and television sets are ubiquitous, and employment and incomes are on the rise, but, writes Kristof, "ambitions are spiraling at an even faster clip." Mainland Chinese, Taiwanese, and Japanese smugglers have created an international migration network for smuggling illegal migrants abroad, mostly to the United States. For a large sum of money (immigrants reportedly paid as much as $50,000 to make the clandestine trip to the United States aboard the *Golden Venture*), smugglers arrange boat passage to the United States, where the migrants are then employed in an illegal underground economy at low wages, often under intolerable working conditions. But enough of the migrants do well to perpetuate the belief in China that emigrants can become rich. "We Fujianese think of the United States as a kind of heaven," said a worker whose older sister married a Chinese-American and is now living in Washington, D.C. "We worship the United States. I would love to go and work there, if only I could find a way."

It should be noted that most immigrants from Fujian go to Taiwan, not to the United States. Migrants may not earn as much, albeit still more than the $35 monthly pay typical in Fujian, but it is easier to cross the 150-kilometer Taiwan Strait on a fishing boat and less expensive than traveling to the United States. Taiwanese authorities estimate that in the five-year period from 1988 to 1993, as many as 50,000 illegal migrants have entered Taiwan, mostly from Fujian province. Paradoxically, some Taiwanese authorities prefer Southeast Asians to meet their labor shortages rather than mainland Chinese, who are easily assimilated and hence difficult to control.[33]

The Chinese case illustrates how modernization in the broadest sense (industrial growth, the expansion of communication and transportation, increased education) increases the propensity for both internal and international migration. The American historian Marcus Lee Hansen noted that there are three conditions for migration: freedom, desire, and means.[34] A rise in per capita incomes in China, Eastern Europe, and the states of the former Soviet Union will provide the financial means to would-be migrants as long as governments provide the freedom to leave. Large-scale emigration is particularly likely from a region with a tradition of emigration and already established linkages to the world outside. People from Fujian province, for example, have been emigrating since the seventeenth century to Taiwan, Singapore, Malaysia, and Indonesia. Similarly, there are close ties

32. Nicholas D. Kristof, "Where Chinese Yearn for 'Beautiful' U.S.," *New York Times,* June 20, 1993, p. 1.
33. *Far Eastern Economic Review,* August 5, 1993, p. 24.
34. Thistlethwaite, "Migration, Ethnicity," p. 37.

between specific villages and towns in the Caribbean and Mexico that have sent generations of young people to the United States and between towns in North Africa and Turkey and enclaves in Western Europe. The experience of Fujian province suggests that as the economies of other regions improve, the desire and the financial means for emigration will grow.

EMIGRATION AND MACROECONOMIC POLICIES

In addition to forced emigration and restricted emigration, governments use a variety of policies to encourage emigration in order to achieve various macroeconomic objectives. One of these is to provide partial relief for unemployment. In the mid-1970s, for example, more than 10 percent of the labor force in Portugal, Algeria, Morocco, and Tunisia emigrated to Western Europe. Similarly, large portions of the Mexican labor force found employment in the United States. In addition, 2 to 3 million South Asians were employed in the Persian Gulf before the Gulf War. Although such migrants constitute a minuscule fraction of the entire labor force of the sending countries, they represent a substantial proportion of the labor force from their home regions. It is estimated, for example, that a half million workers from the Indian state of Kerala, which has a population of 25 million and a high unemployment rate, have migrated to the Gulf states for employment. Similarly, selected regions of Jordan, Egypt, Turkey, Pakistan, Yugoslavia, Spain, Italy, Greece, and Colombia are significant suppliers of migrant workers.

In general, Third World governments encourage migration to ease unemployment among the lower-income, less skilled classes rather than from among the better-educated. At times, however, governments also promote a brain drain. Several Asian and Middle Eastern governments, responding to the demands of their middle classes, invested large sums in higher education (including medical and technical schools), thereby producing more graduates than could be absorbed by their respective economies. Though governments often publicly lament the brain drain, they may actually promote emigration for their middle class. For example, the Egyptian government has sought opportunities to export teachers to other Arab countries. The Korean government, through a state agency called the Korea Overseas Development Corporation, has run free language courses for potential emigrants, provided courses for those with special skills (nurses, computer programmers) who need to pass specialized accreditation tests, and offered loans of up to $200,000 for those who intend to start businesses abroad. With help from the International Labor Organization, Nepal established a program for the training of skilled workers for the construction industry to improve its capacity to export labor to the Middle East. The Republic of the Philippines expanded its medical schools to meet the demand for certain categories of medical personnel in the United States.

In addition to being a means of easing employment pressures, migration has also benefited countries through the flow of remittances. Remittances from migrants are of great economic importance to countries of emigration and are a factor in the development of government policies to encourage people to go abroad for employment. In 1982, developing countries received an estimated $40 billion in remittances. By 1989, the total value of official remittances worldwide was $65.5 billion, a figure higher than the $51 billion provided in official development assistance in 1988.[35] Furthermore, for some labor-exporting countries, such as Yugoslavia, Greece, Turkey, Italy, Portugal, Morocco, Pakistan, India, Egypt, and Yemen, remittances have been equal to a third or more of total earnings from exports. For several countries, remittances from emigration made up the total deficit in the balance of payments. Such remittance flows are so critical to the economic well-being of Mexico and El Salvador that proposed legislation by the United States to halt the flow of illegal migrants and to force illegal migrants to return to their countries of origin raises concerns in these countries about the effects on their balance of payments and unemployment rates. In the late 1980s, the government of El Salvador noted that Salvadorans in the United States sent between $350 million and $600 million home each year, a figure greater than the official U.S. aid program to the country. The Salvadoran government also estimated that a half million Salvadorans (about 10 percent of the country's total population) had entered the United States illegally.

Other examples also illustrate the importance of remittances. In response to an announcement by the United Arab Emirates that Indian migrants who overstayed their work permits or entered illegally would be sent home, the government of India sent a high-level delegation to dissuade the UAE from taking any hasty action. Governments in Southeast and East Asia have been competing for turnkey projects in the Middle East that would involve the sending of "package labor" consisting of construction workers. And Sri Lanka sent a cabinet officer to the Middle East to explore the manpower requirements of Gulf governments so that they could educate and recruit workers to meet those requirements.

Aside from their impact on the balance of payments, remittances provide substantial benefits to families who stay home. These funds can be used for purchasing food, land, housing, and consumer durables, as well as for education and sending other family members abroad. Remittances may lead to productive investment because family members put capital into agriculture, create new businesses, or set aside savings that may then be recycled for investment. Some studies also report that migration is a source of class mobility for returning migrants and for their families.[36]

A third economic reason for governments to encourage emigration is that it can be an instrument for relieving the state from bearing the costs—political as well as economic—of social welfare. In the eighteenth and nineteenth centuries, several European governments encouraged emigration as a way of easing the social and political burdens on the political system created by poverty and crime. It has been estimated that in one century, beginning in 1788, England exiled 160,000 of its criminals to Australia, conveniently getting rid of prisoners and reducing the cost of maintaining prisons.[37] In the early part of the nineteenth century, the British government also viewed emigration as a way of relieving the costs of the Poor Law. Emigration was advocated by both the Poor Law Committee and the Irish

---

35. Sharon Stanton Russell and Michael S. Teitelbaum, *International Migration and International Trade* (Washington, D.C.: World Bank, 1992), p. 1.

36. Philip L. Martin, *The Unfinished Story* (Geneva: International Labor Organization, 1991), p. 44.

37. Robert Hughes, *The Fatal Shore* (New York: Knopf, 1987), p. 2.

Committees of the House of Commons to relieve pauperism, particularly in Ireland. Consistent with this view, Thomas Malthus, writing in the 1817 edition of his *Essay on the Principle of Population,* described emigration as a useful "temporary relief" during times of contraction in employment. In seven years of famine, from 1847 to 1854, fully 1.6 million Irish emigrated, mostly across the Atlantic.[38] Robert Owen advocated emigration as a way of decreasing the supply of labor and hence increasing wages.[39] The 1834 amendment to the Poor Law gave local government boards authority to use public funds to assist emigration. Poor Law authorities sent orphans abroad, particularly to Canada. British authorities also viewed migration as a benefit to their colonies and argued for colonization as a way of redistributing population in the empire and of promoting production and trade in the colonies.

Nor was Britain alone in regarding emigration as a means of reducing the costs of social welfare. In Germany, from which 1.5 million emigrated between 1871 and 1881, local officials believed that "a large body of indigent subjects constitute a social danger and a serious burden on meager public funds; better let them go."[40] Thus European politicians and intellectuals generally viewed the exodus with favor. Indeed, one American scholar wrote in 1890 that "there is something almost revolting in the anxiety of certain countries to get rid of their surplus population and to escape the burden of supporting the poor, the helpless and the depraved."[41]

Today such population dumping is not a significant element in the flow of migrants from the Third World to advanced industrial countries. Indeed, the education and skill levels of many of the emigrants calls attention to one last economic benefit of emigration: the use of migrants to obtain technology. Until recently, it was assumed that the brain drain entailed a loss of technological skills on the part of developing countries. It remains true that doctors, engineers, and scientists have been recruited by the West from developing countries; however, many developing countries now recognize the brain drain as a brain overflow, the result of an investment in education that exceeds the capacity of the economy to absorb skilled labor. Moreover, there is increasing recognition that some skilled migrants do return, capital in hand, with technologies that have been acquired from the West. Though the diffusion of electronics, telecommunications, and nuclear technologies to developing countries is largely the result of the commercial purchase of technology or investment by multinational corporations, it also partly reflects the role played in technology transfers by students and other short-term migrants to the West. Some countries have even systematically sought out their citizens abroad for investment and technology transfer: The People's Republic of China actively encourages overseas Chinese to invest in China, and the Indian government provides incentives to nonresident Indians for direct investments and joint ventures. Moreover, a single instance of technology transfer can be of extraordinary international importance, as

38. H. J. M. Johnston, *British Emigration Policy, 1815–1830* (Oxford: Clarendon Press, 1972), p. 165. Malthus also regarded remittances to Ireland from Irish emigration as a way of relieving distress for those who remained.

39. W. A. Carrothers, *Emigration from the British Isles* (London: Cass, 1965), p. 223.

40. Walker, *Germany and the Emigration,* p. 16.

41. Richmond Mayo-Smith, *Emigration and Immigration* (New York: Johnson Reprint, 1968; originally published 1890), pp. 197–198.

is the case of the role played by a Pakistani nuclear physicist who acquired nuclear technology while working in the Netherlands.

CRITICS OF EMIGRATION

The proponents of international labor migration argue that it is beneficial to both sending and receiving countries as an equilibrating mechanism for shifting labor from labor-surplus low-wage areas to labor-short high-wage areas, a shift that pushes wages up in the one and down in the other and thereby stimulates investment and productivity in both. The low-income sending country is believed to be a net gainer from emigration. Benefits include relief from unemployment, improvement in the wages of residents who remain behind, stimulation of technological investment and innovation as the labor supply declines, remittances that benefit a country's foreign exchange, increased availability of resources for investment, extra income that families can invest in health and education, a gain in exports as overseas migrants buy from the home market, and the opportunity for migrants to acquire new skills, attitudes, and technologies that may prove useful when they return home.

Each of these presumed benefits can and has been viewed in a negative light by scholars, journalists, and government officials in developing countries. Remittances, it is argued, are used for wasteful consumer expenditures rather than invested in productive activities. Migrants and their families hunger for foreign-made goods whose import reduces the foreign exchange benefits that accrue from remittances. Critics further argue that remittances induce inflation by pushing up the price of land, housing, and consumer goods. Nor, it is said, is the flow of technology associated with migration necessarily beneficial because laborsaving technologies may increase unemployment rates. The presumed skill benefits of returnees are discounted on the grounds that the ones who return are likely to be "failed migrants" who were unable to adjust to the labor market of the host country or to have acquired skills that are too job- or industry-specific to be of use in the home country.

Labor migration in general is seen by some critics as having more negative than positive consequences. Emigrants, argue the critics, tend to be young, innovative, and energetic, thereby draining a country's human resources. The loss of unskilled rural laborers reduces the agricultural labor supply, and the loss of skilled workers lowers the quality of industrial labor. Furthermore, investment by the home society in the education of people who migrate benefits only the receiving country, which has borne none of the costs. The departure of workers does not lead to an increased investment in technology because sending countries have little capital to invest, and when laborsaving technologies are introduced, they only worsen the employment plight of returned migrants.

Finally, say the critics, for the sending society, the gains from emigration are short-term. If migrants remain abroad or are joined by their families, remittance flows eventually cease. Return migration increases only when employment opportunities have declined in the receiving country, which means, in this global economy, that they have declined in the sending country as well. Thus receiving countries transfer their unemployment back to the sending country at a time when the sending country is least able to provide employment to nationals who return.

According to the critics, then, emigration is primarily a mark of dependence because it creates a dependent relationship between sending and receiving countries. Sending countries develop a need for remittances to satisfy a deficit in their balance of payments. Furthermore, the sending country is forced to adjust its labor market and educational system to the demands for labor by advanced industrial countries. On the individual level, migrants and their families develop a taste for, or dependence on, Western-made and Western-type consumer goods, or what is referred to as the "cult of consumerism"—a preference for jeans, digital watches, soft drinks, videotapes, stereo sets, and Western-style clothes. Among many young people, employment abroad is regarded as the key to economic success and social status, whereas staying at home promises only failure and poverty. Thus indigenous values and culture are derogated.

Few of these criticisms stand up against empirical scrutiny; the social and economic changes attributed to emigrants generally have other determinants. Consumerism and a preference for Western-made products and Western culture are more often the result of changing patterns of global communication, especially satellite television and movies, than of migration. There is no evidence that emigration has been of such a magnitude as to deplete rural areas of the amount or quality of labor needed to sustain agricultural growth; indeed, some of the highest rates of emigration have been from areas in which the agricultural growth rates is above average for developing countries. Nor is there evidence that high emigration rates are incompatible with rapid industrialization: Italy, with over a million workers employed elsewhere in Western Europe, experienced a 6.2 percent annual growth rate in industry from 1960 to 1970. Similarly, during this same period, Turkey, with 850,000 workers in Western Europe, had a 9.6 percent annual growth rate; Algeria, with 500,000 workers, nearly 20 percent of its workforce, abroad, grew at 11.6 percent; Greece, with 246,000 workers abroad, grew at 9.4 percent; and Mexico, with substantial emigration to the United States, had an industrial growth rate of 9.1 percent.[42]

The argument that remittances are "wasted" because migrants and their families engage in "unproductive" purchases of land and consumer goods is particularly curious. Clearly, a country gains more if migrants use some of their remittances to improve the technology and productivity of agriculture, start businesses, or invest their savings in new or expanding industries. The propensity of migrants to save and to transmit part of their savings to families at home and of returning migrants to bring substantial savings with them makes its reasonable to ask whether these savings contribute to economic growth. The failure of so many migrants to make "productive" investments is often a reason given for the disapproval of migration. Yet this same criterion is not normally applied to others in the society who have experienced substantial increases in income. What is the propensity to save and invest in productive activities on the part of doctors, lawyers, engineers, and other professionals with high and expanding incomes? Or on the part of workers in

42. *World Development Report, 1982* (New York: Oxford University Press. Published for the World Bank, 1982), pp. 110–111.

the industrial sector who have received large salary increases? Or even on the part of the vast numbers of government civil servants in most developing countries? If this criterion is to be applied convincingly to migrants' use of their money, it must also be applied to resident members of the society.

Moreover, any analysis of "productive" investment must be linked to the study of opportunities for such investment. The failure of agricultural families to use remittances in agriculture suggests that there are barriers to productive investment such as the system of land tenure, the high cost of inputs in relation to agricultural prices, and the lack of adequate marketing facilities.

In any event, the question of whether remittances are used productively by migrants is better recast as the question of whether savings are productively invested by banks and borrowers. Given the high propensity of migrants to save, the central question is first whether savings entering the official banking system increase the availability of credit and *then* whether the credit is productively employed—not whether the migrants themselves start businesses, purchase agricultural equipment, or invest in the stock market. Furthermore, investments in agriculture and industry are not the only productive investments; investments in education and health contribute to a growth in human capital. An investment in housing for rental purposes often yields a high return to the investor. And although the purchase of land is often nonproductive, the sellers of land may spend their earnings in productive ways.

For the most part, the criticisms of emigration lack an empirical basis. Rather, such criticisms reflect a deep resentment that many nationalist intellectuals in the Third World feel toward the exodus of their people to industrialized Western countries. The issue of emigration as a mark of dependence is as much a statement about the political and psychological state of the relationship between sending and receiving countries as it is about the economic gains and losses resulting from emigration.

As much and as often as critics of emigration have pointed to its costs, they have not persuaded governments to forgo the benefits of remittances and the reduced unemployment that results from exporting labor. Indeed, even as emigration to Western Europe declined in the early 1970s, many Third World countries competed for opportunities to export their workers to the oil-producing countries of the Middle East. Remittances and the employment benefits of emigration have been seen as so important to the governments of most sending countries that policies adopted by receiving countries to reduce or terminate migration have been viewed with extreme concern.

Emigration is also regarded by some Third World governments as having political benefits, as well as serving economic objectives. Exile or forced migration can be used as punishment for critics of the regime and out-of-favor social classes or ethnic groups. Control over emigration can be a benefit to be distributed as a form of patronage. Emigration can be an instrument for forestalling social and political costs by reducing unemployment. Finally, forced emigration may provide a government with a bargaining chip in negotiations, as a means of exercising pressure on its neighbors for obtaining bilateral assistance. Key centers of power within a government generally recognize the benefits of emigration.

Ideological rhetoric is thus a poor guide to what government elites of the source countries of emigration actually believe. In fact, despite Marxist critics,

many leftist countries have been the most energetic in encouraging and even forcing emigration, and Third World nationalist critics of emigration are also among the
most opposed to entrance restrictions in advanced industrial countries. One is
reminded of the opening of the film *Annie Hall,* when Woody Allen tells the story
of two women complaining about their vacation in a hotel at a mountain resort:
"The food was positively poisonous," said one woman. "Yes," agreed the other, "and
in such small portions."

Like the two women in this story, Third World countries want the portions to
be larger. They actively promote emigration, oppose restrictions on immigration by
advanced industrial and oil-producing countries, and seek political alliances in the
receiving countries to ensure continued access. Thus the tightening of immigration
restrictions by the advanced industrial and oil-producing countries may become a
source of conflict between sending and receiving countries. A particularly sensitive
issue is the question of whether the nationals of a Third World country have the
same opportunities for immigration as others and are given equal rights and benefits as the citizens of the labor-importing country.

Even when migration flows and remittances have diminished, the major effects
of earlier international migrations are felt. Western Europe and North America
have significant numbers of people from the Third World, and the labor-importing
countries of the Persian Gulf have substantial numbers of Arab and Asian migrants.
How these populations are treated by the host society and what role the migrants
and their descendants play in forging economic, cultural, and political links
between the host country and their country of origin are questions that have significant long-term international relations consequences.

Perhaps the most politically explosive issue is looming on the horizon, though
it is currently voiced only by a handful of intellectuals and politicians in the Third
World and in the West. This is the demand for a new international demographic
order in which people from low-income countries would be readily admitted into
countries that are well-off. Although such a demand is unlikely to have any more of
an impact on the policies of advanced industrial countries than earlier calls for a
new international economic order, it may make it more difficult for industrial countries to persuade developing countries to take steps to reduce emigration or to
accept repatriated illegal immigrants and individuals whose claims for asylum have
been rejected.

PREDICTING EMIGRATION

To the extent that labor migration is largely determined by demands in the richer
economies and refugee flows are largely determined by political conditions in the
countries of origin, migration flows are not readily predictable. If recent trends
continue, it seems likely that most international migrations will be predominantly
regional: from North Africa, Turkey, and other Mediterranean states to Western
Europe; from Eastern Europe and the former Soviet Union to Central Europe;
from the Caribbean basin to the United States; from the poorer to the richer countries within Latin America (primarily to Venezuela and Argentina); from South Asia
and the non-oil Arab states to the oil-producing states of the Middle East; from

southern Africa to South Africa; and among the states of the Horn of Africa. Major question marks include whether China will become a major producer of emigrants, whether there will be large-scale movements among the former states of the Soviet Union, whether Japan will open its borders to become a major pole of attraction for migrants, and whether there will be substantial flows among the increasingly prosperous countries of Southeast Asia. A stable, economically expanding South Africa would be a magnet for people from other parts of Africa, but a violent, conflict-ridden South Africa could provoke a large exodus.

Economic integration within the European Union, the North American Free Trade area, and the Asia-Pacific region seems likely to account for much of future regional migration, but it remains uncertain how or even if states will be able to control entry. Demographers have argued that while richer countries will be seeking skilled migrants to meet their technological needs, poorer countries will want to export low-skilled migrants who may well find a niche in the service sectors of developed countries.[43] As states pick and choose whom they want, the pressure for illegal migration thus seems likely to increase. Refugee flows are obviously dependent on political conditions within states, particularly ethnic conflicts and civil wars, and conflicts among states. With an estimated 30 conflicts currently taking place in developing countries and refugee flows from Mozambique, Somalia, Ethiopia, Eritrea, Liberia, Angola, Azerbaijan, Burma, Sudan, Armenia, Rwanda, Tajikistan, Sierra Leone, Burundi, Sri Lanka, Western Sahara, Cambodia, and the former Yugoslavia, there is no indication that the magnitude of population movements will decline in the near future. We could also readily imagine strife within Burma, Iran, Pakistan, South Africa, and the states of the former Soviet Union or conflicts between India and Pakistan, Jordan and Syria, Greece and Macedonia, Serbia and Albania, Eritrea and Ethiopia, Tajikistan and Afghanistan, Bangladesh and Burma, Egypt and Sudan, Libya and Chad, and Thailand and Vietnam. The end of the cold war, moreover, has led to a rise in nationalism, a growth in the military expenditures of many Third World countries, and the proliferation of nuclear weapons and missile capabilities. As is often said, the Third World, Eastern Europe, and the states of the former Soviet Union remain dangerous places. In short, wars between states, ethnic strife, aborted democratic movements, droughts, floods, famines, and economic collapse in debt-ridden countries will all continue to fuel the flight of people across national boundaries.

The response of receiving countries will be critical in determining not only how many refugees are accepted but also whether and how receiving countries are able to resolve the internal conflicts that generate refugee flows. Can they take preventive measures to ameliorate conflict? Will they, individually or collectively, take action to restore order within and among states? What actions, if any, could be effective? Moreover, how receiving countries respond to an increasing number of both unfounded and legitimate requests for asylum, their own needs for labor, claims for family reunification through immigration, and illegal entrants will shape much of the world's future migration. The responses to international migration on the part of several advanced industrial societies will be considered in the next chapter.

43. John Salt, "The Future of International Labor Migration," *International Migration Review*, Winter 1992, p. 1077.

chapter 3

THE MIGRATION CRISIS IN THE NATION-STATE

Virtually all industrial societies are struggling with the problems of how to respond to pressures for increased migration and how to deal with migrants, legal or illegal, who live in their midst. Although the issues are generally similar—whether to admit refugees, how to deal with unfounded claims for asylum, what to do about illegals, whether and how to integrate existing migrants—countries that regard themselves as nonmigrant homogeneous nation-states have usually dealt with these issues differently than countries of migration. In this chapter, we will examine the migration crisis as it affects three such countries: Germany, Italy, and Japan. Germany is Europe's front-line state, no longer facing a hostile bloc to the east but rather a raft of countries producing refugees and asylum seekers eager for entry. Since the late 1980s, Germany has been the recipient of the largest number of asylum seekers in Western Europe. In 1992, fully 438,000 asylum seekers entered Germany, compared to 210,000 for the remainder of Western Europe. Members of the European Community (EC) recognized that any effort to reduce the flow into Western Europe and, in particular, to distinguish between newcomers who genuinely needed protection and those who sought asylum simply to migrate depended on the policies adopted by the German government. Italy presented the European Union (as the EC has been known since late 1992) with a second problem, an influx not only of asylum seekers but also of illegal migrants from the Third World. Italy is a country with little experience regulating entry, for in the not-too-distant past it was primarily a country of emigration. And like two other members of the European Union, Spain and Portugal, it remains a relatively easy entry point from the south. Our third case, Japan, provides us with an example of a country that sought to preserve its ethnic homogeneity after the Second World War by closing itself to migration but has recently been attracting migrant workers, mostly illegals, from China and Southeast Asia. Japan must now decide whether to adopt some kind of guest worker policy and, if so, whether the result would be the settlement of an immigrant class that would challenge Japan's self-image of ethnic homogeneity. All three countries have traditionally regarded themselves as nation-states with a common national identity, though national identity, firmly entrenched in Japan, remains a matter of contention in Germany and Italy. Migration thus opens the question of whether there can be multiple cultural identities. All three countries, historically countries of emigration, not immigration, now face an influx of unwanted migrants

Table 4   FLOW OF ASYLUM SEEKERS INTO SELECTED COUNTRIES, 1980–1992

Country	Asylum Seekers (thousands)				
	1980	1984	1988	1991	1992
Austria	9.3	7.2	15.8	27.3	16.2
Belgium	2.7	3.7	4.5	15.2	17.6
Denmark	0.2	4.3	4.7	4.6	13.9
Finland	—	—	0.1	2.1	3.6
France	18.8	21.6	34.3	47.4	28.9
Germany	107.8	35.3	103.4	256.1	438.0
Greece	—	0.8	9.3	2.7	2.0
Italy	—	4.6	1.4	24.5	2.6
Netherlands	1.3	2.6	7.5	21.6	17.1
Norway	0.1	0.3	6.6	4.6	5.2
Portugal	1.6	0.2	0.3	0.2	0.6
Spain	—	1.1	4.5	8.1	11.7
Sweden	—	12.0	19.6	26.5	83.2
Switzerland	6.1	7.4	16.7	41.6	18.1
United Kingdom	9.9	4.2	5.7	67.0	—

Note: 1992 data are provisional. A dash indicates that data are unavailable.

Source: Organization for Economic Cooperation and Development.

and asylum claimants. Can they—should they—adopt immigration policies, and if so, what criteria should be used to decide whom to admit?

By way of contrast, we will also look at a fourth case, Australia. Unlike Germany, Italy, and Japan, Australia has historically been a country of immigration, but it has also regarded itself as a homogeneous nation-state whose immigrants were primarily from the British Isles. Australia, too, has been concerned with issues of migration and absorption, but its approach has been sharply different from that of the other three countries. Australia has chosen to expand its migration intake and to diversify its sources and in the process become a more multicultural society. An examination of these four cases thus highlights the nature of the migration crises faced by nation-states but also suggests that there are a variety of alternative responses.

Before we turn to the cases, let us examine the debate over refugee, asylum, and migration policies within the European Union.

ONE NATION, ONE STATE VERSUS MULTICULTURALISM

The concept of the nation-state—a country made up of a single people with a shared history, culture, and language—first developed in Western Europe. Minorities were expected to assimilate, and those who did not, such as Bretons and

Basques with their own language and Jews, Hussites, Huguenots, and (in England) Roman Catholics with their nonmainstream religions, did not fare well. Even to this day, although religious diversity is now permitted, the idea of cultural homogeneity remains a central feature of many European countries.

Throughout the nineteenth century and into the twentieth, France and Germany attracted large numbers of immigrants from other European countries, immigrants who were, as with other minorities, expected to become fully assimilated. It is estimated that as much as one-third of the population of France can trace its origins to the immigration of a grandparent. Italian and Spanish immigrants were expected to become assimilated into French society and culture and did in fact do so. Similarly, Polish migrants to Germany lost their Polish identity. Within a generation or two, migrants to Germany and France were completely absorbed. The hyphenated Frenchman or German had no place in either society.

In recent years, migration from the Third World has placed the concept of cultural homogeneity under attack throughout Western Europe. With millions of migrants from the Mediterranean countries and other former colonies, the countries of Western Europe are less certain as to whether the new migrants can or should be assimilated. Many countries are wrestling with the question of whether monoculturalism should be replaced with multiculturalism and, if so, what it means to be multicultural. A similar debate has shaped political discourse in Australia and Canada, once bastions of British culture, and the issue of multiculturalism has also become an issue in U.S. education. Multiculturalism has a variety of different meanings, ranging from the question of whether symbols of cultural difference should be permitted (should Muslim girls in French schools be permitted to wear the chador?) to the issue of bilingualism and multicultural curricula in schools.

Yet even as multiculturalism can be a positive acceptance of cultural diversity, it can also be a form of enforced separation, a way of inducing minorities to return to their country of origin. For example, the German government has been particularly reluctant to assimilate its Turkish and Yugoslav migrants, hoping that many of them will return home. Some European countries (like France) have permitted locally born children of migrants to become citizens at birth (the notion of *jus solis*), whereas others, like Germany, retain the historic principle that nationality is a matter of inheritance (*jus sanguinis*). These differences have become internationally significant since the European Union decided that citizens of countries within the union will have the right of free circulation. French-born North Africans who have acquired French citizenship can reside anywhere in Europe, but German-born Turks, few of whom have German citizenship, cannot. Differences among European countries with respect to citizenship laws, the admission of refugees, tolerance for undocumented aliens, and willingness to admit ethnic kinfolk from neighboring countries matter, if there are to be no boundaries between Western European states. However, common rules concerning whom to admit, what rights migrants should have, whether multiculturalism or assimilation should be the goal, and who should be granted citizenship are difficult issues because they are at the very core of the idea of national sovereignty. Until agreement is reached on many of these matters, the ideal of a common European home will remain incomplete.

The problems of harmonizing immigration policies and sorting out whether migration means multiculturalism are compounded by the recent massive influx of migrants and refugees from the east. An influx of Albanians into Italy, Eastern

Table 5   FLOW OF FOREIGNERS INTO SELECTED COUNTRIES, 1980–1991

Country	Foreign Newcomers (thousands)											
	1980	1981	1982	1983	1984	1985	1986	1987	1988	1989	1990	1991
Belgium	46.8	41.3	36.2	34.3	37.2	37.5	39.3	40.1	38.2	43.5	50.5	54.1
France	59.4	75.0	144.4	64.2	51.4	43.4	38.3	39.0	44.0	53.2	102.4	109.9
Germany	523.6	451.7	275.5	253.5	295.8	324.4	378.6	414.9	545.4	649.5	649.3	664.4
Luxembourg	7.4	6.9	6.4	6.2	6.0	6.6	7.4	8.2	9.1	9.1	10.3	—
Netherlands	78.5	49.6	39.7	34.4	34.7	40.6	46.9	47.4	50.8	51.5	60.1	62.7
Sweden	—	—	—	18.3	14.1	13.4	19.4	19.0	24.9	28.9	23.9	17.4
Switzerland	70.5	80.3	74.7	58.3	58.6	59.4	66.8	71.5	76.1	80.4	101.4	109.8
United Kingdom	69.8	59.1	53.9	53.5	51.0	55.4	47.8	46.0	49.3	49.7	52.4	53.5

Note: Data, except for France and United Kingdom, are from population registers. Asylum seekers are excluded. For France, up to 1989, inflows include permanent workers, holders of provisional work permits, and family reunification; from 1990, data are not comparable to previous years; new registrations have been made (inflows of spouses of French nationals, parents of French children, refugees, self-employed, and others eligible for a residence permit). For Germany, figures though 1990 refer to western Germany; 1991 refers to Germany as a whole. A dash indicates that data are unavailable.

Source: Organization for Economic Cooperation and Development.

Europeans into Germany, and even eastern Germans into western Germany has created concern among the local populations. It should be noted that even before 1989, migration into Western Europe was rising, in large part due to family reunification and job seeking. Europe is already anxious about its large Muslim population—as expressed through popular support in virtually every Western European country for antimigrant right-wing parties, whose principal targets are Muslim migrants and their children. Moreover, continued civil conflicts in the former Yugoslavia and economic deterioration and the rise of right-wing nationalist movements in the former Soviet Union might result in an expanded refugee flight westward. Such an influx places a heavy burden on housing, employment, and social services; heightens xenophobic fears in societies already stressed by migration from the south; and generates tensions between new immigrants from the east and the old immigrants from the south. A large-scale increase in requests for asylum has heightened anxieties throughout the European Union.

A variety of policy instruments for keeping unwanted migrants and refugees from entering the European Union have been entertained, including border controls, employer sanctions, employment-generating investment in Eastern Europe, expansion in trade, and inducements to sending countries to keep their people at home. If these attempts fail, even stronger nativist sentiments are likely to develop throughout Western Europe, with an increase in the strength of antimigrant political parties and xenophobic behavior. The prospects of successfully incorporating the present generation of migrants and their children into the political, social, and economic life of the countries in the European Union are substantially greater if these states feel that they have effective control over entry than if the flows are unregulated.

REFUGEES IN THE EUROPEAN UNION DEBATES

It is in this context that we need to understand the efforts by the European Community to deal with the refugee influx. One such effort was made in July 1992. The Ad Hoc Group on Immigrants of the European Community, which consists of politicians and civil servants from the member nations' interior ministries, proposed a communitywide refugee policy that would make it difficult for refugees from the Third World to enter the European Union. The proposed definition would be used by all member countries when deciding whether to accept or reject a claim for refugee status. It reaffirmed the existing policy that refugees must stay in the first safe country they reach. It added that "intercontinental movements of asylum seekers are seldom necessary for protection reasons," thus implying that Europe would prefer refugees to remain in their own continent. This attitude places the heaviest burden on the neighbors of refugee-producing states—what human rights organizations called a "beggar thy neighbor" approach. The implications of this proposal affect both non-European and European states bordering on refugee-producing regimes. Bosnians who flee to Germany could not then seek asylum in France or Belgium; indeed, Bosnians would find it difficult to enter Germany, for they would first have to pass through other former Yugoslav republics and Austria. Similarly, Tamils who fled Sri Lanka could not fly from India, the country of first asylum, to Europe, and Afghan refugees could not fly from Pakistan to a European country.

Obviously, countries of first asylum opposed any such blanket policy, insisting that others share the burden of caring for refugees. Human rights advocates also argued that refugees should not be repatriated to any other country unless it was clear that the other country had a satisfactory minimum set of procedures for reviewing asylum claims, including acceptable appeal procedures. Furthermore, these advocates insist that there be minimal procedural safeguards so that one state does not return refugees to another without being assured that adequate procedures are in place for reviewing asylum claims. According to Amnesty International, many Western European countries have deficient asylum procedures.[1]

Other examples of efforts to deal with the refugee influx are bilateral rather than multilateral agreements. In September 1992, the German interior minister signed a pact with Romania allowing Bonn to send back most of the 43,000 Romanians who had entered Germany in 1992. The German government also negotiated with Czechoslovakia and with Bulgaria to persuade them to take back refugees who had been refused political asylum. Asylum seekers from Romania, Czechoslovakia, and Bulgaria have had the lowest acceptance record of all the Eastern European and Third World asylum seekers arriving in Germany since 1989.

In addition to developing common entry policies, the countries in the European Union have sought to harmonize adjudication policies, particularly regarding what are called "manifestly unfounded claims" for asylum. These asylum claims began to grow in the mid-1980s and accelerated sharply after the collapse of communism in Eastern Europe and the outbreak of civil conflict in the former republics of Yugoslavia. Many individuals left Eastern Europe and less developed countries not for fear of political persecution but to improve their economic well-being. These individuals regarded employment prospects at home as poor and believed that they could do better in any of the countries in Western Europe, despite the recession.

In an effort to reduce the number of unfounded claims, one Western European country after another developed policies that would discourage asylum requests and would enable repatriation of failed applicants as quickly as possible, thereby avoiding additional claims on the welfare system. One policy alluded to earlier has been to develop a classification of "safe countries," countries in which people are presumed not to be at risk of persecution and therefore from which claims for asylum will not be accepted. Human rights advocates have criticized this approach, arguing that the list would invariably be guided by foreign policy considerations; countries would seek to be placed on the list, and those that are excluded from the list would regard exclusion as a politically hostile act.[2] Moreover, such lists cannot respond to changing conditions; a country regarded as safe at one time might later engage in persecution. Officials charged with adjudicating claims would

---

1. These included Ireland, Italy, and Austria—usually because officials reviewing claims have no special knowledge of international refugee law or conditions in the asylum seekers' country of origin or because they were not provided access to legal counsel. Amnesty International also regards the accelerated procedures adopted by Switzerland, the United Kingdom, and Belgium as unsatisfactory usually because they relied on lists of "safe countries" or imposed limits on appeals. See Amnesty International, *Europe: Human Rights and the Need for a Fair Asylum Policy* (London: Amnesty International, 1991).

2. Ibid.

presume, at least initially, that individuals arriving from certain countries were making unfounded claims and would not give them the full hearing that would be given to refugees from other countries. Germany is one of several Europeans countries that have a "safe countries" list.[3]

The European Union also attempted to reduce asylum claims directly by encouraging the United Nations High Commissioner for Refugees (UNHCR) to deal with displaced persons, or individuals in flight within their own country, thereby discouraging these people from becoming refugees. The UNHCR has not normally dealt with displaced persons unless asked to do so by the government under which such persons live because such intervention is considered a violation of the sovereign rights of states. Moreover, the UNHCR was widely criticized for assisting displaced persons in Bosnia who sought to leave. Was the agency thereby enabling the Serbs to engage in a policy of "ethnic cleansing" by facilitating the departure of Bosnian Muslims from the country? By October 1992, an estimated 700,000 refugees had fled Bosnia, primarily to Germany and other Western European countries whose governments were resolved not to admit more. Dr. Sadako Ogata, the UN High Commissioner for Refugees, declared that the United Nations would not assist in the process of ethnic cleansing and would seek to help displaced persons in Bosnia and other former Yugoslav republics. While Amnesty International and other organizations concerned with human rights welcomed the UNHCR's willingness to help displaced persons, they also noted that such activities could contradict the body's principal role of ensuring the right of asylum. Does an interest in preventing displaced persons from becoming refugees lead the UNHCR to discourage those who want to leave a country to seek asylum? If individuals within the country ask UN personnel to arrange their exit, will the UNHCR assist them to leave if it regards its principal task as encouraging people to stay?

This same issue arose in Iraq, where the United Nations sought to provide a safe haven for Kurds in an effort to prevent them from fleeing the country. Turkey was adamant that it not be flooded with refugees from Iraq, which would increase the strains between its own large Kurdish population (many of whose members support the creation of an independent Kurdish state) and the government of Turkey. In large part because of pressure from Turkey, the Western allies, with UN approval, declared a no-fly zone, prohibiting Iraqi aircraft from overflying Kurdish areas where they might engage in surveillance, strafing, or bombing. By protecting

3. Under a new asylum law passed by the German parliament in May 1993, refugees from a country that Germany considers free of persecution will be immediately sent home. Both Romania and Bulgaria are on the list that Germany considers free of persecution. In an effort to stop the flow of asylum seekers from the Third World who come to Germany by way of Poland, Germany will also turn away refugees who arrive at the border. The German government has agreed to pay Poland $76.4 million dollars as compensation and negotiated a similar accord with the Czech Republic (*New York Times,* May 27, 1993, p. A8). The new law was approved with the support of the opposition Social Democratic Party, which initially opposed tightening the country's asylum law but relented as popular resentment grew and more and more foreigners sought asylum. In 1992, in addition to the 438,000 people who entered Germany in search of asylum, 250,000 war refugees arrived from the Balkans. Fewer than 5 percent of applicants for asylum are considered qualified due to persecution. Though the rest can be expelled, they are often able to stay on for months or even years at government expense while their cases are reviewed. An unknown number of illegal immigrants also enter, many by swimming across the Oder River from Poland. In June 1992, similar asylum legislation was passed by the Austrian government. The law states that anyone who comes through a "safe" country can be deemed to have found protection there. Austria has also posted an increased number of troops to try to seal the Hungarian border.

Kurds within Iraq, the United Nations discouraged and even prevented Kurds from leaving the country. Human rights groups welcomed efforts to protect the Kurds within their own territory but were concerned that international agencies might prevent Kurds from leaving.

The countries of the European Community took steps to harmonize their procedures for examining asylum claims in 1988 when they agreed to the Dublin Convention, which provides that an asylum application lodged in any one of the EC member states will be examined by only one contracting state. A subsequent convention signed in December 1991 on the crossing of external borders provides for common procedures on visa requirements and imposes sanctions on transport operators that carry people without visas. Five EC member states also signed what is known as the Schengen Supplementary Agreement in June 1990, under which they agreed to dismantle controls at their common borders and to follow the provisions affecting asylum seekers in the two EC conventions. The Maastricht Agreement of December 1991 would enable EC institutions to take over responsibility for harmonizing immigration and asylum policies for the member states, including developing common procedures for dealing with asylum claims, the return of asylum seekers to "safe" countries of first asylum, and dealing with "manifestly unfounded claims" from asylum seekers from countries of origin considered "safe."

While agreeing in principle to the idea of harmonization, many human rights advocates were concerned that the European Community, in its eagerness to accelerate adjudication procedures and to reduce unfounded claims, would not pay adequate attention to human rights considerations. For example, sanctions on airlines that carry passengers without correct travel documents could prevent genuine asylum seekers from leaving their country, as they might not be able to obtain passports from their home governments or officially seek visas from countries into which they proposed to flee.[4] Furthermore, airlines would then face the responsibility of determining whether someone is a genuine refugee, a task that airlines, with no expertise in adjudicating claims, are not equipped to handle. Finally, financial penalties for allowing unfounded or undocumented asylum seekers on planes provide strong incentives for airlines to reject all passengers without documents, even if their claims of persecution are genuine.

GERMANY: GENEROSITY AND XENOPHOBIA

No industrial country has faced as severe a crisis over international migration as Germany. The fall of the Berlin Wall and the reunification of Germany, the collapse of Soviet control over Eastern Europe, and the breakup of Yugoslavia and of the Soviet Union have all combined to make Germany a front-line state not against a

---

4. Amnesty International, *Europe,* p. 5. Amnesty International regards visa requirements as obstructing asylum claims because asylum seekers have been refused entry if their travel documents were not in order. However, since it would be unrealistic for states to abolish visas to protect genuine asylum seekers who are unable to obtain travel documents, Amnesty concludes that governments at least ought to declare "that they will ensure that the visa requirements and sanctions on transport operations . . . will not obstruct asylum-seekers who need to seek protection in one of the contracting states" (p. 9).

Table 6   FOREIGN RESIDENTS IN WEST GERMANY BY COUNTRY OF ORIGIN, 1990

Country of Origin	Number of Residents (thousands)	Country of Origin	Number of Residents (thousands)
Turkey	1,675.0	France	83.3
Yugoslavia	652.5	Morocco	67.5
Italy	548.3	Romania	53.1
Greece	314.5	Hungary	35.1
Poland	241.3	Tunisia	25.9
Austria	181.3	Bulgaria	11.4
Spain	134.7	Finland	10.3
Netherlands	111.0	Algeria	6.7
United Kingdom	94.8	Other countries	820.8
Iran	89.7	Total	5,241.8
Portugal	84.6		

Note: Foreign population figures include children born in West Germany to foreign parents but do not include naturalized citizens. "Other countries" category includes large numbers of people from the former Soviet Union.

Source: Organization for Economic Cooperation and Development.

cold war adversary but against a flood of refugees and migrants. The major crisis in Germany, as defined by German authorities, has been the problem of manifestly unfounded claims by asylum seekers, that is, of large numbers of people who do not qualify for asylum under German law or under the UN convention on refugees but who nonetheless seek entry into the country. The response of Germans to that crisis has in turn created negative images of Germany in much of Europe and the United States.

Paradoxically, Germany has been more open to refugees than any other industrial nation. Its refugee intake in recent years has ranked first in the industrial world. There are 750,000 "German refugees" in Germany, a peculiarly German category made up of two groups: the *Übersiedler,* Germans from East Germany who fled to the West after the Berlin Wall was erected in 1961 but before the collapse of the East German regime in 1989, and *Aussiedler* (resettlers), ethnic Germans from Poland, Romania, and the Soviet Union. In the broadest sense, an *Aussiedler* can be any ethnic German living abroad who has one grandparent of German nationality or who lives in prewar German territory to the east that is now outside the borders of the modern state. *Aussiedler* thus have a claim to citizenship on the basis of their Germanness, not as asylum seekers. In 1990 alone, nearly 400,000 *Aussiedler* came in. An estimated 3.5 million people of German origin live in eastern and southeastern Europe and the successor states to the Soviet Union.

In addition, 5,241,800 non-German foreigners, known as *Ausländer,* resided in Germany in 1990. In 1991, the number rose to 5,882,000, with significant increas-

Table 7   FOREIGN RESIDENTS IN THE UNITED KINGDOM BY COUNTRY OF ORIGIN, 1990

Country of Origin	Number of Residents (thousands)	Country of Origin	Number of Residents (thousands)
Ireland	638	Bangladesh	38
India	155	France	38
United States	102	Western Africa	37
Italy	75	Spain	24
Caribbean and Guyana	70	Portugal	21
Central and Eastern Europe (including former USSR)	57	Northern Europe	17
		Other countries	468
Pakistan	55		
Germany	41	Total	1,875
Eastern Africa	39		

Note: Figures do not include naturalized citizens. Estimations are based on annual labor force survey.

Source: Organization for Economic Cooperation and Development.

es in the number from Turkey, former Yugoslavia, Poland, and Romania. Many of the migrants entered Germany as *Gastarbeiter,* or guest workers, in the 1950s and 1960s in response to labor needs during the postwar recovery. Germany, France, Sweden, Switzerland, and the Benelux countries experienced labor shortages after 1945, a time of rapid economic growth when there had been a decline in the number of people in the labor force—the result of low birthrates in the 1930s and high wartime death rates. Western European countries then imported immigrant labor from North Africa, Turkey, and Yugoslavia. By 1973, France and West Germany had 2.5 million foreign workers each; Switzerland, 600,000; and the Benelux countries, a third of a million. Between 1946 and 1950, the United Kingdom admitted 300,000 people from the European continent and thereafter met its labor needs through immigration from the Commonwealth. In 1971, the United Kingdom had 1,121,000 residents born in the Commonwealth and in Pakistan; by 1981, this number had risen to 1,474,000, and by 1990, to 1,875,000.[5] In the early 1990s, more than 15 million foreigners resided in Western Europe. Foreigners constituted 4.2 percent of the population of Western Europe, compared to 7.8 percent in the United States.

Both the United Kingdom and the Continental countries took steps in the 1970s and early 1980s to end the influx of migrants, policies that paradoxically

5. David Coleman and John Salt, *The British Population* (Oxford: Oxford University Press, 1992), pp. 451–452.

Table 8   FOREIGN POPULATION IN SELECTED COUNTRIES IN WESTERN EUROPE, 1980–1991

| Country | Foreign Population (thousands) | | | | | |
	1980	1985	1988	1989	1990	1991
Austria	283	272	299	323	413	512
	(3.7%)	(3.6%)	(3.9%)	(4.2%)	(5.3%)	(6.6%)
Belgium	—	846	869	881	904	922
		(8.6%)	(8.8%)	(8.9%)	(9.1%)	(9.2%)
France	—	—	—	—	3,607	—
					(6.4%)	
Germany	4,453	4,379	4,489	4,846	5,242	5,882
	(7.2%)	(7.2%)	(7.3%)	(7.7%)	(8.2%)	(7.3%)
Italy	299	423	645	490	781	897
	(0.5%)	(0.7%)	(1.1%)	(0.9%)	(1.4%)	(1.5%)
Netherlands	521	552	624	642	692	733
	(3.7%)	(3.8%)	(4.2%)	(4.3%)	(4.6%)	(4.8%)
Sweden	422	389	421	456	484	494
	(5.1%)	(4.6%)	(5.0%)	(5.3%)	(5.6%)	(5.7%)
Switzerland	893	940	1,006	1,040	1,100	1,163
	(14.1%)	(14.5%)	(15.2%)	(15.6%)	(16.3%)	(17.1%)
United Kingdom	—	1,731	1,821	1,949	1,875	1,750
		(3.1%)	(3.2%)	(3.4%)	(3.3%)	(3.1%)

Note: Figures for Germany are for West Germany through 1990; 1991 figures cover Germany as a whole. A dash indicates that data are unavailable. Figures do not include naturalized citizens.

Source: Organization for Economic Cooperation and Development.

resulted in additional migration as individuals sought to meet government deadlines (as in the United Kingdom) or as wives and children joined their spouses (as in France and Germany). By the mid-1980s, it was clear that Europe no longer had guest workers but rather had permanent settlers whose full social, economic, and political integration had yet to take place.

In the 1950s and 1960s, Germany signed contracts with Italy, Spain, Greece, Turkey, Morocco, Portugal, Tunisia, and Yugoslavia to import foreign workers. The largest number of workers to come to Germany came from Turkey (about 20 percent), Yugoslavia (15 percent), Italy (14 percent), and Greece (7 percent). In 1973, the importation of labor was stopped, but the foreign population continued to grow as immigrant workers brought their families. Second and even third generations of "immigrants" were born in Germany, swelling the ranks of the *Ausländer* further because none of these individuals are entitled to citizenship by birth.

Cancellation of the guest worker program closed off the only way for an ordinary migrant to enter Germany legally. As it became more difficult for would-be migrants to enter Germany, the number of applicants for refugee status increased. These included asylum seekers both from Eastern Europe and, by the late 1970s, from the Third World. With the collapse of Communist regimes in Eastern Europe and in the Balkans, these regions became major producers of asylum seekers. The total number of asylum seekers into Western Europe increased from 230,000 in 1988 to 550,000 in 1991 and 660,000 in 1992. In each year, Germany was the largest single recipient.

A survey conducted by the German newsmagazine *Der Spiegel* in 1992 reported that 96 percent of Germans considered the influx of refugees a "foreigner problem."[6] According to the survey, a large majority of Germans endorsed antiforeigner sentiments, including statements that foreigners "abuse our social system" (77 percent agreed), "heighten Germans' housing shortage" (74 percent), "increase unemployment among Germans" (60 percent), and "pose a danger on the streets" (59 percent).

To the world outside Germany, the "foreigner problem" was not the influx of refugees—which had reached nearly 60,000 per month by mid-1992—but violent attacks by German citizens on asylum seekers, refugees, migrants, and foreign workers. One particularly shocking incident occurred in September 1991 in Hoyerswerda, a small town in eastern Germany, when a gang launched an assault on a hostel for refugees while local residents watched impassively or cheered. A similar attack occurred in Rostock, also in eastern Germany, in the summer of 1992. These incidents revived the image of the "ugly German" hostile to foreigners, even though only a small number of people took part in the attacks and they were decried by the German government and by most Germans.

Official political discourse in Germany emphasizes that, the large foreign population notwithstanding, *Deutschland ist kein Einwanderungsland* (Germany is not a country of immigration). *Überfremdungsangst* (fear of overforeignization) dominates the rhetoric of Germany's growing antimigrant right-wing movements, the Republikaner and the NPD. The German media use words like *Asylschwemme* (asylum flood), *Lawine* (avalanche), *Zeitbombe* (time bomb), *Springflut* (spring flood), and *Asylschnorrer* (asylum parasite).[7] Many Germans, facing growing unemployment, higher rents, and a decline in social benefits, feared that foreigners were taking their jobs and apartments and draining resources from the welfare state. Many Germans were also angry that the government permitted asylum seekers to receive social welfare benefits, which led to the widespread belief that many asylum seekers were "parasites."

A great many Germans sense that a large proportion of people who seek asylum enter not only because of the opportunities for employment at higher wages than can be earned at home but also to take advantage of Germany's highly developed welfare system. Stories abound of abuses of the welfare system by asylum seekers. A Göttingen secondary school teacher told me of an Iranian woman who requested asylum upon arrival in Germany and then went immediately to a well-known surgeon for treatment of a thyroid condition. This surgeon, to whom the

---

6. *International Herald Tribune,* October 27, 1992, p. 1.

7. Jeffrey M. Peck, "Refugees as Foreigners: The Problem of Becoming German and Finding a Home" (diss., United Nations University/WIDER, 1992), pp. 16, 22.

woman had been referred by her doctor in Tehran, performed an operation and placed her in a local hospital for nearly four weeks at the cost of approximately DM 400 per day. The cost for the doctor, the operation, and hospital care came to nearly DM 20,000, all of which was borne by the welfare system. After the woman was released from the hospital, she informed the doctor that she was returning to Tehran.

In another case, also in Göttingen, an unidentified Eastern European refugee was killed in an automobile accident. When the authorities traced him, they found that he had seven names, each of which was registered in a different *Land* (state), enabling him to collect seven welfare benefits of DM 800 per month. In a third incident, an asylum seeker crossing the border, unwilling to give his real name, called himself Coca Cola, and was then able to collect welfare benefits under this assumed name, though the *Land* authorities recognized that the presumed refugee was mocking the government. These stories, reminiscent of accounts elsewhere of abuses of welfare systems, are widely repeated in Germany to point to weaknesses in a refugee system that allows claimants to acquire welfare benefits immediately upon arrival before the validity of their claims can be assessed. As it may take several years for an asylum case to be settled, this practice can be quite costly.

To reduce the drain on the state welfare system, the German government permitted foreigners to work, starting in August 1991. Many Germans now complain that asylum seekers and refugees are taking jobs from unemployed Germans, although most foreigners take jobs that Germans tend to shun, such as garbage collector, road sweeper, or manual factory worker.

The right to political asylum is enshrined in Article 16 of the Basic Law of the Federal Republic of Germany. In addition to providing asylum to foreigners with a fear of political persecution, Germany also admits as "tolerated refugees" immigrants who fear return to a war-torn or economically distressed region where they would be endangered. In this sense, Germany has had one of the most generous asylum and refugee policies of any industrial country.

At the same time, Germany does not, as we have noted, regard itself as a country of immigration or automatically grant citizenship to German-born children of migrants, readily naturalize immigrants, or even seek to integrate them into German society. Only people of German descent are automatically accorded membership in the German nation. Strains of xenophobia in Germany—although perhaps no worse than in some other parts of Europe—have evoked images of German nationalism and sent a chill throughout Europe and the United States.

As both the number of asylum seekers and the number of attacks against foreigners grew, the political debate within Germany intensified. Chancellor Helmut Kohl proposed that Germany revise its liberal asylum law to enable the government to use federal forces to turn back refugees from countries that Germany considers free of oppression.[8]

The opposition Social Democratic Party (SPD) initially opposed efforts to amend Article 16 of the Basic Law, expressing concern that the government was giving in to antimigrant neo-Nazis. The German government, however, took the

---

8. *International Herald Tribune*, November 2, 1992, p. 5.

position that there must be accelerated asylum procedures to deal with the "mani-festly unfounded" cases.

As discussed in detail earlier, human rights advocates argue that the various proposals to deal with unfounded claims infringe on legitimate claims. So even though the hurdles proposed by the Federal Republic of Germany (many of which were also proposed by the European Commission) seem likely to reduce the massive number of unfounded claims, they also make it more difficult for refugees who warrant asylum to receive it. In the broadest language of public policy, how does one provide an entitlement based on a legally specified need when large numbers of unqualified individuals abuse the system? Moreover, what can governments do with individuals whose cases have not yet been reviewed because of an overload on the asylum system—place them in some form of detention with provisions for public assistance or allow them to seek employment? Alternatively, can the government streamline procedures to hasten the review of asylum claimants (for example, by compiling a list of "safe countries"), or would this lead to many unjust rejections?

German concern over unwanted migration has now been extended to the several million ethnic Germans living in the former Soviet Union. Some of these individuals are descendants of people who migrated to Russia in the eighteenth century at the invitation of Catherine the Great (herself a German) to help develop Russian farming. Others trace their origin to the Hapsburg Empire. Prior to World War II, the largest concentration of ethnic Germans could be found in the autonomous Volga German Republic on the border of Kazakhstan, but in 1941 Stalin disbanded the republic and deported the Germans to Central Asia and Siberia. Today, the old territory of the Volga Republic is largely Russian, with only a small number of Germans. Nearly half of those in the former Soviet Union with the designation "German" in their passports now reside in Kazakhstan.

Since 1987, these Germans have been moving to Germany at the rate of 150,000 to 200,000 each year. About 650,000 applications for admission into Germany are pending, and it is believed that given the opportunity, virtually all who are by passport designation or by claim of German origin (the latter, given the high rate of intermarriage, may be as many as 5 million) would migrate to Germany. Many of these individuals do not speak German.

A number of policies aimed at preventing more migration of ethnic Germans to Germany have been adopted. In particular, the Russian government has offered to reestablish the autonomous Volga German Republic. Under an agreement signed in 1992, the German government is financing the resettlement of ethnic Germans from Central Asia to the republic. The German government hopes that large-scale investment in the Volga region—in housing, schools, clinics, industry, and rural construction—will convince the ethnic Germans to stay in Russia rather than emigrate to Germany. It remains uncertain, however, whether the Russian Germans can be persuaded to settle in a region now predominantly occupied by Russians in the face of a resurgence of Russian nationalism when the legal option of "returning" to Germany exists. In a further effort to slow the flow, the German government now requires that ethnic Germans complete a detailed application form in German and that each case be individually reviewed. The German government has also established a de facto admission quota (approximately 250,000 annually).

In 1993, the German government reexamined its refugee and citizenship policies. Refugee and asylum laws were revised to enable the government to halt unrestricted entry to newcomers claiming asylum. As mentioned earlier, under the new law, the government can bar entry to people who come from (or through) countries that the government considers "safe," or unlikely to give rise to legitimate claims of fear of persecution. All countries bordering on Germany are now considered "safe"; this new *cordon sanitaire* in effect shields Germany from any refugee influx across its land borders.

Chancellor Helmut Kohl also announced steps to make German citizenship easier to obtain. Parliament passed a new citizenship law to enable foreign nationals who have lived legally in Germany for 15 years to obtain citizenship and those between 17 and 23 years of age to obtain citizenship if they have lived in the country for eight years and attended school for at least six. Although this is still short of the principle of *jus solis,* the new rules open the door somewhat wider to Turks and other immigrants and their children, though perhaps not wide enough to ensure the incorporation of the immigrant population into German society. The leader of the opposition Social Democrats, Johannes Rau, though welcoming the proposed change in citizenship rules, took issue with Chancellor Kohl's insistence that rightist violence against foreigners was the result of a permissive press, lack of tough police controls, and "liberal education policies." He concluded that "we don't need to tighten our laws; we need to change our attitudes."[9]

ITALY: EUROPE'S UNDERBELLY

From the end of the Second World War to 1974, Italy remained a country of emigration. An estimated 1 million Italians left for the western hemisphere and for Australia, and another 840,000 found jobs elsewhere in Europe, mainly in France, Belgium, and Switzerland. But by 1975, Italy had become a net immigration country. Migration was not a significant policy issue for Italy, however, until Albanians began coming in the early 1990s. Whereas Germany has had a liberal refugee policy, Italy's refugee policy has been among the most restrictive of the European countries. For most of the postwar period, Italy rarely admitted refugees as residents, a position the government justified on the basis of the country's widespread poverty and unemployment. Italy was, however, a transit country for refugees en route to the United States, Canada, Australia, and the Scandinavian countries. Most were Europeans from Communist countries, but a small number of refugees from the Third World were also allowed to enter, including Vietnamese boat people picked up by Italian ships in the China Sea, Chileans fleeing the Pinochet regime, and Afghans. As of 1991, the total foreign population of Italy was under 900,000, or 1.5 percent of the population.

Under the dictatorship of Enver Hoxha, Albania had remained a Stalinist state after World War II even as reform movements were developing in Eastern Europe. Only after the Hoxha's death in 1985 did Albania enter a period of political open-

9. *New York Times,* June 17, 1993.

Table 9   FOREIGN RESIDENTS IN ITALY BY COUNTRY OF ORIGIN, 1991

Country of Origin	Number of Residents (thousands)	Country of Origin	Number of Residents (thousands)
Morocco	90.6	Greece	17.5
United States	60.9	Brazil	17.3
Tunisia	47.6	Argentina	15.1
Philippines	41.1	Spain	14.7
Germany	40.3	Romania	14.0
Former Yugoslavia	34.7	Sri Lanka	13.9
United Kingdom	27.9	Ghana	12.9
Senegal	27.8	Iran	12.8
Albania	27.0	Ethiopia	12.6
France	25.1	India	12.3
Egypt	22.7	Somalia	12.1
China	22.0	Other countries	235.7
Poland	19.3	**Total**	**896.8**
Switzerland	18.7		

Note: Figures do not include naturalized citizens.

Source: Organization for Economic Cooperation and Development.

ness, permitting general elections to take place in March and April 1991. Even so, the elections took place in a climate of fear, under pressure from local party functionaries. Consequently, the country voted to return the former Communist Party (now renamed the Party of Labor) to power. Albania's economy remained in a desperate state. Agricultural productivity declined, and there was a general sense of hopelessness. In 1990, Albanians started to leave the country, and in July of that year, Western embassies in Tirana, the capital, were besieged by Albanians seeking visas. Members of the Greek minority in southern Albania sought and obtained political asylum in Greece, and in March 1991 an exodus from Albania to southern Italian ports began. In Italy, generous local citizens provided the Albanians with food and shelter, but as the influx continued the Italian government took steps to halt the flow. Italian authorities offered the Albanians 50,000 lire ($40) each and new clothes if they would return home. When monetary incentives proved ineffective, the government adopted a policy of forced repatriation. Scenes of the flight of Albanians by sea, their arrival in Italian ports, and their forcible repatriation by the Italian government were dramatically captured by European television. The Italian government then offered to increase its financial aid to Albania and persuaded the Albanian government to prevent boats from leaving its ports with immigrants.

The issue of refugees should be seen in the broader context of a growing migration flow into Italy. A study prepared by the Agnelli Foundation noted that through the 1980s, Italy was receiving a substantial influx of illegal migrants even in the absence of a significant labor shortage; indeed, much of the migration had been to southern Italy, a region with a high level of unemployment.[10] (Northern Italy satisfies its labor needs by importing labor from the south or by encouraging northern industries to move south.) The Agnelli study noted that with the closing of European borders to economic immigration, the request for political asylum had become the preferred—indeed, the only—legal way for immigrants to enter Europe. As a result, Italy receives a large number of immigrants and asylum claimants from the Cape Verde Islands, Chile, China, Ghana, Egypt, Morocco, Nigeria, the Philippines, Sri Lanka, Tunisia, and Eastern Europe. Refugees awaiting resettlement in a third country are not permitted to work, but in practice illegal employment is common. Italy's migration law (the "Martelli law," named after the deputy prime minister at the time of its enactment) limited entry into the country. Before the Martelli law was passed in 1990, an estimated 600,000 to 1 million foreigners resided in Italy illegally. The Martelli law granted amnesty to thousands of illegal immigrants and proposed that an annual quota be fixed each year for immigration (it was to be zero for both 1991 and 1992). As a result of the amnesty decision, the number of legalized foreigners in Italy increased from 490,000 in 1989 to nearly 900,000 in 1991, with significant increases in the numbers from Morocco, Tunisia, the Philippines, Senegal, and Egypt. The right of asylum was extended to non-European refugees, but punitive measures were imposed on airlines that transported non-EC national without documents. The Italian government also admitted substantial numbers of Yugoslav refugees but limited the entrance of Albanians on the grounds that Yugoslavs were more likely than Albanians to return home when conditions improved. Critics of the Italian government pointed to the discriminatory and discretionary nature of decisions on migrants and refugees and the absence of an adequate procedure for determining who is entitled to asylum.

Facing an influx from Eastern Europe, Africa, and other Third World regions, Italy has sought to end its reputation as an easy entry point for refugees and for illegal migrants by rejecting people at its borders and by expelling illegals.[11] Support for an antimigrant policy has come from the Lega Nord, one of Italy's most rapidly expanding political parties. In municipal elections in 1993, the Lega won 40 percent of the vote in Milan. Its share of the national vote for the Chamber of Deputies was 8.7 percent.

Control over entry from North Africa has also been a major issue in Spain. Illegal migrants from North Africa, Ethiopia, Somalia, Ghana, and Nigeria come by boat from the Moroccan coast. The cost of a trip from Morocco to Gibraltar ranges from $150 to $750. In May 1991, Spain agreed to fall in line with European Community regulations by requiring visas from North Africa. Previously, North Africans came as tourists, found work, and stayed on illegally. The government also granted amnesty to an estimated 130,000 illegal immigrants. In all, Spain in 1991 had 200,000 non-EC foreigners and an estimated 300,000 illegal African immigrants, half of them Moroccans. Many live in shantytowns and are employed as

10. "Immigration Policies for Italy and Europe," *XXI Secolo,* December 1991.
11. Jenny Hills, "Italy's New Refugee Policy," *RPN,* June 1992, pp. 23–24. See also Amnesty International, *Europe,* pp. 13–14.

casual farm laborers, picking fruits and vegetables. Illegals continue to arrive on rickety boats from Morocco, attracted by jobs that pay around $30 per day, considerably more than they can earn in North Africa and enough to send some money to their families. The number of illegal migrants from Algeria has also grown as the Algerian economy has deteriorated. In an effort to halt the flow, the Spanish government has persuaded Morocco to stop small boats from bringing illegal immigrants across the Strait of Gibraltar.

As Germany has been the gateway from the east, Spain, Italy, and France have been the gateway from the south. All three countries have taken steps to reduce the flow of asylum seekers and, in the case of France, to halt the migration of workers, yet the flow of illegals has apparently increased. In all three countries, the great concern is that political conditions in Algeria, Morocco, Tunisia, and Egypt, particularly the growth of fundamentalist Islamic parties, could precipitate large-scale flight across the Mediterranean.

JAPAN: CAN ANYONE BECOME JAPANESE?

Half a world away, Japan, another country that shares the belief that the nation and the state coincide, is also wrestling with questions of how to deal with refugees, guest workers, and illegal migrants. At issue in these debates are Japan's labor force requirements as its economy grows and its population ages, its obligations under international law, and its relations with other countries of Asia. At their most basic level, however, these issues can be reduced to a controversy over the appropriateness of the Japanese self-image as a closed, ethnically and racially homogeneous society in an era in which Japan has become a global economic power.

Post–World War II Japan adopted a very different set of migration policies than the countries of Western Europe did. As indicated in our discussion, Western Europe encouraged migration and imported labor to supplement its slow-growing labor force. Facing a similarly tight labor market, the Japanese chose not to import labor but instead to encourage firms in need of low-skilled, low-wage labor to move abroad. Japan gave a higher priority than European countries to cultural and social factors in determining how to satisfy a structural economic need. As a result, Japan stood virtually alone, outside of any of the global international migration systems.[12] In 1991, Japan's foreign population was 1,219,000, or slightly under 1 percent.

From the Meiji Restoration in 1868 until the onset of World War II in 1940, Japan, like the countries of Western Europe, was actually a labor-exporting country. Large numbers of Japanese migrated to the West Coast of the United States, Hawaii, Brazil, Argentina, Bolivia, Uruguay, Peru, and the Japanese colonies of Manchuria, Korea, and Taiwan.[13]

12. In Mary M. Kritz, Lin Lean Lim, and Hania Zlotnik (eds.), *International Migration Systems* (Oxford: Clarendon Press, 1992), several of the authors note that the Japanese government was opposed to migration despite a demand for less skilled service workers that could be satisfied by migration from other Asian countries.

13. As many as 500,000 Japanese migrated to South America; see Masami Sekine, "Guest Worker Policies in Japan" *Migration,* Winter 1992–1993, p. 52.

Table 10   FOREIGN RESIDENTS IN JAPAN BY COUNTRY OF ORIGIN, 1991

Country of Origin	Number of Residents (thousands)	Country of Origin	Number of Residents (thousands)
Korea	693.1	Canada	5.9
China and Taiwan	171.1	Malaysia	5.6
Brazil	119.3	Australia	5.4
Philippines	61.8	Indonesia	4.6
United States	42.5	Germany	3.8
Peru	26.3	Pakistan	3.7
United Kingdom	11.8	Other countries	48.7
Thailand	8.9	Total	1,218.9
Vietnam	6.4		

Note: Foreigners staying in Japan for less than 90 days are excluded.

Source: Japanese Ministry of Justice.

Migration into Japan began in the 1930s, when Japan imported workers from Korea to meet wartime labor shortages. This was the first experience Japan had had with a significant nonindigenous racial and linguistic minority. Even in this instance, however, incorporation of the migrant population into Japan was never a consideration. The Koreans were guest workers intended, as in postwar Europe, to meet short-term labor needs; they were not regarded as immigrants to be incorporated into Japanese society.[14]

Migration into Japan after the war was neither encouraged nor welcomed. This exclusionary attitude derives from Japan's self-image as a country whose citizens can trace their lineage to an antique past. "Japaneseness" has long been regarded not so much as a matter of race but rather as a reflection of qualities that are inbred, inherent, even divine, and that cannot be acquired by others, regardless of how long they reside in the Japanese islands. Consistent with this attitude, Japan adopted a distinct insularity until the mid-nineteenth century, when Commodore Perry's black ships arrived. Even after the Meiji Restoration, when Japan set out to internationalize itself and create a modern society by borrowing from Europe and the United States, the Japanese continued to view themselves as a unique culture and society into which outsiders could never be incorporated.

That is why postwar Japan chose to export industries and develop its technology rather than to import labor. Companies that required unskilled and semiskilled labor unavailable in Japan were encouraged to move their plants abroad.

14. At the end of World War II, Japan had approximately 2 million Korean residents, who had been employed during the war. Most returned to Korea, but about 700,000 still remain. Many have become Japanese citizens, but they continue to be regarded by most Japanese as foreigners or aliens; see ibid., p. 67.

Consequently, Japan's automobile industry created platforms in South Korea for the production of components. Similarly, in the 1980s, Japanese firms expanded into Indonesia, Thailand, Singapore, and Malaysia. Foreign investment and the employment of labor abroad thus became, in effect, a substitute for the importation of labor. In other instances, the Japanese government, working with Japanese industries, encouraged the development of technologies that would reduce the demand for unskilled workers in manufacturing, thereby removing any need for immigrants. Among the advanced industrial countries, Japan alone entered the 1970s with a homogeneous population, no large numbers of foreign workers, and no significant ethnic cleavages.[15]

Starting in the mid-1970s, three factors led to a reconsideration of Japan's policies toward immigrants: an influx of Vietnamese refugees, the increasing presence of illegal low-wage foreign migrants, and the emergence of a legal skilled migrant population.

The first Vietnamese refugees arrived by boat in 1975, forcing Japan to develop formal channels to deal with new arrivals. Although at the time Japan lacked a refugee policy, the minister of justice granted a small number of these refugees permission to enter the country. A more formal approach toward refugees subsequently evolved. In 1981, Japan signed the Geneva Convention Relating to the Status of Refugees.[16] On January 1, 1982, the Immigration Control and Refugee Recognition Act was promulgated, and the government established a quota of 10,000 for Indochinese refugees. In subsequent years, the Japanese government followed the UNHCR guidelines for Indochinese but was less sympathetic to political refugees from other areas of the world. Between 1979 and 1989, Japan admitted 6,337 Indochinese (4,380 Vietnamese, 878 Laotians, and 1,079 Cambodians) and only 38 non-Indochinese refugees.[17] Refugees were sent to resettlement centers, where they were taught Japanese and then helped to find jobs in small and medium-sized firms.

Tolerance had its limits, however, and in June 1989, a new screening process was put in place to stop the flow of Indochinese boat people. This policy was a response to a growing antiforeign sentiment in the country and an increasing abuse of the refugee system. The Japanese were particularly alarmed by the arrival of mainland Chinese posing as Indochinese. These Chinese "boat people" were regarded as economic immigrants seeking higher wages than could be earned in China.[18] Procedures introduced in September 1989 enabled the government to

15. The Ainu and the Barakumin constitute Japan's major ethnic minorities, but both are small in number, indigenous, and largely ignored in the country's political life. As mentioned in note 14, some 700,000 people of Korean descent continue to live in Japan, quite apart from the Japanese, providing a constant reminder to many Japanese that they are too incapable of absorbing foreigners to warrant establishing a new migration policy. See George A. De Vos and William O. Wetherall, *Japan's Minorities* (London: Minority Rights Group, 1983).

16. Although Japan acceded to the 1951 convention, the Japanese courts ruled that *refoulement* (expulsion) was permitted under its refugee and immigration law if the minister of justice finds the application of the principle of *non-refoulement* "seriously detrimental to the interests of Japan and the security thereof." See Louis B. Sohn and Thomas Buergenthal (eds.), *The Movement of Persons Across Borders* (Washington, D.C.: American Society of International Law, 1992), p. 135.

17. Mizuno Takaaki, "The Refugee Quandary," *Japan Quarterly*, January–March 1990, p. 90.

18. Saito Yasuhiko, "Impostor Refugees, Illegal Immigrants," *Japan Quarterly*, January–March, 1990, p. 88.

return Chinese from Fujian province in agreement with the Chinese government. This policy also served as a warning to Indochinese and other potential asylum seekers and refugees that resettlement in Japan would be difficult, thereby encouraging them to seek admission elsewhere.[19]

Officially, the Japanese government maintains that Japan is too small and too densely populated to accommodate significant numbers of refugees, no matter how legitimate their claims. Alternatively, Japan is prepared to provide financial support to the UNHCR as an expression of its willingness to be internationally cooperative and to share the burden of refugees equitably. Japan's contributions to the UNHCR, other international agencies, and the governments of Thailand and the Philippines for refugee assistance ranged from $50 million to $105 million per year in the 1980s [20] and increased to more than $200 million annually by the 1990s. Nevertheless, some human rights advocates criticized Japan's response to the refugee crisis as unsatisfactory, given the large number of refugees worldwide and in particular the many Indochinese refugees in Southeast Asia in need of resettlement in the 1980s. Moreover, Japan has been strict in applying refugee criteria, seeking repatriation whenever possible, and has not been particularly hospitable to refugees who have been settled. In fact, the small number of refugees presently admitted to Japan often subsequently seek admission to European or North American countries, which are regarded as more accepting of minorities.

A second factor that forced Japan to confront the migration issue was a growth in illegal migration. In the mid-1980s, it became apparent that Japan was receiving a significant number of illegal migrants, largely from Southeast Asia. The media began to report that a growing number of illegal female guest workers were being recruited as disco dancers, waitresses, hostesses, and massage parlor prostitutes.[21] Reasons cited for this trend include an increase in the number of Japanese women entering into higher-status employment and a welfare system that makes unskilled low-wage jobs unacceptable to the Japanese themselves. Many female guest workers initially entered legally (on a Certificate for Public Entertainment or as students) and then stayed on illegally. In addition, small manufacturing companies and the construction industry recruited unskilled male manual laborers—in spite of a government ban on unskilled guest workers. This occurred because small manufacturing companies preferred to hire low-paid illegal guest workers than to invest in high-technology equipment.[22]

---

19. Many migrants from Fujian subsequently sought entrance into the United States, demonstrating the way in which the migration and refugee policies of one country play a role in shifting flows to other countries.

20. Yoshio Kawashima, "Japanese Laws and Practices on Indo-Chinese Refugees," *Osaka University Law Review,* February 1991, p. 1.

21. Sekine, "Guest Worker Policies," p. 54.

22. Ibid., p. 57. One survey found that one in seven small to medium-sized firms in Japan employed foreign workers, mostly without papers (*Economist,* June 2, 1990, p. 36). The Japan Food Service Association, with 336 member firms, asked the government to establish an official guest worker system. The Tokyo Chamber of Commerce proposed a scheme for importing 600,000 guest workers on two-year contracts. Initially, many of the illegals were Pakistanis and Bangladeshis who arrived in Japan after the cut in oil prices led to a drop in the employment of foreigners in the Middle East. Subsequently, South Koreans went to Japan, then Chinese boat people. Thai and Filipina "hostesses" were imported, many into the Japanese underworld. The Japanese government has sought to reduce the influx by suspending its visa exemption agreements with Pakistan and Bangladesh and closing down Japan's phony language schools, which enabled immigrants to get two-year study visas.

By 1992, the number of illegals in Japan was estimated at around 280,000.[23] Facing growing numbers of illegals, Japan has had to consider questions of whether the status of such immigrants should be legalized or whether a guest worker program should be initiated to subvert illegal labor recruitment. Opponents point to Germany, France, and Switzerland, where guest worker programs have left a legacy of permanent settlers and have created problems of integration, housing, education, and social services and the potential for ethnic conflict. More important, opponents note that the Japanese "traditionally regard themselves as a homogeneous society . . . [and] worry that traditional Japanese culture will be destroyed by the introduction of other cultures."[24] As an alternative, they suggest that the use of robots, highly mechanized automatic equipment, factory automation, and office automation can reduce the need for unskilled labor in both the manufacturing and construction industries, and labor-intensive industries can be transferred to developing countries where low-wage unskilled workers are readily available. Among the opponents of migration are union officials, who believe that the use of guest workers will result in a secondary labor market of workers outside the trade union movement and that a dual labor market would result in a general depression of wage levels for all workers.

In an attempt to address the illegal immigration problem, Japan passed the New Immigration Control and Refugees Recognition Act in June 1990, imposing penalties (of up to 2 million yen and three years' imprisonment) on employers who recruit illegal workers. This legislation makes exceptions for the employment of highly professional and skilled workers from abroad but does not provide a guest worker scheme for restaurants, pubs, hotels, and motels or permit the recruitment of unskilled migrant workers.

Some scholars and journalists have called for a rethinking of Japan's policies—not only on the grounds that Japan needs unskilled workers to meet the needs of employers but also because Japan has become internationalized and therefore ought to incorporate migrants, refugees, and guest workers. "Japan must overcome its ethnocentric and closed-minded attitudes to foreigners by accepting people from different cultures. Japan would benefit from their influence and develop a more creative culture," writes Masami Sekine.[25] An attack against homogeneity also comes from journalist Mizuno Takaaki, of the *Asahi Shimbun:* "Japan, which had

23. These estimates, and those given elsewhere in this paragraph, are from Surya B. Prasai, "Asia's Labour Pains," *Far Eastern Economic Review,* April 29, 1993, p. 23. Prasai is the information specialist for the International Labor Organization's regional office in Bangkok and author of *Third World Priorities for the '90s* (Chicago: University of Chicago Press, 1990). Other newly industrialized countries of East and Southeast Asia have also had an influx of illegal workers: Singapore has between 200,000 to 300,000 illegals, mainly from Malaysia, the Philippines, Sri Lanka, and Thailand; the Malay peninsula has attracted 470,000 illegal migrants; Sabah reportedly has 140,000 illegal migrants from Indonesia; Thailand has an estimated 200,000 illegals, largely from Burma; Korea has 46,000 illegals, mainly Filipinos, Chinese, and Nepalese; and Taiwan has an estimated 60,000 illegal workers, with many coming in regularly from the mainland.

24. Sekine, "Guest Worker Policies," p. 61.

25. Ibid., p. 60. In a similar vein, Koichi Koizumi writes that "as an unforeseen by-product of the acceptance of Indochinese refugees, definite progress has been made towards alleviating prejudice towards other categories of foreigners, such as Koreans and Taiwanese, who have settled in Japan" ("Refugee Policy Formation in Japan," *Journal of Refugee Studies,* 1992, no. 2, p. 134). Saito Yasuhiko, professor of international law at Tokyo Universities, also writes that "the question is not how to keep unskilled

until now unquestioningly defined itself as a homogeneous society, may be on the brink of having to accept a new self-image as a society composed of people of diverse origins. It can foster that image by acknowledging the beacon of hope that it is for refugees and laborers alike—and acting accordingly."[26]

Some Japanese business organizations have also argued that the acceptance of foreign workers would open up Japanese society internationally while coping with a labor shortage.[27] One Japanese labor economist, Kazutoshi Koshiro, economics professor at Yokohama National University, points to the decline in the birthrate and the aging of the Japanese population in the 1990s and beyond as a demographic development that will cause a chronic labor shortage.[28]

For some Japanese, the relevant experience is that of Australia, another industrial country on the periphery of the Asian mainland that dropped its restrictive "white Australia" immigration policy in response to global criticism and concern that it was alienating Asian countries with which it sought trade and good relations. A more open Asia-oriented guest worker, migration, and refugee policy, they argue, is good international politics. But for other Japanese, the experience of Great Britain, Germany, France, and Switzerland confirms their own deeply held view that a migration and refugee policy that makes Japan a more heterogeneous society will have undesirable social, cultural, and political consequences.[29]

Japan will clearly face additional difficulties in the future as it attempts to develop coherent migration policies. Japan's citizenship laws are a more fundamental indication than migration and refugee policies of how Japan approaches the issue of heterogeneity. Japan, like Germany, grants citizenship on the basis not of birth but of descent. Thus Koreans born in Japan of Korean nationals residing in Japan do not automatically become Japanese citizens. Although many are Japanese-

---

workers out but how to take them in. . . . The world is smaller than ever before; people, products, money and information move freely without regard to national borders. Japan has already done much to open its doors to the international flow of products, money and information. All that is left is to open up to the flow of people. . . . By the 1990s, Japan, like it or not, will have to conform to this global trend. If it is to remain an integral part of the international community, it cannot continue to resist being an exception" ("Impostor Refugees," p. 85).

26. Takaaki, "Refugee Quandary," p. 93.

27. Tadashi Hanami, "Discrimination in the U.S. and Japan from a Legal Viewpoint," *Journal of American and Canadian Studies,* p. 16. Hanami defends the restrictive position toward guest workers, noting that the countries of Western Europe have since reversed their policies on guest workers following the oil crisis of 1973.

28. "No matter how much businesses tighten their belts and automate their operations, no matter how many women and older people join the labor market, and no matter how many companies switch to overseas production, many fields will have to depend on foreign workers. These will include construction, transportation, nursing, some parts of the manufacturing industry and care-givers for the elderly. Japan will have to expand the permissible range of foreign labor in these areas." Kazutoshi Koshiro, "Labor Shortage and Employment Policies in Japan," paper prepared for the Second Japan-ASEAN Forum on International Labor Migration in East Asia, Tokyo, September 1991, p. 7.

29. Hanami writes, "In a Japanese context, the lesson from U.S. immigration history is that Japan should also establish a policy based on the interests of 'natives' with humane considerations such as principles of family reunion and preferential acceptance of refugees. But there is no reason to accept unskilled persons without qualifications only from humanitarian and so-called 'international' considerations" ("Discrimination," p. 21). For a pro-immigration view, see Haruo Shimada, *Japan's "Guest Workers"* (Tokyo: University of Tokyo Press, 1994). Shimada advocates a "work and learn" program that will enable Japanese employers to employ and train foreign workers temporarily.

born second- and third-generation descendants of Koreans brought to Japan in the 1930s or 1940s, they are classified as resident aliens. Even when, under a 1965 agreement with the government of South Korea, the Japanese government granted permanent residence status to a majority of the Koreans, citizenship was not granted. Thus of the estimated 700,000 Koreans living in Japan in the 1980s, approximately 75 percent were born and brought up in Japan. Nor does naturalization mean acceptance of Koreans in the wider society; Korean ancestry can limit school admissions, employment, and club memberships.[30]

At present, the issues of illegal migrants, refugees, and citizenship remain far less politically salient in Japan than in Western Europe, given the relatively low numbers of foreigners living in Japan. However, the intensity with which most Japanese regard "Japaneseness" as primordial suggests that small changes in the number and composition of foreigners in Japan can have unexpectedly large political and social consequences.

AUSTRALIA: FROM BRITANNIC TO MULTICULTURAL

In contrast to Germany, Italy, and Japan, Australia has traditionally been an immigrant country, its population almost entirely derived from the British Isles. As one Australian wit put it, Australia recruited migrants from the four corners of the world—Scotland, Ireland, Wales, and England. In fact, Australians remained so loyal to Britain and the British crown that they sent soldiers to fight in Britain's colonial wars. Australia's economy, moreover, was an adjunct to the British economy, providing wool for Britain's mills and meat for its kitchens. These ties were shattered during World War II, when it became clear that the British navy, after its defeat at Singapore, was no longer able to protect Australia. Japanese aircraft bombed Darwin, and only the United States Navy stood in the way of a Japanese invasion. The subsequent withdrawal of Britain from its overseas possessions, the British entry into the European Community, and the decline in British migration to Australia forced Australians to rethink their national identity and their immigration policies. Concerned that Australia would be vulnerable if its population remained low and in need of labor for its expanding postwar economy, the Australian government broadened its admission policies to encourage immigration from the entire European continent. This new policy was still the "white Australia" policy and was much criticized by outsiders for its blatant racism. Nonetheless, it initiated the diversification of Australia's population as migrants entered from Greece, Italy, Yugoslavia, Germany, and the Netherlands.[31]

---

30. De Vos and Wetherall, *Japan's Minorities*, p. 11. For a historical review of Korean settlement in Japan see Michael A. Weiner, *Race and Migration in Imperial Japan* (London: Routledge, 1994).

31. For accounts of Australia's migration policies, see Katharine Betts, *Ideology and Immigration* (Carlton, Victoria: Melbourne University Press, 1988); Charles Price, *Southern Europeans in Australia* (Melbourne: Oxford University Press, 1963); Robert Hughes, *The Fatal Shore* (New York: Knopf, 1987); James Jupp, *Immigration* (Sydney: Sydney University Press, 1991); and Gary P. Freeman and James

Table II   AUSTRALIAN IMMIGRATION PLANNING LEVELS BY CATEGORY, 1991–1992

Category	Immigrants Permitted (thousands)
Family	56.0
Skill	
Employer nominations	7.0
Business migration	5.0
Special talents	0.5
Independents	30.0
Special eligibility	0.5
Refugees, humanitarian, and special assistance	
Refugees and global humanitarian	8.0
Special assistance	4.0
Total	111.0

Note: "Family" category includes estimated onshore residence approvals of 9,000, and "Employer Nominations" category includes labor agreements and estimated onshore residence approvals of 2,000.

Source: Australian Department of Immigration, Local Government and Ethnic Affairs.

In the years to follow, as Australia began to refocus its trade policies toward East and Southeast Asia, many Australians came to regard the whites only policy as a principal deterrent to the creation of a secure economic and political environment for their country. Some intellectuals also argued that Australia's cultural parochialism and the persistent tendency to pattern itself after the United Kingdom could best be overcome if Australia further diversified its migration intake. Consequently, in the late 1960s and early 1970s, the whites only policy was ended, and the entry doors were widened. The government put in place what it regarded as a "balanced" intake based on a number of multiple concerns: family unification to enable the children and parents of existing migrants to enter the country; furthering economic growth by recruiting skilled people needed by the economy; and humanitarianism, which would facilitate the entry of refugees. A detailed point-quota system was put into place. Under this system, close family members can readily obtain admission, and more distant family members are given preferences for admission if they meet the skill or educational requirements.

Jupp (eds.), *Nations of Immigrants* (Melbourne: Oxford University Press, 1992). On multicultural policies, see the chapters in Freeman and Jupp by Stephen S. Castles, "Australian Multiculturalism: Social Policy and Identity in a Changing Society," and by Louis De Sipio and Rudolfo de la Garza, "Making Them Us: The Political Incorporation of Culturally Distinct Immigrant and Non-immigrant Minorities in the United States."

Table 12   FOREIGN-BORN POPULATION IN AUSTRALIA BY BIRTHPLACE, 1971 AND 1991

Origin	Number of Residents (thousands) 1971	1991
Europe	2,196.5	2,410.4
United Kingdom and Ireland	1,088.2	1,222.0
Italy	289.5	261.6
Yugoslavia	129.8	167.2
Greece	160.2	145.8
Germany	110.8	121.0
Other Europe	418.0	492.8
Asia	167.2	898.3
New Zealand	80.5	287.5
Africa	61.9	186.1
America	55.8	158.2
Other or not stated	17.5	—
Total	2,579.3	3,940.5

Note: 1991 data are provisional. Table reflects shifts in immigrant population that occurred after the effective end of the "white Australia" policy in 1973. Data for 1971 are those of the census. Data for 1991 are broadly comparable to the census but may tend to overestimate. A dash indicates that data are unavailable.

Source: Organization for Economic Cooperation and Development.

Employers can nominate individuals whom they wish to employ under the skilled quota, and there is also a quota for those with business skills who seem likely to invest and create employment for Australians.

As a result of these policies, the annual intake of family migrants in the 1980s to early 1990s ranged from 44,000 to 80,000; skilled migrants, 10,000 to 52,000; and humanitarian (refugee) migrants, 12,000 to 13,000. The total annual intake in most years has ranged from 92,000 to 136,000, or between 0.6 and 0.7 percent of Australia's population, one of the highest immigration rates in the world. Even when unemployment was high, as in 1992–1993, the planned intake was 80,000, slightly under one-half of 1 percent. In 1991, fully 3.9 million (22.7 percent) of Australia's population was foreign-born, making it a country of immigration second only to Israel, where immigrants or children of immigrants comprise 40 percent of the population. The largest single source of migrants to Australia continues to be the United Kingdom (14 percent), followed by Hong Kong, Vietnam, New Zealand, the Philippines, India, China, Taiwan, Malaysia, and Sri Lanka. The majority of new migrants now come from Asia. In 1991, there were nearly 900,000 Asian-born migrants in Australia.

In recent years, Australia's immigration policy has been subject to criticism. The high immigration rate, especially the high proportion of Asians, has generated antimigrant sentiment. Some Australians express concern over the increasingly non-British, nonwhite composition of the population; others, predominantly environmentalists, argue that migration prevents Australia from achieving the ideal of low or zero population growth. The familiar argument that during high unemployment, immigrants take jobs from the native population can also be heard, even though there is little evidence to support it. The first of these criticisms, fear of multiculturalism, is, however, the most significant. In the mid-1980s, people began to refer to the "Asianization of Australia," and the leader of the opposition party called for a "One Australia" policy, regarded by some as a call for a return to a whites only immigration policy. Despite these attitudes, however, Australian society has proved remarkably resilient in absorbing its immigrant population and in minimizing ethnic cleavages, particularly in light of the growth of antimigrant nativist political parties in Europe and the Third World.

A number of factors have eased the absorption of migrants into Australia. Most important is the capacity of the Australian government to control the intake and to minimize the amount of clandestine migration. In this regard, Australia has some geographic advantages because it is an island and relatively distant from places of large-scale emigration. But the sea has not prevented Chinese, Cubans, and Haitians from landing on North American shores or North Africans from going by boat to Italy or Spain. Hence we must look at other factors to understand Australia's success. In particular, Australia has devised a number of strategies for a more tightly controlled entry than other developed countries.

The first such policy is a universal visa system. All visitors (other than those from New Zealand) who wish to enter the country are required to obtain a visa. This policy enhances control by letting visa officers know which countries' citizens overstay in Australia, thereby enabling the government to develop a "risk factor" profile, a list of countries that send a large number of people who overstay. The universal visa system also prevents individuals from flying into the country without a visa and then requesting asylum. Airlines flying to Australia risk fines unless they check passengers for visas before allowing them to fly.

A second strategy of the Australian government is to insist that all requests for asylum be made offshore. The Department of Immigration, Local Government and Ethnic Affairs has posted officers with responsibility for reviewing claims for asylum in Australian embassies and consulates abroad. The few individuals without visas who do succeed in coming ashore and claiming asylum are not permitted to settle or to make claims on the welfare system pending review of their cases; since 1989, they have been placed in detention camps. This last strategy has been criticized by human rights groups, which contend that the conditions in these camps are unsatisfactory, detention denies individuals their freedom, and the review process is long, sometimes lasting several years. The government, however, defends the camps, reporting that only 8 percent of those who seek asylum successfully pass through the review process and are found to be legitimate refugees. Furthermore, since the detention system was put in place, there have been fewer onshore requests for asylum, indicating that the centers have served to deter unfounded claims.

Notwithstanding its tight immigration controls, Australia has been relatively generous in its admission of refugees, both so-called Convention refugees subject to political persecution and refugees who suffer discrimination or are fleeing violence. As with ordinary migrants, some preference is given to those who have close links to Australia, such as relatives of Australian residents or persons educated in the country. But there is also a small, separate humanitarian quota allowing Australian nongovernmental human rights and refugee groups to nominate candidates for admission. Since World War II, Australia has admitted and settled 500,000 refugees and displaced persons—a figure proportionately among the highest in the world.

In general, in terms of skill level and education, the quality of the migrants and refugees in Australia is high. A large proportion of migrants were employed as managers, administrators, professionals or paraprofessionals, or tradespersons prior to migrating. Nearly 70 percent of the migrants arriving in 1991–1992 were skilled, well above the 43 percent level of skill in the Australian workforce. Many of the migrants have found employment as secondary school teachers, computer professionals, general managers, registered nurses, office secretaries, and electrical engineers. According to a study prepared by the Department of Immigration, Local Government and Ethnic Affairs, a higher proportion of migrants of English-speaking background held positions in the professions and trades than the Australian-born. The study also reported that long-established migrants had unemployment rates that were lower than those of the Australian-born.[32]

The Australian government thus pursues a dual track: a generous admission policy with priority to refugees and to others who by virtue of their skills and their family, employer, and organizational connections in Australia are most likely to adapt readily, and tight controls so as to prevent the entrance of persons who do not qualify under the rules or who try to circumvent offshore visa application procedures. Immigration officials insist that the incoming flow must be controlled and, above all, must be seen as such by the public at large. The use of detention camps, the willingness of the government to repatriate rejected asylum seekers, and the insistence on offshore reviews are all regarded as essential to maintaining public support for existing levels of migration.

The Australian government has declared that it is committed to a policy of multiculturalism and has even created an office of multicultural affairs, located in the prime minister's office. The precise implications of multiculturalism are unclear, but at a minimum the Australian government has articulated the rights of all Australians (indigenous tribal populations as well as those of migrant origin) to express their individual cultural identity. Multiculturalism is a frequent theme in speeches given by the prime minister and cabinet officers. In addition, the government funds after-school language programs for children who wish to preserve or acquire the language of their parents and takes a positive view of bilingualism. Universities maintain multicultural programs to "deparochialize" Australians and to instill cultural pride in migrant communities. Government funds also go to ethnic associations; to the national Ethnic Community Council, run largely by members of the older migrant communities from Greece and Italy; and to a multicultural

---

32. Australian Department of Immigration, Local Government and Ethnic Affairs, *Population Flows* (Canberra, 1993), pp. 24–27.

television channel known as SBS. SBS is aimed specifically at encouraging immigrants to retain their cultural heritage; it broadcasts comprehensive international news programs, foreign films (with English subtitles), and special programs for immigrants and their descendants. SBS also maintains separate foreign-language radio broadcasts, which are listened to almost exclusively by the migrant communities. Finally, to prevent racial discrimination, several laws have been passed, and a monitoring group, the Human Rights and Equal Opportunity Commission, has been set up.

As part of its absorption policy, Australia has established easy naturalization rules. The residency requirement was dropped in the early 1980s from four years to two. Immigrants must pass a test in basic English, but those over the age of 50 are exempt. The children of legal residents have automatic birthright citizenship.

One final indication of the attention Australia gives to issues of migration and absorption is that the minister of immigration is a member of the cabinet. Immigration is seen as a matter of national policy linked to employment, ethnic relations, social welfare policies, human rights and discrimination, and foreign policy. The immigration issue is thus never off the national agenda. It arises when the Department of the Attorney-General has to adjudicate claims for discrimination; when the prime minister has to decide whether to grant temporary or permanent asylum, as it did to 20,000 Chinese students following the Tiananmen Square incident; when the government has to negotiate with the United States and Britain over such matters as Indochinese boat people; and when the Department of Education has to make decisions regarding multiculturalism. The Department of Immigration, Local Government and Ethnic Affairs is thus quite large, with senior officers responsible for migration settlement, providing grants-in-aid to migrant welfare organizations, controlling entry of persons into Australia, handling onshore claims for refugee status, providing liaison with international organizations dealing with refugee issues, granting citizenship and determining eligibility, and examining the economic, social, and environmental impact of migration. The ministry also funds the quasi-autonomous Bureau of Immigration Research.

Though harassment of and discrimination against foreigners, especially Asians, remains a feature of Australian life, Australia has avoided the large-scale antimigrant violence and xenophobia experienced by Western Europe. The explanation, as we have seen, lies in two major factors: first, a policy that has brought into the country a migrant population with high levels of skills and education that enable most migrants to move readily into the labor market without creating the ethnic division of labor that has characterized many other migrant-receiving societies, and second, a system of controlling admission that has reassured most Australians that their borders are not out of control. The result is a remarkably high level of public support for continued migration, easy naturalization, and some form of multiculturalism.

The contrast between the Australian experience and that of Germany, Italy, and Japan has little to do with the labor requirements of each of these societies. All but Italy experienced similar labor shortages following World War II, and current levels of unemployment are as high in Australia as in Europe. Rather, the contrasts are due to differences in conceptions of national identity—specifically, whether a nation is built on the notion of cultural homogeneity or cultural diversity and whether the notion of pluralism extends from the political to the cultural realm. The Australian experience suggests that national identity is not necessarily written in stone; societies can and do redefine themselves. Australia has done so; Germany, Italy, and Japan have not.

In the next chapter, we will examine more closely factors that facilitate or impede the absorption of migrants. We will first consider how two groups of countries, the Persian Gulf states and the countries of Western Europe, each sought to use migrants in the labor force without incorporating them in the society and polity. Then we will explore nativism as a set of political beliefs that has shaped attitudes toward immigrants in the United States, Western Europe, and several developing countries. Finally, we will examine how citizenship rules and other policies facilitate or impede migrant absorption.

THE ABSORPTION
OF MIGRANTS

Can Vietnamese migrants be made into Americans, Russians into Israelis, Turks into Germans, Bangladeshis into Englishmen? Can Nepalis be made into Bhutanese, Indonesians into Malaysians, Koreans into Japanese? Such questions underscore the complexity of the issues raised by the changing ethnic composition of countries as a result of international population movements. Most of the developed countries are becoming ethnically diverse, and the ethnic composition of developing countries is changing as well. The absorption, incorporation, integration, and assimilation—the terms themselves suggest complexity, ambiguity, and contention—of migrants and refugees has therefore become a major issue in both advanced industrial countries and the Third World.

In examining the factors that influence absorption, it is important to distinguish between immigration policies and immigrant policies. The former refers to policies dealing with admission, the latter to policies on the treatment of migrants once they have entered the country. Both clearly affect the absorption process: Immigration policies determine which people enter, their characteristics, from where they come, and in what numbers, while policies toward immigrants determine whether they and their families have access to education, housing, employment, welfare benefits, and citizenship. This chapter focuses primarily on policies toward immigrants.

The capacity of countries to absorb migrants reflects differences in the characteristics of the migrant-receiving countries, the policies they adopt, the receptivity of the host population, the structure of the labor market in the host society, the capacity of migrants to find a niche in the labor market, and the preferences of the migrants themselves. The process of absorption therefore varies so greatly from one society to another that policy "lessons" can be transferred only with difficulty. What has worked for the United States, a country of immigration, may not be relevant for Germany or France, the policies of Western Europe may not be relevant for the states of the Persian Gulf, and absorption issues for Nepal, Fiji, Bhutan, and Bangladesh will differ markedly from those of developed countries. But each country facing a large population influx, welcomed or not, must wrestle with the question of its meaning for national identity and cultural pluralism.

This chapter focuses on four aspects of the process of migrant absorption. The first is the issue of categories: How do societies categorize migrants and their relationship to the local population, and how do these social constructs shape thinking?

Second, how and why have so many societies imported guest workers as a way of avoiding the issues of absorption? Here we will compare the experiences of the oil-producing Gulf states with those of Western Europe to suggest why and how the Gulf states but not the European states have managed to avoid the issue of absorption. Third, we explore why fear of too great an influx of foreigners has historically been so central to government policies toward immigration, even in acknowledged countries of immigration. A comparison of nativist responses in the United States, Western Europe, and several Third World countries lets us consider whether there is a threshold of acceptable migration and, if so, whether we can determine what it is.[1] Fourth, we examine some of the key factors that appear to be important in the absorption process, focusing on advanced industrial societies.

TYPES OF MIGRANTS

The absorption process differs among the various categories of migrants. Illegals who slip into the underground economy, legal migrants entitled to permanent residence and citizenship, and guest workers who stay but are expected to leave—each presents a different problem for absorption. What distinguishes among them is legitimacy: the legitimacy of their entry and of their claim for permanent inclusion in the community.

Both the legal and popular vocabularies reflect differences in how societies think about these various categories of migrants and their claims to rights and benefits. In Germany, as discussed earlier, there are *Übersiedler*, Germans from East Germany who fled to the West between 1961 and 1989; *Aussiedler*, ethnic German "resettlers" from Poland, Romania, and the Soviet Union; and *Ausländer*, or non-German foreigners, including *Gastarbeiter*, or guest workers. Similarly, in Great Britain, the British Nationality Act of 1981 distinguishes among British citizens, British dependent territory citizens, British overseas citizens, British subjects, and British protected persons. It also delineates two main types of immigration status: patrial (with the "right of abode") and nonpatrial.[2] The United States admits different categories of immigrants and refugees as well. Refugees may be granted "temporary protected status" (TPS) or "extended voluntary departure" (EVD); among ordinary migrants, there are green card holders, who have the right to remain and become naturalized citizens, and "replenishment agricultural workers," who can stay and work for only a limited period.

Not only are there categories that distinguish among migrant groups, but there are also terms to describe differences between migrants and natives. The use of these terms further highlights the complexity of absorbing people considered outsiders by locals, even though they may have lived in the community for generations. In Malaysia, a distinction is made between *bhoomiputra* and non-*bhoomiputra* (indigenous and nonindigenous peoples); in Indonesia, there are the indigenous *pribumi* (Indonesians) and the non-*pribumi*, primarily Indonesian Chinese.

---

1. By nativism, I mean attitudes and policies favoring native inhabitants over immigrants; nativism does not necessarily imply xenophobia, a fear or hatred of foreigners.

2. Ann Dummett and Andrew Nicol, *Subjects, Citizens, Aliens and Others* (London: Weidenfeld & Nicolson, 1990).

Similarly, in India, distinctions are made between people who originate from the locality ("sons of the soil") and those who are migrants or descendants of migrants from other parts of India.[3] These various terms tell us a great deal about who is regarded as part of the community and who is not, and they define what rights and benefits should be given not only to migrants but often to their descendants as well. These terms, as we shall see, often illuminate variations in the capacity of societies to absorb immigrants.

GUEST WORKERS: AVOIDING ABSORPTION

The principal objective of guest worker policies is the desire of policymakers to import labor that does not have to be absorbed into the social or political system. Guest worker policies have been put in place in Western Europe, in the oil-producing states of the Persian Gulf, and in other regions of the world.

As stated in Chapter 3, Western Europe imported millions of guest workers from North Africa, Yugoslavia, Greece, southern Italy, and Turkey to cope with labor shortages in the 1960s. Similarly, the oil-rich countries of the Middle East imported an estimated 3.6 million foreign workers from Arab countries and from Asia by the early 1980s. Two other oil-producing states, Nigeria and Venezuela, also imported workers. An estimated 2 million workers entered Nigeria from the neighboring countries of Togo, Benin, and Ghana (most of whom were subsequently expelled in 1983), and Venezuela admitted approximately 1 million workers, mostly from Colombia. Singapore recruited 50,000 workers from Indonesia and Malaysia. Vietnamese were employed in Soviet Siberia and in several Eastern European countries. There are also substantial seasonal flows in many parts of central Africa and in South and Southeast Asia and, until recently, substantial daily flows of workers across the Green Line into Israel from the West Bank and Gaza.

Though these migrants often form only a small proportion of the labor force of the sending country, their proportion in the labor force of the receiving country has often been quite large. In the Gulf states, the proportion of foreign workers is unusually high: 39 percent in Bahrain, 45 percent in Oman, 71 percent in Kuwait, 81 percent in Qatar, and 85 percent in the United Arab Emirates. The number of foreign workers in Kuwait and in Saudi Arabia declined markedly during the Gulf War,[4] but according to most reports, large numbers of foreign workers returned after the war ended.[5] In the early 1990s, fully 9 percent of the workforce in

3. In many local languages, distinctions are drawn between locals and nonlocals. Tribals in the state of Bihar, for example, call themselves *adivasis* ("original" people), as distinct from *dikus*, or outsiders. In the region around Hyderabad, locals call themselves *mulki* and outsiders non-*mulki*. In India's north-eastern state of Assam, a local person is *Ahomiya* (culturally Assamese) or *thalua* (which includes both Assamese and indigenous tribals), while people who come from outside are *Ona-Ahomiya* (not Assamese) or *pamua* (non-Assamese landowners). None of these terms is neutral.

4. An ILO study reported a decline in the annual flow of contract migrant workers to the Middle East from the major Asian labor-exporting countries even before the Gulf War, from 1,007,000 in 1983 to approximately 700,000 in 1986. Rashid Amjad, *To the Gulf and Back* (New Delhi: International Labour Organisation, Asian Employment Programme, 1989), p. 6.

5. Nasra M. Shah, *Economic, Demographic, Sociocultural and Political Dynamics of Emigration from and within South Asia* (Unpublished study prepared for the Mid Project Meeting of the IOM/UNFPFA project on Emigration in Developing Countries, 1994), pp. 67–68.

Table 13   ASIAN MIGRANT WORKERS IN THE MIDDLE EAST BY COUNTRY OF EMPLOYMENT, 1975–1983

Country of Employment	Migrant Workers in Residence		
	1975	1980	1983
Bahrain	17,050	90,905	85,777
Iran	1,227	1,608	17,636
Iraq	10,656	55,567	—
Jordan	52	11,098	4,269
Kuwait	33,156	152,691	217,554
Libya	5,173	208,848	185,085
Oman	58,623	150,383	261,773
Qatar	33,222	68,004	93,871
Saudi Arabia	34,176	699,761	1,736,614
United Arab Emirates	166,362	470,867	536,410
Yemen	—	8,860	215,022
Other countries	—	11,911	47,686
Unspecified by country	526	52,269	218,095
Total	360,223	1,982,772	3,619,792

Note: A dash indicates that data are unavailable.

Source: United Nations Economic and Social Commission for Asia and the Pacific.

Germany and France consisted of migrant workers, 7 percent in Austria and Belgium, and an astonishing 24 percent in Switzerland.

A tight labor market in itself does not necessarily result in a decision to admit immigrants. If a high demand for labor persists for a period of time, wages may rise, previous nonparticipants (such as women) may enter the labor market, employers may shift from labor-intensive to capital-intensive investments, the level of technology may be modified to reduce labor use, and labor-intensive industries may close down or move abroad. Alternatively, if countries believe that the tight labor market is temporary—either because of a short-term economic boom or an earlier temporary decline in population growth rates—employers may be permitted to import labor. The approaches taken by countries that choose to admit migrants to meet labor needs vary, especially regarding temporary versus permanent admission. Usually, formal contracts between workers and employers specify wages and working conditions, duration of stay, and who should bear the costs of return. But beyond these formal contracts are social contracts between the state and the immigrants, specifying what, if any, social benefits immigrants will receive, as well as migrants' rights regarding length of stay, freedom to change employers, entitlement to bring family members, and possibilities for permanent residence and citizenship.

The countries of Western Europe and the Persian Gulf adopted a policy of admitting temporary rather than permanent migrants for a number of reasons. The most commonly cited reason is that these governments viewed the labor shortages as temporary. Western European governments assumed that the tight labor market of the 1950s and early 1960s would end when the large numbers of citizens born immediately after the war entered the labor force. Similarly, the Gulf countries imported large numbers of workers to handle what they presumed was a temporary surge in construction after the 1973 oil boom.

Sociologists and economists have suggested deeper structural explanations for the use of temporary foreign workers. Foreign workers can be a cushion in economies that experience fluctuations in employment and can be forced to leave as unemployment increases.[6] Furthermore, foreign workers enable industrial societies to fill labor needs in dead-end, low-status, low-wage sectors of the economy (what some economists call the "secondary labor market") without perpetuating sharp class cleavages within the native population.[7] In fact, if social policy is directed at providing the national population with dignified jobs, good working conditions, reasonable wages, and respectable social status, one could theoretically reduce inequalities within one's own society by importing foreign workers.[8]

Economics aside, a major reason for admitting guest workers rather than permanent migrants was to avoid having to become an ethnically plural society. Most Europeans subscribed to the notion that their countries should contain a single nationality, sharing a common language, culture, and, in some instances, religion. The governments of West Germany, France, Norway, Denmark, Sweden, and the Netherlands were not inclined to create heterogeneous societies, and Belgium and Switzerland were reluctant to increase or alter their heterogeneity. Similarly, the Gulf states regarded themselves as homogeneous Arab societies.

An alternative for the labor-short, oil-rich Gulf states that would not have jeopardized their homogeneity would have been to admit permanent migrants from neighboring countries, congruent with a pan-Arab perspective. But the Gulf governments evidently feared that Arab migrants might bring in antimonarchical ideologies such as Nasserism, Baathism, and Islamic fundamentalism, pervasive at the time in the Middle East, thereby undermining the existing regimes. Palestinians were denied the right to become citizens of the Gulf states partly out of concern for the dilution of their claims for a Palestinian state but also because host governments feared that the newcomers might attempt to transform the local political system.

6. W. R. Böhning, *Studies in International Labour Migration* (London: Macmillan, 1984).

7. Michael J. Piore, *Birds of Passage* (Cambridge: Cambridge University Press, 1979).

8. The result, of course, can be precisely the opposite of what is intended if guest workers displace native workers at the lower end of the labor market. Few issues in the study of migration have been as contentious and as unresolved as the question of whether guest workers and illegals take jobs that the local poor do not want because wages are lower than the income that can be obtained through the welfare system. For competing views, see Michael Fix and Jeffrey S. Passel, *Immigration and Immigrants* (Washington, D.C.: Urban Institute, 1994), and George J. Borjas, "Immigrants, Minorities, and Labor Market Competition," *Industrial and Labor Relations Review?*, pp. 382–392. Fix and Passel contains a useful bibliography on the controversy.

A fundamental premise behind both the Western European and Gulf policies of admitting guest workers was that labor would be regarded as a commodity. From this perspective, the preferred workers were those who came without their families, made little use of public services, and did not put economic or political demands on employers or the state. Foreign workers were more likely to conform to these ideals than permanent migrants.

Persian Gulf and Western European Policies Compared

A central legal and political issue regarding temporary foreign workers, therefore, is the question of what rights and benefits they are to be given by the host country. The way in which this question is resolved has an important impact on the relationship between governments of receiving and sending countries, on the political behavior of the foreign workers, and ultimately on the question of whether migrant workers become permanent residents. A comparison of the differences in the policies adopted by the Persian Gulf states and those adopted by the countries of Western Europe helps us understand why the strategy of importing guest workers has thus far avoided the issue of migrant absorption in the former but not in the latter.

The volume of migration to the Gulf was extraordinarily high. Among the five small countries of the Gulf—Kuwait, Qatar, Bahrain, the United Arab Emirates (UAE), and Oman—approximately two-thirds of the labor force is imported; prior to the Gulf War, half of the labor force in Saudi Arabia was imported as well.

Although Gulf governments initially regarded immigrant workers as a means of fulfilling short-term labor needs, it is clear that migrants are now structurally integrated into their economies. So-called temporary labor migrants are used to fill permanent jobs in the health and education sectors, the expanding industrial sector, and even government services. Furthermore, the oil-producing states have constructed new industries and public-sector entitlements that, for the foreseeable future, will require a labor force larger and more skilled than they themselves can provide from among their own citizens.

Despite the apparent permanence of guest workers, the Gulf governments rejected the notion that foreign workers should be politically and socially integrated into their societies. On the contrary, they have been committed to creating a sense of insecurity and impermanence among the migrants even as the migrant process has, for all practical purposes, become enduring.[9] The Gulf states pursue the following specific policies toward their migrant workers:

- Regardless of how long they reside in the country, migrant workers cannot ordinarily become citizens, nor can their locally born children become citi-

9. Even as oil prices declined, the countries of the Gulf continued to recruit foreign labor. In Bahrain, for example, the number of Indian nationals increased from 50,000 in 1981 to 77,0900 in 1986; see F. J. Khergamvala, "Indians Least Hit by Gulf Recession," *The Hindu*, International Edition, May 2, 1987. A study of Kuwait reports that declining oil revenues before the Gulf War were not accompanied by any significant decline in the employment of foreign workers largely because the demand for maintenance and operational staff to service the new infrastructure and industries continued to expand; see J. S. Birks, I. J. Seccombe, and C. A. Sinclair, "Migrant Workers in the Arab Gulf: The Impact of Declining Oil Revenues," *International Migration Review*, Winter 1986, pp. 799–814. Foreign workers fled Kuwait following the Iraqi invasion, and immediately following the war, Kuwait expelled a large number of Palestinians. When reconstruction started, Kuwait once again imported large numbers of foreign workers, many from South Asia.

zens. Citizenship may be bestowed only in rare cases by the ruling sheikhs. This policy is nondiscriminatory and is applied to migrant Arabs who have spent many years in the Gulf (including locally born Palestinians) as well as to non-Arabs.

- Except in Oman and the UAE state of Dubai, nonnationals are usually not permitted to own a business, purchase a house, or acquire land. Import licenses and franchises are also given only to citizens, even if such business-es are actually financed and managed by foreigners.

- There is no free labor market. Migrant workers receive work permits only after obtaining "no objection certificates" (NOCs) from the government. The permits, though renewable, are of limited duration. Furthermore, migrants may not change jobs without the consent of both their employer and the Ministry of Labor and Social Affairs. If foreign workers change employment without consent, they risk deportation. Migrant workers can also be deported for "incitement of workers to strike or to refrain from work-ing" or "physical or verbal attacks on employers or supervisors."

- The political rights of foreign workers are restricted. They may not form or join trade unions or hold public meetings.[10] Thus in most of the Gulf, asso-ciations of migrant workers are confined to social functions. In addition, public manifestations of religious activities such as religious processions among non-Muslims are forbidden. Violations of these rules or any laws may lead to expulsion. In such cases, nonnationals do not have the right of appeal.

- Social welfare benefits given to citizens are generally not extended to for-eigners. Free medical care, free universal education from primary school through university, and low-cost housing are provided to the local population but not to migrant workers, except in Kuwait. Foreign communities are, however, permitted to set up privately financed schools for their own chil-dren, and individual employers often provide medical facilities for their for-eign employees.

- Migrant workers are not permitted to bring their wives and children unless their wages are above a level specified by the government. As a result, unskilled and semiskilled workers are generally unable to bring their families.

- To reduce even further the chances that migrant workers will want to stay, recruitment of guest workers has increasingly tended to favor non-Arabs. Asians are less likely than Arab guest workers to make demands on employ-ers and, due to language differences, do not interact socially or politically with the locals. The percentage of non-Arabs in the labor force, mainly Asians, rose from 12 percent in 1970 to 41 percent by 1980. In 1985, fully 63 percent of Gulf migrants were Asian.[11]

These policies do more than simply establish the temporary position of the migrant workers; they institutionalize a pattern of dualism (with its implications of opposing principles) as distinct from pluralism (with its implications of equality). The contrast with the policies adopted by the labor-importing countries of Western Europe is quite striking. Like the countries of the Persian Gulf, France, Germany,

10. In Kuwait, they may join unions, but only after they have been in residence for five years.

11. Sharon Stanton Russell and Michael S. Teitelbaum, *International Migration and International Trade* (Washington, D.C.: World Bank, 1992), p. 24.

Switzerland, Belgium, and the Netherlands also admitted foreign guest workers rather than immigrants.[12] In contrast to the countries of the Persian Gulf, Western European governments offered foreign workers many of the same rights and benefits provided citizens. Foreign workers are not tied to their employers but are free to change jobs. They are entitled to the same health, education, unemployment, and social security benefits as citizens. Children of migrants are taught in the local language. Migrant workers who have been employed for a specified period are not required to leave the country when they are unemployed. Moreover, the authority of the government to expel a migrant worker is prescribed by law and subject to a variety of legal appeals.

Since the late 1960s, moreover, Belgium, France, Germany, Switzerland, and the Netherlands have granted migrants the right of political participation through consultative councils composed of migrant workers. These advisory bodies enable migrants to take part in decisions involving education, cultural affairs, sports, housing, and social and health services. Political rights were enhanced in the mid-1970s with the granting of voting rights in local elections in Sweden, Finland, Denmark, Norway, and the Netherlands. The German, French, and Swiss governments did not give voting rights to migrant workers but did guarantee public liberties, including freedom of speech and the right to join and form associations.

European governments eased restrictions on the entry of family members. In Germany, in fact, public policy unwittingly induced migrants to bring wives and children by changing the qualifications for income supplements: Once provided to migrants for each child in Germany or abroad, supplements are now provided only for children residing in Germany.[13] The result was a major influx of migrant children; by 1980, there were as many as 450,000 Turkish children in Germany. In comparison to the Gulf states, European governments have had much more liberal policies toward the families of migrant workers.

Some European governments provided additional benefits to migrants. In the Netherlands, additional teachers were provided in schools where there were substantial numbers of non-Dutch children. In Sweden and Norway, funds were granted to migrant organizations to enable them to support cultural and social activities and publish their own journals. And in Germany, a supplementary housing program was created for migrant workers.

Ironically, Western European countries were committed to the notion that foreign workers and their dependents should eventually return home, but the policies they implemented made it increasingly easier and more attractive for foreign workers to remain. This occurred in part because employers, concerned with maintaining a stable labor force, were opposed to the practice of worker rotation, and in time governments ceased to require that workers return home after a specified

12. The United Kingdom was an exception in that it admitted immigrants from its former colonies in the West Indies, East Africa, and South Asia and did not make use of guest workers. Sweden also considers itself a country of immigration. The Netherlands has many immigrants from its former colonies Indonesia and Suriname but also admitted foreign guest workers.

13. Hermann Korte, "Labor Migration and the Employment of Foreigners in the Federal Republic of Germany Since 1950," in *Guests Come to Stay,* ed. Rosemarie Rogers (Boulder, Colo.: Westview Press, 1985), pp. 36–37.

period. Moreover, even though the rise in the price of oil and a decline in the demand for labor in Western European encouraged migrants to return home, governments were unwilling to use force.[14] Consequently, most migrants and their dependents remained. By the late 1970s, it was apparent that migrant workers and their families had become permanent minorities in countries that had made no provision for their permanent settlement.

The policies of the Gulf states, although illiberal from a Western perspective, have been more consistent with the goal of preventing temporary migrants from becoming permanent settlers. Nonetheless, even the Gulf states appear to have had only limited success in preventing migrants from becoming permanent settlers. This suggests that workers are prepared to stay in countries with higher wages and more employment opportunities than exist at home, even when severe political, economic, and social restrictions are imposed on them. Guest worker programs, except when administered by governments that are prepared to expatriate workers who are no longer needed, have not proved to be an effective way of satisfying the need for labor while avoiding the need for the permanent absorption of migrants.

NATIVISM AND IMMIGRATION POLICIES

Fear of "too great" an influx of foreigners remains central to all government policies on immigration and a factor in the capacity of countries to absorb immigrants. Admission policies, of course, vary widely. Some countries admit no migrants, while others have annual quotas. Some countries base their admissions primarily on labor needs, while others emphasize family reunion or broader humanitarian considerations. Some countries pay no attention to race, religion, language, or culture in determining who can enter, while others are guided by explicit notions of ethnic affinity. Some countries grant entrants all the rights of citizenship, others extend various political rights and social benefits just short of citizenship, and still others provide substantially fewer rights and benefits than those given to citizens.

Although it is commonplace for scholars to regard some of these responses in pejorative terms—as discriminatory, chauvinist, racist, and xenophobic—it is essential to recognize that every society, without exception, imposes some limits on how many people will be admitted and who they may be. There is, however, no economic, political, or sociological theory that specifies what would constitute an appropriate level of immigration or what kind of immigrants would be most desirable and acceptable to the local population. What is economically desirable to employers may be socially and politically unacceptable to the rest of the local population. For example, employers are more resistant to restrictions on migration and more tolerant of illegal migrants than the general population. For employers, migration can be a mechanism for keeping wages down, discouraging unionization, and, especially when migrants are illegal, obtaining a more pliable, harder-working

---

14. By contrast, the oil-producing states have been prepared to expel unwanted guest workers. Nigeria and Libya both sent workers home in large numbers in the mid-1980s. Saudi Arabia expelled its Yemeni population during the Gulf War, and Kuwait expelled its Palestinians. Fear of expulsions makes the home governments of guest workers reluctant to press for improved working conditions.

labor force at lower cost. These very elements make migration undesirable to local labor. Furthermore, what may be beneficial in the short term (for example, when there are acute labor shortages) may be regarded as undesirable later when unemployment is high. The initially supportive attitudes of Western Europeans toward migrant workers changed in the late 1970s and 1980s as economic growth rates declined and unemployment rose and as it became clear that "temporary" workers were unwilling to return home. France gave birth to a new party, the National Front, that expressed militant opposition to North African migrant workers. In Germany, there were manifestations of anti-Turkish sentiment, and in Switzerland, several referenda on forced repatriation were barely defeated.

A review of historical and contemporary political movements created to halt further immigration or to force return migration suggests how nativism can impede the absorption of migrants.

Nativism Versus Pluralism in the United States

It is instructive to start with a description of antimigrant nativist movements in the United States—not because the United States has been particularly egregious in the restrictions it has placed on immigrants but for the very opposite reason. The United States has admitted more immigrants than any country in the world, and since 1965, it has been among the least restrictive with respect to the ethnic composition of its immigrants. Moreover, from the very beginning of its history, it has been an immigrant country. One of the charges made against the crown in the Declaration of Independence is that Britain imposed restrictions on migration into the colonies. From 1821 to 1924, some 40 to 50 million Europeans migrated to the United States.

Nonetheless, U.S. history is replete with antimigrant political movements. Popular hostility to immigrants and immigration grew in the 1830s and 1840s with the rise of the anti-Catholic Know-Nothing Party. By the middle of the nineteenth century, there was increased opposition to Irish, Italians, Slavs, Jews, and Asians, particularly the Chinese in California. Moreover, opposition to migrants did not come from fringe elements alone but had an honorable place in the American intellectual tradition. Indeed, nativism became a respectable attitude among American social scientists, economists, social theorists, and humanists by the end of the nineteenth century. Social Darwinism, eugenics, a nationalist concern with the preservation of American values and culture, and, at times, sheer racism and anti-Semitism shaped the thinking of many distinguished American figures.[15]

Nativist sentiment led to restrictions on the entrance of Chinese and other Asians into the United States. Thousands of Chinese had migrated to California in

15. According to John Higham, *Strangers in the Land* (New York: Atheneum, 1963), p. 40, in 1888, the American Economic Association offered a prize of $150 for the best essay on the theme "The Evil Effects of Unrestricted Migration." Francis A. Walker, president of the Massachusetts Institute of Technology, the American Statistical Association, and the American Economic Association and superintendent of the U.S. censuses of 1870 and 1880, used his considerable reputation and statistical skills to argue that the foreign-born were replacing the native-born through demographic competition. To compete with cheap foreign labor, he wrote, native-born Americans were reducing their family size rather than lowering their standard of living. He argued that migrants created unrest in the labor force and were a threat not only to American prosperity but also to social and political stability. He further voiced the fear that the immigrant flows consisted of peoples who were unassimilable to American values. "The

the 1850s following the discovery of gold, and many Chinese were subsequently engaged to work on the railroads, as domestic servants, and in industry. A combination of racial animosity and fear of competition on the part of white workers led to physical attacks against the Chinese and pressure in California to exclude the Chinese from both further immigration and naturalization. In 1882, the Chinese Exclusion Act was passed, the first of a series of measures that restricted the entrance of Chinese into the United States and precluded Chinese living in the United States from becoming naturalized citizens. Similar efforts were made to exclude the Japanese. In 1907 and 1908, a so-called gentlemen's agreement was signed under which the Japanese government vowed to limit migration to the United States to nonlaborers.

The nativist movement enjoyed its greatest intellectual respectability in the 1920s. Some of the most prominent intellectuals of the time were avowed nativists and social Darwinists: Henry Fairfield Osborn, president of the American Museum of Natural History; Ellsworth Huntington, Yale professor and author of *The Character of Races;* Robert M. Yerkes, president of the American Psychological Association and author of *Psychological Examining in the United States Army* (which unfavorably compared the intelligence of Negroes and the foreign-born with that of native-born white Americans); William MacDougall, another psychologist concerned with race and intelligence and an ardent eugenicist; Carl Brigham, author of *A Study of American Intelligence;* and Abbott Lawrence Lowell, president of Harvard, who advocated restrictive quotas for the admission of Jews into Harvard.

The Immigration Act of 1924 represented a victory for the nativists. Its national-origins clause stipulated migration quotas that limited entrance to 2 percent of the number of foreign-born residents of each nationality in the United States in 1890. Exemptions were made from these quotas only for the wives and minor children of U.S. citizens, not of aliens. This legislation, and the political mood that underlay it, made migration difficult through the early 1940s, even as refugees sought to escape from Nazi Germany.

The migration doors were reopened with the passage of new legislation in 1952 that provided for occupational preferences, and the 1965 Immigration Act permitted entry of up to 20,000 persons per year from any country, giving preferences to individuals with skills and to family unification. Additional legislation permitted the entrance of significant numbers of refugees. From the mid-1960s to the present, between 500,000 and 1 million migrants and refugees have entered the United States each year. Almost all of the recent migrants came from Asia, Mexico, Central America, and the Caribbean. The foreign-born population of the United States grew from 9,619,000 in 1970 to 19,767,000 in 1990.

Nativism in the United States was only marginally linked to the issue of job competition. The target of the nativists was not the *number* of migrants who came

---

entrance into our political, social and industrial life of such vast masses of peasantry," wrote Walker, "degraded below our utmost conceptions, is a matter which no intelligent patriot can look upon without the greatest apprehension and alarm. These people have no history behind them which is of a nature to give encouragement. They have none of the inherited instincts and tendencies which made it comparatively easy to deal with the immigration of the olden time. They are beaten men from beaten races, representing the worst failure in the struggle for existence. Centuries are against them, as centuries were on the side of those who formerly came to us."

Table 14   FOREIGN-BORN POPULATION IN THE UNITED STATES BY BIRTHPLACE, 1960–1990

Birthplace	Number of Residents (thousands)			
	1960	1970	1980	1990
Europe	7,233.7	5,712.0	5,149.3	4,016.7
Germany	989.8	833.0	849.4	711.9
United Kingdom	833.1	686.1	—	640.1
Italy	1,257.0	1,008.5	831.9	580.6
Poland	747.8	458.1	418.1	388.3
Former Soviet Union	690.6	463.5	406.0	333.7
Portugal	57.7	91.0	211.6	210.1
Ireland	338.7	251.4	197.8	169.8
Yugoslavia	165.8	153.7	153.0	141.5
France	111.6	105.4	120.2	119.2
Greece	159.2	177.3	211.0	117.4
Hungary	245.3	183.2	144.4	110.3
Other countries	1,637.1	1,300.8	1,605.9	493.5
Canada	952.5	812.4	842.9	744.8
Mexico	575.9	759.7	2,199.2	4,298.0
Caribbean	—	—	1,258.4	1,938.3
Cuba	79.2	439.0	607.8	737.0
Dominican Republic	—	—	—	347.9
Jamaica	—	—	—	334.1
Central America	48.9	315.5	353.9	1,134.0
El Salvador	—	—	—	465.4
South America	89.5	255.2	561.0	1,037.5
Asia	449.3	824.9	2,539.8	4,979.0
Philippines	104.8	184.8	501.4	912.7
Korea	11.2	38.7	289.9	568.4
Vietnam	—	—	231.1	543.3
China	99.7	172.1	286.1	529.8
India	12.3	51.0	206.1	450.4
Japan	109.2	120.3	221.8	290.1
Other countries	112.1	258.0	803.4	1,684.4
Africa, Oceania, other, and not stated	309.1	500.6	1,175.4	1,649.0
Total	9,738.1	9,619.3	14,079.9	19,767.3

Note: Due to rounding, individual cells may not sum to totals. A dash indicates that data are unavailable.

Sources: U.S. Census Bureau; Organization for Economic Cooperation and Development.

but their *composition*. Nativists regarded Catholic, Greek Orthodox, Oriental, and Jewish migrants as disrupting a preexisting American culture, which they regarded as "Nordic," white, and Protestant. Nativism coincided with periods in which there was a growth of patriotic Americanism. For many intellectuals in New England, migration was an offense by aliens who threatened their class, their religion, their country, their race, and their political conservatism—all the values of class and country that they regarded as quintessentially American.

The strength of nativists' sentiment in the United States is demonstrated by their success in restricting immigration for three decades, from the 1920s until after World War II, and for their imposition of racial criteria for an even longer period. Nonetheless, it is important to recognize that pluralists, not nativists, have shaped the American vision—a vision that asserts the value to American life and culture of a continuous infusion of immigrants and emphasizes the composite character of American cultural identities and the value of cultural diversity. It is also important to recognize that many of the very groups that were the targets of nativist hostility—Jews, Irish, Italians, Poles, Japanese, Chinese—are now integrated into American life, with average levels of income, education, and professional accomplishment that are no lower and are often higher than for Americans of Anglo-Saxon origin.

Nativism in Western Europe

A similar tension between nativists, with their image of a homogeneous culture, and pluralists, with their acceptance of and even enthusiasm for cultural diversity, can be observed in Western Europe. Opposition to migrants is a major feature of contemporary Western European politics. In country after country, as we have seen, political parties have assumed an antimigration stance and candidates for public office have called for restricting the entry of asylum seekers, tightening control over illegals, and even the repatriation of guest workers. Still, to put the matter in perspective, in no European country has an antimigrant xenophobic political party assumed power, and in no European country has legislation been passed expelling guest workers. Germany, notwithstanding its image as a center for nativist sentiment, has been host to hundreds of thousands of asylum seekers from Eastern Europe and from the Third World and to this day remains the home of millions of guest workers and their domestically born children.

The growth of nativist sentiment in Western Europe is associated with four major factors: (1) the recession and growing unemployment in the 1980s; (2) the apparent permanence of guest workers, whose children have now become numerically prominent in urban schools; (3) the sharp increase in the number of asylum claimants and illegals; and (4) the increased cost burden that asylum claimants, refugees, and illegals place on a welfare system that is already in financial crisis.[16] There are, of course, great variations among European countries in both the extent

16. All factors but the second are also relevant in the United States. In the past few years, the impact of migrants on the welfare system has become an issue (especially in California and Florida) because state and local governments bear heavy costs delivering health services, education, and housing to migrants, refugees, and illegals that central authorities do not fully cover. The distribution of these costs is also an issue in Germany, another federal system.

of nativist sentiment and the political form it takes. There have been violent attacks by right-wing "skinheads" against refugees and immigrants in Germany, referenda (defeated) in Switzerland calling for the expulsion of guest workers, and physical attacks against Indians and Pakistanis in Britain and against Algerians in France. Nativist sentiment has been more muted among the Scandinavian countries and surprisingly mild in parts of southern Europe (Spain, Portugal, and Italy) that have experienced an influx of illegal migrants from sub-Saharan Africa.

One feature of nativist sentiments in Western Europe warrants special notice. The presence of non-Europeans in Europe has raised the issue of cultural and religious pluralism. France has historically been an immigrant country, but its immigrants have been assimilated into the French language and culture. Germans do not characterize their country as an immigrant country, but in fact there is a history of immigration from Poland, and similarly the pattern has been one of total assimilation into the German language and culture. Contemporary antimigrant sentiments in Europe have their antecedents in historical conflicts over religion, which, far more than language, has led to internal warfare, pogroms, extermination, expulsion, and segregation into ghettos.[17] Protestants were expelled from France, and German Jews were regarded as outside the German *Volk* in spite of their secularism and cultural and linguistic identification with Germany. The effective integration of Muslim guest workers and their families now living, for all practical purposes permanently, in Western Europe is similarly inhibited by religious differences. For many Europeans, nativism as hostility to foreigners is more often directed at those who worship other gods than those who speak other tongues or belong to other races.[18]

More broadly, as we have noted earlier, many Europeans remain ambivalent as to what they expect from their immigrants. At times they would like migrants to "become" German and French; at other times they want migrants to retain their distinctive language, culture, and identity. The latter attitude is not necessarily an indication that Europeans, enmeshed in the tradition of the nation-state, have developed a new sense of pluralism. On the contrary, some Europeans hope that nurturing the separate cultural and national identity of immigrants will encourage them eventually to return home. Cultural pluralism, in this form, can thus paradoxically be an expression of nativism rather than, as in the United States, a manifestation of the idea of a civic culture.

Nativism in Developing Countries

Nativism is by no means confined to advanced industrial societies. An unwillingness to incorporate migrants into society is a feature of many Third World countries. As discussed earlier, the Gulf countries are quite clear as to the preferred future of

17. The conflicts between Croatians, Bosnians, and Serbs is a case in point, for the fault lines are primarily religious rather than linguistic.

18. In private conversations, many Europeans express the view that the migrant "problem" is with Muslims, not with other immigrants. In France, for example, the absorption of Vietnamese is not regarded as problematic as that of the absorption of North Africans.

their migrants from Asia. Migrants are to remain Indian, Pakistani, Sri Lankan, Bangladeshi, Filipino, Chinese, Korean, and Thai, and when they are no longer needed, they are to return home. Neither assimilation nor cultural pluralism is the model of the future; separation and return are the ideal.

Gulf Arabs have, however, expressed concern that in the "interim," they may be at cultural risk because there is the danger that their children, often cared for by Asian nannies, may imbibe alien ideas or be affected by non-Islamic religions.

Among some low-income developing countries, the fear of immigrants is even more acute than in the Gulf states, with high levels of violence between migrants and the local population. Tension is greatest in countries where immigration has been on such a large scale that the local population is fearful of becoming a minority.

India's experience with migration provides a telling example. A concern that the indigenous population may become a minority has been a central issue in India's northeastern state of Assam, where there has been a long history of immigration from the neighboring Bengali-speaking region.[19] Bengali migration to Assam dates to the middle of the nineteenth century, when Assam was part of the province of Bengal in an undivided India. Educated Bengalis in the legal profession, journalism, medicine, and teaching moved to Assam, which the British (in part under Bengali influence) regarded as a cultural outpost of Bengal. In the second half of the nineteenth century and the early years of the twentieth, however, a nationalist movement, directed against both the Bengali settlers and the British, developed in Assam. This struggle persuaded the British that a separate province of Assam should be created.

Despite this change, the Bengali problem in Assam became even more acute as large numbers of Bengali Muslim peasants moved to Assam in search of land. In fact, the number of Bengali Muslims became so large that in 1947, when Pakistan and India were formed from the undivided British colony, a referendum was held in the Muslim areas of Assam contiguous to East Pakistan, and Assam was partitioned between the two new states.

In the first election in independent India in 1951, the Assamese were finally able to get exclusive control of the state government. Once in power, they took steps to ensure the predominance of the Assamese, the "sons of the soil." Assamese was made the official language of the state, and the Assamese were given preference in employment in the government bureaucracy. From time to time there were even physical attacks against non-Assamese merchants from other parts of India.

Subsequently, the continued influx of peasants from East Pakistan to Assam in search of employment and land was viewed with alarm by the Assamese. When a massive influx of refugees took place in 1972, as a result of a civil war between the Bengalis of East Pakistan and the central government of Pakistan, the Assamese warmly supported India's armed attack against Pakistan. And when the war ended, the Assamese supported the government's policy of expelling the refugees to Bangladesh (as the independent East Pakistan was now known).

Illegal migration from Bangladesh to Assam continued throughout the 1970s. This became manifestly apparent in 1979 when the Government of India Election

19. Myron Weiner, *Sons of the Soil* (Princeton, N.J.: Princeton University Press, 1978).

Commission published the electoral rolls for the state on the eve of parliamentary elections. At this time, the increase in voter registration was far greater than what could be accounted for by natural population increase or by any evidence of migration into Assam from other parts of India. The Assamese concluded that Bangladeshis had immigrated illegally and that the Bengali electorate was now sufficiently large to erode and perhaps even destroy the political domination of the Assamese. They therefore called on the central government to remove the illegal Bangladeshis from the electoral rolls and force them to return to Bangladesh. The central government, however, felt unable to distinguish between Bengali-speaking migrants from Bangladesh and those who had come to Assam earlier, either from East Pakistan or the Indian state of West Bengal. The proposal was therefore rejected, creating an impasse that led to a violent political upheaval in the state. Sections of the Assamese community, especially students, launched attacks against the Assamese and central governments and against the Bengalis, thereby forcing the government to cancel the parliamentary elections. Subsequently, the central government committed itself to sealing the borders against further illegal migration and promised to take a large proportion of the illegal migrants off the electoral rolls. In 1986, new state elections were held and were won by the Assam Gana Parishad, an antimigrant Assamese party committed to a platform of removing illegal Bangladeshis from the state. More recently, the issue of illegal migration from Bangladesh continued to fester and influence both local and national politics. Most notably, in 1993, the Bharatiya Janata Party, the leading opposition party, declared that the expulsion of illegal Bangladeshis from India would be a central plank in any forthcoming national parliamentary election. Moreover, a recent influx of Bangladeshis into Delhi has led central government officials and politicians to view the migration as a national problem, not merely a regional one.

Similar nativist sons-of-the-soil political movements can be found in other developing countries. Fear of becoming a minority and losing political control was the major factor in a political coup by the Fijian military against a democratically elected government with an Indian-dominated majority. Fijian commitment to democracy seemed secure until a non-Fijian community took power. Many Fijians felt that the loss of political power might result in their becoming like the Maoris in New Zealand or the Kanaks in New Caledonia, two native peoples in the Pacific overwhelmed demographically, politically, and socially by immigrant communities.

Fear of immigrants has become a widespread phenomenon in much of the Third World, sometimes linked to fear of loss of land or employment and sometimes to concerns over becoming demographically (and hence politically and culturally) overwhelmed by large numbers. In the Pakistani province of Sind, for example, the local population has been adamantly opposed to the immigration of Biharis in Bangladesh who wish to "return" to Pakistan. Sindhis are fearful that a further influx of non-Sindhis into their province (on top of an earlier migration of Muslims from India) would weaken their already precarious political control. A similar concern over migration is strong in two other countries of South Asia— Bhutan, which fears that the influx of Nepalis will reduce the local Tibetan population to a minority, and Nepal, which fears that its cultural and political hegemony in the southern parts of the country will be eroded by continued immigration from northern India.

Is There a Threshold of Acceptable Migration?

There is undoubtedly a threshold of acceptable migration, but it varies both among countries and over time within a particular country. For example, as discussed earlier, before 1973 Australia pursued a "white Australia" immigration policy but then subsequently admitted large numbers of migrants from Asia. Today, 22.7 percent of the population is foreign-born, and yet, compared with other countries, Australia has not experienced a major backlash against migration. Since World War II, there has been a major increase in migration (especially from Asia) to the United States, in some years nearly a million migrants, but only recently have there been calls for restrictions and even then mainly on illegal migrants. A nativist outburst against overforeignization erupted in Switzerland in the mid-1980s, but not until the foreign-born population reached over 1 million, or 16 percent of the population. In contrast, a similar reaction took place in Germany with only 7 percent of the population foreign-born. Conflicts between the Fijians and Indians did not erupt even when the Indian population reached 49 percent, yet in Sri Lanka the majority Sinhalese community imposed restrictions on the Tamil population when the latter constituted less than 20 percent of the population.

Each of these variations has a specific explanation. The changing educational composition of Asian migrants, as well as changing attitudes on race issues, eased acceptance of Asians in Australia and the United States. Switzerland's multiethnic character made the acceptance of migrants easier than for Germany; more recently, the growth of unemployment throughout Western Europe made new migration unacceptable. The Sinhalese Buddhist clergy played an important role in convincing people to fear the Tamils in Sri Lanka, even though the Tamils were in no position to exert political control. In contrast, in Fiji, there were no traditional leaders playing a comparable role; the Fijian response was triggered by the political rise of the Indians.

In short, specific explanations can be found for any of the reactions we have observed against immigration. These include whether or not there is a tradition of cultural pluralism; the country's history of immigration; current levels of unemployment; the ability of the native population to compete with migrants in the labor market; the religious, linguistic, racial, and class composition of the migrants; the stock of earlier migrations; and the real (or perceived) possibility of the migrant community's asserting political control. Such contextual explanations, rather than a general theory, seem more useful in determining what constitutes a politically acceptable level of immigration.

Furthermore, the rate of immigration in itself does not seem to be a particularly critical factor in the readiness of the native population to accept migrants and their children. High immigration into the United States, Canada, and Australia has not resulted in a wave of xenophobia, yet antimigrant right-wing parties have flourished throughout Western Europe even in countries where immigration and asylum rates are low. There are several plausible explanations, beyond sheer numbers, for the attitudes held toward migrants. Immigrant societies, with a history and an ideology of immigration, are less likely to produce xenophobia than countries that do not regard themselves as immigrant societies (even if historically they have had large numbers of immigrants). Furthermore, multiethnic societies are more likely than homogeneous societies to have a tolerance for the additional cultural diversity produced by migrants. If the migrants are predominantly from a single country or cultural region, they are more likely to be perceived as a cultural threat than if they are themselves culturally diverse. An uncontrollable influx of illegals or refugees is perceived as more threatening than an influx of the same magnitude through the usual immigration processes. A persistent high unemployment rate with no decline in sight will increase the hostility toward migrants at the lower end of the native labor force, even if there is little evidence of large-scale displacement. There are, of course, exceptions to each of these generalizations, but the experience of most countries of immigration suggests that these are more critical determinants for how migrants and natives relate to one another than simply the magnitude of the migration flow.

One further observation should be made: Migrant communities are invariably in competition both with the native population and with one another—over places in the educational system, rental housing, control of retail trades, and jobs, especially during an economic recession. In fact, xenophobic antimigrant political groups typically thrive in working-class neighborhoods during recessionary periods when they attract support from young native toughs resentful of both state support for migrant minorities and the successes of the migrants at a time when they themselves are not doing well. The highly publicized attacks against South Asians by white teenage skinheads allied with the British National Party and against Gypsies and Turks by young neo-Nazis in Germany took place under these conditions.

Competition for scarce housing and jobs may also exacerbate relations between migrant communities and indigenous ethnic minorities—not only because some groups are more successful than others but also because the media often hold up the successful minorities to berate the unsuccessful. The attacks by blacks against Korean shopkeepers during the Los Angeles riots of 1992 is a case in point.

What can be said with certainty is that every country does have a limit on the number and composition of immigrants that it finds acceptable. During a recession, xenophobia generally rises as "foreigners" are blamed for unemployment, crime, homelessness, and the plight of the poor. But what constitutes a foreigner is a socially defined notion tied to conceptions of community and citizenship that shape whether and how immigrants and their children are absorbed into a society. It is to the issue of immigrant absorption that we now turn.

ABSORPTION: CITIZENSHIP AND RIGHTS

The capacity of a society and a polity to absorb migrants is largely determined by three factors: (1) the willingness of the society to absorb migrants, (2) the structure of the labor market, and (3) the commitment of migrants to their new society. Of these factors, the most critical is probably the first.

Countries that share the Western heritage of the Magna Carta, the Bill of Rights, and parliamentary institutions generally converge when it comes to defining the rights of citizens. Over time, these rights have evolved from the basic notion of protecting individuals against the state to the more complex notion that the state should provide individuals with certain entitlements. However, no such convergence in views exists on the question of *who* should be admitted into citizenship.

Historically, as mentioned earlier, immigrant countries such as the United States, Canada, Australia, and New Zealand have welcomed large numbers of immigrants and incorporated them as citizens, whereas Japan and most of the countries of Western Europe have been restrictive in the granting of citizenship to migrant guest workers and their locally born children.

These differences illustrate that even though the conception of citizens' rights is derived from common liberal and social democratic principles, the questions of which migrants should be admitted, what kind, and whether they should be granted citizenship are more deeply embedded in each individual country's political culture and history.

Countries have a variety of options open to them with respect to the admission and granting of rights to migrants. The most restrictive is not to admit migrants at all and to base citizenship on descent. Less restrictive options include admitting migrants to fill temporary labor needs, limiting their stay, and providing only minimal welfare benefits essential to their economic performance; permitting migrants to stay indefinitely and granting them many (if not all) of the entitlements provided to citizens but excluding them (and their children) from citizenship; and finally, enabling migrants to become naturalized citizens or granting birthright citizenship to the locally born children of immigrants.

As we have seen, migrants cannot be truly incorporated into the host society as long as they are viewed as temporary residents. Guest workers may be treated well, given accommodations, provided employment, and offered access to many of the benefits of the welfare system, but they will be regarded as outsiders in the cultural, social, and political sense as long as they are seen as temporary sojourners. Consequently, citizenship rules are an extremely important aspect of immigrant absorption.

Citizenship can be acquired in several ways. The most common is by birth, either by place of birth (*jus solis*) or line of descent (*jus sanguinis*). Both conceptions are matters of ascription. Citizenship can also be acquired through naturalization, a privilege granted by the state. Furthermore, in some societies, aliens may claim citizenship as a right upon compliance with the terms set by law, while in others, citizenship may be conferred only at the discretion of state authorities.[20]

It makes a significant psychological difference if native-born children of foreigners are regarded by indigenes (and by themselves) as Americans, Israelis, British, or French at birth, rather than having to wait until the age of 18 to acquire formal citizenship. Citizenship at birth implies, and indeed grants, unconditional equality. Individuals who must wait until they reach maturity to choose their citizenship may be under pressure from friends, relatives, and their parents' home government not to "surrender" their foreign identity.

America's Liberal Absorption Process

Compared with most other countries, the United States has been quite willing to absorb and accept immigrants, as indicated by its liberal citizenship policies. In the United States, individuals become citizens in any one of three ways: by virtue of having been born in the United States, by birth abroad if their parents are citizens,

20. Richard Plender, *International Migration Law* (Leiden, Netherlands: Sijthoff, 1972).

or by naturalization if they comply with the conditions specified by law, which include five years of permanent residence, understanding the English language, and having a minimal knowledge of U.S. history and government. The first of these, the *jus solis* rule, has been interpreted broadly by the courts to confer citizenship on anyone born in the United States, including the native-born children of illegal aliens and short-term visitors.[21]

Liberal citizenship rules have not always characterized the U.S. attitude toward immigrants. Legislation passed in 1882 excluded from citizenship migrants from China, Japan, Burma, Malaya, Siam (Thailand), Korea, India, the Philippines, and portions of the Near and Middle East. Racial tests for citizenship were justified on the grounds that certain peoples came from civilizations "inimitable" to the principles of democracy and were therefore incapable of assimilation into the American way of life. As a result of this act, Asian migrants were converted into guest workers, permitted to remain and work in the United States but prohibited from bringing family members.[22] However, efforts by several states further to restrict Asian migrants by preventing them from purchasing property were struck down by federal courts on the grounds that such legislation violated the Fourteenth Amendment.[23]

Racial restrictions on naturalization were ended more than a half century later with a 1943 act that eliminated the ban on the immigration and naturalization of Chinese, a 1946 act that lifted restrictions against Filipinos and East Indians, and the 1952 MacCarran-Walter Act, which ended all racial tests for citizenship. The category of aliens ineligible for citizenship was thus abolished. In subsequent acts, Congress also abolished national origin quotas for immigration, admitted migrants who satisfied U.S. labor force needs or were rejoining family members, and admitted refugees with a "well-founded fear of persecution." The general thrust of legislation in the United States over time has therefore been to make immigration less ascriptive and to facilitate the naturalization of all who entered as immigrants.

In the 1980s, a total of 8.5 million people (nearly half of whom came from Asia) were admitted into the United States. A substantial (and increasing) portion of these came under family unification provisions of the law, but some were admitted under the quota of 20,000 persons per year per country. In the 1980 Refugee Act, the United States set an annual refugee ceiling and set quotas for various regions of the world. Certain categories of refugees (such as asylum seekers and temporary parolees) are not entitled to federal benefits, but most are treated in the same legal fashion as immigrants and are given permanent legal status, which permits them to seek citizenship.

Immigrants to the United States have a *right* to become citizens. Consequently, approximately two-thirds of migrants living in the United States for five years or longer are naturalized.[24] Each year, at least a quarter of a million additional indi-

---

21. Peter H. Schuck and Rogers M. Smith, *Citizenship Without Consent* (New Haven, Conn.: Yale University Press, 1985).

22. Restrictions on bringing family members and brides is one of the most effective ways of preventing the growth of an immigrant population. The number of Asians in the United States would be far larger had nativists not successfully imposed these restrictions.

23. The Fourteenth Amendment provides that no state shall "deprive any person of life, liberty or property without due process of law; nor deny to any person within its jurisdiction the equal protection of the laws." Note the use of the word *person* rather than *citizen*.

viduals are naturalized. Naturalized citizens have the same rights as native-born Americans, except that they cannot become president.

Beyond citizenship rights, immigrants in the United States are legally entitled to certain protections and benefits in accordance with the Fourteenth Amendment. The Supreme Court has ruled that legal resident aliens are entitled to most of the benefits of the welfare state (*Graham* v. *Richardson,* 1971) and that state governments cannot deny employment to aliens for most state civil service jobs (*Sugarman* v. *Dougall,* 1973), even though they may impose restrictions on eligibility when there is a substantial and necessary public purpose.[25] The Immigration Reform and Control Act (IRCA) of 1986 goes even further, banning all discrimination in employment against lawful aliens. Furthermore, most federally sponsored social welfare programs, including Aid to Families with Dependent Children, welfare payments, food stamps, old-age assistance, aid to the disabled, supplemental security income, and federally supported housing, are available to resident aliens. Some congressional acts, however, do restrict benefits for aliens (Medicare, for example).[26]

Illegal aliens are also entitled to certain rights and benefits as well. The Supreme Court struck down a Texas law that sought to deny access to public education to children of illegal aliens (*Plyler* v. *Doe,* 1983). This ruling was based on the fact that although the children and their illegally resident parents could one day be deported, it was unlikely that this would ever happen.[27] However, the Supreme Court has been careful not to extend many benefits to illegal aliens. In any event, federal and state agencies rarely check the legal status of aliens, so illegals often

24. On U.S. naturalization, see Louis De Sipio, "Social Science Literature and the Naturalization Process," *International Migration Review,* Summer 1987, pp. 390–405; Richard A. Easterlin, David Ward, William S. Bernard, and Reed Ueda, "Naturalization and Citizenship," in *Immigration* (Cambridge, Mass.: Harvard University Press, 1982), pp. 106–159; Linda W. Gordon, "Asian Immigration Since World War II," in *Immigration and U.S. Foreign Policy,* ed. Robert W. Tucker, Charles B. Keely, and Linda Wrigley (Boulder, Colo.: Westview Press, 1990), pp. 169–191; David S. North, "The Long Gray Welcome," *International Migration Review,* Summer 1987, pp. 311–326; Harry P. Pachon, "Naturalization," *International Migration Review,* Summer 1987, pp. 299–310; and Alejandro Portes, "Illegal Immigration and the International System," *Social Problems,* April 1979, pp. 425–438.

25. For example, state governments can make citizenship a condition of employment in the police and in public schools. The federal government can also deny resident aliens employment in the federal civil service if there is a clear public reason for doing so. See Douglas C. Bennett, "Immigration, Work, and Citizenship in the American Welfare State" (paper presented at the annual meeting of the American Political Science Association, Washington, D.C., August 1986).

26. Governor Pete Wilson of California has called for a constitutional amendment to change the rule under which children born in the United States to illegal aliens are automatically U.S. citizens. He has also called for a more rigorous enforcement of the federal law that prohibits giving welfare to illegal aliens and opposes giving health care or insurance to illegal aliens in any national health plan, though he would not deny illegal aliens emergency health care at hospitals.

27. The Supreme Court ruled that the Fourteenth Amendment to the Constitution provides equal protection under the law to all *persons* and makes no distinction between citizens and aliens. Hence even illegal inhabitants are entitled to legal protection and to benefits provided under the law. U.S. courts have also ruled that children born in the United States of illegal migrants have the right to opt for U.S. citizenship when they become of age (see Schuck and Smith, *Citizenship Without Consent*). If the distinction between the rights and benefits provided to citizen and noncitizen inhabitants has become blurred in European law, in the United States there has been a further tendency to blur the distinction between illegal and legal residents.

have access to welfare benefits. Other court rulings have indicated that illegal migrants threatened with deportation are covered by the equal protection clause, in addition to being entitled to some protections against unreasonable searches and seizures and the protection of the Fair Labor Standards Act, including minimum-wage protection.

The United States has also extended liberal citizenship policies to illegal as well as legal immigrants. The IRCA offered citizenship as a form of amnesty to unlawful aliens who had been in the country continuously since December 31, 1981. Moreover, it has also been possible for individuals granted temporary asylum to convert their status to immigrant.

Thus, in the United States, the thrust of congressional legislation, court rulings, and administrative practices has been to reduce the differences between the rights and benefits of citizens and those of aliens and even illegals. The primary difference remaining between legal resident aliens and citizens is that aliens cannot vote, run for public office, or serve on juries. Noncitizens can also be denied access to certain public jobs. Deportation of aliens is uncommon, limited largely to convicted criminals. In short, the American practice has been to treat as equals—with respect to both legal rights and many social benefits—all permanent residents of the United States, whether they be native-born Americans, naturalized citizens, legal aliens (including refugees), or illegal migrants.

However, there are indications that this trend is being reversed. In an effort to press Washington to take more forceful measures to halt illegal migration, in 1994 California voters approved a ballot initiative (Proposition 187) that prohibited access of illegal aliens to public services including education and nonemergency health care. Other states are considering similar measures, and some members of Congress have called for limiting the rights of aliens to public benefits.

Germany, Israel, France, Australia

The migration and citizenship policies of other democracies and the conceptions that underlie them differ substantially from those of the United States and each other. They differ with respect to both how citizenship is attributed at birth and how citizenship can be acquired.

In contrast to the welcoming approach adopted by the United States, Germany has pursued exclusive citizenship policies and has limited the rights of noncitizens, reflecting the sentiment that "Germany is not a country of immigration." Germany does not automatically grant citizenship to children of migrants born in Germany or readily naturalize immigrants who seek to become citizens. Only people of German descent are freely accorded membership in the German nation,[28] and only Germans can be of German nationality.[29]

28. Kay Hailbronner, "Citizenship and Nationhood in Germany," in *Immigration and the Politics of Citizenship in Europe and North America,* ed. William Rogers Brubaker (Lanham, Md.: University Press of America, 1989), pp. 67–79.

29. One anecdote illustrates this attitude. The German media described the three victims of a fatal fire-bombing of longtime Turkish residents in Mölln, near Hamburg, as "Turks," including a 10-year-old who was born in Germany and had never lived anywhere else. The incident dramatized the central feature of German citizenship law, which grants citizenship at birth exclusively on the basis of descent and regards naturalization as exceptional.

German citizenship law has deep historical and cultural roots. In the eighteenth and nineteenth centuries, when Germany was politically fragmented, Germans developed a sense of nationhood that was independent of the state. German nationality rested on a linguistic and cultural identity, not a political one. The notion of a single nationality and a single German citizenship persisted even with the partition of Germany and the creation of two German states after the Second World War. Thus the East Germans and ethnic Germans from Poland who fled to the Federal Republic were not regarded as refugees but simply as Germans entitled to move to the Federal Republic and to claim German citizenship.

Contemporary citizenship law reflects these nationalistic roots and is contained in the Nationality Law of 1913. This law permits all descendants of German citizens to adopt German citizenship. Because the Federal Republic of Germany did not recognize the division of Germany, all East Germans and millions of ethnic Germans settled in Eastern Europe and the Soviet Union had a statutory right to enter the Federal Republic and claim citizenship.

In contrast, the Turks, Yugoslavs, and Italians who entered Germany as migrant workers were not regarded as potential citizens. Foreign citizens living in Germany have no legal *right* to naturalization and can be naturalized only at the discretion of the German government.[30] Furthermore, naturalization is possible only for those who have resided in Germany for ten years, speak German, are committed to the democratic order of the Federal Republic, have a cultural attachment to Germany, and have surrendered their emotional and political attachment to their home country.[31] These requirements, combined with the limits imposed at the discretion of administrative authorities, have led to a low naturalization rate. Few of the 5.9 million non-EC foreign immigrants in Germany have become naturalized citizens, though a majority of the migrants have resided in Germany for more than a decade. Furthermore, an estimated 70 percent of the 1 million foreign children born in Germany do not hold German citizenship.

There is, however, one point of convergence between the German and American policies: Noncitizens have rights. They are entitled to political rights, including freedom of association, the right of assembly and demonstration, and freedom of speech. Migrants also have a right to reside in Germany, which entitles them to the same access as citizens to employment in the labor market and equal wages. The children of migrants have the same rights to education as German citizens. Lastly, no distinction is made between citizens and noncitizens with respect to access to social services, including unemployment insurance, old-age pensions, accident and disability insurance, health benefits, and vocational training. The primary legal differences that exist between citizens and noncitizens are that the latter cannot vote or run for public office, are restricted from employment in some public positions, and are exempt from serving in the military.

Israel, like Germany, bases citizenship on descent. Under the 1950 Law of Return, Israel regards all Jews as having the right to enter and settle in Israel. Jewish migrants automatically acquire Israeli citizenship. Individuals are Jews by virtue of their descent from a Jewish mother; they do not need to share a common

---

30. Hailbronner, "Citizenship and Nationhood," p. 68.

31. Hailbronner writes that "political activities in emigrant organizations are usually taken as evidence against a permanent attachment to Germany" (ibid., p. 69)

language or culture, nor do they need to be religious adherents to be regarded as Jewish. Furthermore, Arabs who resided in Israel when the state was formed and their Israeli-born children are also citizens of Israel, although Arabs who resided in Israel before independence and subsequently left do not have the right to return. Israel thus has two rules of citizenship by birth: People born in the country to parents who are nationals are automatically citizens irrespective of religious or ethnic affiliation, and people born abroad are entitled to immigrate and claim nationality if they are Jewish.

Israel's Law of Return has generated conflict within Israel and abroad as to who is a Jew. For Orthodox Jews, only the child of a Jewish woman is a Jew, regardless of the religion of the father. This definition, the basis for Israeli immigration law, puts Israel at odds with the Jewish Reform movement in the United States, whose rabbinical organization declared in 1983 that children of mixed marriages, no matter which parent was Jewish, would be presumed to be Jewish if they participated in "appropriate and timely public and formal acts of identification with the Jewish faith and people."[32] Neither Orthodox nor Conservative rabbis have accepted the Reform position; they argue that the Reform position removes a reason for a non-Jewish wife to convert to Judaism and that liberalization widens the gap between American and Israeli Jews. Moreover, marriages between Reform and Orthodox Jews become problematic because they raise the question of whether the Reform member of the marriage is in fact Jewish by biological descent. Thus one unanticipated consequence of the Israeli law of immigration and citizenship is that it has generated divisions within the Jewish community over how pluralistic Judaism is with respect to such matters as conversion, intermarriage, and the relative roles of biology and choice.

One fundamental difference between Germany and Israel, however, is that while both have, in effect, a law of return that gives preference to people defined by the state as belonging to the community, Germany has admitted non-Germans who do not meet the requirements, whereas Israel has largely restricted its immigration to Jews and hence has not had to deal with the issue of absorbing non-Jewish immigrants.[33]

In general, countries like Germany, Israel, Switzerland, the Netherlands, and Japan that follow the concept of *jus sanguinis* make naturalization difficult, while countries that subscribe to the notion of *jus solis* tend to be more liberal on questions of citizenship. In the Netherlands, for example, locally born children acquire the citizenship of their parents, and only the third generation of locally born children of noncitizens obtain Dutch citizenship at birth. Migrants can, however, become citizens after five years of residence if the migrant has "a reasonable knowledge of Dutch" and "sufficient acceptance by Dutch society."[34] In Switzerland,

32. *New York Times,* August 7, 1993, p. 28.

33. A small number of non-Jewish refugees have been given asylum, mostly notably Bosnian Muslims and Vietnamese.

34. Tomas Hammar (ed.), *European Immigration Policy* (Cambridge: Cambridge University Press, 1985), p. 68.

Table 15   NATURALIZATION RATES IN SELECTED COUNTRIES, 1990

Country	Number of New Citizens	Rate	Country	Number of New Citizens	Rate
Austria	9,199	2.9	Spain	7,049	1.7
Belgium	—	0.2	Sweden	16,770	3.7
Denmark	3,028	1.9	Switzerland	8,658	0.8
France	54,366	1.5	United Kingdom	57,271	2.9
Germany	—	1.0	Australia	127,857	—
Luxembourg	—	0.8	Canada	104,267	—
Netherlands	12,790	2.0	United States	270,101	2.3
Norway	4,757	3.4			

Note: Naturalization rates for the European countries are calculated on the basis of naturalizations of foreigners in most recent year available as a percentage of the total nonnaturalized stock in the preceding year. Figures for France include acquisition of nationality by decree or by declaration; children acquiring nationality as a consequence of parents' naturalization or through automatic acquisition of nationality on reaching legal majority (for those born in France to parents who are both foreigners) are excluded. The naturalization rate for the United States is calculated on the basis of naturalizations as a percentage of total foreign-born noncitizen population as reported in the 1990 census; children of foreign parents acquiring nationality as a result of birth in the United States are excluded. A dash indicates that data are unavailable.

Source: Organization for Economic Cooperation and Development.

migrants can be naturalized only by vote of the communal parliament or, in the small communes, by an assembly of the citizens, a procedure that keeps the rate of naturalization exceedingly low.[35] The locally born children of migrants are subject to the same procedure. (An exception to this generalization is Sweden, which makes naturalization easy, though it has a tradition of *jus sanguinis.*)[36]

France, which subscribes to *jus solis,* also has comparatively generous citizenship laws. Before the naturalization law was modified in 1993, locally born children of migrants could automatically become French citizens at the age of 18 if they had resided in France for five years and had not been convicted of a crime. Children born in France were automatically French citizens at birth if at least one parent was born in France or a French colony (such as Algeria) prior to independence. (The "foreign" population of France, as of 1990, was 3,607,000, but that figure does not include the foreign-born or their children who have become French citizens.) Ethnicity plays a less important role in determining citizenship in France than it does elsewhere in Europe.

35. Hans Joachim Hoffmann-Nowotny, "Switzerland," in ibid., p. 222.

36. Tomas Hammar, "Citizenship, Aliens' Political Rights, and Politicians' Concern for Migrants: The Case of Sweden," in *Guests Came to Stay,* ed. Rosemarie Rogers (Boulder, Colo: Westview Press, 1985), pp. 85–107.

Table 16   FOREIGN RESIDENTS IN FRANCE BY COUNTRY OF ORIGIN, 1990

Country of Origin	Number of Residents (thousands)
Portugal	645.6
Algeria	619.9
Morocco	584.7
Italy	253.7
Spain	216.0
Tunisia	207.5
Turkey	201.5
Yugoslavia	51.7
Poland	46.3
Other countries	780.7
Total	3,607.6

Note: Figures do not include naturalized citizens.

Source: Organization for Economic Cooperation and Development.

That has not always been the case, however. The belief that nationality depends on blood was widely held in France throughout the nineteenth century.[37] Not until passage of a new French national law in 1889 was the principle of *jus solis* adopted. This change was dictated in part by the adoption of conscription, which led many French hawks to argue for turning into French citizens the 1 million foreigners (mainly Belgians and Italians) then living in France so that several hundred thousand young men could be drafted into the military. The French came to believe that foreigners born in France could be assimilated into French life and culture and that the secular schools and the military were powerful assimilating institutions.[38]

France absorbed large numbers of migrants from Italy, Spain, and Portugal in the second half of the nineteenth century and from Poland, Czechoslovakia, and the Ukraine during the interwar period. Nonetheless, France did not then (and does not now) regard itself as an immigrant country.[39] Postwar migration to France consisted heavily of North Africans, Portuguese, and Spaniards. As was the case elsewhere in Western Europe, many French assumed that the migrants would in time return home. From 1974 to the early 1980s, the French government actively

---

37. William Rogers Brubaker, *Immigration and the Politics of Citizenship in Late Nineteenth Century France* (Cambridge, Mass.: Society of Fellows, Harvard University, 1989), p. 24.

38. Ibid., p. 34.

39. Gérard Noiriel, "Difficulties in French Historical Research on Immigration," in *Immigrants in Two Democracies,* ed. Donald L. Horowitz and Gérard Noiriel (New York: New York University Press, 1992), pp. 66–79.

encouraged migrant workers to return home. In contrast to European countries like Germany, however, when it became clear that the migrants had come to stay, the French government chose to pursue a policy of inclusion, providing citizenship to the children of migrants residing in France and admitting into citizenship immigrants who assimilate to the mores and customs of France and demonstrate linguistic competence. In addition, immigrants who had French nationality because they were born in French territories could now request "reintegration" into French nationality.[40]

Strong opposition to French immigration and citizenship has come from the National Front, the antimigrant political party led by Jean-Marie Le Pen. The National Front has called for the abolition of *jus solis*. In the 1986 elections, conservative parties called for legislation that would set conditions for the acquisition of citizenship by the French-born children of foreign nationals residing in France. This proposed legislation was subsequently withdrawn as a result of popular opposition from parties of the left and a coalition of religious, student, and human rights organizations. However, the issue of whether the children of foreign-born parents should have to request citizenship at maturity remained a subject of debate. New legislation was approved by the French parliament following the victory of conservatives in the 1993 elections. It provided for the deportation of illegal immigrants and tightened the conditions for granting political asylum. The most important reform was a provision that young people born in France of foreign parents must now formally request French nationality between the ages of 16 and 21. Previously, citizenship had been granted automatically at the age of 18. Opposition to the government's new policy came from Social Affairs Minister Simone Veil and other members of the government, but a bill to allow the police to make identity checks on anyone whose "behavior" suggests that he is foreign was passed by 463 votes to 96 in the overwhelming conservative National Assembly. "Rather than facial characteristics," said the Gaullist deputy who authored the amendment, "I wanted police to concentrate on cultural signs, such as reading the *New York Times* in the street. If you are reading the *New York Times* in the street, you may be presumed to be a foreigner."[41] Public opinion polls reported that large majorities supported the government's new restrictions. France's high unemployment (3 million people, or 10.9 percent of the labor force) has evidently been a major factor in support for the new policies.[42]

Among the other industrial democracies, Australia, as discussed earlier, was explicitly restrictive with respect to the ethnic and racial characteristics of the people it chose to admit as immigrants and then as citizens. In an effort to increase its population, Australia promoted large-scale immigration after World War II. The Australian government was committed to maintaining a homogeneous British-like population, but when it was unable to attract enough immigrants from Great Britain, the country was opened to continental European immigrants:

40. Brubaker, *Immigration and the Politics of Citizenship*, p. 114.

41. *New York Times*, June 23, 1992, p. A12.

42. In 1990, France had 3.6 million immigrants out of a population of 57 million (6.3 percent). Interior Minister Charles Pasqua declared that zero immigration was the government's policy.

"We seek to create a homogeneous nation," said an Australian minister of immigration. "Can anyone reasonably object to that? Is not this the elementary right of every government, to decide the composition of the nation? It is the same prerogative as the head of a family exercises as to who is to live in his own house."[43]

In 1972, Australia formally ended its "white Australia" policy with the passage of an immigration law that stated that policy was to be based on the "avoidance of discrimination on any ground of race, color of skin, or nationality."[44] That policy shift was, as noted earlier, in part the result of pressure on Australia to end its racial criteria for migration—especially from the countries of Southeast Asia with which Australia was trying to improve relations—and in part in recognition of the fact that Asia rather than Europe was the most likely source of future immigration.[45] In effect, Australia had shifted from a *jus sanguinis* policy, based on a conception that only British could settle in Australia, to a more inclusive conception of who could become Australian.

Citizenship in Australia is now easily acquired after two years of residency. Because there are few additional benefits associated with citizenship, migrants who choose to become naturalized are simply identifying themselves with Australia and proclaiming their public allegiance.[46] As with other traditional immigrant countries, such as the United States and Canada, Australia regards immigration into the country as tantamount to admission into citizenship.

Postcolonial Citizenship

Among the newly independent states of the Third World, citizenship has often been particularly contentious and problematic. The rules of citizenship have been a major source of conflict not only within countries but also between countries as certain categories of people have been denied citizenship or had their citizenship withdrawn by the newly independent postcolonial rulers. Postcolonial Uganda withdrew citizenship from its South Asians; Ceylon (Sri Lanka) withdrew citizenship from tea estate workers from South India; Burma withdrew citizenship from its Indian migrants. Similar circumstances have arisen in the newly independent former republics of the Soviet Union. Estonia passed legislation in June 1993 declaring that only pre-1940 residents and their descendants were automatically citizens; all others had to apply. Such a policy could result in substantial displacement because in 1940, only 8 percent of Estonia was ethnically Russian, whereas in 1993, it was 28 percent. Under pressure from Western European governments, the Estonians subsequently modified the law, but they maintain quotas on the number

43. Joseph H. Carens, "Nationalism and the Exclusion of Immigrants: Lessons from Australian Immigration Policy," in *Open Borders? Closed Societies?* ed. Mark Gibney (Westport, Conn.: Greenwood Press, 1988), p. 45.

44. Ibid., p. 44.

45. Charles Price, "Australia," in *The Politics of Migration Policies,* ed. Daniel Kubat (New York: Basic Books, 1973), pp. 3–18.

46. A study reveals that Asian migrants value Australian citizenship more highly than immigrant Britons. Immigrants from the Third World are twice as likely as immigrants from English-speaking countries to become Australian citizens. M. D. R. Evans, "Choosing to Be a Citizen: The Time-Path of Citizenship in Australia," *International Migration Review,* Summer 1988, p. 252.

of people who can become naturalized.[47] Furthermore, Estonia, Latvia (where ethnic Latvians constitute a bare majority), and Lithuania have all imposed language requirements for Russians who seek naturalization and have made it clear that they would welcome the emigration of their resident Russians. Citizenship laws in the Baltic states have created anxieties for the Russians living in each of these states. In all, there are 25 million Russians living outside of Russia in former Soviet republics. In Kazakhstan, Russians constitute 38 percent of the population; in Latvia, 34 percent; in Estonia, 30 percent; in Ukraine, 22 percent; in Belarus and Moldova, 13 percent; and in Turkmenistan, 9 percent.[48]

Easy access to citizenship by migrants does not prevent the rise of conflicts between migrants and the native population. Opposition to the foreign-born has been a Europe-wide phenomenon, even among countries with generous rules of naturalization and birthright citizenship. But it is hardly a coincidence that the most severe antiforeign attacks in Europe have taken place in Germany, the country that is so restrictive regarding the naturalization of foreigners and where popular attitudes equate German nationality with German descent. It is also clear that the legal status and rights of Russian migrants (and their descendants) is one of the most explosive issues in what the Russians call the "near abroad" successor states of the Soviet Union. The ease with which migrants can acquire citizenship and nationality is by no means the only determinant of whether immigrants and their children are integrated into the society and whether conflicts erupt between migrants and natives, but it is clearly a critical factor.

The Labor Market

The structure of the labor market is another factor that influences whether migrants and their children are economically and socially incorporated into the host society. Are migrants and their children confined to jobs that natives do not want and offer few opportunities for advancement? Is there an assumption by the host society that the children of uneducated migrants are fit only for the same menial jobs held by their parents? Do the teachers of migrant children regard them as less able than the children of native-born citizens, fated for menial work?

The selective recruitment of migrants to fill menial positions in an economy in which new technologies are being rapidly acquired and cognitive skills and education are essential for mobility is likely to lead to a bifurcated society, with migrants locked into positions at the lower end of the labor market, helots in the economy and in the social and political order. Such circumstances appear to be developing in the United States, where unskilled migrants today function in a very different kind of economy than such migrants did at the turn of the twentieth century. In the early 1900s, individuals with little education but with personal drive had far greater opportunities for mobility than at present, when high levels of education are required for social mobility. For this reason, some observers have argued for a selective U.S. immigration policy that gives priority to individuals with the high levels of education, skills, and financial resources that will facilitate their absorption

47. *Economist*, July 31, 1993, p. 45.

48. 1989 Soviet census.

into the labor market. The long history of prejudice against Asians in the United States notwithstanding, Asian migrants to the United States (who now exceed the annual legal intake of migrants from Latin America) have been more readily incorporated into the American economy and society than the less educated migrants from Mexico, Puerto Rico, and most other areas of the Caribbean. A large proportion of the migrants entering the United States from India, Hong Kong, Taiwan, South Korea, and the Philippines are sufficiently well educated to fit into high-wage positions in the labor market. The average educational level of Asian Indians in the United States, for example, is higher than that of white Americans. As a group, Asian Indians have high rates of naturalization, and their children do better in school and in the labor market than the less educated migrants from Latin America. Intergenerational mobility is a key element in the assimilation process. Its absence often reinforces ethnic and racial subordination even in the absence of discrimination.

Although educated migrants may be more successful than the less educated, a large part of the immigration into industrial societies is of the less skilled, migrants who can take care of the elderly, mind children, work in restaurants and small businesses, clean houses, and take on the many menial jobs that have become unattractive in countries in which welfare benefits are only marginally lower than the minimum wage. A recent study of educational levels among immigrants to the United States found that 40 percent of immigrants from Latin America have less than nine years of education, compared with 20 percent of European, 15 percent of Asian immigrants, and only 9 percent of the native population. However, a high proportion of immigrants from Asia have advanced degrees.[49]

The demand by many employers for low-skilled, low-wage workers remains a critical determinant of the continued influx of illegals into the United States, Japan, and Western Europe. The intake of the unskilled, both legal and illegal, has also had a negative impact on the willingness of societies to assimilate immigrants. Given that cultural assimilation is related to the socioeconomic and educational status of immigrants, an unskilled immigrant labor force employed in the low-wage dead-end sector of the economy (and in some instances further marginalized by its illegal status) is unlikely to experience much generational mobility. Yet left to its own devices, the labor market in advanced industrial countries is as likely to recruit the unskilled across international boundaries as the highly educated—precisely the opposite of what most scholars and policymakers would regard as an optimum migration intake both for national economic growth and for the ease of migrant integration into the country's political and social system. For this reason, some industrial societies now have two distinct classes of migrants: those admitted legally under a set of policies likely to facilitate successful absorption (such as family reunification, educational level, financial resources, and employment needs in universities and high-tech industries) and illegal "undocumented" migrants or low-skilled asylum seekers who, by virtue of their characteristics or their legal status, are less amenable to social and political absorption.

---

49. Fix and Passel, *Immigration and Immigrants,* pp. 32–33.

The Preferences of Immigrants

Another key determinant of integration is whether the migrants themselves desire it. If migrants (and refugees) anticipate returning home and, furthermore, if they regard the host society merely as a temporary place in which to acquire income or escape violence or persecution in their homeland, they are not likely to want to go through the process of redefining their identity or acquiring citizenship in a new country.

The willingness to change one's identity or to add a second identity by declaring allegiance to a new country is shaped first and foremost by the willingness of the host culture to accept immigrants into the community. As long as the host culture regards immigrants as permanent aliens and denies them citizenship, migrants will feel the need to cling to their original identities. Germans often make the point that Turkish migrants do not want to become German citizens, so it is unnecessary for Germany to liberalize its naturalization laws. But how many individuals would want to join a club that bars them from entry? Migrants—and especially their children—do have a choice of identities, but if the host society ascribes an identity to them—in this case, an alien identity—it becomes exceedingly difficult for the migrant to be absorbed or to assimilate into the adopted country. Migrants and refugees permanently admitted into a country where they are provided with protection and assistance are likely to feel a sense of gratitude and therefore to identify readily with the new country.

Another critical determinant of the attitude of migrants toward adaptation to the host society is whether they are socially or politically rejected by their country of origin. Refugees are more likely to grasp the opportunity to acquire a new identity if they know that they cannot return home. Examples abound: Jews from Eastern Europe readily adapted to their American homeland in the late nineteenth and early twentieth centuries. Armenians from Russia and Turkey, Greeks from Turkey, Baha'is from Iran, Indians from Uganda, Hindus from Pakistan, Muslims from India, Jews from North Africa, and other "rejected" peoples have also eagerly sought citizenship in new homelands in the United States, Britain, Canada, Australia, Greece, India, Pakistan, and Israel.

The creation of a migrant enclave in the new homeland is sometimes regarded as an impediment to the social process of assimilation, particularly with respect to learning the language and culture of the host society. Yet at the same time, enclaves often provide havens that enable migrants to adjust to their new environment. The impact of ethnic enclaves on the absorption of migrants is affected by a number of factors. It makes a difference if enclaves become permanent ghettos to which migrants are restricted because of the housing and employment practices of the larger community or, alternatively, a way station through which socially mobile members of the immigrant community move freely. In general, self-segregation into neighborhoods has not been a barrier to assimilation when migrants and their children are able to acquire the same education as others in the society and to find employment outside the community; but self-segregation accompanied by limited education and employment opportunities (or by the failure of the community to avail itself of these opportunities) typically sustains separateness and generates conflict between the migrants and indigenes as well as among the various migrant communities.

A related factor that influences the attitudes of migrants toward absorption is their own linguistic assimilation. How eager is the migrant community to learn the language of their hosts? The process of linguistic assimilation occurs most rapidly when migrants need the language to find employment. Consequently, migrants are more likely to invest in language learning if there is an adequate return on the investment through employment in the local labor market where the host language is required. Furthermore, language learning will take place more rapidly if the stream of migration is not large and continuous. Once the migration stream has ended or been substantially cut back, linkages to the homeland are more likely to be reduced. Conversely, a constant infusion of substantial numbers of people from the homeland who bear with them their language and local news may weaken the resolve of the migrants to acquire a new identity, particularly if many of the newcomers regard themselves as temporary sojourners. For similar reasons, proximity, easy access to the homeland, and a high migration return rate may also slow the pace of identity formation.

State policies can influence and encourage language acquisition. If the state funds schools taught in the language of the migrants or creates a separate language stream within the school system, the rate of language acquisition is likely to be slower than if children are placed in schools where the language of instruction is that of the host society. Such language "tracking" can have long-term disadvantages for migrant children, discouraging their future assimilation into the host society as well. Children educated principally in their parent's language are likely to be handicapped in the labor market, limited to occupations that serve their own community.

Whereas in most countries, governments regard language learning as a key to absorption, there is considerable disagreement as to whether absorption is made easier or more difficult if the host society attributes some value to the culture of the migrant community. Many French have argued, for example, that assimilation must be total—that the French government need not give any recognition to the migrant's language and culture and that it is the task of the migrant to acquire the French language, learn French history and literature, and identify with French values. In contrast, traditional immigrant societies, such as Canada, Australia, the United States, and Israel, have been more willing to grant some degree of cultural autonomy to migrants, accepting the organization of groups along ethnic lines and treating the articulation of ethnic demands as legitimate. In some instances, these countries have also gone beyond tolerance and have embraced some of the elements of the immigrant culture, borrowing from the language and cuisine of migrant groups and, most important, conferring respect on the migrant cultures. Paradoxically, such policies aimed at encouraging pride in one's own culture may make assimilation easier. If the host culture looks down on the migrant's culture, the undermining of the migrant's self-esteem may impede development of the self-confidence necessary for assimilation and social mobility.

The marked differences among states with respect to treatment of minority cultures have generated much political controversy; multiculturalism is an ill-defined and contentious concept that arouses great passions. What aspects of their own culture do migrants seek to maintain, and are their preferences acceptable to the host society? Advocates regard multiculturalism as a set of positive state policies that encourage migrant communities to maintain their own language, culture, identity, and history and to act as a cohesive political force. Hence some multiculturalists call for bilingual education not as a transition to migrants' learning the language of the host society but as a means of sustaining their own linguistic and cultural identities. They may also call on the government to fund the community's cultural activities and to enable communities to organize politically and elect their own members to legislative bodies. Such policies, advocates assert, are both humanitarian and beneficial because they enable the migrant community to maintain its identity within the broader context of a multicultural society and to minimize the tensions that might otherwise develop between the migrants and their native-born children. In contrast, critics of multiculturalism object to state policies that they believe will induce a sense of separateness between migrants and their hosts. Bilingual education, they argue, may marginalize the children of migrants in the labor market. Furthermore, separate electoral representation, while enabling ethnic communities to elect their own leaders to legislative bodies, may marginalize migrants by making it unnecessary for politicians to try to win electoral support among a variety of ethnic groups.

Multiculturalism is a hot topic of debate in the new Europe. Several years ago, the French were divided on the question of whether a Muslim girl could come to class covering her head with a scarf. This act was interpreted by many French secularists as an attack against the secular basis of the French school system and by feminists as a symbol of Islamic repression of women. However, others used the incident to argue for the right of Muslims to assert their religious identity, even in public institutions. In Great Britain, the debate over multiculturalism has centered around demands by Muslims for government funding of private Muslim schools on the grounds that the state already provides support to private Christian and Jewish schools. While some British agree that funds should be provided to religious educational institutions on a nondiscriminatory basis, others are concerned that state funding of Muslim schools may nurture intolerant religious fundamentalism. In the United States, the debate over multiculturalism centers in part on the issues of multicultural curricula in the schools and on bilingual education. Such policies are seen by advocates as a means of inculcating pride and by critics as a way in which ethnic community leaders may induce young people to resist cultural assimilation. Whether multiculturalism, variously defined, impedes or facilitates the absorption of migrants may ultimately depend not only on the policies themselves but also on whether the host society takes a positive view of the notion that migrants should be permitted (or encouraged) to maintain their own distinctive identity.

Both within and among each of the migrant communities in the United States there are also major differences in attitudes toward bilingual education and hence toward how integration should be accomplished (if at all). Russian and Asian migrants resist government programs that require their children to attend classes in their native tongue, preferring instead to immerse their children in English-speaking classes, which they see as the fast track toward higher education and economic advancement. But many (though by no means all) Spanish-speaking Americans are eager to place their children in Spanish-speaking classes to preserve their Mexican-American, Puerto Rican, Cuban-American, or Latin American identity.

The willingness of migrants to be absorbed and their own conception of what absorption means are inextricably linked with what the host society expects of its new citizens. A major source of tension between migrants and their hosts in many societies is in fact the lack of clarity on this issue. Presumably, a country should require that all citizens speak the national language; that they be committed to the country's political values, processes, and institutions; that they have some knowledge of the country's history and culture; and that they accept the obligations of citizenship. Yet a country need not expect any of its citizens to give up their religion or put aside any other languages or eating habits or social practices that are not at variance with national laws, regardless of whether such actions sometimes differ from those of the majority. Nevertheless, it has been particularly difficult for many societies to accept the idea that cultural or religious identity and nationality need not be one and the same. Today, an individual can be French, German, or Austrian and be a Muslim, an Englishman can be a Hindu, and a Swiss can be a Tibetan Buddhist. Similarly, a German can speak Turkish or Serbo-Croatian, and a Frenchman or Belgian can speak Arabic. Yet many European countries endured contentious centuries and even wars to accept the simple notion that Protestants and Catholics could coexist in the same country. Consequently, it is even more difficult for many Europeans to accept that migrant citizens can retain a sense of identity and pride in the country and culture of their parents and grandparents.[50]

Nevertheless, whatever term we choose, cultural pluralism or multiculturalism, some form of it is already in place in the United States, Canada, Australia, and Israel. In each of these countries, it is considered legitimate for members of migrant communities to speak their own language (in addition to the dominant language), sing their own songs, dance their own dances, and observe their own holidays. It is also considered legitimate for migrant communities to form their own associations, lobby for their interests in the legislative and executive branches of government, and take positions on issues of foreign policy involving relations between their government and that of their forebears. Canada and Australia even provide funds for ethnic groups to sustain their activities.

Although some multicultural policies may encourage migrants to resist assimilation, potent elements in many host societies induce young people to want to assimilate. In Western societies, the power and appeal of the mass media, music, lifestyle, consumerism, and popular culture are so great that the children of migrants find it difficult to resist cultural incorporation. In most Western countries at least, migrant communities are bound, in the course of time, to assimilate much of the local culture and lose some of their own. Even if the host society accepts

---

50. Early in the twentieth century, when the Hapsburg and Ottoman empires held sway over diverse cultures, it was acceptable to swear allegiance to the crown but not necessarily to identify with German or Turkish culture. Loyalty to the monarch was regarded as compatible with a variety of group identities; a Bohemian proud of Czech culture, history, music, and artistic traditions was seen as no less a subject than a Viennese proud of his cultural heritage. For centuries, Greeks, Turks, Albanians, Bosnians, Serbs, and Bulgarians shared membership in a common political union in which each community maintained its own autocephelous church, language, and personal law. There was no presumption or requirement of a common culture. But clearly, the shift from subject to citizen in central and southeastern Europe eroded an acceptance of cultural diversity within a single state.

many elements of the culture of the immigrant community, the terms of exchange between migrants and their hosts are unequal. The host culture surrounds the migrants and generally offers rewards in the form of employment and respect to those who speak the local language and share many of the features of the host culture. In contrast, the host societies threaten with economic and social marginalization migrants who do not speak the language or who fail to adopt the elements of the culture required for educational success. Painful as it is, immigrants must accept some loss of culture by their children and grandchildren as part of the price of avoiding marginalization.

Can citizenship be secular, nondenominational, devoid of cultural content—in other words, can it be a purely political conception? Few Europeans feel comfortable with such a notion because it runs counter to the widespread idea that citizenship, nationality, and culture are the same—that a German citizen is German in culture and common descent and that a French citizen is French in culture as well as a believer in the political values enshrined in the French Revolution. In contrast, for Americans, national identity rests heavily on a set of political beliefs; to become a naturalized American, one must take a test in the Constitution and swear allegiance to a flag and a nation, not to a culture, religion, or language.

I asked an Israeli Arab from Haifa how he identified himself. "I am," he replied, "an Israeli citizen and a Palestinian national." To the same question, my downstairs neighbor in Brookline, Massachusetts, a naturalized American citizen from Korea, replied, "A Korean-American." So are his children, all born in the United States. A Parisian friend, an academic who came to France from Romania as an adolescent, describes himself simply as French. Here, then, we have three very different notions of the relationship between nationality and citizenship.

For most Western Europeans, it is inconceivable that one could have, as the Israeli Palestinian does, the nationality of one country or people and the citizenship of another. Nor could one be Algerian-French, Turkish-German, or Yugoslav-Swiss in the hyphenated American style with its implications of dual nationality. The experience of traditional countries of immigration suggests that migrants and their children can live in one country and still have a relationship to another country. There is clearly nothing sacrosanct about the relationship between nationality and citizenship. In fact, many migrants to Western Europe and elsewhere may acquire naturalized citizenship while still retaining a sense of identity with their country of origin and even perhaps dreaming of returning someday. Does such a relationship threaten the interests of either country?

The world is full of people away from home, their legal status often in limbo, their national identities uncertain. They are denizens or naturalized citizens of one country but do not choose, or may not be permitted to choose, the national identity of their host. Such anomalies are partly the result of the policies of governments that admit people to work but do not grant citizenship. But often they result from the preferences of the migrants themselves, who want to retain the culture of their homeland and to transmit that culture to their children but who also seek the right of permanent residence or citizenship in another country. Acceptance and toleration of ethnic diversity and dual identities (and sometimes dual citizenship) permit further divergence between ethnicity or culture, on the one hand, and citizenship, on the other. Moreover, sending countries contribute to the gap by forcing patriotic opponents into exile or by encouraging individuals to leave for employment but maintain ties and send remittances.[51]

The term *absorption* suggests a fixed center, a sponge, so to speak, that takes in and transforms what is being absorbed. But the host society can itself be modified, even transformed, by the migrant presence as it comes to accept cultural differences in the framework of a common citizenship. Should worldwide migration flows continue, country after country will have to decide what it expects of its migrants in the way of cultural absorption and, in turn, how much cultural pluralism it is prepared to accept. Thus international population movements transform the social structure of the receiving societies as well as the character structure of the migrants.

The recent experiences of advanced industrial societies suggest a set of hypotheses as to the factors that facilitate the absorption of migrants into the economy, the culture, the social system, and the polity of the host society: when the host society regards the migrants as permanent members of the society by readily granting citizenship and the migrants in turn readily accept citizenship and a new identity; when the children of the migrants are at birth considered citizens and provided with the same educational opportunities given to the children of the native-born; when the characteristics of the migrants are particularly suitable for mobility within the host country's labor market; when the host economy is expanding and thereby providing opportunities for the migrants, as well as reducing competition between migrants and natives; when the structure of the labor market provides opportunities for migrants who seek occupational mobility; when the host society does not denigrate (even if it does not elevate or even recognize) the culture and values of the immigrant community; when the migrant stream is diversified or the numbers from one source are not so large and continuous as to enable the migrants to build permanent self-contained enclaves where migrants can employ one another, speak the same language, and insulate themselves from the larger society; when the influx of migrants and refugees is regarded by the host society as controllable; and when the state does not require or promote (although it may permit) separateness in schools, employment, or housing. It is striking to see how many of these factors—though by no means all—can be affected by state policies. Governments determine the magnitude and sources of migration and the skills characteristic of migrants, influence (though they cannot always control) the level of illegal migration, decide who will be granted citizenship and what rights and benefits should be given to various categories of migrants, and encourage or discourage integration by their housing, education, and language policies. Still, when one considers how complex and often divided the political forces in most countries are in choosing policies that can promote integration, and how difficult it is for governments to fine-tune these policies—especially in a slow-growth economy—we can appreciate why the integration of immigrants in most countries remains so problematic and, in the short term, so ridden with conflict.

51. Indians abroad, said Prime Minister Rajiv Gandhi, "should not be considered as a brain drain but as a bank on which the country could draw from time to time." *Hindustan Times*, November 23, 1988.

chapter 5

MIGRATION RULES AND INTERNATIONAL RELATIONS

In July 1993, several ships carrying over 650 Chinese were spotted by the U.S. Navy off the California coast. U.S. immigration officials concluded that the Chinese migrants, mostly young men from China's coastal provinces, intended to request asylum to ensure themselves of an extended stay in the United States while their claims were reviewed and, if rejected, appealed. During the interim, these migrants would find jobs, become indentured, and even turn to crime to pay the $20,000 to $50,000 fee charged by the smugglers who had arranged the trip and to earn remittances to send back to their family. Many would no doubt fail to attend their hearings, instead disappearing into the growing underground of illegal migrants.

Consequently, armed with a recent Supreme Court decision permitting the halting of ships suspected of violating American laws even in international waters, the Navy and Coast Guard interdicted the ships. The U.S. Immigration and Naturalization Service (INS) sent officials to the ships, gave the Chinese questionnaires to prove that they were political refugees, and concluded that all but one were not. Although human rights advocates argued that the Chinese should be allowed to enter the United States and get a fair hearing on their claims of persecution, administration officials were concerned that unless the ships were halted, the stream of illegal migrants would continue. Other ships, in fact, had earlier offloaded their human cargoes in New York and in California.[1] Moreover, the INS was already overloaded with a backlog of asylum claimants and expected another 120,000 requests that year, 90 percent of whom were likely to be ruled ineligible.

1. On June 6, 1993, a shipload of 263 Chinese aliens ran aground off Rockaway, in the New York City borough of Queens. The ship, a tramp steamer called the *Golden Venture*, came via a tortuous route from the East China coast to Thailand, Kenya, around the Cape of Good Hope, and on to New York. When the ship ran aground and its passengers swam to shore, seven died. It was believed that a tightening of regulations on the West Coast—immigration officials were detaining passengers for long periods instead of releasing them to await hearings—led smugglers to switch their ships to East Coast ports. The number of asylum claimants from China increased significantly after President Bush, in a 1989 order, announced that immigration agents must give special consideration to Chinese fleeing that country's population control policies, which can impose sterilization or abortion on couples who have more than one child. "We get 18-year-olds who've never been married who tell us they want to have two kids and that's why they're here," explained an INS official (*New York Times,* June 7, 1993, p. B5). According to one estimate, 100,000 illegal Chinese have entered the United States since 1992 (*Far Eastern Economic Review,* April 8, 1993, p. 17).

If the Chinese were allowed to enter the United States, they would have to be given a hearing and could not be immediately repatriated.

In an effort to deal with this problem, the U.S. government asked the Mexican government to allow the Chinese to land in Mexico. Since Mexico does not have an asylum review procedure comparable to that of the United States, Mexico could immediately send the Chinese back by plane. After a week of negotiations, the Mexican government agreed. Within days after their arrival, Mexico deported the Chinese to Fujian province in southeastern China, from which most of them came. It was also reported that the Mexicans had arrested some of the ship's officers for smuggling. U.S. officials then negotiated with the Chinese foreign ministry for assurance that the repatriated migrants would not be imprisoned. "After they return to China, they will not be penalized," an official of the Fujian Civil Affairs Bureau said. "The authorities will do some ideological work with them and they can return home. There will not be any kind of fine." However, a few weeks later, it was reported that many of the immigrants had been sent to "reeducation camps."

Together, the U.S., Mexican, and Chinese governments had taken steps to thwart future illegal flows of Chinese to the United States. This incident therefore illustrates one way in which states negotiate with one another to control international migration. As we shall see, there are a variety of ways in which states can influence one another's migration policies and foreign policies. We will also look at how international migrants themselves influence the behavior and policies of both host and home governments and the relations between those governments. Even though international migration clearly has a significant impact on relations between states, scholars have done little to incorporate population movements into the theoretical literature on international relations. Nor, for that matter, has much attention been devoted to how state actions shape population movements in ways that lead states into conflict or cooperation. This chapter is intended to illuminate these areas.

We start from three simple propositions. The first is that national migration policies affect a country's international relations. Migration policies often provoke conflict, but under some conditions they may also lead to consultation and cooperation between governments. The second is that the immigration and emigration policies of governments—their exit and entry rules—are no longer solely a domestic issue but are increasingly influenced by the actions and policies of other countries. The third is that international migrants often become a political force in both host and home countries, with the capacity to influence not only emigration and immigration policies but also relations between the sending and receiving countries.

We will initially deal with these issues by considering the concept of sovereignty as it relates to neoclassical economic ideas. There are two simple reasons for doing so. First, the notion of sovereignty is, as suggested earlier, central to understanding the role of states in influencing international migration; and second, sovereignty in matters of international migration, as in many other areas of state policy, has been eroding, and we need to understand how and why if we are to comprehend the relationship between international migration and international relations.

SOVEREIGNTY AND ECONOMIC LIBERALISM

However difficult it may be to define what constitutes a sovereign state, on one point there is universal agreement: States claim the exclusive authority to decide who may enter and who may become a citizen. A colony whose imperial rulers decide who can enter is not sovereign. This theme is reflected in the American Declaration of Independence, which charged the British crown with, among other things, "obstructing the Laws for Naturalization of Foreigners; refusing to pass others to encourage their Migrations hither, and raising the Conditions of New Appropriation of Lands." Similarly, the Chinese believed that they had lost sovereignty when European powers acquired extraterritorial rights and the right to control entry to port cities. Africa's loss of sovereignty was even more extreme. The imperial powers not only decided who could enter and whether there could be permanent settlers but also imported indentured labor and even forcibly exported indigenes as slaves.

Although neoclassical economic liberals advocate free trade and the free flow of capital as a means of providing for efficient resource allocation to the benefit of all, they do not advocate the free movement of peoples. It is not because the free movement of peoples is inefficient. In fact, a world in which labor could move freely to wherever the demand was greatest and in which labor supply and demand could be matched without regard to international boundaries might very well be economically more efficient. But it would no longer be a world of sovereign states.

Thus even the most ardent neoclassical economists recognize that when it comes to the movement of people, considerations other than the efficient use of resources come into play. In the absence of state controls over immigration, one country could peacefully invade another through colonization. If 35 million hardworking Chinese were allowed to settle in Burma, the Burmese economy might very well prosper, and the Burmese themselves might be economically better off. But the country would no longer be Burma. The Burmese would no longer be able to control the central cultural symbols of their national life or to maintain political control over their own state.[2]

A policy of open entry is precluded by policymakers' and citizens' concern for the preservation of a particular national identity (or identities) and widely shared values and for maintaining control over political institutions. However, countries may offer open entry to outsiders with whom their population shares a close ethnic affinity. For example, the People's Republic of China was the primary haven for Vietnamese refugees of Chinese extraction; India has readily accepted Hindus from Pakistan and Bangladesh; Israel admits Jews from anywhere in the world under its Law of Return; France opened its doors to *pieds-noirs* from Algeria, including those who had never lived in France; and the Arab states on the western shore of the Persian Gulf permit their citizens to move freely from one state to another. Countries also selectively admit people with whom they have had historic ties or toward whom they feel a sense of obligation or guilt. Hence the United States has admitted refugees from Vietnam, the Netherlands has admitted people from its former colony of Timor, and the United Kingdom has admitted Indians from East Africa as well as citizens of other Commonwealth nations.

There are indications that in some countries attitudes toward entry have become more flexible. The decision of the European Union to permit citizens of

2. By contrast, an influx of tens of thousands of well-to-do Hong Kong Chinese into Vancouver, British Columbia, has been an economic asset without constituting either a political or cultural threat to Canada.

member nations to move about freely represents a historic step toward the elimination of full local sovereignty; it also represents a major move toward the redefinition and enlargement of national identities to encompass a European nationality. The United States and Australia are among a small number of countries in which national origins and ethnicity have been superseded by educational and occupational considerations as determinants of entry. Western European and Gulf states also once made it easy for foreigners to enter the labor force, but unlike the United States, they made a sharp distinction between the qualifications for holding a job and those for becoming a citizen.[3]

Nonetheless, these examples suggest that entry rules are only marginally shaped by economic considerations, even for countries that are relatively open to the flow of trade, capital, and technology. How people define their national identity and their receptivity to other peoples with different identities shape the entry rules set by governments and condition the way governments respond to changes in the demand for labor.

RULES OF ENTRY

States differ markedly with respect to rules of entry. In broad terms, there are currently five types of rules.

1. *Unrestricted entry rules.* Although no country freely permits entry to everyone, some countries grant virtually unrestricted entry to citizens of neighboring countries. A cohesive ethnic group may be freely allowed to move back and forth across borders, as has historically been the case for Pashtun-speaking tribals traversing the Afghanistan-Pakistan border. Similarly, prior to unification, West Germany freely admitted anyone from East Germany, and members of the European Union allow their citizens to move freely from one member country to another. In the nineteenth century, U.S. borders were almost entirely open.

2. *Promotional entry rules.* Countries may actively promote entry in an effort to increase their population or temporarily to fill a demand for labor. The countries of the western hemisphere, Australia, and New Zealand promoted entry throughout the nineteenth and early twentieth centuries, as did the Western European countries in the 1950s and 1960s and the countries of the Persian Gulf in the 1970s and 1980s. Israel, in fulfillment of its nationalist ideology to create a homeland for all Jews, promotes the immigration of Jews irrespective of their country of origin. Promotional policies invariably involve some principles of selectivity—by education and skill levels or ethnicity.

3. *Restrictive or permissive entry rules.* Governments may discourage or even oppose immigration but nonetheless permit entry under highly selec-

3. For an analysis of the relationship between migration and citizenship in the Middle East, see George Dib, "Migration and Naturalization Laws in Egypt, Lebanon, Syria, Jordan, Kuwait and the United Arab Emirates, Part 2: Naturalization Laws," *Population Bulletin of the United Nations Economic Commission for Western Asia,* June 1979.

tive rules such as permitting family reunification or selectively admitting small numbers of highly skilled individuals.

4. *Unwanted entry rules.* Governments may allow entry by people that it does not want due to legal or moral obligations (asylum seekers with a well-founded fear of persecution) or the impossibility of preventing their entry (a massive refugee influx, illegal migrants). These are often entry "rules" only in the sense that governments do not or cannot take steps to halt the flows.

5. *Prohibition entry rules.* Governments may rejected all migrants and refugees and effectively seal their borders against illegal entrants.

RULES OF EXIT

There are five types of exit rules.

1. *Prohibition exit rules.* Governments may prevent their citizens from leaving. Totalitarian states invariably deny their citizens the right of exit, concerned that they would thereby lose an important instrument of political control. In contrast, democratic regimes subscribe to the notion that citizenship implies the right to leave.[4] Note that even though regimes disagree on the relevance of the concept of sovereignty to rules of exit, they do agree that all states have the right to regulate entry.

2. *Selective exit rules.* Governments may allow citizens to leave selectively, permitting the exit of those with some characteristics but prohibiting the exit of others. For example, governments may restrict the emigration of individuals possessing certain skills, as when the Egyptian government restricted the emigration of doctors. Communist states usually prohibited citizens from leaving to seek employment abroad or to change their citizenship but from time to time relaxed these prohibitions. Before 1989, for example, the East German government permitted some of its citizens to migrate to West Germany, and earlier the Soviet Union selectively permitted Jews to leave for Israel.

3. *Permissive exit rules.* Governments may freely permit their citizens to leave as long as they have performed the obligations of citizenship (have paid their taxes, served in a conscript military, not broken the law, and so on). Western democracies ordinarily treat the freedom to leave as a fundamental right of citizenship, though in practice such rights can be circumscribed by currency regulations.

4. *Promotional exit rules.* Governments may encourage citizens to seek employment abroad to relieve unemployment or to increase remittances. Some governments have even developed education programs to provide citizens with skills that could enhance their opportunities for finding

---

4. The Helsinki Declaration and the UN Declaration of Human Rights stipulate the right of all citizens to leave their country.

employment abroad. For example, Sri Lanka, Pakistan, Bangladesh, and India all promote emigration to the Middle East. In the past, the government of Turkey promoted emigration to Germany, and the Algerian government promoted emigration to France.

5. *Expulsion exit rules.* Governments may expel individual citizens or induce entire groups of people to leave by threatening their safety and income if they remain. Expulsion rules can be directed at political dissidents, a threatening social class (such as the middle class in Cuba after the Castro revolution), or an ethnic minority (Indians in East Africa, Chinese in Vietnam). Refugee movements that seem to be the side effects of internal political upheavals or famines are often quite deliberate consequences of state policies, ways in which regimes choose to deal with class enemies or dissident ethnic minorities.

ACCESS RULES AND MIGRATION THEORY

Rules of exit and entry are important variables influencing the magnitudes, characteristics, and directionality of international migration. These rules make up one of the four clusters of variables that shape international migration. The others are (1) differential variables, such as wage differentials, differences in employment rates, and differences in land prices between sending and receiving countries; (2) spatial variables, such as distance and transportation costs; and (3) affinity variables, such as religion, culture, language, and kinship networks. Differential and spatial variables are usually the concern of economists; spatial variables are of particular interest to geographers; affinity variables attract the interests of sociologists and anthropologists; and access variables are the concern of political scientists and students of international relations.

Differential, spatial, and affinity variables have been the subject of extensive research, but less attention has been given to the study of the determinants of exit and entry rules. The policies of some individual countries have been studied. However, except for the work by Aristide Zolberg, Astri Suhrke, and Michael Teitelbaum,[5] there is little systematic comparative and theoretical work on such issues as how and why states make their access rules, the interplay between domestic and international considerations, the relationship between regime types and access rules, and how rules are affected by internal political transformations.

All too often, the theoretical literature on international migration tends to treat access variables as exogenous or as a kind of interference or noise in a process. Economists, in particular, tend to assume the primacy of differential, distance, and affinity variables, excluding access variables from their analysis. At times, of course,

5. Aristide R. Zolberg and Astri Suhrke, "Social Conflict and Refugees in the Third World: The Cases of Ethiopia and Afghanistan" (paper presented at the annual meeting of the American Political Science Association, Washington, D.C., 1984); Aristide R. Zolberg, "International Migrations in Political Perspective," in *Global Trends in Migration,* ed. Mary M. Kritz, Charles B. Keely, and Silvano M. Tomasi (New York: Center for Migration Studies, 1981); and Michael S. Teitelbaum, "Immigration, Refugees and Foreign Policy," *International Organization,* Summer 1984, pp. 429–450.

the options available to policymakers are sharply constrained by these variables. Where differentials are high, affinities are close, and distances are small, a country usually faces difficult decisions (and limited choices) about its access rules (for example, the United States in relation to Mexico, India in relation to Bangladesh); where differentials and affinities are low, even though distances are small, neighboring countries often need not be concerned about their rules of entry (as in France and Germany prior to World War II). But in other circumstances, rules of access can be decisive in shaping the volume, characteristics, and sources of migration. As we have seen earlier, Japan and Australia have used control over entry relatively effectively, though income and employment differentials with their neighbors are very great indeed.

But even entry rules are not decisive. Individual decisions by migrants are obviously influenced by the rules of entry. What is less obvious, however, is that migrants also consider the exit rules of countries to which they contemplate migration. In fact, migrants are usually reluctant to seek entry into countries that have restrictive exit rules if similar economic opportunities are available in countries that freely permit exit. Similarly, migrants may consider whether their decision leaves open or precludes subsequent migration. In the 1970s and 1980s, for example, Jewish emigrants from the Soviet Union, considering whether to migrate to the United States or Israel, often chose the United States, knowing that the option of moving to Israel remained open, whereas the reverse decision might preclude further migration. Similar considerations may explain why there has also been a small (but surprising) migration of Russian Jews into Germany.

Researchers have not paid adequate attention to how potential migrants and refugees choose their destination, particularly how their knowledge about access rules influences their decisions. Information about new legislation, changes in administrative rules, new court decisions, new airline regulations, and government decisions on interdicting boats appears to be disseminated rapidly to would-be migrants and refugees. How such information is disseminated, through whom it is disseminated, and precisely how it affects individual and family decisions are not well understood, though governments are increasingly making policies on the assumption that they will in fact deter migration.

In addition to affecting the migration decisions of individuals, the access rules adopted by a government are also likely to have significant consequences both for the movement of capital and for the adoption of technology. Governments are generally better able to control the exit and entry of people than they are of the flow of capital. By restricting the entry of people when the demand for labor has risen, a government may also unintentionally induce an outflow of capital. Hence the Japanese government's policy of prohibiting Japanese firms from recruiting labor abroad (a decision made for cultural and political, not economic, reasons) was a factor in the decision of some Japanese firms to relocate plants abroad. In contrast, the decision of the French and German governments to import Algerian and Turkish workers may have slowed the relocation of industrial plants abroad. Similarly, a decision to employ or not to employ imported labor has an impact on the pace of technological innovation; firms that can cut costs by using low-wage immigrants are less likely to adopt laborsaving technologies. An important area for future research is precisely how a change in the access rules affects the other factors of production.

ACCESS RULES AND INTERNATIONAL CONFLICT

Understanding access rules is important from another perspective. They affect not only international migration but also international relations. The congruence or incongruence of rules between states can influence the patterns of international conflict and cooperation. A brief consideration of emigration-immigration intersections may suggest some of these patterns.

When one state promotes entry and another state promotes exit, as when one country wants to import labor from a country that is willing to export it, the two countries have compatible objectives. They are then able to negotiate such matters as wages, conditions of employment, rules for expatriation, and arrangements for remittances. The Algerian-French arrangements in the 1960s are an example.[6] When several countries are involved in the exchange, multilateral arrangements are also possible, as in the case of the Gulf states. Cooperation may also take place in matters other than the movement of labor. For example, one country may want to promote the exodus of an ethnic minority, while another country in which the concerned ethnic group is the majority may want to promote its entry. This may be done by formal agreements, such as took place among several countries in the Balkans in the 1920s, or by a tacit understanding.

Conversely, when one state permits, promotes, or compels emigration to a state that prohibits entry, the situation is potentially highly conflictual.[7] Migration from Bangladesh to northeastern India has been a source of conflict between the two countries, as has the migration of refugees from Afghanistan to Pakistan. Illegal migrations from Mexico to the United States have also created tensions, albeit not to the same extent as in South Asia.

When one country prohibits or restricts emigration that another country seeks to promote, migration policies may become a bargaining chip in a large negotiation package. Both the United States and Israel promoted the entry of Jews from the Soviet Union when the Soviet Union no longer permitted the exit of significant numbers of Jews. The United States then made a concerted effort to influence Soviet emigration policies by linking Soviet policies toward emigration with trade issues. At the same time, Israel linked emigration to an exchange of ambassadors and any future Soviet participation in a Middle East peace process. Thus migration policies became a bargaining chip between countries with incompatible policies.

Countries with strained relations may effectively seal their borders to population movements to avoid further conflicts. For decades, the longest border in the world was sealed from both sides, with the People's Republic of China prohibiting exit and the Soviet Union prohibiting entry. As a result, population movements

6. For an examination of how migration affected French-Algerian relations, see Mark J. Miller, "Reluctant Partnership: Foreign Workers in Franco-Algerian Relations, 1962–1979," *Journal of International Affairs,* Fall–Winter 1979, pp. 219–237, and Stephen Adler, *International Migration and Dependence* (Farnborough, England: Gower House, 1977).

7. For an account of forced migration as an instrument of both domestic and foreign policy, see Michael S. Teitelbaum, "Forced Migration: The Tragedy of Mass Expulsions," in *Clamor at the Gates,* ed. Nathan Glazer (San Francisco: Institute for Contemporary Studies, 1985); on the law of asylum, see Michael S. Teitelbaum, "Political Asylum in Theory and Practice," *Public Interest,* Summer 1984, pp. 74–86. See also Guy S. Goodwin-Gill, *International Law and the Movement of Persons Between States* (Oxford: Clarendon Press, 1978).

Table 17   EXIT AND ENTRY RULES

Entry Rules	Exit Rules				
	Expulsion	Promotion	Permission	Selection	Prohibition
Unrestricted	NC	NC/Coop	NC	V	V
Promoted	NC	Coop	Coop	V	Cflt
Selective	V	V	V	V	V
Unwanted	Cflt	Cflt	NC	NC	NC
Prohibited	Cflt	Cflt	NC	NC	NC/Coop

Note: Coop=cooperative; NC=nonconflictual; V=variable (usually dependent on the content of the selectivity rules); Cflt=conflictual.

between the two countries did not take place despite the very substantial income and employment differentials. With the breakup of the Soviet Union and the termination of restrictive exit rules by the successor states, population movements in the region are likely to increase, exacerbating strained interstate relations. For example, flows between Kyrgyzstan and China, Tajikistan and Afghanistan, and Azerbaijan and Iran, as well as greater movement among the successor republics themselves, may well become sources of conflict.

Expulsions need not cause international conflict if the receiving country is concerned with the promotion of migration or is at least willing to permit free entry. The mass population exchange between India and Pakistan in 1947 and 1948, which involved as many as 14 million people, did not lead to international conflict over this issue because both countries respected the wishes of ethnic minorities to settle where they constituted a majority. The forcible exit of Jews from North Africa to Israel in the 1950s was not a source of international tension. In contrast, the forcible exit of many Arabs from Israel in 1948 has been followed by an interminable conflict between Israel and its Arab neighbors.

The table above illustrates the ways in which exit and entry rules can lead to conflict or cooperation among states, depending on whether they have compatible or incompatible rules. The horizontal axis denotes exit rules, and the vertical axis, entry rules.

The examples cited suggest that the compatibility of exit and entry rules have consequences not only for the flow of international migrants but also for relations among states. For this reason, states increasingly recognize that under some circumstances (both when rules are incompatible and when they are compatible), it is in their interests to negotiate migration policies with other states, for they can no longer regard their own exit and entry rules as strictly internal matters.

INTERNATIONAL RELATIONS AND THE RULES OF ACCESS

Exit and entry rules have already become a matter of international negotiations, as in the case of the European Union whose members negotiated regulations regarding population movements within and among themselves. A number of multilateral conventions on labor migration have also been established by the International

Labor Organization, although their effect on the rules set by governments seems negligible. More important, the entry rules set by one country may be implicitly shaped by the exit rules set by another. For example, prior to reunification, West Germany permitted free access to individuals coming from East Germany, while East Germany restricted people from exiting.[8] But when the East Germans permitted Turks, Sri Lankans, and Pakistanis to enter and freely exit through Berlin, the West German government became concerned about the growing number of migrants seeking status as political refugees. The dismantling of the Berlin Wall, the reunification of Germany, the fall of the Eastern European regimes, the deterioration of political and economic conditions in the east—especially in the Balkans—and the consequent new freedom to exit subsequently inundated Germany with migrants seeking entry under Germany's generous asylum law. As a result, Germany reformulated its entry rules to make them more restrictive. Changes in exit rules in the east brought about a change in entry rules in the west.

Similarly, the Austrian and Italian governments permitted refugees to enter from the Soviet bloc, but only because of the willingness of third countries to permit permanent entry; Austria's and Italy's rules of entry were thus conditional on the entry rules of others. When other European countries declared that refugees should remain in the country of first asylum, both Austria and Italy made their entry rules restrictive.

Migration policies were the centerpiece of negotiations between the United States and Cuba in August 1994 after President Fidel Castro let it be known that his government would permit people to leave on their own small boats. By the end of the summer, an estimated 35,000 "rafters" were picked up by the U.S. Coast Guard as they headed for Florida. Concerned that the refugee influx would generate political turmoil in the United States (with political consequences in Florida), President Clinton reversed a 28-year-old policy of granting automatic political asylum to Cubans. The Cuban government offered to halt the exodus in return for the end of the U.S. embargo on Cuba and for the sharp increase of legal migration of Cubans to the United States. The U.S negotiators refused to negotiate an end to the embargo but agreed to admit 20,000 Cuban immigrants yearly. The Cuban government accepted the offer and then barred its citizens from leaving by boat. The negotiations thus resulted in changes in U.S. entry rules from a refugee-driven set of rules to an immigration-driven set of rules, in return for a change in Cuban exit rules.

Once again, it needs to be emphasized that access rules are not merely the political expression of economic forces, however important these may be. Global economic changes may, of course, influence governments to change their access rules. For example, the oil price rise created labor shortages in many oil-producing countries while inducing other countries to export labor to improve their balance of payments through remittances. Agricultural and industrial policies may lead to an increase in the demand for labor or to a large labor surplus, putting pressure on a government to ease its entry or its exit rules. But it would be a mistake to think

---

8. East Germany did permit citizens over 65 to exit if they would forgo state-provided social security benefits, a historically familiar policy of using emigration as a device for reducing social welfare costs.

that the choices governments make are necessarily dictated primarily by economic considerations.[9] Indeed, governments seeking to maximize values other than economic growth often choose entry and exit rules that economists would regard as inefficient. A productive minority may be expelled by a government to improve the status of a politically dominant ethnic group. Or a government may restrict entry because it fears the political consequences of unwanted immigration, even though it recognizes that the migrants would contribute to national wealth.

Access rules should be understood as more than the formally prescribed legal norms and the procedures and mechanisms for enforcing these norms. Written rules are intertwined with administrative capacity, the willingness of states to enforce legal norms, the expectations states have of one another, and the reputations states have for behaving in a particular manner.[10] Consider the reputation of states with respect to expulsions. Any country can expel illegals, but it is politically easier for authoritarian countries than for democracies. For example, during and after the Gulf War, Kuwait and Saudi Arabia expelled migrants without domestic or international protest. Saudi Arabia expelled Yemenites when the government of Yemen declared its support for Iraq, and Kuwait expelled Palestinians for their support of and collaboration with the Iraqi invaders. Communist regimes have had a reputation for expelling dissident social classes or for creating conditions that induced large numbers of people to flee: Cubans after the Castro revolution, Chinese from Vietnam, refugees from Cambodia and Laos, Tibetans after the Chinese Communist occupation, Czechs and Hungarians after their governments' crackdown on dissidents, and Afghans after the Communist coup and the Soviet invasion.[11] The establishment of an authoritarian government clearly increases the possibility of flight; so may other kinds of regime changes.[12]

It is also easier for a government to expel a minority group with which the dominant ethnic group has no affinity than to expel one with close ties. For example, it was not politically difficult for Uganda to expel its Indian population. It is

9. Neoclassical economists and Marxists share a tendency to explain international migration primarily in terms of changes in the global economy or particular patterns of capitalist development in both sending and receiving countries. For an analysis of Mexico-U.S. migration using this latter perspective, see Alejandro Portes, "Illegal Immigration and the International System: Lessons from Recent Mexican Immigration to the United States," *Social Problems*, April 1979, pp. 425–438. See also W. R. Böhning, "Elements of a Theory of International Economic Migration to Industrial Nation-States," in *Global Trends in Migration*, ed. Kritz et al. (New York: Center for Migration Studies, 1981).

10. For a discussion of the ways in which reputations of states affect their relations, see Robert O. Keohane, *After Hegemony* (Princeton, N.J.: Princeton University Press, 1984).

11. For this reason, many governments were automatically alarmed at the prospect of a Communist takeover in a neighboring state because they expected such a regime change to provoke a large population exodus.

12. The policy of inducing certain categories of unwanted people to leave is not confined to Communist regimes, nor is it a recent development. In the nineteenth century, the British pursued a policy of inducing indigents to emigrate to relieve the state of the costs of having to provide for the poor; see H. J. M. Johnston, *British Emigration Policy, 1815–1830* (Oxford: Clarendon Press, 1972). The British also had a policy of ejecting prisoners: Crowding in British jails in the 1770s and 1780s led the crown to ship convicts to Australia. Cuba followed a similar policy when it sent some of its prison population on boats to the United States in 1980 from the port of Mariel. For a discussion of induced or forced emigration from Third World countries, see Chapter 2.

politically more difficult, however, for India to expel illegal Bengali-speaking Muslim migrants from Bangladesh, for Pakistan to expel Pashtun-speaking refugees from Afghanistan, or for Bangladesh to expel Muslim refugees from Burma.

The foregoing analysis suggests that future research should be conducted into how states make their access and entry rules, how states influence one another in shaping these rules, and how these rules in turn affect relations between states. It would be useful to focus on particular regions, for considerations of proximity are often crucial in setting entry and exit rules.[13] We might take a closer look at the South Asia region, where international migrations are largely unwanted by receiving countries. As a result, conflicts over population movements tend to be great, leading to high-level politics involving heads of state and top officials. War even erupted in the region over unwanted migration when India invaded Pakistan in large part over the massive influx of refugees from East Pakistan. A number of the actions pursued by states in the region (Pakistan toward Afghanistan and the Soviet Union, India toward Bangladesh and Sri Lanka) can also be understood in part in the context of the efforts of these states to prevent or mitigate the effects of unwanted population movements.

Another region in which migration rules and international relations are closely entwined is the Middle East, where population flows have, in the main, been approved by both sending and receiving countries. In these cases, negotiations on migration matters are generally at a low level, involving government bureaucrats. It has also been possible to deal with migration issues at a multilateral level through the Gulf Cooperation Council (GCC). Together, the Persian Gulf governments have attempted to adjust their labor policies on the basis of assumptions concerning future population movements and have explored possibilities for integrating some of their development policies, taking into account the relationship of these policies to migration. In 1991, however, when Iraq invaded Kuwait, members of the GCC joined the Western powers in a war to force an Iraqi withdrawal, the issue of migrants moved from low to high politics as governments saw migrants in the context of security rather than labor needs.

Conflicts over migration have also become important in the Caribbean basin, a region that includes the island states of the Caribbean, Central America, and the southern part of the United States. Unwanted flows into the United States from El Salvador, Nicaragua, Haiti, and Cuba have been an important element in U.S. policies toward each of these countries. President Clinton's decision to invade Haiti if its military rulers refused to step down and restore the elected president was in large measure aimed at halting the outpouring of refugees into the United States.

Perhaps the least understood and least researched aspect of international migration is how the foreign policies of states intentionally or, more often, unintentionally influence population movements from other states. Clearly, many foreign policy decisions by governments (military action, sanctions, trade policies) can

---

13. For a comparative review of European policies on entry and exit in the 1960s and 1970s, see W. R. Böhning, "Immigration Policies of Western European Countries," *International Migration Review,* Summer 1974, pp. 155–164, and Ray C. Rist, "The European Economic Community and Manpower Migrations: Policies and Prospects," *Journal of International Affairs,* Fall–Winter 1979, pp. 201–218.

result in a population exodus or can induce another government to change its exit policies. We shall return to this theme later.

THE NEW TRANSNATIONALS

International migrants have become important political actors influencing both the political processes of the countries in which they reside and the relationship between their country of residence and their country of origin. In recent years, scholars have become aware of the important role played by international nonstate institutions, especially transnational corporations and global religious institutions, in the internal development of states. These transnational nonstate institutions often also shape relations among states. International migrants play a similar role. We will consider some of the political roles played by international migrants with respect to both how they shape the politics of their home and host countries and how they shape relationships between home and host countries.

In the three-actor situation of migrant, host government, and home government, there are great variations in where the initiative for political action lies. Migrants are often pawns—admitted into a country as temporary guest workers, politically powerless, then repatriated when no longer needed by the host country with often little more than a whimper of protest from the home country. But in other circumstances, migrants have become naturalized citizens, their numbers and wealth have grown, and they have become politically articulate, able to affect the politics and policies of the host country—including its migration and refugee policies and its relationship with the migrants' countries of origin. Between these two extremes, moreover, migrants and refugees play a wide range of political roles, depending on factors such as the degree of political freedom offered by the host country, their numbers and place in the economy of the host country, the circumstances under which they left their home country, and the political relationship of the host and home countries.

Migrants and their descendants have sought to influence migration policies in their country of residence. They have sometimes promoted policies intended to benefit the economy or foreign policy interests of their country of origin. Alternatively, they have been critics of their country of origin and have pressured their host government to try to influence the domestic politics of their country of origin. The variations in political actions by migrants is reflected in the many active migrant groups worldwide, including Sikh secessionists in the United Kingdom, immigrant Filipino opponents of President Marcos in the United States, anti-Turkish Armenian terrorists in the United States and Western Europe, Turkish fundamentalists in Germany, Polish immigrants and their descendants in Chicago, Cuban refugees in Florida, Nicaraguan refugees in the United States, immigrants from Timor in the Netherlands, Yemenites in Saudi Arabia, and Croatians in Germany. Almost everywhere, migrants have become a political factor that governments of both sending and receiving countries must take into account.[14]

14. For a study of the role played by expatriate communities in international relations, see Gabriel Sheffer (ed.), *Modern Diasporas* in *International Politics* (London: Croom Helm, 1986).

Note that the term *migrant* is itself problematic because in some societies, it refers not only to individuals who have migrated from another country but also to their descendants born in the host society. There are approximately 100 million people in the world who were born in one country and reside in another. Many of these migrants and the descendants of earlier generations of migrants constitute diasporas, that is, ethnic groups that retain ties to their "original" homelands.[15] The major contemporary diasporas are the Chinese, Indians, Lebanese, Palestinians, Greeks, Gypsies, Armenians, Jews, Irish, and Africans, but new transnational migrant communities are constantly in the process of being constructed. There are now significant Filipino and Korean populations in the United States and Tamils, Tibetans, Iranians, Ukrainians, and Poles in North America and Western Europe who have maintained their identity and ties with their homelands. How these international migrants, and the larger diasporas to which they often belong, are mobilized, by whom, and for what causes can have profound political implications for both the countries of origin and destination, as well as for relations among countries.[16]

MIGRANT STRATEGIES

A useful starting point for examining the political role of migrants is to consider what migrants want. Let us examine their ambitions in four broad areas.

Migrant Claims on the Host Country for Rights and Entitlements

Invariably, the first claim of migrants on the host country is for rights and entitlements. Migrants are universally concerned with policies that affect their ability to stay, seek employment, change jobs, acquire property, gain access to public benefits, seek redress under law, and become naturalized citizens. In addition, they are concerned with the policies of the host country that affect future immigration, particularly whether they are permitted to bring in their relatives, how open the migration doors are to people from their country of origin, and whether they themselves

15. Until modern times, the term *diaspora* had theological connotations, referring to the dispersion of the Jews whose return to the Promised Land would, according to Protestant theologians, usher in Christ's second coming. However, it is now widely used to refer to the global dispersion of people from a common homeland.

16. The relationship between the disaspora and the home country is no better illustrated than in the complex relationship between American Jews and Israel. American Jews have been active as lobbyists in Washington, as financial supporters to the government of Israel and to a variety of contending political parties within Israel, and as a source of immigrants to Israel. Their impact on Israeli politics is at least as great as their influence on American politics. A dramatic example of the former is the role played by Rabbi Meir Kahane, a Brooklyn-born Jew who migrated to Israel to become a major figure among settlers on the West Bank, and his close associate, Dr. Baruch Goldstein (who also migrated from Brooklyn), whose killing of dozens of Muslim worships in Hebron in February 1994 threatened to destroy the peace process between Israel and the Palestinians. American-born migrants to Israel constitute 15 percent of the settlers on the West Bank and a high percentage in the militant movements.

are free to enter, exit, and reenter. Migrants may also be concerned with broader questions related to their cultural autonomy: Can they freely practice their religion, use their native language in dealing with the government, and maintain cultural institutions, or are they required to assimilate to the culture of the host society?

The greater the political rights of migrants, the more readily they can make claims on the political system. As noted earlier, migrant workers in the Middle East, knowing that they can be summarily repatriated by their authoritarian host governments, are in a weak position to make claims. In contrast, migrants (although not illegal migrants) in Western Europe, the United Kingdom, Canada, Australia, and the United States are in a better position to make claims. Moreover, in this latter group of countries, migrant communities are often able to find allies within the host population who are sympathetic to their claims for political rights and greater cultural autonomy and who can organize to promote these claims.

The more rights given to migrants, the more emphatic will be their claims to entitlements. Naturalized citizens in particular are free, like other members of the society, to voice their claims. Their ability to voice their claims as an ethnic group, however, depends on whether the society accepts the notion of cultural pluralism— the legitimacy of an ethnic minority to maintain its identity and assert political demands through that identity.

In the United States, ethnic politics is a historically well established feature of the political system. As a result, new generations of migrants from Asia and Latin America can legitimately press their claims in education, housing, and social welfare. Furthermore, migrants in the United States can and do lobby on immigration legislation, attempt to influence policymakers on behalf of or in opposition to their country of origin, and put forth their own ethnic candidates for public office. Similarly, in other traditionally migrant countries, migrant communities are well organized to make claims on their own behalf. In Canada, Australia, the United Kingdom, and several Scandinavian countries, the government actually provides financial support to ethnic groups to enable them to pursue cultural activities and even to lobby the government. Immigrant communities may become more organized and more articulate in making claims in Europe in the future if the nation-states of Europe accept the principle that migrants can maintain their ethnic identities even after becoming citizens.

In making claims on their host countries, migrants may solicit support for their countries of origin. Such support is more often provided to migrants living in democratic countries than to those living in authoritarian countries because governments of sending countries want to minimize the risk of forcible expulsions from the latter and know that they can appeal to the political conscience of the former. Consequently, the Algerian and Turkish governments actively work with and provide support to their citizens in France and Germany and are sensitive to the mistreatment of their citizens. In contrast, the governments of India, Pakistan, Bangladesh, and Sri Lanka provide considerably less support for their migrant workers in the Persian Gulf states for fear that these countries would respond by not admitting their migrants or by replacing their migrants with those of other countries. The political system of the host country, rather than the political system of the home country, is the more important variable in predicting whether migrants will receive political support from their country of origin.

Migrant Claims on the Home Country
and Home Countries' Claims on Migrants

The linkage between migrants and their country of origin is highly variable. The migrant community itself may be divided in its attitude toward the government of the home country, as were overseas Chinese when China fell under Communist rule, overseas Iranians during the Khomeini Islamic revolution, and overseas Indians when Mrs. Gandhi declared a national emergency and suspended democratic rule. Ethnic divisions within the migrant community may also shape its relationship with the home country: The attitudes of Tamils from Sri Lanka, Sikhs from India, and Chinese from Malaysia differ from those of other ethnic groups from the same countries.[17] The ethnicity, or group identity, of people who come from multi-ethnic societies is not necessarily the same as their nationality. Armenian and Kurdish migrants from Turkey or Jewish migrants from Poland clearly have a different group identity than migrants who belong to the majority ethnic group in these countries. Similarly, a Sikh migrant may emphasize his religious identity and dissociate himself from an Indian identity, and a Tamil from Sri Lanka may prefer to regard himself as a Tamil rather than a Sri Lankan. In extreme cases, a secessionist movement in the country of origin may lead members of an ethnic community abroad to redefine their group (and ultimately national) identity.

Migrants may attempt to influence directly the internal affairs of their countries of origin. Influence may take the form of economic and political support through investment, active promotion of trade, facilitation of technology transfer, and funding of governing political parties. However, influence can also take the form of hostility toward the home government and support for dissidents and, where they exist, opposition political parties. Hostility generally arises when migrants regard the home government as politically repressive or antagonistic to their ethnic or religious communities. That is why many Filipinos in the United States actively supported Aquino's efforts to overthrow the Marcos regime, many Turks in Germany support fundamentalist groups at home, and many Sikhs in Canada, the United States, and the United Kingdom support secessionist Sikh groups in India.

If portions of the migrant community are opposed to the government of their own country of origin, there will be strains between the sending and receiving countries. The position taken by Third World governments toward their migrant populations is also complicated and ever-changing. They may view cultural and religious linkages with satisfaction (as for the Indian government's promotion of Indian culture among overseas Indians) or with concern (as for the Turkish government's attitude toward the growth of Islamic fundamentalism among Turkish migrants in Germany). The kinds of cultural links that develop between migrants and their country of origin may not only shape relations between diasporas and their homeland but may also influence the patterns of cultural pluralism in the countries in

17. It is worth noting that migrants from a country that permits its citizens to travel abroad to visit relatives are likely to be less hostile to their country of origin than those from a country that restricts travel. Compare the relatively positive attitude of Hungarians in the United States toward their home country in the 1970s and 1980s with those of Soviet emigrants to the United States at the time.

which the migrants have settled.[18] It should also be noted that Third World countries, initially concerned primarily with the flow of remittances, have become increasingly interested in the role that migrant business managers and professionals play in investment and the transfer of technology. The governments of China and India, for example, now actively work with their overseas communities to promote investment and technology transfers.[19]

The greater the political cleavages in the home country, the more likely it is that migrant groups will themselves be politically divided so that different factions of the migrant community will support different factions of the opposition at home. Relations between host and home governments are invariably strained by such political activity on the part of migrants. The home government will be displeased when money (not to mention arms) is sent to dissidents and when its policies become the target of media criticism influenced by migrants in host countries. For example, the Indian government protested when the BBC permitted Sikh secessionists to air their views on the assassination of Indira Gandhi. Similarly, the British government has pressed the United States to take measures to prevent Irish-Americans from providing support of any kind to the Irish Republican Army.

Migrants and the Foreign Policy of the Host Country

Migrants may attempt to influence their host governments to intervene in the internal affairs of their countries of origin—especially to promote human rights, religious freedom, democratization, self-determination, or political independence.[20] Such efforts have a long history in the United States. In the early twentieth century, migrants from Central and Eastern Europe were enthusiastic supporters of President Wilson's doctrine of self-determination, which was aimed at breaking up the Austro-Hungarian and Ottoman empires. Similarly, many American Jews supported the efforts of Central and Eastern European Zionists to create a Jewish state in Palestine. Today, Third World migrants in the United States are particularly active in advocating foreign policy positions toward their countries of origin. Examples include Armenians who seek restitution from Turkey for atrocities committed earlier in the century, Palestinians who want the United States government to support their claim for a Palestinian state, Cubans who press the United States to maintain an embargo against the Castro regime, Tamils who want the government of Sri Lanka to give autonomy or independence to the Tamil minority, and Sikhs who make a claim for autonomy or independence in India. Similar move-

18. For early prescient views on the problems of creating cultural pluralism in Europe as it was being shaped by the presence of migrant workers, see Gary P. Freeman, *Immigrant Labor and Racial Conflict in Industrial Societies* (Princeton, N.J.: Princeton University Press, 1979), and Ray C. Rist, *Guestworkers in Germany* (New York: Praeger, 1978).

19. The governments of mainland China and Taiwan in fact compete for political and financial support among the estimated 30 million overseas Chinese.

20. Migrants to the United States have also played an important role in opposing interventions abroad. Indeed, as pointed out in Robert W. Tucker, Charles B. Keely, and Linda Wrigley (eds.), *Immigration and U.S. Foreign Policy* (Boulder, Colo.: Westview Press, 1990), immigrant communities were an important force for American isolationism prior to the two world wars. However, since the Second World War, migrant communities have been a major political force for internationalism and intervention.

ments have been mounted in Western Europe by Palestinians, Tamils, Sikhs, Timorese, Kashmiris, Greek Cypriots, and South Moluccans.[21]

Migrant groups are particularly active in pressing the United States government to promote human rights in their home countries. These efforts often receive widespread support because Americans are generally sympathetic toward demands for human rights abroad. Filipino-Americans urged President Reagan to withdraw his support for the Marcos regime and to press for free elections. Korean-Americans lobbied for the United States to urge Korea to hold free elections. South African blacks in the United States, although small in number, have had a powerful ally in the American black community in their press for the dismantlement of apartheid and for independence for Namibia. Currently, many Chinese students in the United States want Congress to withhold most-favored-nation status from China.

One tactic often employed by migrant groups to convince host governments to intervene in the politics of home governments is to support the claim for refugee status and asylum by those who leave. Migrants in the United States, Canada, and Western Europe have used these tactics with varying degrees of success. By persuading the German, British, and U.S. governments that they have a "well-founded fear of persecution" and obtaining asylum, Tamil, Sikh, Chilean, or Chinese migrants have in effect elicited formal criticism of the home country governments.

Migrants, as we have already suggested, can also be supportive of their home governments. Ethnic Americans have been extensively involved in advocating positive policies toward countries with which they continue to have emotional ties. German-Americans tried to dissuade the United States from supporting the British and French in World War I; Greek-Americans pressed the U.S. Congress not to provide arms aid to Turkey; Asian Indians have pressed Congress not to provide arms aid to Pakistan; Jewish-Americans have supported assistance to Israel; and African-Americans advocate economic aid and debt relief for the nations of Africa. It will be interesting to see whether migrants and their descendants in Europe will play a similar role in attempting to influence their host governments' policies toward their countries of origin. The support for an independent Croatia by Croatians in Germany in 1991, for example, may foreshadow similar movements by immigrants elsewhere in Europe.

The Collective Claims of Transborder Peoples

In the Third World, the most politically sensitive migrant flows involve peoples divided by international boundaries. Transborder peoples often have a different view of international boundaries from that of governments or other migrant com-

21. Overseas migrants are often more zealous in their support for secession, irredentism, and independence than people at home. An awkward issue for the home community and government is how to respond to the demands of the overseas population and in particular whether to give overseas citizens (and their children) the right to vote. One interesting example was the unwillingness of the government of Puerto Rico and its major political parties to grant nonresidents of Puerto Rican heritage the right to vote in a plebiscite on the future of the island, questioning the "Puerto Rican-ness" of those who left. The island has a population of 3.7 million, and it is expected that by the year 2000, the Puerto Rican populations of the U.S. mainland and the island will be about equal. Many mainlanders insist that they will eventually return to the island and should therefore have a say in its future status. *New York Times*, August 23, 1993, p. B1.

munities. Borders are often regarded as barriers to the day-to-day contact sought by an ethnic group. Ethnic community members may seek to marry, trade, and participate in religious festivals or community holidays across these borders. Furthermore, their merchants, marriage brokers, mendicants, mullahs, and musicians often ignore international boundaries. Consequently, a transborder people may seek to rearrange boundaries so that the ethnic group can be incorporated into a neighboring country or form a new country. Irredentism, secession, and open borders are therefore among the claims often made by transborder communities. The list of such groups in the Third World is long: Somalis in Somalia, Ethiopia, Djibouti, and Kenya; Kurds in Iran, Iraq, and Turkey; Pashtuns in Afghanistan and Pakistan; Tajiks in Afghanistan and Tajikistan; Baluchis in Iran, Afghanistan, and Pakistan; and Bengalis in Bangladesh and northeastern India. Various advocates of "pan" movements (pan-Arab, pan-African, pan-Slavic) have also demanded the right freely to cross international borders, thereby challenging the fundamental belief in state sovereignty held by national elites.

Porous borders enable members of an ethnic group divided by an international boundary to move freely back and forth and to maintain social cohesion; yet one or both governments may eventually regard this free movement as threatening to their security, to their capacity to control trade, and especially to measures to achieve national integration. Even population movements across international boundaries once regarded as benign are increasingly regarded as problematic.[22]

The breakup of the Soviet Union and the creation of independent republics with populations that span the new international borders also open up possibilities for irredentist movements, boundary disputes, ethnic conflicts, and return migrations. Each of these may prove to be a source of interstate conflict in which migrant communities play a significant role.

The foregoing discussion illustrates some of the new domestic and foreign policy issues that have arisen as a consequence of the emergence of transnational peoples and their increasing politicization. In particular, it should be emphasized that transnationals link internal and international politics. A government hosting a migrant population must consider the political reactions of its migrants to making changes to its foreign policy. In June 1994, for example, the government of Japan indicated to the United States that it would be difficult to impose sanctions on North Korea for its violations of the nuclear nonproliferation treaty because Japan's North Korean migrant population (estimated at 250,000) sent remittances (an estimated $1.8 billion per year) to their relatives at home. The Japanese government reported that it was not in a position to impose banking controls on remittances (especially since remittances could be funneled through banks in third countries) and that it was also concerned that the Korean migrants might disturb public order (through protests or even terrorism). Similarly, during the Afghan war, the Pakistan government had to consider the reactions of its many Pashtun refugees (and its native Pashtun population) in deciding whether or not to close the borders to new

---

22. See Myron Weiner, "Transborder Peoples," in *Mexican Americans in Comparative Perspective,* ed. Walker Connor (Washington, D.C.: Urban Institute, 1985); see also Fredrik Barth (ed.), *Ethnic Groups and Boundaries* (Boston: Little, Brown, 1969). *Boundaries* is used by Barth in the sense of a community's self-definition in relation to others as well as in the legal and geographic sense.

refugees or to prevent the return to Afghanistan of armed Pashtuns. It has also been suggested that Germany took into account the presence of its Croatian migrants in setting its policies toward the breakup of Yugoslavia and the recognition of the Republic of Croatia.

THE CHANGING POLICY PROCESS

We return, then, to the venerable notion of state sovereignty and to suggest that it is being transformed under the new reality of international population movements. It is old news that states are becoming interdependent and face more and more international constraints on domestic policies. Global trends in international transportation, technologies, weapons, and the structure of the global economy have eroded earlier notions of sovereignty. What is unique about international migration, however, is that it changes the very composition of a country's population and therefore, potentially, domestic policies. It brings the outside in, as it were, even as it also involves sending insiders out. The result is not merely an impersonal interaction involving monetary systems, trade flows, or acid rain but deeper, affective interactions involving human beings.

As international migration has become more salient among policymakers and as policymakers have become more aware of the international relations aspects of decisions involving migrants, new bureaucratic agencies have become involved in the decision-making process. In most countries, migration had been a subject of concern primarily in ministries and departments of labor and home affairs. But as the issue of migration has become a matter for bilateral or regional negotiations, a shift in power has begun to take place from these agencies to those concerned with external affairs and defense. The bilateralization of migration has also become linked to other bilateral issues—trade, aid, investment, water resources, environment—thereby involving even more bureaucratic agencies in considerations of migration. Consequently, any examination of the internationalization of migration issues must entail a close study of the changing intrabureaucratic relationships in both sending and receiving countries.

Moreover, the issues now raised by international migration are no longer matters for the national governments alone—as any state or local official in Assam or Texas or Frankfurt will affirm. Indeed, as we look at both sending and receiving countries, it is striking to see how many actors have entered into the political struggles over migration. We should end this chapter, then, with a final proposition that the internationalization of migration issues is changing intrabureaucratic relationships and introducing new and often conflicting interests into considerations of policies affecting migration in both sending and receiving countries. In consequence, if scholars are to have a useful input into policy, they must be cognizant of the policymaking process in which decisions are made, the actors who participate in that process, and the political constraints on policies.

The movement of international migration issues to the top of the political agenda and the issues thereby raised both within and between governments is particularly pronounced when migration becomes perceived as a threat to national security and regime stability, the theme of our next chapter.

chapter 6

SECURITY, STABILITY, AND INTERNATIONAL MIGRATION

Security is an elusive concept that calls up governments' concerns to protect their territory and population against threats to the stability of the regime, to social well-being, or to the important societal values of the country. A large influx of refugees or unwanted migrants can strain the economy, upset a precarious ethnic balance, generate internal violence, or threaten a political upheaval at the national or local level. In recent years, migration and refugee issues, once solely the concern of ministries of labor or immigration, have become recognized as affecting a country's security and stability and for this reason have engaged the attention of heads of states, cabinets, and key ministries in defense, internal security, and external relations. The most dramatic example of international migration affecting the security of a state was the exodus of East Germans to Austria through Czechoslovakia and Hungary in July and August 1989. The flow precipitated the decision of the German Democratic Republic to open its western borders, which in turn resulted in a massive migration westward, the subsequent fall of the East German government, and the absorption of the German Democratic Republic by the Federal Republic of Germany. It was flight, not an invasion, that ultimately destroyed the East German state.[1]

Examples abound of other migration and flows that have generated conflicts within and between states and have therefore risen to the top of the political agenda. Among these are the rise of right-wing antimigrant political parties throughout Western Europe; the conflict between the United States and Great Britain over the forcible repatriation of refugees from Hong Kong; the U.S.-Israeli controversy over the settlement of Soviet Jews on the West Bank; the placement of Western migrants by Iraq at strategic locations to prevent air strikes during the Gulf War; the anxieties in Western Europe over a possible influx of migrants from Eastern Europe and the former Soviet Union; the threat by Palestinian radicals to launch terrorist attacks against airlines carrying Soviet Jews to Israel; the invasion of Rwanda by armed Tutsi refugees in Uganda who wanted to overthrow the Hutu-

---

1. For an informed eyewitness account of how the exodus of East Germans in the summer and fall of 1989 led to the dismantling of the Berlin Wall and the reunification of Germany, see Timothy Garton Ash, "The German Revolution," *New York Review of Books,* December 21, 1989, pp. 14–18.

dominated government; the mass killing of Tutsis by Hutus and the subsequent overthrow of the Rwandan government by the armed Tutsi-dominated Patriotic Front; the successful defeat of the Kabul regime, after 13 years of warfare, by the Afghan *mujahideen;* and the large-scale flight of Haitians and Cubans for the coast of Florida. In each of these instances, one or another government was concerned over its internal stability, its international security, or, in some ill-defined way, its national interests.

It is wise to remind ourselves that most of the world's refugees flow to, as well as from, developing countries and that most migration occurs from one developing country to another.[2] Many of these flows readily arouse security concerns: Tibetans facing an influx of Chinese; Fijians concerned over an earlier influx from India; Kazakhstan, Latvia, and Estonia concerned over earlier migration flows from Russia; India's state of Assam concerned with large-scale migrations from Bangladesh; and tiny Bhutan coping with an influx from Nepal. In each instance, there are understandable fears of being culturally or politically overwhelmed.

ALTERNATIVE PARADIGMS

It is the thesis of this chapter that state policies toward emigration and immigration are often shaped by concerns over internal stability and international security. There is a substantial literature by economists on the ways in which economic differentials within and between countries influence migration,[3] as well as literature by political scientists on the ways in which conflicts within countries generate refugee flows.[4] But little systematic comparative attention has been given to the ways in which international population movements create conflicts within and between states, that is, to population flows as an independent rather than a dependent variable. A study of these effects is necessary to understand why states and their citizens often have an aversion to international migration even when there are economic benefits.

A stability and security perspective on policy requires a more concentrated focus on political changes within states as a major determinant of international population flows and on migration and refugee flows both as a cause and as a consequence of international conflict.

2. The best annual data sources on international refugees and displaced persons are *World Refugee Survey,* published in Washington, D.C., by the U.S. Committee for Refugees, and *The State of the World's Refugees,* published in New York by Penguin Books for the United Nations High Commissioner for Refugees.

3. See Sidney Klein, *The Economics of Mass Migration in the Twentieth Century* (New York: Paragon House, 1987); Brinley Thomas, *Migration and Economic Growth* (Cambridge: Cambridge University Press, 1973); Charles Poor Kindleberger, *Europe's Postwar Growth* (Cambridge, Mass.: Harvard University Press, 1967), esp. chap. 9; and Theodore W. Schultz, "Migration: An Economist's View," in *Human Migration,* ed. William H. McNeill and Ruth S. Adams (Bloomington: Indiana University Press, 1978), pp. 377–386. These works deal with the benefits and costs as well as the determinants of migration. For a useful bibliography on the economics of migration, see Julian L. Simon, *The Economic Consequences of Immigration* (New York: Blackwell, 1989).

4. Among the most comprehensive treatments of the major world regions that have produced refugees in the twentieth century are Aristide R. Zolberg, Astri Suhrke, and Sergio Aguayo, *Escape from Violence* (Oxford: Oxford University Press, 1989), and Michael R. Marrus, *The Unwanted* (New York: Oxford University Press, 1985).

A security and stability framework can be contrasted with an international political economy framework, which explains international migration primarily by focusing on global inequalities, the economic linkages between sending and receiving states (including the movement of capital and technology and the role played by transnational institutions), and structural changes in labor markets linked to changes in the international division of labor. The two frameworks have much in common. Both turn our attention from individual decision making by migrants to the larger social, political, and economic context within which individuals act; both are interactive frameworks emphasizing the linkage between migration processes and other global processes; and both pay close attention to the behavior of states and to the importance of borders. A security and stability framework, however, gives somewhat greater importance to state decision making than the political economy approach, which too often regards the state as a weak actor buffeted by larger global forces.

The two frameworks direct us to study different aspects of international migration, to ask different questions, to offer different explanations for international flows, and to create different conceptual tools for analysis. Though they are at times complementary, the frameworks often yield different outcomes. A more narrowly economic perspective, for example, may lead the analyst to regard the movement of people from a poor country to a rich country as mutually advantageous (the former benefiting from remittances, the latter from needed additions to its labor force), whereas a security and stability perspective of the same migration flow may lead one to point to the political risks associated with changes in the ethnic composition of the receiving country and the attendant international strains that result if there are clashes between natives and migrants. Alternately, an economic perspective might lead the analyst to conclude that migration results in a brain drain from the sending country and worsens unemployment and housing shortages in the receiving country, whereas a security and stability framework might lead the analyst looking at the same migration flow to argue that internal security and international peace can be enhanced because the migrants are an ethnic minority unwelcome in their home country but readily accepted by another country. The movement of people may be acceptable to both countries even though each incurs an economic loss. Thus cost-benefit analyses may yield different assessments and policies, depending on which framework is chosen.

Much of the contemporary literature on international migration focuses on global economic conditions as key determinants of population movements.[5] Differentials in wages and employment opportunities—a high demand for labor in

<hr>

5. For a neo-Marxist perspective, see Saskia Sassen, *The Mobility of Labor and Capital* (Cambridge: Cambridge University Press, 1988); Alejandro Portes and John Walton, *Labor, Class, and the International System* (New York: Academic Press, 1981); Stephen Adler, *International Migration and Dependence* (Farnborough, England: Gowen Publishing House, 1977); and Stephen Castles and Godula Kosack, *Immigrant Workers and Class Structure in Western Europe* (London: Oxford University Press, 1973). For other political economy interpretations, see Charles Poor Kindleberger, *Europe's Postwar Growth: The Role of Labor Supply* (Cambridge, Mass.: Harvard University Press, 1967).; Michael J. Piore, *Birds of Passage* (Cambridge: Cambridge University Press, 1979); W. R. Böhning, *The Migration of Workers in the United Kingdom and the European Community* (London: Oxford University Press, 1972); W. R. Böhning, *Studies in International Labour Migration* (London: Macmillan, 1984); Julian L. Simon, *Economic Consequences of Immigration;* and George J. Borjas, *Friends or Strangers* (New York: Basic Books, 1990).

one country and a surplus of workers in another—stimulate the movement of labor. According to economic theories of migration, individuals will emigrate if the expected benefits exceed the costs, with the result that the propensity to migrate from one region or country to another is viewed as being determined by average wages, the cost of travel, and labor market conditions. As a result, it is argued, changes in the global economy, such as a rise in the world price of oil or shifts in terms of trade and international flows of capital, will increase the demand for labor in some countries and decrease it in others. Moreover, the development strategies pursued by individual countries may lead to high growth rates in some and low growth rates and stagnation in others. Uneven economic development among states and a severe maldistribution of income within states may induce individuals and families to move across international boundaries to take advantage of greater opportunities.

These economic explanations, however, neglect two critical political elements in international population movements. The first, discussed in Chapter 2, is that international population movements are often impelled, encouraged, or prevented by governments or political forces for reasons that may have little to do with economic conditions. In fact, international population flows in Africa and South Asia are determined only marginally by changes in the global or regional political economy. Second, even when economic conditions do create inducements for people to leave one country for another, *governments* are often decisive in whether their citizens will be permitted to leave and whether immigrants will be permitted to enter, and their decisions are frequently based on noneconomic considerations. Moreover, governments vary in their capacity to control entry. States that are capable of defending themselves against missile, tank, and infantry attacks are often unable to defend themselves against the intrusion of illegal migrants infiltrating across a border in search of employment or safety. Governments want to control the entry of people and regard their inability to do so as a threat to sovereignty. Any effort to develop a framework for the analysis of transnational flows of people must therefore also take into account the political determinants and constraints on these flows.[6]

6. Among the studies that focus on the political determinants of refugee flows, the most comprehensive is Zolberg et al., *Escape from Violence.* Few other studies so directly consider the relationship between population flows and the political processes within and between states that create them. For a study of the *effects* of migration, especially on foreign policy, see the particularly useful set of essays edited by Robert W. Tucker, Charles B. Keely, and Linda Wrigley, *Immigration and U.S. Foreign Policy* (Boulder, Colo.: Westview Press, 1990); also see Michael S. Teitelbaum, "Immigration, Refugees, and Foreign Policy," *International Organization,* Summer 1984, pp. 429–450. For an examination of how refugee flows affect and are affected by international relations, see Gil Loescher and Laila Monahan (eds.), *Refugees and International Relations* (New York: Oxford University Press, 1989), and Leon Gordenker, *Refugees in International Politics* (New York: Columbia University Press, 1987). Note that the standard works in international relations and in the political economy of international relations do not discuss international migration and refugee flows. See, for example, Robert O. Keohane and Joseph S. Nye, *Power and Interdependence* (Boston: Little, Brown, 1977); Robert Gilpin, *The Political Economy of International Relations* (Princeton, N.J.: Princeton University Press, 1987); Kenneth Waltz, *Theory of International Politics* (Reading, Mass: Addison-Wesley, 1979); Stephen D. Krasner, *Defending the National Interest* (Princeton, N.J.: Princeton University Press, 1978); and Robert O. Keohane, *After Hegemony* (Princeton, N.J.: Princeton University Press, 1984).

A security or stability framework complements rather than replaces an economic analysis by focusing on the role of states in both creating and responding to international migration. The object of this chapter is to identify the circumstances in which security or stability considerations become paramount in how states deal with issues of international migration. We will first describe some of the conditions under which refugees and economic migrants are regarded as threatening to the security or stability of either receiving and sending countries and then describe some of the ways in which states have reacted when facing population movements they regard as threatening.

MIGRATION PERCEIVED AS THREAT

Migration can be perceived as threatening by governments of either population-sending or population-receiving communities. But what constitutes a threat is a matter of perception, which differs from one society to another. For example, an ethnically homogeneous society may place a higher value on preserving its ethnic character than a heterogeneous society and may therefore regard a population influx as a threat to its security. In a somewhat different vein, providing a haven for people who share one's values (political freedom, for example) is important in some countries but not in others; consequently, in some countries, an influx of "freedom fighters" may not be regarded as a threat to security. Moreover, even in a given country, what is highly valued may not be shared by elites and counterelites. The influx of migrants regarded as radicals may be feared by a monarch but welcomed by the opposition. One ethnic group may welcome migrants, while another may be vehemently opposed to them. The business community may be more willing than the general public to import migrant workers.

Similarly, countries differ in whether or not they regard the mistreatment of their citizens abroad as a threat that calls for state action. Some countries are prepared to take armed action in defense of their overseas citizens; others prefer not to antagonize a government that has enabled many of its citizens to find employment and become a source of much-needed remittances.

Any attempt to classify types of threats therefore raises the question, threat to whom? We also quickly run into the need to distinguish between real and reasonably perceived threats, on the one hand, and paranoid notions of threat or mass anxieties, on the other. But even these extreme notions are elements in the reaction of governments to immigrants and refugees. It is necessary to find an analytical stance that neither dismisses all fears as xenophobic and racist nor regards all anxieties over immigration and refugees as a justification for exclusion.

Before turning to an analysis of how, why, and when states or their citizens regard immigrants and refugees as potential threats, it is necessary to note that certain apparent explanations of the responses of population-receiving countries are of limited utility. One such explanation is economic absorptive capacity. It is plausible that a country with little unemployment, a high demand for labor, and the financial resources to provide the housing and social services required by immigrants should regard migration as beneficial, whereas a country low on each of these dimensions should regard migration as economically and socially destabilizing. Nevertheless, using these criteria, one might expect Japan to welcome migrants and Israel to reject them, when in fact the opposite is the case.[7]

A second plausible but unsatisfactory explanation is the volume of immigration. A country facing a large-scale influx should feel more threatened than a country experiencing a small influx of migrants. From this perspective, one might have expected West Germany to regard a trickle of Sri Lankan Tamils in the mid-1980s with equanimity but to move swiftly to halt the 1989 influx of 2,000 East Germans daily or assume that the countries of Africa would feel more threatened by an onrush of refugees and hence be less receptive than the countries of Western Europe confronted with a trickle from the Third World. Again, however, the opposite has been the case.

Economics does matter, of course. A country willing to accept immigrants when its economy is booming may be more inclined to close its doors in a recession. But economics does not explain many of the differences between countries, nor does it explain the criteria that countries employ to decide whether a particular group of migrants or refugees is regarded as acceptable or threatening. The magnitude of the flow may matter, but again, it depends on who is at the door.

A third and more plausible explanation for the willingness of states to accept or reject migrants is ethnic affinity. A government and its citizens are more likely to be receptive to those who share the same language, religion, or race and to regard others as threatening. But what constitutes ethnic affinity is, again, a social construct that can change over time. Australians and Americans no longer regard Asians as unassimilable, as they once did. Many Western Europeans now regard Eastern Europeans as fellow Europeans who are more acceptable as migrants than people from North Africa. Who is or is not "one of us" is historically variable. To many nineteenth-century American Protestants, Jews and Catholics were not "one of us," and today, for many Europeans, Muslims are not "one of us." Moreover, what constitutes cultural affinity for one group in a multiethnic society may represent a cultural, social, and economic threat to another: Note the hostile response of some African-Americans in Florida to Cuban migrants,[8] the Indian Assamese response to Bangladeshis, and the Pakistan Sindhi response to Biharis. Perceived cultural affinity—or its absence—clearly plays a critical role in how various communities respond to a population influx; this is a theme to which we shall return.

There are five broad categories of situations in which refugees or migrants may be perceived as a threat to the country that produces the emigrants, to the country that receives them, or to relations between sending and receiving countries. The first is when refugees and migrants are regarded as a threat—or at least a thorn— in relations between sending and receiving countries, a situation that arises when refugees and migrants are opposed to the regime of their home country. The sec-

7. In fact, when Soviet Jewish migration reached 200,000 in one year, there were "euphoric expectations of a million-and-a-half newcomers within two or three years," wrote the editor of the *Jerusalem Post* (cited in David Bar-Illan, "Why Likud Lost—and Who Won," *Commentary*, August 1992, p. 28).

8. The ambivalent attitude of African-Americans toward immigration is described in Lawrence H. Fuchs, "The Reactions of Black Americans to Immigration," in *Immigration Reconsidered*, ed. Virginia Yans-McLaughlin (New York: Oxford University Press, 1990).

ond is when migrants or refugees are perceived as a political threat or security risk to the regime of the host country. The third is when immigrants are seen as a cultural threat or, fourth, as a social or economic problem for the host society. And the fifth—a new element growing out of recent developments in the Persian Gulf region—is when the host society uses immigrants as an instrument of threat against the country of origin.

REFUGEES AND IMMIGRANTS AS OPPONENTS OF THE HOME REGIME

Conflicts create refugees, but refugees also create conflicts. An international conflict can arise when a government classifies individuals as refugees with a well-founded fear of persecution and has therefore implicitly accused their country of origin of engaging in persecution. In other words, the mere granting of asylum can create an antagonistic relationship. For example, the January 1990 congressional debate over whether Chinese students should be permitted to remain in the United States because of the threat of persecution in China was regarded by the People's Republic of China as interference in its internal affairs. President Bush was prepared to permit graduating students and other Chinese in the United States to remain by extending their visas rather than granting asylum, but many members of Congress wanted to grant formal asylum status to condemn China for its human rights violations.

The United Nations High Commissioner for Refugees maintains that the granting of refugee status does not necessarily imply criticism of the sending country by the receiving country, but this contradicts the conception of the refugee as having a fear of *persecution*.[9] Moreover, democratic regimes generally allow their refugees to speak out against the regime of their country of origin and to send information and money back home in support of the opposition. The host country's decision to grant refugee status thus often creates an adversarial relationship with the country that produces the refugees, even if the motives of the receiving country are humanitarian. In the most famous asylum episode of the past century, Iranian revolutionaries took violent exception to the U.S. decision to permit the shah of Iran to enter the United States for medical reasons. Iranians regarded it as a form of asylum and used it as an occasion for taking American hostages.

A refugee-receiving country may also actively support the refugees in their quest to change the regime of their country of origin. Refugees are potentially a tool in interstate conflict. Numerous examples abound: The United States armed Cuban refugees in an effort to overthrow the Castro regime at the Bay of Pigs and armed *contra* exiles from Nicaragua; the Indian government armed Bangladeshi "freedom fighters" against the Pakistan military and provided military support for Tamil refugees from Sri Lanka; Pakistan, Saudi Arabia, China, and the United States armed Afghan refugees to force Soviet troops to withdraw from Afghanistan; China

---

9. For an analysis of the UNHCR's concept of protection, see Gordenker, *Refugees*, pp. 27–46.

provided arms to Khmer Rouge refugees to help overthrow the Vietnamese-backed regime in Cambodia; and Palestinian refugees received Arab support against Israelis. Refugee-producing countries may thus have good reason for fearing an alliance between refugees and governments that they regard as their adversaries.

Nonrefugee immigrants can also be a source of conflict between receiving and sending countries. A diaspora made up primarily of refugees is, of course, likely to be hostile to the regime of the country from which they fled. But even economic migrants may become hostile, especially if they live in democratic countries and the government of their homeland is repressive. For example, many overseas Chinese turned against the Chinese government in 1989 when the regime repressed demonstrations in Tiananmen Square. Thereafter, many overseas Chinese backed dissidents in China and pressed their host governments to stop supporting the Chinese government. The government of China became increasingly concerned that overseas Chinese could be a force for mobilizing opposition to the regime at home.[10] Numerous other diasporas have sought to undermine the regime of the home country, including South Koreans and Taiwanese in the United States (who supported democratic movements at home), Iranians in France (Khomeini himself during the reign of the shah and opponents of Khomeini's Islamic regime thereafter), Asian Indians in North America and the United Kingdom (after Prime Minister Indira Gandhi declared an emergency), Indian Sikhs (supporting secession), and dissident Sri Lankan Tamils and Northern Irish Catholics.[11]

The home country may take a dim view of the activities of its citizens abroad and hold the host country responsible for those activities. But host countries, especially if they are democratic, are loath to restrict migrants engaged in lawful activities—especially if some of the migrants have already become citizens. The home country may even plant intelligence operators abroad to monitor the activities of its migrants and may take steps to prevent further emigration.[12] The embassy of the home country may also provide encouragement to its supporters in the diaspora. Consequently, the diaspora itself may become a focal point of controversy between

10. In March 1990, the Chinese government sealed Tiananmen Square after receiving word that overseas Chinese, using fax machines, had encouraged dissidents to protest peacefully by gathering in large numbers in the square. For a history of Communist China's early relationship with its diaspora, see Stephen Fitzgerald, *China and the Overseas Chinese* (Cambridge: Cambridge University Press, 1972).

11. For an analysis of the role played by Asian migrants and their descendants in the United States in supporting movements for democratization or for self-determination in their home countries, see Myron Weiner, "Asian Immigrants and U.S. Foreign Policy," in *Immigration and U.S. Foreign Policy*, ed. Tucker et al.(Boulder, Colo.: Westview Press, 1990), pp. 192–213. For an analysis of the political role of other diasporas in the United States, see Yossi Shain, "Democrats and Secessionists: U.S. Diasporas as Regime Destabilizers," in *International Migration and Security*, ed. Myron Weiner (Boulder, Colo.: Westview Press, 1993).

12. On the role played by the Taiwanese security apparatus in attempts to thwart support for Taiwanese independence sentiments in the Taiwanese community in the United States, see Weiner, "Asian Immigrants," p. 197.

13. Examples include conflicts between Turkish Muslim fundamentalists and their opponents in Germany and, earlier, among Indians in Britain who were divided in their attitude toward Prime Minister Indira Gandhi's government after she declared an emergency in 1975 and arrested members of the opposition.

the home and host countries, among contending groups within the diaspora, or between portions of the diaspora and the home government.[13] In this way, struggles that might overwise take place only within a country become internationalized if the country has a significant overseas population.

REFUGEES AS RISKS TO THE HOST COUNTRY

Governments are often concerned that the refugees to whom they give protection may turn against them if they are unwilling to assist the refugees in opposing the governments of their countries of origin. Paradoxically, the risk may be particularly high if the host country has gone so far as to arm the refugees against their country of origin. Guns can be pointed in both directions, and the receiving country, in arming refugees, takes the risk that these refugees will seek to dictate their policies toward the sending country. For example, the decision by Arab countries to provide political support and arms to Palestinian refugees from Israel created within several Arab states a population capable of influencing their own foreign policies and internal politics. Palestinians became a political force in Lebanon in ways that subsequently made them a political and security problem for Lebanon, Syria, Jordan, Israel, France, and the United States. The security threat resulting from the presence of Palestinians in Kuwait was particularly acute in the 1991 Persian Gulf War. Palestinian support of Iraqi invaders in Kuwait was a significant asset to Iraq, for some of the 400,000 Palestinians in Kuwait held important positions in the Kuwaiti administration. The decision after the war by the Kuwaiti government to expel Palestinians reflected its view that Palestinians had become a security threat.[14] During the Gulf War, the Saudi government expelled an estimated 1.0 to 1.5 million Yemenites because the government of Yemen supported the Iraqi regime.[15] In Pakistan, armed Afghan refugees limited the options available to the Pakistani government in its dealings with the governments of Afghanistan and the Soviet Union. The Pakistani government armed the Afghans to pressure the Soviets to withdraw their forces and agree to a political settlement but as a result could not sign any agreement with the Soviet or Afghan governments that was unacceptable to the armed Afghans within its own borders.

Refugees have launched terrorist attacks within their host countries, illegally smuggled arms, allied with the domestic opposition against host government policies, participated in drug traffic, and in other ways eroded governments' willingness to admit refugees. Palestinians, Sikhs, Croats, Kurds, Armenians, Sri Lankan Tamils, and Northern Irish, among others, have been regarded with suspicion by intelligence and police authorities of other countries, and their requests for asylum have been scrutinized not only for whether they have a well-founded fear of perse-

14. For an analysis of the changing attitudes of Kuwaitis toward Palestinian migrants and toward foreign workers in general, see Jill Crystal, *Kuwait* (Boulder, Colo.: Westview Press, 1991), pp. 166–169.

15. An estimated 5.5 million people from 40 countries were temporarily or permanently displaced by the Gulf War. The other major displaced peoples were Kurds, Kuwaitis, Palestinians, and South Asians. Elizabeth N. Offen, "The Persian Gulf War of 1990–1991: Its Impact on Migration and the Security of States" (master's thesis, MIT, 1992).

cution but also for whether their presence might constitute a threat to the host country.

These fears, it should be noted, are sometimes exaggerated, and governments have often gone to extreme lengths to protect themselves against low-level threats.[16] However, these fears are not without foundation, especially in the context of increasing international terrorism.

IMMIGRANTS AS A THREAT TO CULTURAL IDENTITY

As discussed earlier, how and why some migrant communities are perceived as cultural threats is a complicated issue, initially involving how the host community defines itself. Cultures differ with respect to how they define who belongs to it or can be admitted. These cultural norms govern whom the society lets in, what rights and privileges are given to those who are permitted to enter, and whether the host culture regards migrants as potential citizens. A violation of these norms (by unwanted immigrants, for example) is often regarded as a threat to basic values and in that sense is perceived as a threat to national security.

Chapter 4 developed the argument that norms regarding who belongs to a society are embedded in the laws that determine who, by virtue of birth, is entitled to citizenship and who can be admitted into the community as a naturalized citizen. Notions of consanguinity, embedded in the view of the nation as a people with a common descent, shapes the capacity of many states to absorb immigrants. Where notions of consanguinity dominate citizenship law, the government can readily distinguish between an acceptable and an unacceptable influx even without regard to the numbers or to the condition of the economy. Countries with norms of consanguinity find it difficult to incorporate ethnically alien migrants and refugees into citizenship and are likely to have political groups that advocate sending immigrants home even though expulsion may impose severe economic consequences on the host country.

A norm of indigenousness may also be widely shared by a portion of a country's population and even incorporated into its legal system. This norm prescribes different rights for those who are classified as indigenous and those who, irrespective of the length of time they or their ancestors resided in the country, are not so classified. An indigenous people asserts a superior claim to land, employment, education, political power, and the central national symbols that is not accorded to others who live in the country. As described earlier, the indigenes—called *bhoomiputras* in Malaysia, "sons of the soil" in India, and native peoples in some societies—may assert exclusive rights denied to others. Such assertions often rest on the notion that they as a people exist only within one country, while others have other homelands to which they can return. Thus the Sinhalese in Sri Lanka, the Malays

---

16. One of the more extreme responses was the McCarran-Walter Immigration Act passed by the U.S. Congress in 1952, which excluded any aliens who might "engage in activities which would be prejudicial to the public interest, or endanger the welfare, safety or security of the United States." The Immigration and Naturalization Service interpreted the act to go beyond barring known or suspected terrorists to excluding writers and politicians known to be critical of the United States.

(*bhoomiputras*) in Malaysia, the Assamese in Assam, and the Melanesians in Fiji subscribe to an ideology of indigenousness that has, in various guises, been enshrined in the legal system and shapes the response of these societies to immigrants. The *bhoomiputras* in Malaysia regarded the influx of Chinese and others from Vietnam as so threatening as to lead the Malaysian government to reject Vietnamese boats carrying refugees even when vessels were in danger of sinking. Similarly, the Assamese rejected the influx of Bengalis, Indian-born Nepalis, and Marwaris from other parts of India (as well as immigrants from Nepal and Bangladesh), fearing that any resulting demographic change would threaten their capacity to maintain the existing legal arrangement under which native Assamese are provided opportunities in education and employment not accorded to other residents of the state.[17]

Countries in which societal membership is based on notions of indigenousness or consanguinity are likely to have a greater sense of threat from migration than societies that have a political definition of membership. U.S. naturalization law, for example, requires applicants to demonstrate their knowledge of the U.S. Constitution and form of government and to swear allegiance to the principles of the Constitution. Political knowledge and loyalty, not consanguinity or indigenousness, are the norms for membership. It is in part because the United States has political rather than ethnic criteria for naturalization that it has been more supportive of immigration and in the main has felt less threatened by immigration than most other countries.

Legal definitions of citizenship aside, most societies react with alarm when there is unregulated large-scale illegal immigration of people who do not share their culture and national identity. Examples abound. Illegal migration into the Sabah state of Malaysia from the Philippines and Indonesia—amounting to 400,000 or more of Sabah's 1.4 million population—has created anxieties there. Malaysia is particularly uneasy because the Philippines lays claim to Sabah and some Filipino leaders insist that so long as the dispute continues, Malaysia has no right to consider Filipinos illegal aliens. If the Filipinos acquire citizenship, it has been noted, they might win a third or more of Sabah's parliamentary seats and pursue a merger with the Philippines. The Philippines might thereby acquire through colonization what it is unable to win through diplomatic or military means.[18]

Colonization as a means of international conquest and annexation can in fact be the deliberate intent of a state. The government of Morocco moved 350,000 civilians into Western Sahara in an effort to occupy and claim disputed territory.

---

17. For an analysis, with examples, of the notion of indigenousness as providing the basis of group legitimacy, see Donald L. Horowitz, *Ethnic Groups in Conflict* (Berkeley: University of California Press, 1985), pp. 202–216.

18. Concern about colonization can also be an internal affair in multiethnic societies. Territorially based ethnic groups may consider an influx of people from other parts of the country a cultural and political threat. Hence the Moros in Mindanao revolted at the inmigration of people from other parts of the Philippines, Sri Lanka's Tamils oppose settlement by Sinhalese in their region, Nicaraguan Misquito Indians object to the migration of non-Misquito peoples into their territory on the Atlantic coast, and a variety of India's linguistic communities regard inmigration as a form of colonization. In some cases, such settlements can provoke internal conflicts between migrants and indigenes that lead to international consequences.

The Israeli government provided housing subsidies to its citizens to settle on the West Bank. After the annexation of the Turkic regions of Central Asia in the nineteenth century, the czarist and Soviet regimes encouraged Russian settlement, and a similar policy of settling Han people has been pursued by the Chinese government in Sinkiang province and Tibet.

Finally, many governments are concerned that migration may lead to xenophobic popular sentiment and to the rise of antimigrant political parties that could threaten the regime. Under such circumstances, governments may pursue antimigration policies in anticipation of public reactions.

IMMIGRANTS AS A SOCIAL OR ECONOMIC BURDEN

Societies may react to immigrants because of the economic costs they impose or because of their purported social behavior, such as criminality, welfare dependency, or delinquency. Societies may also be concerned because the people entering are so numerous or so poor that they create a substantial economic burden by straining housing, education, and transportation facilities. In advanced industrial societies, services provided by the welfare state to migrant workers, permanent migrants, or refugees may generate local resentment. In less developed countries, refugees may illegally occupy private or government lands; their goats, sheep, and cattle may decimate forests and grazing land; and they may use firewood, consume water, produce waste, and in other ways come to be regarded as an ecological threat.

A particularly contentious political issue is whether migrants and refugees impose high costs on the social services of advanced industrial societies and, if so, who bears the costs. Most studies in the United States, Canada, and Australia report that the costs of migration for the welfare state are not high and that over the long term, migrants contribute their share of these costs through the tax system. But taxes may be paid to the central government, whereas local governments provide the services. Refugees, moreover, may generate higher costs because governments usually provide them with housing and other benefits that are not ordinarily given to immigrants. Illegals fall into still a different category; they may not pay taxes, but they also minimize their use of health and welfare services for fear of detection. Still, there are costs.

Migrants and refugees often have a disproportionate impact on particular regions of the receiving country. Wherever migrants, refugees, and illegals are concentrated, the infrastructure costs for the community, with respect to schools, public transportation, and health services, are often high. In the United States and other federal systems, these costs are often borne disproportionately by state and local governments, which have principal responsibility for primary and secondary education and for the administration and partial financing of health and welfare services. Though the central government determines how many migrants and refugees will be admitted, collects their income taxes, and is responsible for the prevention of illegal migration, local authorities of the geographic areas affected by a population influx invariably bear much of the cost. State and local communities often regard migrants as competitors for dwindling government resources. Some local communities resent using property taxes to pay the cost of schooling illegals and refugees. State governments also view migrants as unwarranted financial burdens on public services. Texas, California, Arizona, Florida, and New Jersey have filed suits against the federal government seeking financial redress for the billions of dollars they have spent on educating illegal aliens, paying their Medicaid costs, and imprisoning illegal aliens convicted of crimes.

The willingness of governments and local populations to bear these costs is likely to be low if it is believed that the government of the sending country is engaged in a policy of population dumping—exporting its criminals, unwanted ethnic minorities, and surplus population at the cost of the receiving country. The United States distinguished between Cubans who fled the Communist regime in the 1960s, whom it welcomed, and Cuban convicts removed from prisons and placed on boats for the United States in the 1980s, whom it did not.[19] After the 1947 partition, India accepted Hindus from Pakistan who preferred to live in India but regarded as destabilizing and threatening the forced exodus of East Pakistanis in the early 1970s. India saw this latter exodus as a Pakistani effort to turn West Pakistan into the majority province by dumping East Pakistanis into India. Governments also distinguish between situations in which ethnic minorities are permitted to leave (Jews from the Soviet Union) and those in which minorities are forced to flee (Bulgarian Turks, Sri Lankan Tamils) and are more likely to accept the former than the latter.

The fears of advanced industrial countries notwithstanding, however, population dumping has not been a significant element in the flow of migrants from the Third World to advanced industrial countries. To the extent that population dumping has occurred, it has largely involved ethnic minorities who have fled primarily to neighboring developing countries.

Forced population movements of ethnic minorities took place in Eastern Europe during the interwar period, placing enormous economic and social strains on the receiving countries, taking a heavy toll on the migrants themselves, and worsening relations among states. But because there was an element of exchange, and minorities moved to states in which their ethnic community was a majority, settlement was possible and violent international conflict was avoided. In 1922 and 1923, Greeks fled Turkey and Turks fled Greece. An estimated 1.5 million people from both nations were involved. In a related population exchange in 1923, the Greek government, in an effort to Hellenize its Macedonian region, forced the exodus of its Bulgarian population. As the Bulgarian refugees moved into Greek-speaking areas of Bulgaria, the local Greek population fled southward to Greece.[20] The world's largest population exchange was in South Asia, where 14 million people moved between India and Pakistan between 1947 and 1950. Because each

19. For an account of the history of Cuban migration to the United States from 1959 until the Mariel boatlift in 1980, see Gil Loescher and John A. Scanlan, "U.S. Foreign Policy, 1959–1980: Impact on Refugee Flow from Cuba," *Annals of the American Academy of Political and Social Science*, May 1983, pp. 116–137. See also Jorge I. Dominguez, "Cooperating with the Enemy? U.S. Immigration Policies Toward Cuba," in *Western Hemisphere Immigration and United States Foreign Policy*, ed. Christopher Mitchell (University Park: Pennsylvania State University Press, 1992), and Felix Masud-Piloto, *With Open Arms* (Totowa, N.J.: Rowman & Littlefield, 1988).

20. Marrus, *Unwanted*, pp. 96–109.

country respected the wishes of the other's ethnic minorities to settle in the country in which they constituted a majority, the exchange took place without causing a conflict.[21] Similarly, the forced exit of Jews from North Africa to Israel in the 1950s was not a source of international conflict, as the refugees were welcomed by Israel.

Paradoxically, the arrival of a relatively small number of refugees may elicit alarms by government officials if they believe that it presages a larger flow. One reason governments hesitate to grant refugee and asylum status to people fleeing economic ills or even violence at home—as distinct from having a personal "well-founded fear of persecution"—is concern that the number of asylum requests would then increase. Policymakers argue that to admit even a small number of refugees because of political conditions or violence at home would be to open the door to larger numbers than the society is prepared to admit and impose social, cultural, and economic costs that neither the population nor the government is willing to bear. Governments may therefore become restrictive in anticipation of future costs.

MIGRANTS AS HOSTAGES

Actions taken by the governments of Iran, Iraq, and Libya all demonstrate how migrants can be used as an instrument of statecraft to impose restraints on the actions of home governments. The actions of Iraq are perhaps the most notable illustration of this strategy. Following the invasion of Kuwait on August 2, 1990, the government of Iraq announced a series of measures using migrants as instruments for the achievement of political objectives. In an effort to deter the United States and its allies from launching air strikes against military facilities where hostages might be located, the Iraqis declared that Westerners living in Iraq and Kuwait would be forcibly held as a shield against armed attack. The Iraqi government also indicated its willingness to treat the migrants of countries that did not send troops to Saudi Arabia (such as India) more favorably than the migrants of countries that did (such as Pakistan and Bangladesh). Subsequently, the Iraqi government declared that food would not be provided for Asian migrants (including Indians) unless their countries sent food supplies and medicines in violation of the United Nations embargo.

Although the Iraqi strategy of using migrants for international bargaining was unique, the mere presence of migrants in a country from which they could be expelled has been for some time an element affecting the behavior of the migrants' home country. Since the late 1970s, the countries of South Asia have been aware of their dependence on migration to the Gulf region and have recognized that any sudden influx of returning migrants would create a major problem for domestic security by causing an end to remittances, creating balance-of-payments problems, threatening with destitution families dependent on migrant income, and introducing large numbers of returnees into labor markets that were already experiencing substantial unemployment. Since the Gulf War, in fact, all of these fears have mate-

21. The population exchange proved violent, as the various communities slaughtered one another. However, it was neither the exchange nor the killings that led to war between India and Pakistan. The Indo-Pakistani war of 1947–1948 was over the disputed territory of Kashmir.

rialized. Sending governments, which are generally aware of such potential consequences, have hesitated to criticize host governments for the treatment of migrant
workers.[22] When workers have been expelled for strikes and other agitational activities, home governments have sought to pacify their migrants abroad—and the host
government—in an effort to avoid further expulsions. In fact, to placate host governments, home governments often remain silent even when workers' contracts
have been violated. Consistent with this approach, the initial reaction of some governments with migrants in Kuwait and Iraq was first to see whether their migrants
could remain and to ensure the safety of their citizens and only later (if at all) to
support international efforts against Iraqi aggression.

More recently, there were reports that Libya threatened to expel migrants of
any government that voted for the UN Security Council resolution invoking sanc-
tions against Libya for its failure to extradite two men accuse of terrorism in the Pan
American Airlines flight that exploded over Lockerbie, Scotland. The target of
Libya's threat was clearly Egypt, which had 1 million citizens working and living in
Libya.

A security threat is, of course, often a matter of perception. What are the
enemy's capabilities? What are its intentions? Perceptions similarly shape decision
makers' assessments of whether refugees and migrants constitute a security threat.
Time and again we have seen that the assessments made by various governments of
the threat posed by a population influx can be quite different. With the rise of
antimigrant right-wing parties in France, Germany, Italy, Switzerland, and elsewhere in Europe, European governments have virtually halted migration and made
entry difficult for refugees from Third World countries. In contrast, the United
States, Canada, and Australia—all traditional immigration countries—have strong
pro-immigrant constituencies that have sustained pro-immigration policies even in
the midst of substantial unemployment.[23] Moreover, perceptions of risk change.
Prior to the invasion by Iraq, Kuwait had a larger number of guest workers than
native workers but did not feel insecure in their presence. But as a result of the
invasion and the support to Iraq reportedly given by some migrant communities,
the government and citizens of Kuwait now have a different assessment of the
political risks of foreign workers and are concerned both with their numbers and
their national origin. Moreover, a country's concern that a refugee influx is the

22. For a description of working conditions of South Asian migrants in the Persian Gulf and the reluctance
of South Asian governments to protest the mistreatment of migrants, see Myron Weiner, "International
Migration and Development: Indians in the Persian Gulf," in *Population and Development Review*, March
1982, pp. 1-36. For accounts of the benefits to Asian countries of migration to the Gulf, see Godfrey
Gunatilleke (ed.), *Migration of Asian Workers to the Arab World* (Tokyo: United Nations University, 1986),
and Rashid Amjad (ed.), *To the Gulf and Back* (New Delhi: International Labour Organisation, 1989).

23. These countries have their anti-immigrant sentiments as well. Patrick Buchanan, candidate for U.S.
president in the 1992 Republican primaries, was opposed to migration, and there is considerable public sentiment for reducing legal immigration and limiting the rights of both aliens and illegal migrants to
social services. The Australian debate is more pertinent for its focus on the security dimensions of migration: Australian advocates of migration argued that Australia's security is improved by opening its doors
to migrants from Asia; opponents have been concerned with multiculturalism and population growth.
See Katharine Betts, *Ideology and Immigration* (Carlton, Victoria: Melbourne University Press, 1988),
and Robert Birrell, Douglas Hill, and Jon Nevill (eds.), *Populate and Perish?* (Sydney:
Fontana/Australian Conservation Foundation, 1984).

result of population dumping by its neighbor—clearly a matter of perception of intentions—is likely to be greatest when there is a history of enmity between sending and receiving countries, as in the case of Pakistan and India. Countries almost always feel threatened if their neighbor seeks to create a more homogeneous society by expelling its minorities—the phrase now is "ethnic cleansing"[24]—but there can be (and have been) circumstances when a population exchange or an orderly return of an ethnic minority can be regarded as nonthreatening by the receiving country.

How governments assess each other's intentions with respect to both economic migrants and political refugees is thus critical to how conflictual population movements may become. A government is more likely to accommodate a refugee flow from a neighboring country if it believes that the flight is the unfortunate and unintended consequence of a civil conflict that if it believes that the flight of the refugees is intended.[25] Similarly, a government's response to reports that its citizens abroad are maltreated will depend on whether it believes that the host country is culpable.

Perception, however, is not everything. As we have seen, there are genuine conflicts of interests among countries on matters of migrants and refugees. Countries quarrel over each other's entry and exit rules. Some countries want people that another will not let go, and some countries force out those whom others do not want.[26] Consequently, how states react to international population flows can itself be a source of international conflict.

CONFLICT-PRODUCING RESPONSES

Facing unwanted and uncontrollable flows of migrants and refugees and unable effectively to seal their borders, governments have often had to adopt threatening and coercive measures to halt the flows. The Indian government pressured the government of Bangladesh to halt Bangladeshi land settlement in the Chittagong Hill Tracts, which had caused local Chakma tribals to flee into India. The Indian government is in a position to damage Bangladeshi trade and to affect the flow of river waters if the Bangladesh government is not accommodating. Similarly, when Burmese Muslim refugees moved from the Arakan region of Burma into Bangladesh as a result of a Burmese government policy of settling non-Muslim Burmese in Arakan, the Bangladeshi government threatened to arm the Burmese Muslim refugees unless settlement was halted. In both these cases, the threats worked to reduce or even, for a while, halt the flow. In another example, the Arab League argued that the influx of Soviet Jews into Israel could constitute a threat to

---

24. The older expression "unmixing of peoples" was reportedly used by Lord Curzon to describe the situation during the Balkan Wars. Marrus, *Unwanted*, p. 41.

25. Europe stiffened its views toward Serbia when it became clear that Serbs were seeking to force the exodus of Croatians and Bosnians; many German officials then concluded that their willingness to accommodate refugees was enabling the Serbs to achieve their objective of clearing areas of non-Serbs.

26. The influence of rules of entry and exit on patterns of conflict and cooperation among states is examined in Chapter 5.

international peace and security under the UN charter.[27] Palestinians consequently threatened international carriers who agreed to carry Soviet Jews to Israel.

Coercive diplomacy to induce a country to halt actions that are forcing people to flee may be more effective when there are collective international sanctions. However, it has been exceedingly difficult for countries burdened by refugee flows to persuade the international community that sanctions should be imposed on the country producing the refugees.

Governments have also resorted to armed intervention to change the conditions in the sending country so as to halt emigration. In 1971, an estimated 10 million refugees fled East Pakistan into India following the outbreak of a civil war between the eastern and western provinces of Pakistan. The refugee flow was regarded by India as the result of a deliberate policy by the Pakistani military to resolve Pakistan's internal political problems by forcing East Pakistan's Hindu population into India. Many Indian officials believed that the Pakistani government was thereby seeking to change the demographic balance in favor of West Pakistan by shifting millions of East Pakistanis to India. The Indian government responded to this perceived threat by sending armed forces into Pakistan; its occupation of East Pakistan forced the partition of the country, and within months India had sent the refugees home.

In two other instances in South Asia, armed support for refugees has been used as an instrument of policy by the receiving country. The Pakistani government armed some of the 3 million Afghan refugees who entered Pakistan following the April 1978 Communist coup in Kabul and the subsequent Soviet invasion of Afghanistan in December 1979. The aims of the Pakistani government were to force a Soviet withdrawal, bring down the Soviet-supported Communist regime, and repatriate the refugees. The other instance of intervention was the initial Indian support for the Tamil Tigers, a militant group fighting against the Sri Lankan government. The Indian government supported Tamil Tiger refugees in India and enabled arms to flow into Sri Lanka in an effort to force a political settlement between the Tamils and the Sri Lankan government. In the end, however, the ethnic conflict worsened and the refugee exodus continued, prompting direct intervention by the Indian military.

The high level of threat or violence employed among the countries of South Asia in dealing with unwanted migration and refugee flows may foreshadow similar behavior elsewhere. The factors at work in South Asia include the ethnic affinity between the migrants and the people of the region into which they have migrated (a factor affecting the decision of refugees to flee and also increasing the anger of the receiving population), the adversarial relationship among some of the countries in the region, the porosity of borders, and the lack of administrative, military, and political capacity to enforce rules of entry. Facing large uncontrollable and unwanted population movements, governments in the region have looked for ways to influence the exit policies of their neighbors.

The Kurdish revolt in Iraq after the Gulf War provides another example of the use of force to deal with an unwanted refugee flow. As Kurdish refugees entered Turkey, the government of Turkey made clear its unwillingness to add to its own

Kurdish population and used its troops to seal the borders. The United States, Great Britain, and other allies in the war used their military power to force Iraq to place the Kurdish region under allied protection; the intervention enabled an estimated 1.5 million Kurds who had fled to Iran and Turkey to return and to form their own government.[28]

With the outbreak of war among the successor states of Yugoslavia and an outpouring of Croatian and Bosnian refugees to Germany, Hungary, Austria, and other former Yugoslav states, there have been calls for armed intervention by NATO or by the United Nations.[29] But the countries most affected by the refugee influx were least able to take armed action, and those that could take armed action were unprepared to bear the potential high human costs of intervention when they did not perceive a threat to their national self-interests.[30]

The large-scale exodus of Haitians in the summer of 1994 provides us with a final example of how a refugee flow can lead the receiving country to contemplate the use of force. So long as the United States was engaged in the interdiction of boats carrying refugees, Washington was content with a policy of seeking to persuade President-in-Exile Aristide and the coup leaders in power in Haiti to agree to a political settlement. But when domestic pressures grew within the United States to halt the interdiction and an increasing number of Haitians sought to leave the country, the United States pressed for sanctions in an effort to force the Haitian leaders to step down. However, by worsening economic conditions within Haiti, an increasing number of Haitians took to boats in an effort to get to the United States. As the flow increased, the United States sought to find other places than Florida to accommodate the boat people, but as the numbers continued to increase, the pressure for armed intervention grew. In September 1994, President Clinton

28. Allied intervention to protect the Kurds is a rare instance of a UN-sanctioned military intervention to protect a minority within a country. For a useful account of the history of the efforts by the Kurds to create a state of their own, see Gérard Chaliand (ed.), *People Without a Country* (London: Zed Press, 1980). The Kurds have reportedly created their own government in the territory within the allied protected security zone; *New York Times*, August 12, 1992, p. 1.

29. For useful brief historical and contemporary accounts of refugee movements throughout the Balkans, see Hugh Poulton, *Minorities in the Balkans* (London: Minority Rights Group, 1989).

30. Who has an interest in intervention for the purpose of ending a refugee flow? Only the country that receives the flows, or others as well? These questions have vexed U.S. policymakers in deciding whether and what kind of intervention is justified in Bosnia and by whom. The Clinton administration has wavered over the question of whether or not the United States has an interest in the war in Bosnia or whether the primary concern should be that of the countries of Western Europe. In February 1994, the United States declared its willingness to take part in NATO air strikes around Sarajevo, with the refugee flow as one reason for intervention. President Clinton said that he had concluded that "our nation has clear interests at stake in this conflict." He offered three reasons: (1) It is in U.S. interests that NATO remain "a credible force for peace in post-cold-war Europe," (2) "we have an interest in stemming the destabilizing flows of refugees that this horrible conflict is creating," and (3) "we clearly have a humanitarian interest in helping to prevent the strangulation of Sarajevo and the continuing slaughter of innocents in Bosnia." He went on to place limits on the nature of U.S. involvement by saying that "these interests do not justify unilateral American intervention in the crisis, but they do justify the involvement of America and the exercise of our leadership." *New York Times*, February 10, 1994, p. A14.

announced that U.S. troops would invade Haiti unless Lt. General Raoul Cedras and other officials of the military regime stepped down. Former President Jimmy Carter negotiated with Haitian military authorities to avert an American invasion. An agreement was signed; 20,000 American troops landed in Haiti; and on October 10, 1994, Cedras resigned as commander in chief of the Haitian armed forces. Once again, we have an example of how a refugee flow can generate an acute conflict between countries.

In each of these instances, the high profile and conflictual nature of population movements has engaged the attention of foreign and defense ministries, security and intelligence agencies, and heads of government. The very form and intensity of response to these unwanted migrations is itself an indication that such population flows are regarded as threats to security or stability. The responses also suggest that states do not regard refugee flows and emigration as a purely internal matter, despite the assertion of many members of the United Nations that countries do not have the right to interfere in the internal affairs of states that produce refugees, even when there is a perceived threat to the security and stability of countries on whom the burden of unwanted refugees falls.

Although the notion of sovereignty is still rhetorically recognized, a variety of internal actions by states are increasingly regarded as threats by other states. The spewing of nuclear waste and other hazardous materials into the atmosphere and the contamination of waterways that flow into other countries are no longer regarded as internal matters. In the same spirit, a country that forces its citizens to leave or creates conditions that induce them to do so has internationalized its internal actions.

A conundrum for Western liberal democratic regimes is that they are reluctant to insist that governments restrain the exit of citizens simply because others are unwilling to accept them. Western liberal democracies believe in the right of emigration by individuals, but they simultaneously believe that governments retain the right to determine which migrants will be permitted to enter, in what numbers. Liberal regimes may encourage or even threaten countries that produce refugees and unwanted immigrants in an effort to change the conditions that induce or force people to leave, but they are reluctant to press governments to prevent people from leaving or to force people to return home against their will.[31] They do not want regimes to prevent political dissidents or persecuted minorities from leaving their country; rather, they want governments to stop their repression.

As a matter of political realism, then, a significant increase in the flow of refugees or of unwanted illegal economic migrants is likely to lead the governments of population-receiving countries to consider various forms of intervention to change the domestic factors that force or induce people to leave their homeland. If nationals of one country violate the boundaries of a neighboring country, they and their government should expect other countries to intervene in their internal affairs.

---

31. However, in a stunning public reversal of policy the United States in August 1994 agreed to increase the legal flow of Cuban immigrants in return for a Cuban government promise to prevent rafters from leaving the country.

chapter 7

INTERNATIONAL NORMS AND INSTITUTIONS

The presumed sovereign right of states to decide whom to admit, in what numbers, and with what entitlements is now constrained by international institutions, international agreements, and international norms of conduct. This chapter examines international agreements and norms in an effort to understand how they are developing and to assess their impact on the behavior of states. We will then describe the conflicts that have emerged between humanitarian international institutions and governments concerned with their own national self-interests.

A simple listing of all the international institutions and agreements that now affect international population movements would fill the pages of this chapter, so only the most important ones will be discussed here.[1]

International efforts to deal with refugees began after the First World War, when the League of Nations appointed Fridtjof Nansen as high commissioner in charge of addressing the problem of Russian refugees in Europe.[2] The League subsequently created a high commission for refugees leaving Germany in the 1930s, but this organization failed to provide protection for Jews and others fleeing Germany. Shortly before the end of the Second World War, the newly formed United Nations created the UN Relief and Rehabilitation Agency (UNRRA) to facilitate the resettlement of millions of refugees displaced by the war. A separate UN organization, the UN Relief and Workers Agency for Palestine Refugees (UNRWA), was given responsibility for the Palestinians. The UNRRA was replaced by the International Refugee Organization (IRO) in 1947, and the IRO was in turn folded into the United Nations High Commissioner for Refugees (UNHCR) in 1951.

Today the UNHCR, headquartered in Geneva, is the foremost international institution with responsibility for refugees around the world. In its efforts to protect refugees, it is guided principally by the 1951 Convention Relating to the Status of Refugees, which was subsequently expanded and modified by a 1967 protocol.

---

1. The literature on this subject is vast. An exceptionally useful recent introduction to the subject is provided by Louis B. Sohn and Thomas Buergenthal (eds.), *The Movement of Persons Across Borders* (Washington D.C.: American Society of International Law, 1992).

2. His most memorable accomplishment was the creation of the Nansen passport, which enabled stateless refugees to travel.

The convention states that a refugee is a person who "owing to a well-founded fear of being persecuted for reasons of race, religion, nationality, membership of a particular social group or political opinion, is outside the country of his nationality and is unable, or unwilling, to avail himself of the protection of that country." This definition is the centerpiece of international law dealing with refugees.

The UNHCR, like its predecessors, was initially concerned primarily with refugees in Europe, but it soon expanded to take responsibility for the protection of the new waves of refugees resulting from civil wars, revolutions, dictatorships, and interstate conflicts that emerged among the newly independent postcolonial states.

Also headquartered in Geneva is the International Organization for Migration (IOM), founded in 1951 as the Intergovernmental Committee for European Migration (ICEM). The IOM, with 46 member states and 35 observer states, functions outside the United Nations system and is concerned with the transfer of migrants, refugees, and displaced persons across international boundaries, providing assistance to asylum seekers and the stateless, and helping those who wish to be repatriated. The IOM initially focused on the movements of populations from Europe to North America and Latin America, but by 1980 its operations had become worldwide. A 1989 amendment to the organization's constitution eliminated all geographic limitations and broadened the range of its activities. During the Gulf War, the IOM assisted in the return of foreign workers stranded in the Gulf region and provided assistance to an estimated 600,000 persons. The IOM also works with the UNHCR and with members of the European Union to develop information campaigns aimed at discouraging emigration.

Although not established to deal with migration issues, the International Labor Organization (ILO), which was founded in 1919, has also become active in the field. In response to the worldwide increase in the number of migrant workers, the ILO has developed the Migration and Population Branch to focus on the treatment of migrants in the context of global labor markets. Furthermore, the ILO, in conjunction with representatives from government, employers, and unions, prepares conventions on the protection of migrant workers with binding obligations on ratifying states. As such, it is concerned with *migrant* policies, not *migration* policies. To date, two conventions have been prepared: one in 1975 on the basic human rights of migrant workers and an expanded version in 1990 on the prevention of discrimination against foreign workers and their families. However, these conventions have been ratified primarily by European countries and therefore do not affect the countries of the Persian Gulf, which make extensive use of migrant workers. The ILO has also been concerned with reducing emigration pressures from specific regions. In May 1992, the ILO, in association with the UNHCR, sponsored a major conference in Geneva to consider how international aid might be used to reduce the need for emigration.

Other international institutions are peripherally involved in international migration issues. Several organizations provide assistance to refugees and to displaced persons in fulfillment of broader responsibilities for providing humanitarian relief or facilitating development. The Food and Agricultural Organization (FAO), for example, provides disaster assistance; the United Nations Children's Fund (UNICEF) provides help to mothers and children in distress, including displaced persons and refugees; the International Committee of the Red Cross (ICRC) also works with refugees and displaced persons; the World Health Organization (WHO) works in refugee camps; the International Maritime Organization (IMO) facilitates the rescue of refugees at sea; and the Office of the United Nations Disaster Relief Coordinator deals with disasters that lead to refugee flows.

The issue of population movements has also seized the attention of a host of other international and regional institutions concerned with issues of development or with the management and reduction of international conflict. The Conference on Security and Cooperation in Europe (CSCE), with its secretariat in Prague; the European Free Trade Association (EFTA), with its secretariat in Geneva; the coordination group known as the G-24 (all OECD states); the UN Department of Humanitarian Affairs; the United Nations Development Program (UNDP); the United Nations Fund for Population Activities (UNFPA); the World Bank; the UN Economic Commission for Europe (ECE); the Nordic Joint Advisory Group; the Vienna Club (composed of ministers of interior from Austria, France, Germany, Italy, and Switzerland); the International Air Transport Association (IATA) Control Authority; and Interpol have all been dealing with migration, asylum, and refugee issues.

There are also a number of regional institutions and agreements that affect refugees. The most notable of these are among the members of the European Union (prior to late 1992 known as the European Community). The European Committee on Migration operates within the Council of Europe at Strasbourg to facilitate cooperation among EU members on migration and refugee issues. The European Union Ministers have created the Ad Hoc Working Group on Immigration, concerned with developing conventions for the member states of the European Union. And within the Organization for Economic Cooperation and Development (OECD), with its headquarters in Paris, the Working Party on Migration has representatives from 24 states.

Since the mid-1980s, countless meetings of European officials regarding migration have been held, sometimes including participants from the UNHCR, ILO, IOM, and OECD and often leading to various agreements among members of the Community. These meetings multiplied when the cold war ended and there was an increase in the flow of people from Eastern Europe. One government official estimated that 60 to 75 intergovernmental meetings on migration were held during the first half of 1992 alone. The object of these meetings was to find ways to facilitate the free movement of citizens among the members of the European Union; to harmonize (a favorite EU word) refugee, asylum, and migration policies; and to reduce the number of people who seek entry into the European Union from outside, particularly from Eastern Europe. This pointed up the need for standard procedures among member states to control their borders; common rules for visas, transit, and asylum; and an agreement as to international burden-sharing (another favorite term) when there were large-scale refugee flows into any one of the EU members. This last issue became particularly acute when war broke out among the Yugoslav successor states.

The two most notable agreements emerging from the EC discussion are the Schengen Agreement and the Dublin Convention. The Schengen Agreement of 1985 provided for the abolition of internal borders among the signatories (Belgium, France, Germany, Luxembourg, and the Netherlands, and subsequently Italy,

Spain, and Portugal). The Dublin Convention of 1990 ("Determining the State Responsible for Examining Applications for Asylum Lodged in One of the Members States of the EC") established procedures governing which state would handle an asylum request, with the proviso that claimants could not turn to another member state if their asylum requests were rejected by any signatory. The convention was signed by the 12 EC states, but as of late 1992 it had been ratified only by Denmark and Greece.

Outside of Europe, the most important regional agreement dealing with population movements is the Convention Governing the Specific Aspects of Refugee Problems in Africa, adopted by the Organization of African Unity (OAU). This document provides a more generous definition of refugees within Africa than that given in the UNHCR conventions. According to the OAU, the term *refugee* applies to every person who

> owing to external aggression, occupation, foreign domination or events seriously disturbing public order in either part or the whole of his country of origin or nationality is compelled to leave his place of habitual residence in order to seek refuge in another place outside his country of origin or nationality.

There are also many bilateral agreements that set terms for the flow of migrants between countries.[3] There are formal agreements between Germany and Turkey, France and North Africa, India and Sri Lanka, and India and Nepal. Some of these agreements simply provide for the free flow of citizens across national boundaries, others provide for the recruitment of guest workers, and still others provide for the repatriation of refugees, migrant workers, and other former citizens of sending countries.

GLOBAL NORMS

Global norms—tacitly or formally agreed rules of conduct by states—have been evolving to deal with issues of international migration. The foremost statement of global norms, the 1948 Universal Declaration of Human Rights, provides that "everyone has the right to leave any country, including his own, and to return to his country." The 1951 UN Convention Relating to the Status of Refugees calls for the protection of refugees who have fled their country. Countering these agreements emphasizing the rights of individuals are other international agreements emphasizing the rights of states to regulate who enters their borders. In general, states retain the right to set the conditions under which foreigners may enter and reside in their territory. The 1985 Declaration on the Human Rights of Individuals Who Are Not Nationals of the Country in Which They Live, approved by the UN General Assembly, states:

> Nothing in this declaration shall be interpreted as legitimizing any alien's illegal entry into and presence in a State, nor shall any provision be interpreted as restricting the

3. These bilateral and regional migration systems are documented in Mary M. Kritz, Lin Lean Lim, and Hania Zlotnik (eds.), *International Migration Systems* (Oxford: Clarendon Press, 1992). The regions described include the South Pacific, West Africa, France and Africa, the Caribbean, and Turkey and Germany.

right of any State to promulgate laws and regulations concerning the entry of aliens and the terms and conditions of their stay or to establish differences between nationals and aliens. However, such laws and regulations shall not be incompatible with the international legal obligations of that State, including those in the field of human rights.[4]

Various international agreements prohibit states from adopting entry policies that discriminate on the ground of race, sex, language, or religion. Documents incorporating these provisions include the 1948 Universal Declaration of Human Rights, the 1965 International Convention on the Elimination of All Forms of Racial Discrimination, and the 1966 Covenant on Civil and Political Rights.

The most important international agreements protect refugees, who by definition lack the protection of their own governments. One category of global norms deals with the prevention of refugee flows. First and foremost, the 1948 Universal Declaration of Human Rights prohibits states from expelling their citizens. Similar provisions can be found in various regional conventions, such as the American Convention on Human Rights (1969) and the 1950 European Convention for the Protection of Human Rights and Fundamental Freedoms. Recent statements from officials of the UNHCR emphasize the "right to remain" as a fundamental human right. Nevertheless, despite the widespread assertion of this norm, it is frequently violated. Moreover, none of these declarations contain provisions for international action to punish a state engaged in mass expulsions.

When refugee flows have developed, refugees are accorded protection against expulsion by the principle of *non-refoulement*. The 1951 Convention Relating to the Status of Refugees states:

> No Contracting State shall expel or return *(refouler)* a refugee in any manner whatsoever to the frontiers of territories where his life or freedom would be threatened on account of his race, religion, nationality, membership in a particular social group or political opinion.

Consistent with this norm, the UNHCR asserts that individuals whose requests for asylum have not yet been adjudicated should not be returned home. The principle of *non-refoulement*, in other words, should be applicable not only to refugees but also to foreigners who request asylum.[5] All who seek asylum, therefore, should fall under the protection of the country whose borders they have entered and not be repatriated while their cases are pending. This particular provision has brought the UNHCR into conflict with countries that have returned asylum seekers prior to review or have prevented entry of asylum seekers by interdictions on the high seas or at airports.[6]

---

4. Sohn and Buergenthal, *Movement of Persons,* p. 3.

5. Ibid., pp. 123–129.

6. UNHCR officials were particularly critical of the U.S. policy of stopping Haitians at sea and returning them to Haiti. In June 1993, the U.S. Supreme Court, in an 8-to-1 decision, upheld the administration's policy of forcible repatriation of Haitians intercepted at sea. The court ruled that forced repatriation does not violate the international law of *non-refoulement* because the treaty does not protect refugees outside the nation's borders (*New York Times,* June 27, 1993, p. 1). In a similar effort to circumvent the norm of *non-refoulement,* several European governments (including France and the Netherlands) have declared areas of their main airports "international territory" so that they can return travelers without visas who might otherwise seek an asylum hearing.

There are qualifications to the rule of *non-refoulement*. The 1951 Convention on Refugees states that individuals may be excluded from a country if they represent a danger to the security of that country. It is reasonable, therefore, for governments to distinguish between individuals fleeing from terror and individuals who are terrorists, though as a practical matter it is difficult for governments to make such a distinction when they are overwhelmed with large numbers of claimants for asylum.[7] Furthermore, the 1967 Declaration on Territorial Asylum states that a mass influx of persons may constitute a danger to the country.[8] It is also somewhat unclear whether the principle of *non-refoulement* applies only to those who have been found to be refugees under the convention or whether it should also be applied to individuals whose safety is at risk, even if they are not personally subject to persecution.

It is important to note what has not been included in the international, regional, and bilateral agreements. Internal population movements—including the movement of displaced persons—are treated as the exclusive authority of sovereign states. The UNHCR, the International Red Cross, and other international bodies are precluded from entering a country to deal with displaced populations unless permitted to do so by the affected state. This barrier was broken in 1991 when a UN resolution empowered the UNHCR to provide assistance to the Kurds in Iraq over the objections of the Iraqi government. However, no international agreement sets the conditions under which international institutions can intervene over the objections of states.

In addition, with a few important exceptions, international agreements do not take away the power of states to regulate the flow of migrant workers. States are free to decide who should enter and in what numbers, but international agreements govern the rights and benefits that states should provide to all who are admitted—rules, as noted earlier, pertaining not to the right of migration but to the rights of migrants.

THE CRISIS OF INTERNATIONAL INSTITUTIONS

The growing global crisis in international population movements has led the UNHCR to expand its focus from refugees to a wider range of migration issues. The UNHCR's initial responsibility was to work in countries of asylum to protect people in flight, but it now works in countries of origin. In effect, the UNHCR has become a humanitarian assistance and human rights institution, concerned with the violations of human rights and humanitarian needs within states. This transformation has largely taken place since the end of the cold war, especially with the pas-

---

7. Overwhelmed by the number of people who sought asylum into the United States (150,000 people from 154 countries in 1993), officials of the Immigration and Naturalization Service say that they cannot cope with the growing number of legitimate and illegitimate asylum seekers or readily distinguish victims of political terror from potential terrorists. In an effort to finance the costs as well as to slow the flow to a number that can be managed by asylum review officers, the INS imposed fees on asylum seekers and said that it would delay issuing work permits for 150 days. *New York Times*, February 17, 1994, p. 1.

8. Sohn and Buergenthal, *Movement of Persons*, pp. 131–133.

sage of Security Council Resolution 688 on the Kurds in Iraq and, subsequently, in response to developments in the former Yugoslavia.

UNHCR involvement in Iraq began in April 1991, when the Security Council demanded that Iraq allow international humanitarian assistance organizations to move into "safety zones," under the military protection of the UN coalition. The Security Council concluded that the Iraqi government had launched an attack against its own Kurdish citizens in an effort to subdue them and to force them, if possible, to leave the country. A memorandum of understanding was negotiated between the United Nations and the government of Iraq under which the Iraqi government consented to a UNHCR presence in northern Iraq. This was the first time that the UN Security Council had intervened to protect citizens against their own state, thus establishing a precedent for UN action. The UNHCR and the UN Department of Humanitarian Affairs were then charged with responsibility for providing humanitarian assistance to all who lived in the safe havens so that they would not be forced to leave Iraq.

More recently, the UNHCR has become actively involved in the Balkans. In May 1992, following the breakup of Yugoslavia, the Security Council passed Resolution 752, calling for humanitarian assistance to war-ravaged Bosnia-Herzegovina, backed by UN peacekeepers (UNPROFOR). The UNHCR again took on the role of providing such assistance, under the protection of some 6,000 UNPROFOR troops. As the conflict in Bosnia progressed, the UNHCR faced a major dilemma, concisely expressed by Dr. Sadako Ogata, the UN High Commissioner for Refugees: "To what extent do we persuade people to remain where they are, when that could well jeopardize their lives and liberties? On the other hand, if we help them to move, do we not become an accomplice to 'ethnic cleansing'?"[9] Ogata concluded that the UNHCR had to combine preventive protection in areas of origin with temporary asylum in other countries when people could no longer safely remain at home.

In addition to its activities in Iraq and Yugoslavia, the UNHCR also turned its attention to the question of how best to protect refugees who have returned home—particularly when the conditions at home remain unsatisfactory. In Sri Lanka, El Salvador, Afghanistan, and Angola, refugees returned to violent conditions; in the Horn of Africa, food shortages were still acute; and in Cambodia, human rights concerns remained. As refugees returned home in each of these countries, the UNHCR enlisted the aid of other UN agencies and nongovernmental organizations to assist the former refugees in reconstruction and development, including resuming agriculture, rebuilding bridges and roads, establishing credit institutions, and arranging for shipments of seeds, fertilizers, and pesticides. The UNHCR assumed these varied tasks because the UN Security Council needed an agency that had the staff and experience to work in the field; could provide food, housing, and medical assistance to people in need; and was in a position to work

9. Sadako Ogata, lecture at the Royal Institute for International Relations, Brussels, November 25, 1992.

closely with the secretary general of the United Nations in providing in-country protection and assistance in conjunction with UN peacekeeping operations.[10]

Changes in the activities of the UNHCR reflect changes in attitudes on the part of the United Nations itself and the wider international community. For the United Nations, "humanitarian intervention" has come to mean, in large part, protecting citizens against their own states. Thus the term *intervention,* once suggestive of an imperial act, has now come to encompass the notion of protection in relation to human rights.[11] Consistent with this shift, the UNHCR's role with respect to displaced persons has expanded from *assistance* to encompass the notion of *protection,* a concept hitherto reserved for refugees who lacked the protection of their home government. This transformation in the role of the UNHCR meant an erosion of the principle that the United Nations would not intervene in the internal affairs of states. Indeed, as the UNHCR increasingly became involved in providing humanitarian assistance, monitoring human rights violations, and protecting people their home country, it became apparent that it had gone well beyond its original mandate. Current UNHCR efforts to prevent refugee flows and establish an early-warning system are likely to involve further interventions in the internal political processes of states to protect the human rights of individuals and communities.

Thus by the early 1990s, the UNHCR found itself with a broad agenda: humanitarian assistance, the protection of human rights, reconstruction and development, monitoring the relationship between population movements and the environment, and promoting economic assistance to regions that might otherwise produce refugees and internally displaced persons. These activities are a far cry from the agency's role when it was created in 1951. But even as the UNHCR became more deeply involved in the internal affairs of states under the guise of humanitarianism linked to peacekeeping, Sadako Ogata noted that "humanitarianism can create space and time for political action and can further its implementation, but it can never be a substitute for it."

EUROPE VERSUS THE UNHCR

As the UNHCR's activities expanded, so did the potential for conflict between the UN organization and individual governments. One instance in which UNHCR policies conflicted with governments occurred as a result of the increasing influx of refugees and asylum claimants into Western Europe. Neither states nor international institutions were adequately prepared to cope with the major migration flows

10. Following the Iraqi invasion of Kuwait, the United Nations also created the Department of Humanitarian Affairs (DHA) under the secretary general to coordinate humanitarian relief operations, replacing the United Nations Disaster Relief Coordinator, whose primary concern had been with natural disasters, but the new organization was not given the capacity to conduct field operations.

11. For an analysis of how these norms of intervention have changed, see Laura W. Reed and Carl Kaysen (eds.), *Emerging Norms of Justified Intervention* (Cambridge, Mass.: American Academy of Arts and Sciences, 1993).

that began in the mid-1980s, first from the Third World and subsequently from Eastern Europe. Two types of people were on the move—refugees and the poor. Western Europe found itself facing a flood of asylum claimants, some of whom had a well-founded fear of persecution and thus fit the UN Convention definition of refugees, some of whom were fleeing from war and violence, and some of whom claimed asylum but were primarily seeking a better place to live. Moreover, many in the Third World who did have a legitimate claim to asylum preferred to seek asylum in the more prosperous countries of Western Europe than among their poor neighbors.

As the number of asylum seekers grew, it became increasingly difficult to sort out who qualified. It took longer to review cases, and the costs of providing relief to those awaiting review escalated. Further, when the review process was completed, governments were uneasy about sending back individuals whose claims for asylum had been rejected. This lack of a commitment to repatriate, combined with a review process that could take months or years, in turn enabled many asylum seekers to drift into an underground labor market. In consequence, antiforeign sentiment grew throughout Western Europe, and the distinctions between guest workers, their locally born children, legitimate asylum seekers, individuals with unfounded claims for asylum, and illegal migrants became blurred in the rhetoric of xenophobic political leaders. European governments were politically alarmed. Until the late 1980s, they had to deal with only a trickle of refugees from Eastern Europe while the UNHCR focused on refugees outside of Europe. With the breakup of Yugoslavia and the wars in Croatia and Bosnia, however, the number of asylum claimants increased so dramatically that the individual states of Western Europe and the European Community as a whole were administratively unprepared.

Meanwhile, the UNHCR, as described earlier, became the humanitarian arm of the Security Council to provide assistance in the former states of Yugoslavia. Though its task was to help people remain by providing assistance, it did not at the same time prevent people from leaving. This ran contrary to the hopes and wishes of the countries of Western Europe, which were eager to induce people to remain in their home countries. As a result, barriers to entry were raised throughout Western Europe. Furthermore, many Western European governments criticized the UNHCR's traditional mission of providing assistance and protection in the country of asylum as a stimulus to migration. They preferred a more direct focus on the alternative of humanitarian assistance and in-country protection.

It also became clear that European governments and the UNHCR did not see eye to eye on asylum seekers. The UNHCR staff regarded the majority of asylum seekers as in need of international protection. They took the position that all asylum seekers should receive a full review by host countries according to recommended UNHCR procedures, that individuals who did not meet the definition of refugee under the 1951 convention and 1967 protocol should nonetheless be given temporary asylum if they came from areas of armed conflict and internal upheavals, and that the industrial countries should address the root causes of refugee problems. The UNHCR is also committed to the concept that claimants for asylum who are rejected because they lack a "well-founded fear of persecution" should nevertheless not be sent home if their lives and freedom are in danger. The vast majority of individuals who sought asylum in Western Europe in the late 1980s and early

1990s had their claims rejected as not qualifying under the "well-founded fear of persecution" criterion. Although many of these asylum claimants were permitted to stay on a temporary basis on the grounds that they fled from countries of violence, others were rejected and told to go home. A debate ensued regarding whether rejected asylum seekers should be forcibly repatriated irrespective of their wishes and the principle of *non-refoulement.* UNHCR officials emphasized that the refugees should decide themselves if it was safe; many European governments argued that the judgment to return home should be made by the government.

These conflicts between the UNHCR and European governments persuaded many European leaders that none of the international institutions could satisfactorily assist them in sorting out their refugee and migration concerns. As one European official said privately, "Geneva, where the IOM, the UNHCR, the ILO, the ICRC, and the Human Rights Commission are located, is the humanitarian city. Humanitarian agencies won't do what governments need to do. Our problems can't be handled in Geneva."

Consequently, the countries of Western Europe took measures to address migration and refugee issues outside of the United Nations framework. European leaders saw themselves as confronting two migration- and refugee-related crises. First, they faced an East-West crisis brought about by the economic and political deterioration of Eastern Europe, particularly the former Yugoslavia and the Soviet Union. Upheavals in these regions had generated a population influx into the border states of Central Europe, especially Germany. Second, they faced a North-South crisis due to economic disparities and political conditions in many low-income countries. Such conditions had resulted in increases in asylum claims and illegal migration into Western Europe. Both these crises raised subsidiary questions: What should be done with illegals and individuals whose asylum claims had been rejected? Should individuals whose claims had been rejected by one country be allowed to seek asylum in another? Under what circumstances should individuals be repatriated?

Informal consultations among government representatives from OECD countries began in the mid-1980s. In 1985, the process was formalized into the Intergovernmental Consultations on Asylum, Refugee and Migration Policies in Europe, North America and Australia.[12] Although this body was officially hosted by the UNHCR, the "Consultation," as it came to be known, was often at odds with UNHCR staff.

The recommendations of the Consultation were soon at variance with the UNHCR approach on asylum issues. In response to the waves of asylum seekers who were entering Western Europe from East Berlin, officials from 12 countries met in February 1987 to consider proposals to control irregular movements and deportations and to increase development assistance to countries of origin.[13] Of

12. The participating states are Australia, Austria, Belgium, Canada, Denmark, Finland, France, Germany, Italy, the Netherlands, Norway, Spain, Sweden, Switzerland, the United Kingdom, and the United States.

13. For an account of these and other meetings of the Consultation, see Jonas Widgren, *The Informal Consultations, 1985–1992* (Geneva: Intergovernmental Consultations, 1992).

particular concern were Iranians from Turkey seeking entrance and Tamils fleeing from Sri Lanka. At this time, Jonas Widgren, Sweden's undersecretary of state for immigration, was appointed to serve as coordinator for the Informal Consultations, which reported to the UNHCR but remained outside the normal scope of UNHCR activities. Widgren established an office in Geneva in April 1987. He negotiated with the Turkish government to control outmigration of Iranians from Turkey and to set a quota for the number of Iranians who would be settled in Europe. Although the UNHCR was opposed to the repatriation of Tamils from Europe, negotiations also took place between Widgren and Sri Lanka on the repatriation of Tamil asylum seekers and the provision of assistance to the Sri Lanka government.

Subsequently, the Consultation met frequently to discuss reforms of national asylum systems. Among the topics considered were the acceleration and harmonization of European asylum procedures; the problems of dealing with undocumented asylum seekers; repatriation to Sri Lanka, Turkey, and elsewhere; East-West migration; irregular or illegal migration flows; and the development of long-term strategies.

With the fall of communism in 1989, the issue of East-West migration moved to the top of the Consultation's agenda. In 1990, the EC adopted the Dublin Convention, aimed at avoiding multiple asylum applications among the European states. Consequently, in October 1991, the states participating in the Consultation developed a country assessment approach, modeled after Canada's and aimed at stemming refugee outflows from selected source countries based on an examination of the factors that led to an outflow. The Consultation report noted the necessity of "removing the causes of migratory movements by an adjusted policy in the field of development aid, trade policy, human rights, food, environment and demographics" and asserted a need to strengthen "support for accommodating refugees in their country of origin." The report said that "migration is now seen as a priority issue equal in political weight to other major global challenges such as environment, population growth and economic imbalances between regions."[14] It added that the declaration of the G-7 London summit in 1991 referred to the "growing concern about worldwide migratory pressures" and "the potential destabilizing effects of uncontrolled migration." Donor states, the report noted, might reduce the migratory pressure through "direct investments, freer trade and development assistance when targeted towards market economy and job creation."[15]

Aid would be conditional on "guarantees of democracy, human rights, women's participation, governance, good environment, poverty reduction and population policies" to ameliorate migration pressures. To apply the country assessment (CA) approach, which focused on the countries with the largest number of asylum seekers, the Consultation establishing working groups, headed by the lead states for

14. Unless otherwise indicated, all quotations and figures in this discussion are from Intergovernmental Consultations on Asylum, Refugee and Migration Policies in Europe, North America and Australia, *The Country Assessment Approach and Beyond* (Geneva: Intergovernmental Consultations, 1992), p. 44.

15. In a more sober tone, the Consultation noted that such an effort was a "20–40-year enterprise, not necessarily to be crowned by positive results."

each target country—Germany for Romania, Italy for Albania, the United Kingdom for Ghana, Switzerland for Sri Lanka, the United States for Russia. The task of these groups was to identify the causes of emigration from each of these countries and to seek to address them "through a modest, concrete, short-term, multidisciplinary approach, thereby involving the authorities of the country concerned in a constructive dialogue." In the Romanian case, for example, arrangements were made to promote nonexodus policies. An IOM emigration advice office was established to deter irregular outflows through an information campaign, funding of vocational training for returnees, and support for human rights lawyers in Romania. For Albania, a food and industrial spare parts aid program was put in place, and a joint IOM-UNHCR information program was launched to deter irregular emigration. Ghana, which offered its citizens educational opportunities but few employment opportunities, required microeconomic restructuring programs to create a more market-oriented economy despite the short-term risk of increased unemployment. For Sri Lanka, attention was given to developing a satisfactory repatriation program. All these programs, combined with aid conditionality, were aimed at both deterring exodus and facilitating repatriation.

The Consultation secretariat developed a topology based on the flows of asylum seekers: (1) countries where individuals left primarily because of economic conditions (such as Poland), (2) countries where there were economic grounds for departures but human rights had improved (El Salvador, Ghana, Lebanon, Romania, Turkey), (3) countries where economic conditions were poor and the human rights situation was deteriorating as a result of conflicts (Somalia, Yugoslavia, Zaire), and finally, (4) countries where human rights conditions were more critical than economic considerations (Iran, Sri Lanka).

Consultation meetings also focused on how to deter illegitimate asylum seekers through carrier sanctions, interdiction at sea, visa policies, accelerated procedures for reviewing asylum claimants, implementation of country-of-first-asylum agreements, and the repatriation of rejected asylum claimants. The concept of the "safe country" was developed to facilitate the processing of asylum claims; safe areas were also to be established within countries of origin where applicants could be sent while their cases were pending.

Publicly, the UNHCR and the European participants in the Consultation minimized criticism of one another. The UNHCR hoped that a cooperative approach would enable it to influence European refugee policies, and the Europeans were reluctant to challenge an institution that held the moral high ground. Privately, however, the UNHCR staffers were critical of what they regarded as the increasingly restrictive attitudes and policies of European governments. The UNHCR opposed many of these policies, particularly the creation of safe-country lists. Such lists, UNHCR officials asserted, are undesirable because countries could be placed on the list for political and foreign policy reasons and, more fundamentally, because it shifts the review process away from consideration of individual claims for protection. European officials believed, however, that the UNHCR was not sufficiently sensitive to the problems they were encountering. After all, the number of asylum seekers in Western Europe had grown from under 200,000 in 1985 to nearly 700,000 in 1992. The total annual costs for processing asylum claims and providing assistance had grown from $2.4 billion in 1985 to $8 billion in 1992.[16] Moreover, only a small proportion of asylum seekers were refugees under the provisions of the Geneva Convention, and despite the fact that a majority of them were rejected, most subsequently remained in the host country. The Consultation believed that the arrival of large numbers of applicants without valid claims threatened to erode the entire internationally established right of refugees to obtain protection. Although willing to help refugees, it wanted to reaffirm the principle that individuals had not only the right to leave their country but also, under some circumstances, the obligation to return to their own country; it wanted the principle reaffirmed that asylum and migration policies were matters of national sovereignty; and it sought to emphasize the principle that states had obligations toward their own citizens:

> In addressing the problem of asylum-seekers who had received a full and fair review of their claims but had been rejected, the Consultation asserted that immigration policies formed part of national sovereignty, each state had the right to decide whether to admit foreign nationals, and states had the right to expel aliens.[17]

Countries with large numbers of asylum seekers with invalid claims, according to the Consultation, should be free to decide whether to return the asylum rejectees or admit them as ordinary immigrants, disregarding their asylum claims. However, the latter option was seen by the Consultation as a potential inducement to filing false asylum claims—a problem that could lead to the collapse of the asylum system itself because recognition rates were already low and there was already a heavy backlog of old cases, rising from 159,000 in 1985 to 560,000 in 1991. The major difficulty was that there were no coherent internally acknowledged guidelines as to repatriation, and many states were reluctant to send people home in the absence of clear support from the UNHCR and from other European states. Moreover, many of the countries from which the asylum claimants came were undemocratic and were characterized by ethnic conflicts or violations of human rights. Asylum rejectees came from Bangladesh, Bulgaria, Ghana, Lebanon, Mali, Pakistan, Romania, Turkey, Yugoslavia, and Zaire. It was also difficult to find rejected asylum claimants, for they often found sanctuaries in places of worship or were

16. According to a statistical survey prepared by the secretariat of the Intergovernmental Consultations, a total of 2.9 million individuals had applied for asylum in Western Europe from 1983 to 1992, with an estimated 547,000 in 1991 and 685,000 in 1992. Germany had the largest number of asylum applications, over 400,000 in 1992, with a total of 1.4 million from 1983 to 1992. Other countries with large numbers of applicants included Sweden (253,000), Switzerland (182,000), France (325,000), Austria (145,000), and the United Kingdom (149,000). The largest number of asylum applicants in Western Europe in 1992 originated in the former Yugoslavia; other large numbers came from Turkey, Romania, and Sri Lanka and from Ghana, Somalia, Iran, Lebanon, Zaire, Iraq, Albania, Bulgaria, Nigeria, and Pakistan. Applicants from the former Yugoslavia have been admitted to stay temporarily on humanitarian grounds since the outbreak of the conflict. There are various estimates as to the cost of providing assistance to applicants during the processing period, with most estimates for 1992 around $8 billion, mostly in the form of social assistance and housing, or about $12,000 per person per year for processing, care, and maintenance of each asylum seeker.

17. Intergovernmental Consultations on Asylum, Refugee and Migration Policies in Europe, North America and Australia, *Toward International Recognition of the Need for Consistent Removal Policies with Respect to Rejected Asylum-Seekers* (Geneva: Intergovernmental Consultations, 1992), p. 44.

able to find accommodations among relatives and friends. Nor were countries of origin eager to cooperate with repatriation. The Consultation secretariat consequently called for establishing readmission agreements between sending and receiving countries, accelerating asylum procedures, gathering country-of-origin information, establishing programs for voluntary return in cooperation with the country of origin, and establishing an information campaign reminding their own citizens of the importance of consistently applied asylum policies.

In the end, only a few of the Consultation's proposals were implemented. Two conventions were signed, the Schengen Agreement and the Dublin Convention, both of which prescribed states' responsibilities for handling asylum requests, but neither was ratified by more than a handful of countries. Several governments, most notably Germany, developed their own list of "safe countries" as the basis for reviewing asylum requests. None of the European countries engaged in large-scale repatriation of rejected asylum seekers. Proposals to use development assistance to deter emigration were implemented in only three countries—Romania, Albania, and Russia (for the Volga Republic). What is striking, however, is the persistent effort of the European countries to seek cooperative arrangements among themselves and, in some instances, between sending and receiving countries, rather than to rely, as was previously customary, on unilateral actions. In this sense, states have accepted the principle that refugee and migration policies are not exclusively matters of national sovereignty and that cooperative arrangements are essential if migratory pressures are to be controlled.

It is also clear that asylum and migration policies are no longer regarded as distinct, with the former based solely on the needs of vulnerable individuals in need of protection from persecution and violence and the latter based solely on utilitarian concerns of population-receiving countries. Though states continue to adhere to the distinction between asylum and migration policies, the European states have become aware that both economic emigration and refugee flights are linked one to the other and to conditions in the sending countries. As the number of asylum claimants escalated, it became evident that large numbers of individuals were using the asylum route to migrate. Consequently, recognition rates have declined; in 1987, some 40 percent of applicants were granted asylum; by 1992, the figure had dropped to 25 percent. Rejected applicants were primarily individuals who were using the asylum route to become immigrants. European officials turned their attention to what they called "migratory pressures," the conditions in the Third World and in Eastern Europe that led large numbers of people to want to migrate to European and other industrial countries. What were the major factors in migratory pressures? Population growth? Deteriorating economic conditions? Massive unemployment? Cheap travel? Instant global communication via television? Ethnic conflicts? The conviction grew that, in the words of the European coordinator, Jonas Widgren, "mass displacements of people are a great threat to regional and global security and peace" and "joint thinking is now indispensable in order to avoid a situation in which states are totally out of control of people's movements."[18]

18. Jonas Widgren, "The Need to Improve Coordination of European Asylum and Migration Policies" (address to the Conference of the Trier Academy of European Law, Trier, Germany, March 1992).

Thus for many Western European leaders, the refugee influx is no longer an issue to be addressed only within the UNHCR humanitarian framework. It has to be viewed in terms of the political and security consequences of unwanted population movements.

PREVENTION AND ROOT CAUSES

In her 1991 report to the executive committee of the UNHCR, Sadako Ogata explained that "a better understanding of the different reasons that drive people to move will help to identify the ways in which outflows could possibly be prevented. I should clarify that I define prevention not as building barriers to stop people moving but as removing or reducing the factors which force displacement."[19] European governments, the Consultation, the IOM, and other international agencies agreed with the UNHCR that if unwanted population flows were to be reduced, attention had to be given to conditions in the countries of origin. Thus new buzzwords have emerged in the international community—"root causes," "safety zones," "safe havens," "prevention," "in-country protection," "humanitarian assistance," "human rights," and "measures to avert leaving"—all euphemisms for various types of interventions in the internal affairs of states. The language of sovereignty has increasingly been replaced with notions of international solidarity and the language of intervention.

The UNHCR, along with other international organizations, is constrained as to the nature of its intervention in the internal affairs of states. Indeed, it is technically precluded from intervention—though in practice its officials often act independently of the wishes of the states within which they work. Prevention engages the UNHCR with populations that may seek to exit because of poverty, droughts, or famines as well as civil conflicts. A concern with prevention thus overlaps the responsibilities of the UNDP, UNICEF, the World Food Organization, and all international institutions concerned with development. As the UNHCR has turned to prevention, it has increasingly collaborated with these other UN agencies concerned with relief or development.

The UNHCR field staff is less tied to traditional notions of sovereignty than other UN agencies. To alleviate the suffering of refugees, it traditionally works with local nongovernmental organizations and local authorities, often without clearance from the central government. In several instances, the UNHCR has provided sanctuaries and other forms of safe zones without the sanction of governments. Other UN agencies are less well equipped to take on these responsibilities. The UN Human Rights Commission is little more than an annual meeting for passing resolutions; it has no field staff and no authority to deal with human rights abuses. The International Labor Organization is concerned with the rights of migrant workers, not refugees, and its field staff is insufficient even to monitor abuses of workers' rights.

19. Sadako Ogata, statement to the forty-first session of the Executive Committee of the UNHCR, October, 1991.

The term *prevention* has taken on a variety of meanings, often only vaguely related to an analysis of the determinants ("root causes") of population movements. Prevention now includes the following activities:

- International efforts to settle disputes peacefully within and among states, including any preventive diplomacy to forestall potential refugee-generating situations before flight takes place.
- The creation of early-warning mechanisms for situations likely to generate refugee flights—especially on violations of human rights within countries. These include the use of observers from UN agencies in the field, the international media, and international human rights organizations such as Amnesty International. By monitoring human rights within countries, the international community may be able to put pressure on countries that violate human rights or persecute minorities.
- Humanitarian assistance to internally displaced populations disturbed by human or natural disasters. The focus of such efforts is to enable people to remain in safety in their own homes. The UN high commissioner speaks of the right not to become a refugee or to be coercively displaced: "The right to remain, and the right to return home in safety and dignity, must be given equal importance with the right to seek asylum."[20]
- The establishment under international protection of "safety zones" within countries for internally displaced persons or for communities threatened by violence.
- Improved observance of human rights standards in countries of origin so as to enable refugees to return home safely.

To many observers, these statements regarding prevention constitute little more than the familiar rhetoric of international institutions and are unrelated to the realities of international politics. Who will settle disputes within countries? Who will enforce human rights? Will international agencies provide humanitarian assistance over the objections of governments? Who will enforce safety zones? Who will ensure the safety of rejected or repatriated refugees? Can UN agencies take on any of these responsibilities without the backing of the Security Council? And can UN agencies carry on these tasks without military backing?

THE INTERNATIONAL EXPERIENCE

Of the various efforts by international organizations to prevent or reduce refugee flows, four are particularly noteworthy: (1) the UNHCR's work with displaced persons, (2) the efforts by the UNHCR and other UN agencies to disseminate information on violations of human rights, (3) the IOM information program to deter individuals from leaving their country, and (4) the IOM program to repatriate rejected asylum seekers.

20. Sadako Ogata, statement to the forty-ninth session of the Commission on Human Rights, Geneva, March 3, 1993.

Work with Internally Displaced Persons

In 1992, it was estimated that the number of internally displaced persons world-wide exceeded 24 million and that refugees numbered approximately 18 million. A major concern of the UNHCR has been to provide sufficient relief and protection to the internally displaced so that they would not become international refugees. Its in-country humanitarian assistance programs in Bosnia and elsewhere helped many people in distress remain at home or move to safe areas within their own country. However, without military protection, the UNHCR cannot provide adequate assistance and protection in the midst of armed conflict. It can more readily provide humanitarian assistance to displaced persons in circumstances of drought, famine, and other disasters when neither the government nor any major armed group is hostile to its presence.

Information on Human Rights Violations

The UNHCR and other UN agencies are active in collecting and disseminating information on the violation of human rights, including the mistreatment of minorities. The UNHCR now maintains a computerized database into which it places reports on human rights violations from both its own field agencies and other international institutions, including nongovernmental organizations. The UNHCR provides this information to the media, governments, and nongovernment organizations in the hope that its dissemination will serve to deter regimes from further violations of human rights.

Information for Deterrence

The IOM's major contribution to preventing refugee flows has been to use information for deterrence. Through radio, television, and the print media, the IOM urges would-be migrants and refugees not to leave their country by reporting on new international assistance to their countries and describing the difficulties encountered by individuals who have attempted to emigrate. The IOM had some impact on Vietnam, where a development package was put in place and where would-be boat people were informed that they would be repatriated. But in Albania and Romania, where objective material conditions remain poor and from which flight is comparatively easy, the information campaign has had less success in deterring emigration.

Repatriation of Rejected Asylum Seekers

Closely related to the deterrence program is the IOM program to repatriate individuals who have been denied asylum by a host country. After governments inform screened-out asylum seekers that they may be forcibly repatriated, the IOM offers assistance to enable individuals to reintegrate in the home country. The IOM insists that individuals declare that they have made a voluntary decision to return, for the IOM will not physically remove people, but the threat of deportation and the promise of financial assistance may be applied to induce a "voluntary" decision to return. As one IOM official bluntly (and privately) explained, "Governments do the dirty work of threatening forcible repatriation so that the IOM can arrange a 'voluntary' return with financial assistance. We do not physically remove people—that's the job of governments. We provide postreturn assistance." Several such programs were put in place by the IOM in the 1980s with support from the governments of Switzerland and Italy for the return of unsuccessful Chilean asylum seekers. The IOM has been negotiating the establishment of similar programs with other European governments.

The IOM view on repatriation, which is widely shared by governments, is that individuals whose claims for asylum have been rejected through appropriate legal procedures should be regarded as illegal aliens; in other words, they should no longer be regarded in the context of a refugee protection regime but rather in the context of a migration regime.[21] The IOM agrees with European governments that it is within the sovereign rights of states to remove these aliens from their territory. As illegal aliens, they could either voluntarily return home or be forcibly removed by the government. However, in practice, the problem is more complicated in that rejected asylum seekers may need assistance such as transportation home, food and shelter when they return home, and even some protection if their departure and request for asylum have antagonized their home government. Governments are often concerned that the human rights of returnees be respected by the home country—particularly that returnees not be subjected to punishment, harassment, or degrading treatment that might then impel them, this time justifiably, again to seek asylum. For these reasons, countries that reject refugees may be prepared to provide assistance once the principle of return is reaffirmed.

Thus the IOM return program, in collaboration with host countries, focuses on whether there are appropriate safeguards for returning asylum seekers. Can there be an organized return program, with material assistance, that will enable significant numbers of rejected asylum seekers to be reintegrated into their home country? Will deported individuals be accepted by their country of origin? Although nonrefugees are free to go to any country that will accept them, in practice, only their home country is likely to do so or is legally obligated to readmit them.

Both the IOM and the host countries hope that effective repatriation programs will also serve to deter economic migrants who believe that they can use the asylum route to gain permanent entry into another country. Moreover, if repatriated individuals prove not to be at risk, it becomes easier for countries to reject others who claim asylum. The risk in the IOM program is that financial assistance to rejected asylum seekers could induce individuals to cross the border for the purpose of being repatriated with a financial handout.

Limited as these various programs may be in their overall impact, they nonetheless represent a modest effort by international organizations to reduce unwanted population movements. International institutions are thus attempting to respond to government concerns that population flows are not only a humanitarian

---

21. International Organization for Migration, *Policies and Practices with Respect to Rejected Asylum-Seekers* (Geneva: International Organization for Migration, 1992).

matter but often also a threat to national interests requiring international responses. At present, however, international organizations continue to have greater influence in imposing constraints on the states that receive refugees and immigrants than on states that produce them. Ironically, for many years, Western governments focused on how best to persuade authoritarian countries to permit their citizens to leave. Now the focus has shifted to how best to assist, persuade, induce, or force authoritarian regimes and weak states to change internal conditions and encourage people to stay. Consequently, international institutions are shifting their attention from population-receiving to population-exporting countries, but how effective they can be remains uncertain.

chapter 8

THE MORAL CRISIS

What would be an appropriate *moral* response to a boatload of Bosnians landing on the U.S. coast in search of asylum from their violent homeland? What if the boat contained Chinese claiming asylum on the grounds that their government forbids them from having more than one child? Or unemployed Ghanaians looking for jobs? Or Iraqi Kurdish families concerned about the future of their children? Or Chakmas from Bangladesh who had been pushed off their land? Or Haitians impoverished by a depressed economy and afraid of violence from local thugs? Should some be admitted and some repatriated, depending on the *reasons* for their migrations, or should they all be admitted because they underwent *hardships* coming long distances by sea?

What if these would-be migrants went instead to Western Europe or to developing countries such as Nigeria, India, Mexico, or Turkey or to densely populated Japan or tiny Israel? Should the moral response be the same? Would it matter if many of the migrants were clearly well-off and educated, hoping to find better jobs at higher wages?

In short, do all countries, irrespective of their size, density, economies, polities, social structure, and political ideologies, have the same moral obligations with respect to whom they ought to admit? Or do the United States, Canada, and Australia have a different set of obligations from the countries of Western Europe or the Third World because they are traditional countries of immigration? Are there some universal moral obligations, or are moral obligations incumbent on certain political systems (liberal democracies) but not others, certain economies (well-to-do capitalist countries) but not others, and certain societies (already multiethnic or with a history of migration) but not others?

Some government officials assert that these are fruitless questions. The needs and interests of individual countries, they say, supersede the needs of migrants. Each country, it is argued, should decide on the basis of its own interests and its own moral standards which people to admit, how many, and from where. Morality stops at national borders.

The current political debate, however, suggests that even if morality once stopped at the border, that is no longer the case today. Discussions over asylum policy in the United States and other industrial democracies illustrate the moral contentiousness of migration issues. Some government officials argue that asylum procedures should take place offshore. Asylum seekers, they say, should be required to obtain visas from the embassy of the country they seek to enter. (But, their critics reply, what if it is unsafe to be seen going to the embassy?) Immigration officials should also be posted at the airports of countries producing asylum seekers to review their requests. (Would authoritarian governments permit immigration officials at their airports? Could they adjudicate claims an hour before departure?) Airlines should be penalized for accepting passengers without visas. (Should they require visas even from transit passengers who might then seek asylum?) Asylum seekers coming by sea should be halted by the Coast Guard and the Navy and have their cases reviewed at sea. (Will lawyers be provided?) Asylum seekers coming by land should be sent back if they come from "safe countries" where there is no evidence of persecution or violent conflict. (Who will decide which countries are "safe"?) Barriers could be imposed at borders to prevent illegal entries. (Will every vehicle at heavy trafficked borders be stopped to make sure that everyone has a visa?) Asylum seekers arriving without visas should have asylum reviews at the airports. (Could a satisfactory review have been provided to the 15,000 undocumented aliens who arrived at New York's John F. Kennedy Airport in 1992?) If necessary, asylum seekers without visas should be placed in detention camps. (Will these be like prisons, with barbed wire? Will photographers be allowed?)

Human rights advocates insist on onshore asylum reviews. Anyone who enters by air, land, or sea claiming asylum should be given a full review. (How many will slip away into the underground economy before the review is completed?) Asylum seekers should be placed in public accommodations and provided with financial support. (Should this be at public expense, and for how long?) It does not matter if some people enter fraudulently as asylum seekers as long as genuine asylum seekers are protected. (But what if only a small percentage of those who seek asylum have a legitimate claim?) The security threats posed by fraudulent asylum seekers are exaggerated. (What about the terrorists who bombed the New York World Trade Center? Or drug traffickers?)

Clearly, migration policies can no longer be decided simply on the basis of state sovereignty or the idea that a government need only control its borders. Political considerations must be addressed, stemming from concerns and fears of citizens that too many people are coming in illegally and too few are genuine asylum candidates. And moral concerns must also come into play over the lives of people who are genuinely fleeing persecution and violence.

What should or even can be done to prevent large-scale flight from one country into another? What should the population-receiving country be prepared to do? Provide economic assistance to encourage would-be migrants to stay at home? Provide humanitarian food and medical assistance to displaced persons to keep them from becoming refugees? Impose sanctions on a country that is violating human rights and forcing people to flee? Intervene militarily to disarm warlords, stop ethnic cleansing, and impose peace on warring groups? And can intervention even begin to address all the causes (famines, warfare, genocide, poverty) that lead large numbers of people to flee their homeland?

This chapter and the next examine the debate on these issues among political philosophers, international lawyers, human rights activists, journalists, and anyone else who has wrestled with the question of whether the interests of persons who want to leave their country to seek protection or a better life are paramount to those of states concerned with the protection of the interests of their own citizens.

MORAL REASONING AND PUBLIC POLICY

Underlying much of the debate over migration and refugee policies is the fundamental moral contradiction between the notion that emigration is widely regarded as a matter of human rights while immigration is regarded as a matter of national sovereignty.[1] The United Nations' Universal Declaration of Human Rights and the Helsinki Accords assert a universal right of emigration; yet all governments and international organizations agree that governments have the right to determine whom to admit and to whom citizenship may be granted. But if people are free to leave, where are they to go?[2] Are states obliged to take in migrants from poor countries? Refugees in flight? Are they required to regularize the status of illegals? To grant citizenship to guest workers? Underlying many of these policy questions are fundamental moral issues posed on the one hand by the conflicting claims and rights of the people who seek admission and on the other by the concerns of governments and their citizens to control their borders and protect themselves against what they regard as threats to their security, economic well-being, political stability, and cultural identity. Political theorists have traditionally been concerned with defining the rights and duties of citizens and of residents within national boundaries, only recently with the claims of outsiders who seek admission. Over the centuries, political theorists have defined and expanded our conception of the rights of individuals, but always within the framework of the state. As a result, in liberal democratic societies, the right to move within the country has become as much a right as freedom of speech, assembly, or religion, but international law does not guarantee the right of people to move from one country to another. The question is whether the moral justification for freedom of movement within countries can and should be extended to freedom of movement among countries.

Migration and refugee policies raise moral issues because, directly or indirectly, they involve the exercise of coercion. Within countries, restrictions on the movement of people are decried because they are coercive. However, it is also coercion that prevents people from freely moving across international boundaries. Coercion takes place when ships carrying would-be refugees are halted at sea and sent home, guards prevent undocumented migrants from crossing a border, refugees are confined to camps or forcibly repatriated, illegal migrants are rounded up by the police, employers are fined for hiring illegals, and individuals are arrested for providing sanctuary to unsuccessful refugee claimants.

Whenever coercion is employed by the state to prevent people from doing what they want to do without apparent harm to others, be it within and outside the state, a moral issue arises.

---

1. For the liberal view on the right of emigration, see Frederick G. Whelan, "Citizenship and the Right to Leave," *American Political Science Review,* September 1981, pp. 636–653.

2. A Jewish joke makes the point. A Jew with an exit permit from Germany in 1940 went to a travel agent to seek advice as to where to go. The travel agent pointed to his globe of the world. "You can't go to America," he said. "They just turned back a boatload of refugees from Germany. Switzerland and Great Britain have also closed their doors. The other countries of Europe won't accept Jews either because they are under Nazi occupation. Shanghai will admit Jews, but you can't get there." The Jew looked sadly at the globe and said, "Do you have another globe?"

Migration policy also raises the issue of fairness. Citizenship is determined by country of birth or by the citizenship of our parents, not by choice. Consequently, one's life chances depend on being born in a prosperous country or to parents who are citizens of a prosperous country, where opportunities for advancement are plentiful and persecution is nonexistent. Individuals born in a poor, autocratic country where there are few opportunities and where people who have particular beliefs or belong to particular ethnic or religious communities are treated badly are truly unfortunate. The fact that one's opportunities can be so strongly and permanently constrained by the simple chance of birth seems unfair.

As with most issues of public policy, conflicts over immigration and refugee policies typically reflect group and institutional interests. But behind debates over these policies often lie fundamental moral questions and conflicting moral considerations that are rarely made explicit. With the end of the cold war, both a greater moral and political consensus on universal human rights than ever before and a willingness to consider what international regimes might be created to embody and institutionalize this consensus are emerging. But there is also a widespread recognition that international population movements create major problems for states and that states have a legitimate right to limit these flows when their interests are affected. Thus there is a need to balance state interests with moral considerations in the formulation of migration policies.

In some policy areas—mostly notably in the field of health policies and biogenetics and in policies relating to the use of nuclear weapons—explicit attention has been paid to moral questions. The development of the field of applied ethics has been directed not at offering moral solutions to complex policy issues but rather at identifying the moral questions and specifying the trade-offs among alternative moral principles. The task in the migration and refugee field is similarly to extract the moral assumptions from the policy debates, to identify the dilemmas posed by conflicting moral principles, and to suggest how an explicit examination of moral issues can clarify policy choices. The moral issues with respect to migrants and refugees have been transformed in recent years by the emergence of a movement in support of universal human rights, which transcend international boundaries. Citizens of one country may indeed have moral obligations to those who live outside their boundaries; what these obligations are and how we can weigh them against the claims of our own citizens are fundamental issues.

Moral reasoning differs from other kinds of reasoning about public policies. Typically, policy decisions are based on weighing costs and benefits, evaluating effectiveness, and considering political consequences—all of which have moral implications; but this is not the same as employing moral reasoning. Efforts to apply moral reasoning often flounder in a quagmire of conundrums and moral contradictions. Though these often cannot be resolved, we must at least understand what they are.

There is, first of all, the need to distinguish between personal morality and the application of moral principles to public policy. The moral choices we make as individuals need not, and often should not, be the same as the moral choices made by policymakers. A woman may have a moral objection to aborting her fetus, but that is not an argument for a public policy that bans abortions. One may be a pacifist, but that is not an argument for a public policy of disarmament. One may have a moral aversion to pornography, but that is not an argument for censorship. One may be willing to accommodate a poor immigrant in one's home, but that is not an argument for a policy to admit poor people from other countries. Personal ethics are a poor basis for public choices because they do not take into account the costs that such policies impose on others. Similarly, personal benefits, as from policies that permitted the migration of one's parents to a prosperous nation, are not justification for a liberal migration policy, past or present.

It is also important to distinguish, as Max Weber did, between two kinds of ethics: the ethics of ultimate ends, which pursues an absolute ideal, and the ethics of responsibility, which requires that political leaders choose courses that are often less than ideal. Policymakers must consider not simply whether policies are in some abstract sense moral but also whether there is a reasonable likelihood that morally desirable objectives can be achieved. The morality of an act should be judged by its probable consequences, not by its intent; good intentions are not a sufficient basis for choosing moral policies because many well-intended policies have had bad results. For example, a policy that indicates people to take hazardous risks for desirable ends (say, a policy that leads individuals to flee their country in unseaworthy boats) may have morally unsound consequences.

An apparently morally justifiable policy, moreover, can sometimes lead to costly results and imprudent actions. Policymakers may have to make the difficult judgment of whether military action to provide protection for internally displaced persons will lead to a more costly war that will inflict even greater loss of human life. Support for a persecuted ethnic minority demanding self-determination, for example, might lead to a civil war and large-scale violence. Military intervention in another country to halt persecution or stop violent conflict may also, if it becomes exceedingly costly, lead to premature withdrawal that could result in greater harm to the people originally intended to receive help. Similarly, policies intended to reduce the numbers of people who fall into a particular category targeted for aid (poor, disabled, refugees) may inadvertently increase their numbers. Economists argue that we get more of what we subsidize. For example, when governments offer entitlements to the disabled, the number of people who find ways to get themselves classified as disabled increases. The more benefits we offer asylum seekers (legal aid, free housing, medical care, food, employment), the more people are likely to seek asylum. This is not an argument against helping the disabled, the poor, single parents, asylees, refugees, or any other worthy parties but rather a warning that the greater the entitlements, the narrower must be the definition of who is qualified to receive them. Migration and refugee policies are based on definitional distinctions as to who the beneficiaries are. For each category (asylum seekers, refugees, guest workers, permanent migrants), there are specific criteria to determine who qualifies for what benefits. Both the criteria and the entitlements must be clear, and the logic behind them must be morally defensible as well as administratively practical. Poorly defined criteria combined with generous entitlements are an invitation to abuse.

Moral reasoning also requires that we distinguish between unjust policies and injustices in the implementation of policies. Juries and judges may render unfair verdicts, but it does not necessarily follow that the laws on which these verdicts are based are unjust. Similarly, reviewers of asylum cases may unjustly send someone back home to cruel treatment or even death, but the criteria for granting asylum may be reasonable. Incorrect judgments are often a regrettable effect of just policies and can be addressed by improved procedures or better-trained personnel. Advocates of open borders who use instances of unjust decisions as arguments for admitting all who claim asylum are therefore just as misguided as advocates of total exclusion who point to abuses by asylum claimants as grounds to admit no one. Abuses by either the administrators of laws or the beneficiaries of those laws should not be grounds for adopting policies or procedures that are less just.[3]

Confusion over the morality of policies, as distinct from the morality of implementation, often stems from uneven application of the rules. Policies—and their implementation—should not be arbitrary; they should be reasonably consistent and should be seen as based on principles that people in the society recognize as fair. Just as individuals should not be arbitrarily arrested for a crime or arbitrarily freed, so individuals should not be arbitrarily admitted into a country or arbitrarily rejected. Much of the unease over migration and refugee policies is the result of inconsistent and often arbitrary acts by policymakers or administrators. For example, individuals are sometimes granted asylum if they come from one authoritarian state but not from another. Individuals in identical circumstances may be treated automatically by the United States as refugees, for example, if they came from Cuba, but as economic migrants if they came from Haiti. A consular official may arbitrarily give an entry visa to one person but not to another or may grant asylum to one claimant while denying it to another. Policies that are inconsistent, arbitrary, or patently unfair generate cynicism and become a legitimate basis for public outrage.

Not all the difficulties of applying moral reasoning to public policy are generated by confusion over what aspects of policy—outcomes, implementation, or the policy itself—must be just. Incorporating morality into public policy often entails the consideration of contending morals and making difficult choices among divergent values. On what basis, for example, do we choose between helping the poor in our society and helping the poor who live in other countries? It is morally attractive to treat all human beings equally without regard to their nationality, but is a military commander morally wrong to adopt a military strategy intended to minimize deaths among his own troops at the cost of increasing deaths among his enemies, including civilians? Is it morally wrong for a government to be concerned with the effect of the size and composition of a migrant or refugee influx on the well-being of its own population or to give preference to immigrants and refugees with whom its own citizens have ties of kinship and culture? These judgments often offend people who would apply universalistic criteria, but one ought not to render morally meaningless their basis in the ties of affection that bind families, communities, and citizens together. Issues of moral choice are particularly complex when we try to decide which strangers require our help and how we balance our own needs and self-interests against those of strangers and even enemies. These difficult moral choices arise because resources are always limited and because one person's gain often entails someone else's loss.

---

3. A consistent pattern of abuse by policy administrators or the consistent failure to implement a policy (for example, administrative tolerance of illegal immigration) is, of course, a policy.

Finally, the incorporation of moral reasoning into public policies requires that we decide when moral considerations are applicable. Not all issues of public policy involve moral questions, nor are all questions involving migrants and refugees moral issues. It is important that we not conflate issues of public interest, political ideologies, and fundamental moral rights.

Keeping these elements of moral reasoning in mind, let us now consider some of the public policy issues involving migrants and refugees to which this reasoning might usefully be applied. In the pages that follow, we will examine the moral bases of several specific public policies. Two sets of issues will be considered: first, the morality of various rules of entry—whether borders should be open, restricted, or closed; the criteria for admitting immigrants; and the identification and admission of refugees—and second, the moral treatment of the entrants—the rights of illegals and guest workers and the respective claims of settlers and indigenous peoples.

OPEN BORDERS

At one extreme, a country's entry policy could simply be to open its borders completely, without restriction. Though this approach seems to take the moral high ground by avoiding coercion, it is not clear that it is the most just entry policy by all standards of judgment. To any realist, a safe and prosperous country that declared its borders open risks being overwhelmed by a massive influx of immigrants from poor or violent countries. If the country then provides these immigrants with the same benefits it offers its own citizens (education for children, health care, unemployment benefits, and so on), its social and welfare services may be stretched to the limit. The country's own poor may find themselves pushed aside by migrants prepared to work at lower wages. Furthermore, if the number of migrants is large enough, the local population may find itself outnumbered by people who speak other languages, belong to other cultures, and perhaps seek to change the political system. As the number of migrants grows, the local population may very well become xenophobic, resulting in the growth of antimigrant political organizations, violence, and social disorder.

Poor countries might also be at risk if their borders are open. Peasants from densely populated neighboring countries might freely enter in search of land and employment, thereby putting pressure on the local population. Refugees from civil conflict might cross the border and damage the local ecology by cutting firewood, consuming water, generating waste, and destroying grasslands. The indigenous population might become acutely afraid of domination by the intruding ethnic group, especially if the community is one with which it has a history of enmity.

Any country, rich or poor, that opened its borders might soon find other states taking advantage of its beneficent policy. A neighboring country whose elite wanted a more homogeneous society could now readily expel its minorities; a government that wanted a more egalitarian society could dump its unemployed and its poor; an authoritarian regime could rid itself of its opponents; a country could empty its jails, mental institutions, and homes for the aged. In an extreme case, an overcrowded populous country could take over a hypothetically generous country simply by transferring a large part of its population, and an aggressive country would no longer need tanks and missiles for an invasion.

Notwithstanding these objections, some political theorists argue that liberal democratic societies ought to have open borders or that, short of open borders, a liberal democratic country should take in as many migrants and refugees as its citizenry will allow. The primary criterion for admission, these theorists insist, should not be the needs of the host country but the plight of the people who seek admission.

The work of the philosopher John Rawls provides the starting point for theorists who take this position.[4] Rawls argues that if people knowing nothing of their own personal situations (class, race, ability) could choose the kind of society in which they wanted to live from behind their "veil of ignorance," they would follow self-interest and choose to live in a society in which institutions were constructed to benefit the least well off (Rawls calls this the "difference principle"). In other words, inequalities of wealth, power, and income would be acceptable only insofar as they ultimately benefited the society's least prosperous members. In this aspect, Rawls's theory stems from the assumptions of classical liberalism, with its notions of liberty, justice as fairness, and the right to equality.

For Rawls, the "original position" (starting from a "veil of ignorance") is necessary for thinking about the issues of justice within a *given* society, but other theorists have argued that this approach should be applied universally across *different* societies. Joseph Carens has systematically expounded this position in a number of articles.[5] Others who also argue for a universal theory of justice include Peter Singer, Charles Beitz, Henry Shue, Brian Barry, and two British legal scholars, Ann Dummett and Andrew Nicol.[6]

These philosophers and legal scholars argue that it is purely a matter of chance whether we are born in a country that is peaceful, democratic, and prosperous or in one that is poor, authoritarian, and torn by civil conflict. Starting from the origi-

4. John Rawls, *A Theory of Justice* (Cambridge, Mass.: Harvard University Press, 1971).

5. See the following works by Joseph H. Carens: "Migration and Morality: A Liberal Egalitarian Perspective," in *Free Movement,* ed. Brian Barry and Robert Goodin (London: Harvest Wheatsheaf, 1992), pp. 25–47; "Immigration and the Welfare State," in *Democracy and the Welfare State,* ed. Amy Gutmann (Princeton, N.J.: Princeton University Press, 1988), pp. 207–230; "Refugees and the Limits of Obligation," *Public Affairs Quarterly,* January 1992, pp. 31–44; "States and Refugees: A Normative Analysis," in *Refugee Policy,* ed. Howard Adelman (Toronto: York Lane Press, 1991), pp. 18–29; "Who Belongs? Theoretical and Legal Questions About Birthright Citizenship in the United States," *University of Toronto Law Journal,* 1987, pp. 413–443; "Aliens and Citizens: The Case for Open Borders," *Review of Politics,* Spring 1987, pp. 251–273; "Moral Realism vs. Moral Idealism: The Ethics of International Migration," September 1987, paper presented at Annual Meeting, American Political Science Association, Washington, D.C.; "Nationalism and the Exclusion of Immigrants: Lessons from Australian Immigration Policy," in *Open Borders? Closed Societies?* ed. Mark Gibney (Westport, Conn.: Greenwood Press, 1988), pp. 41–60.

6. See Peter Singer and Renata Singer, "The Ethics of Refugee Policy," in *Open Borders?* ed. Gibney, pp. 111–130, and Peter Singer, *Practical Ethics* (Cambridge: Cambridge University Press, 1979), in which Singer extends his argument for universal equality beyond human beings to other species. See also Charles R. Beitz, *Political Theory and International Relations* (Princeton, N.J.: Princeton University Press, 1979); Henry Shue, *Basic Rights* (Princeton, N.J.: Princeton University Press, 1980); Brian Barry, *The Liberal Theory of Justice* (Oxford: Clarendon Press, 1973); and Ann Dummett and Andrew Nicol, *Subjects, Citizens, Aliens and Others* (London: Weidenfeld & Nicolson, 1990).

nal position, we would all clearly prefer to be born in the peaceful, democratic, prosperous society. From a liberal egalitarian perspective, there are therefore no grounds for limiting membership in any society to the people who happen to be born there. Birthplace and parentage are, as Carens writes, "arbitrary from a moral point of view."[7]

Free migration across open borders would enable people who were born in disadvantaged countries to improve their position by moving to a place where they would have greater opportunity. If, by moving, the worse-off can thereby improve their position, Carens argues, the well-being of current citizens is irrelevant. Carens also says that it is irrelevant if open borders attract an influx of a people from another culture or if the numbers of migrants are large enough to undermine the dominance of the existing culture. The claims of locals, Carens asserts, should not be given priority over the claims of others simply by virtue of their citizenship.

> The best immigration policy from a utilitarian perspective would be the one that maximized overall economic gains. In this calculation, current citizens would enjoy no privileged position. The gains and losses of aliens would count just as much. Now the dominant view among both classical and neoclassical economics is that the free mobility of capital and labor is essential to the maximization of overall economic gains. But the free mobility of labor requires open borders. So, despite the fact that the economic costs to current citizens are morally relevant to the utilitarian framework, they would probably not be sufficient to justify restrictions.[8]

The moral argument for free migration thus grows out of the reality that there are gross economic inequities between states. When differences are vast, freedom of movement would enable individuals to avail themselves of opportunities to improve their income and general well-being and to increase their freedom and safety. From this point of view, both notions of *jus sanguinis* and *jus solis* are fundamentally unfair, for they deny freedom of choice. Why should citizenship rights automatically be conferred on individuals who, through no act of their own, happen to be born in a particular place or to parents who are citizens of that country?

Yet even though the arguments put forth by Rawls, Carens, and others make open borders and free movement seem morally clear-cut, contending moral considerations suggest that open borders may result in great injustices. Michael Walzer asserts that it is also moral to develop policies that preserve a particular way of life.[9] Walzer distinguishes between "members" and "strangers"—people who belong to our political community and those who do not—and he writes that "the theory of justice must allow for the territorial state, specifying the rights of its inhabitants and recognizing the collective right of admission and refusal."[10] Countries, writes

---

7. Carens, "Aliens and Citizens," p. 261.

8. Ibid., p. 263.

9. Michael Walzer, *Spheres of Justice* (New York: Basic Books, 1983). An earlier version of this argument, acknowledged by Walzer, can be found in Henry Sidgwick, *The Elements of Politics* (London: Macmillan, 1891). For a similar conception of community membership and citizenship that rests on the notion of consent, see Peter H. Schuck and Rogers M. Smith, *Citizenship Without Consent* (New Haven, Conn.: Yale University Press, 1985).

10. Walzer, *Spheres of Justice*, p. 44.

Walzer, are somewhat like clubs that can (and should) regulate admissions. *We*, who are members of a community, define who *we* are, what kind of community *we* want to have, and whom *we* should admit into it. We can give membership to strangers, but are not obliged to, except under special circumstances.

If someone is in urgent need and the risks and costs of giving aid are low, we ought to help the injured stranger—out of a sense not of justice but of charity. But giving help—which may lead us to offer the hospitality of our home (or our country)—does not necessarily require that we admit the stranger to membership in our community.

Walzer further argues that people who belong to a community will defend their local politics and culture against strangers and that if the state did not take on this responsibility, we would not end up with a world without walls but rather would "create a thousand petty fortresses. . . . The distinctiveness of cultures and groups depends upon closure and, without it, cannot be conceived as a stable feature of human life. If this distinctiveness is valued, as most people seem to believe, then closure must be permitted somewhat."[11] Walzer therefore finds value in the sovereign state not because it is exclusive but because it provides for greater inclusiveness than would be possible if it did not exist.

Building on Walzer, then, the debate over open borders and the broader issue of whether governments have greater obligations to their own citizens than to others has grown to involve the philosophers who call themselves "communitarians." At a very basic level, the issue for these philosophers is whether "community" is valued and therefore whether members of a community have rights and obligations toward one another that transcend those toward individuals who do not belong to the community. For our purposes, *community* can be defined as coterminous with nationality, and *nationals* can be defined as citizens of a political institution known as the state.

Global egalitarians dismiss the idea of community as an impediment to a just world. "The socialist tradition," explains David Miller, "has been overwhelmingly hostile to nationality as a source of identity, usually regarding it merely as an artificially created impediment to the brotherhood of man."[12] Like the socialists, the globalists (and many with this view would regard themselves as socialists) place the highest value on egalitarianism. Indeed, two major interpreters of liberalism, John Rawls and the legal philosopher Ronald Dworkin, believe that the main idea of liberalism is equality rather than liberty.

Consequently, theorists who subscribe to the ideals of global justice put aside notions of community and the value that a community places on itself—which may be liberty or simply a sense of common identity and mutual obligation.

Neither global egalitarians nor communitarians are wholly consistent in the application of their principles. For example, Walzer contends that Australia, with its vast empty spaces, does not have the right to exclude people driven by poverty from densely populated Southeast Asia and hence should have a generous migra-

---

11. Ibid., p. 39.
12. David Miller, *Market, State and Community* (Oxford: Clarendon Press, 1990), p. 86.

tion policy.[13] Yet he is unwilling to accept the principle that living space throughout the world should be distributed in equal amounts to all individuals.[14] Carens, by contrast, is reluctant to go so far as to say that communities have no right to defend themselves or to take ethnicity into account in determining membership. Given the special historical circumstances, he accedes to Israel the right to give preference to Jews anywhere in the world who seek a refuge. He also concedes to the Japanese the right to close their doors, partly on the grounds that Japan is a densely populated country.[15] Furthermore, Carens is willing, as is another Canadian philosopher, Will Kymlicka, to grant indigenous communities (such as the Indians in Canada) the right to protect and preserve their own communities, even if it means the exclusion of others.[16] And Carens is prepared to see countries place restrictions on immigration when it constitutes a threat to national security or public order—even though he insists that opposition by the natives to migrants (even if their opposition is the source of the disorder) is not acceptable grounds for restricting admissions. Similarly, John Scanlon, another globalist who believes that national borders lack moral significance, concedes that the state might restrict admissions if there is a threat to society, while rejecting the Walzer view that ethnicity or ideology should ever be grounds for admitting or rejecting refugees.[17]

In short, communitarians agree with globalists that we have obligations to people who live outside our borders, and globalists are reluctant to give up complete-

---

13. "The right of white Australians to the great empty spaces of the subcontinent rested on nothing more than the claim they had staked, and enforced against the aboriginal population, before anyone else. That does not seem a right that one would readily defend in the face of necessitous men and women clamoring for entry. If, driven by famine in the densely populated lands of Southeast Asia, thousands of people were to fight their way into an Australia otherwise closed to them, I doubt that we would want to charge the invaders with aggression." Walzer, *Spheres of Justice,* p. 17.

The argument that empty spaces necessitate open boundaries has a long history in American thought; it was used to justify European settlement of Indian territories. In 1890, Richmond Mayo-Smith wrote that "a nation, it is said, has a right to the soil only on condition of making the best use of it, and if it have more land than it really need, it is in duty bound to share it with others. It is on this basis that the colonization of America by the nations of Europe is theoretically justified. The Indians were the original occupiers, and as such they owned the country. But the white men were more highly civilized, and could make better use of the land. What once barely kept a few thousand savages from starvation, now sustains millions of men in an advanced stage of culture." Richmond Mayo-Smith, *Emigration and Immigration* (New York: Johnson, 1968), p. 292. (Originally published 1890).

14. "It would deny that national clubs and families can ever acquire a firm title to a particular piece of territory." Walzer, *Spheres of Justice,* p. 18.

15. Why space should figure into Walzer's or Carens's position seems anachronistic for countries whose attractions are not land but employment. A variation of the argument, one which I suspect neither Walzer nor Carens would accept, is now used by environmentalists to justify policies of exclusion.

16. Will Kymlicka, *Liberalism, Community and Culture* (Oxford: Clarendon Press, 1989), pp. 173–176. Kymlicka seeks to reconcile the apparent contradiction between a notion of justice that implies the distribution of benefits without regard for borders and the notion that community membership has some special value.

17. John A. Scanlan and O. T. Kent, "The Force of Moral Arguments for a Just Immigration Policy in a Hobbesian Universe: The Contemporary American Example," in *Open Borders?* ed. Gibney, pp. 61–107.

ly the idea that sovereign states and the communities they envelop have value. The fundamental difference between globalists and communitarians is that the former believe that there ought to be a presumption of free migration and that the burden of proof should be on advocates of restrictions, whereas the latter believe that states should decide whom to admit based primarily on national self-interest.[18]

For globalists, the highest moral value is distributive justice. The preservation of a nation's existence; its political order, political institutions, and cultural identity; and the well-being and interests of its citizens are all subordinate to the goal of global distributive justice.[19] Global redistribution—through open borders or foreign aid—is regarded not as a humanitarian act but as a moral imperative.

Globalists pay little attention to whether the adoption of their principles in a world comprising sovereign states would lead to an improvement or a worsening of the human condition in any specific country. For example, the adoption of a globalist position on migration by a single country puts that country at risk when other countries choose not to open their borders. As we suggested earlier, migration can then become an act of aggression against the country with open borders as one country disposes of its unwanted on another. Under such circumstances, an open door to migrants might very well do more harm than good to large numbers of people. Moreover, if a state chooses not to give preference to the well-being of its own citizens over the well-being of citizens of other countries, then, as Walzer suggests, local communities and regions within the country might protect themselves by imposing restrictions on entry or discriminating against foreign residents, generating the very opposite result from what the globalists intend.[20]

18. Some globalists are also advocates of global redistribution, "a fair division of natural resources, income and wealth among persons situated in diverse national societies," writes Charles Beitz (*Political Theory*, p. 189), who argues that free movement is a more reliable way of redistributing resources to individuals than state-to-state transfers. Theorists who take this position recognize that freedom of entry would probably be more beneficial to the well-off, who can take advantage of opportunities to move, than to the poor, but they are unprepared to give up the principle of freedom of movement simply because the worst-off are not always the beneficiaries. Aristide Zolberg, in an essay on the ethical dilemmas of migration, concludes by quoting Melville: "If they can get here, they have God's right to come." Aristide R. Zolberg, "Keeping Them Out: Ethical Dilemmas of Immigration Policy," in *International Ethics in the Nuclear Age*, ed. Robert J. Meyers (Lanham, Md.: University Press of America, 1987), p. 293.

19. Indeed, Rawls's focus on distributive justice in a society does not take into account other legitimate moral objectives, such as enhancing opportunities for individuals and creating a social and economic order that will increase national wealth.

20. For a forceful statement of this view, see Timothy King, "Immigration from Developing Countries: Some Philosophical Issues," *Ethics*, April 1983, pp. 525–536. King writes: "If nations fail to impose restrictions on immigration, smaller communities might try to do so. The principles on which these restrictions would be based might be very much less liberal than nationally imposed ones; they might encourage greater segregation by race, income and other individual characteristics. . . . It is possible that the true alternative to the nation-state as a basis for considering migration choices is not the world as a whole but subnational geographic units, and the nation-state is clearly preferable" (p. 533). In contrast with globalists who want open borders to enable the poor to migrate to rich countries, King argues that free migration is realistic only under conditions of near equalization of economic conditions, as in the European Union.

CLOSED BORDERS

Except from the globalist perspective, no country—not even one with low population density or high per capita income—is obligated to admit individuals seeking
employment, higher income, or a better way of life. There are, of course, many sensible reasons why governments might welcome immigrants: They may meet labor
force needs in industry, the service sector, or agriculture; they may bring cultural
diversity and cosmopolitanism to countries whose citizens would like to be less
parochial; they may provide entrepreneurship and other needed skills and talents;
the country may regard itself as a home for people with whom its citizens have historic, cultural, or religious ties; and families of immigrant origin may want to bring
in relatives and other members of their ethnic community. A government may also
choose to open its borders to one or more neighboring countries with which it
shares free trade and similar living standards. But these policies fall within the normal framework of a state's domestic and foreign policies. None implies moral obligation.

In addition, there may be ideological reasons for a country to encourage migration. For traditional immigrant countries such as the United States, Canada, and
Australia, there is a popular ideological presumption in favor of continued migration. The United States, in particular, sees immigration as a way of reasserting the
image of America as a land of opportunity, still capable of offering success and for-
tune to the people it admits. For Israel, the admission of Jews from anywhere in the
world is essential to the Zionist conception of the state as a haven for world Jewry.
The costs of absorption, the availability of housing and employment, and the potential social dislocations are not relevant considerations in deciding whether Jews
should be admitted.

However, in spite of the various reasons why a country might support and
encourage immigration, many governments choose instead to close their borders to
some, or occasionally all, migration. The reasons given for restricting migration are
many. In some countries, local inhabitants are fearful that a large influx of immigrants will overwhelm them, reducing them to demographic minorities and threatening their cultural and political dominance. Other countries fear that migration
will exacerbate problems of overcrowding, poverty, unemployment, and xenophobia.

For societies that do admit migrants, few issues have generated more public
debate than the morality of admitting one class of migrants and not another.
Australia's whites only policy, the pre–World War II U.S. policy of excluding Asians,
and the reluctance of contemporary Germany and other Western European states
to admit Gypsies and Muslims have all come in for criticism. Such policies are
morally questionable because they discriminate in admissions, excluding individuals on the basis of race, religion, or culture.

Somewhat more morally acceptable are preferential policies—by Israel for
Jews, by Germany for people of German origin, by India for Hindus, by Pakistan
for Muslims, by Arab countries for fellow Arabs, by Nepal for people of Nepali origin, and so on. Other kinds of preferences are extended to people with certain
skills, educational levels, local relatives, or financial resources. Supporters of pref-

erential policies argue that according to the communitarian principle, a country has the moral right to admit whomever it wants. Nevertheless, liberals feel uncomfortable when the preferences are based on religion, ethnic origin, or, especially, race.

The line between preferences and discrimination, though it has some merit, is a morally thin one that is easily crossed. A whites only policy reflects not simply a preference for whites but hostility to blacks, Asians, and other nonwhites. In contrast, a national preference for one's ethnic group (Germans, Jews, Nepalis, Arabs, and so on) is to some degree justified by the need or desire to maintain a sense of community. Yet even ethnic preferences are not always moral; a multiethnic society that gives preference to one ethnic community over another is, in effect, making a moral distinction among its own citizens. States can more easily justify preferences in admission policy when their security is at risk. Israelis, aware of the long history of persecution of Jews in countries in which they were a minority, regard their country as a place of refuge for all the Jews of the world and legitimately fear that their country would cease to be a homeland for Jews were its borders open to all Arabs and others who wished to come.

A similar concern for ethnic survival shapes the immigration policies of Bhutan, a small Tibetan kingdom located northeast of India and east of Nepal. For many years, immigrants from the densely populated region of eastern Nepal migrated into Bhutan, eventually leading to concerns that the local Tibetan population might soon be outnumbered. Moreover, if citizenship is granted to the Nepalis and democracy is extended, the Nepalis may vote to overturn the monarchy, and the country will cease to be an independent Tibetan state. The king, with support from his Tibetan subjects, has therefore imposed a series of restrictions on the non-Tibetan population with the intention of halting the flows of Nepalis into the country, as well as to ensure the cultural, political, and demographic hegemony of the indigenous Tibetan population. The government announced that the Tibetan language would be taught in all the schools, that Tibetan dress should be worn by everyone, and that anyone who entered the country after the late 1950s would not be admitted into citizenship.

Clearly, then, the moral issues surrounding closed-border policies are not straightforward. Though preferential admissions policies that are discriminatory result in injustices, in some cases—particularly where there are security concerns—preferences are reasonable. However, even security concerns do not produce clear-cut moral distinctions. For example, is a state justified in denying citizenship to people who have lived there for a generation in the interest of preserving the country's native culture, the dominance of its indigenous population, and the right of that population to choose its own polity?[21] There are no simple answers to such questions.

---

21. Kuwait and other countries of the Persian Gulf take this position as the basis for not extending citizenship to long-term residents, including Palestinians born in the country.

SETTLERS, INDIGENOUS PEOPLES, AND CITIZENSHIP

The rights of native peoples and of settlers who were subsequently imposed on them raise another set of moral conundrums. In numerous regions of the world, indigenous populations have been overrun by foreign settlers. Memories of such "injustices" may last decades, centuries, even millennia. Columbus's voyage to the New World 500 years earlier was recalled in 1992 by the indigenous peoples of North and South America as the beginning of an era of colonization and oppression. In the 1960s, the Dravida Munnetra Kazhagam, a political party in the South Indian state of Tamil Nadu, mobilized popular sentiment against the Brahmanic classes as Indo-Aryan colonizers and oppressors who came to India as migrant invaders in the late second millennium B.C. In our own era, we have witnessed the establishment of the Dutch in the southern tip of Africa; the English colonization of Australia and New Zealand; Han Chinese settlement of Taiwan, Sinkiang, Mongolia, and Tibet; and Russian settlement of the Baltic states and portions of Central Asia. Some people argue, moreover, that even now the process of colonization continues within states, offering as examples Bangladeshi colonization of the Chittagong Hill Tracts traditionally occupied by the Buddhist Chakmas; Burmese colonization of the western Arakan region with its indigenous Bengali-speaking Muslim population; Indonesian settlement of Timor, a former Dutch and Portuguese colony taken over by Indonesia; and Brazilian colonization of indigenous tribal lands in the Amazon.

Indigenous peoples characterize these migrations as *colonization,* whereas migrants prefer to describe themselves as *settlers.* Between the two terms lies a vast normative chasm, with the one word evoking the image of oppression and the other the image of risk taking and innovation. The term *colonizers* suggests illegitimate occupiers of the land who deserve to be expelled by indigenous nationalist freedom fighters, while the term *settlers* implies a permanent right to remain.[22] Moral debates therefore center around whether colonial migrations were historically illegitimate and, if so, whether they should be rectified.

The term *indigenous* evokes the notion of preindustrial native peoples who have lost their ancestral lands and whose distinctive cultures are being or have been destroyed. The United Nations declared 1993 the International Year for the World's Indigenous Peoples, and a United Nations commission has numbered the indigenous people at 200 million worldwide, including the Indian populations of North and South America and tribal peoples of Australia, the Philippines, and the East Malaysian state of Sarawak. The UN Subcommission on Prevention of

---

22. These concepts are social constructs, and which one becomes paramount is an outgrowth of a political process. The Xhosa and Zulu peoples of South Africa, for example, now accept the Afrikaners as settlers, a people who became oppressors but who are nonetheless Africans; they are not regarded as colonists who should be "returned home." (In point of fact, the Xhosa and Zulu are themselves settlers who also migrated into South Africa.) In contrast, French settlers in Algeria were regarded by Algerians as *colons* and were expected to return to France with the end of French rule, as they indeed did.

Discrimination and Protection of Minorities (the "Cobo Report") defines indigenous peoples as follows:

> Those who, having a historical continuity with pre-invasion and pre-colonial societies that developed on their territories, consider themselves distinct from other sectors of the societies now prevailing in those territories, or parts of them. They form at present non-dominant sectors of society and are determined to preserve, develop and transmit to future generations their ancestral territories, and their ethnic identity, as the basis of their continued existences as peoples, in accordance with their own cultural patterns, social institutions and legal systems.[23]

Furthermore, the notion of indigenousness has expanded in recent years to include peoples who were colonized by migrants during a period of imperial rule and for whom the colonizers were not distant Europeans but other people from within the Third World or, in the case of the Soviet Union, Russians or other Soviet peoples. The postcolonial governments of Burma, Sri Lanka, and Uganda regarded earlier generations of migrants from India and their descendants as illegitimate and insisted that they return "home." Similarly, the postcolonial governments of Indonesia, Malaysia, and Vietnam regarded the Chinese as illegitimate.[24]

Today, politically *dominant* communities—not simply politically *subordinate* communities, as in the UN definition—use the notion of indigenousness either to assert a claim to special economic, political, and cultural rights denied others within their own country or to declare the nonindigenes as aliens. The move from subordinate to dominant may be the result of political independence as a disfranchised, previously powerless majority community now assumes political power.

Growing awareness of indigenous peoples has generated an important moral debate. Can one rectify a historic injustice without creating a new injustice? Will the extension of group rights to the indigenous, broadly defined, generate large-scale conflicts within a country? For the republics of the former Soviet Union, each with colonists or settlers from Russia and from other republics, the legitimacy of earlier migrations has become an acutely divisive issue.

Once we speak of indigenous peoples, however defined, we evoke notions of conflicting group rights. When politically dominant Malays, Serbs, Estonians, and Latvians refer to the rights of indigenous peoples, they point to a historic injustice

---

23. United Nations Subcommission on Prevention of Discrimination and Protection of Minorities, *Study of the Problem of Discrimination Against Indigenous Populations* (New York, 1987).

24. The UN definition of *indigenous* specifies that the community must be politically subordinate, a definition that clearly does not fit the politically dominant Malays or many other nationalist communities that have political power. The UN definition focuses on dominant versus subordinate relationships, not European versus non-European. Hence the Sami peoples (or Lapps) of Scandinavia are regarded as "indigenous" peoples of Finno-Ugric ethnic origin who predate the Indo-European invasion of their territory and who now constitute a nondominant group in Norway, Sweden, and Finland. For a useful analysis of the rights claims of indigenous populations and their international standing, see Raidza Torres, "The Rights of Indigenous Populations: The Emerging International Norm," *Yale Journal of International Law,* Winter 1991, pp. 127–175. It is useful to maintain this distinction between, on the one hand, the UN notion of indigenous as preindustrial subordinate peoples and, on the other, the broader nationalist notion of a politically dominant majority who claim to have prior rights to the territory they occupy as their "homeland." It is this latter, broader conception of indigenous that is of concern to us here, not the claims to protection by subordinate peoples.

resulting from the occupation of their lands by outsiders and seek to reclaim for themselves what they believe to be historically theirs. Yet even if indigenous people have a moral claim to some sort of restitution on the basis of having once been overwhelmed by settlers, a morally just policy is not so well defined. The migrant or colonial population, which was once economically or politically dominant, has a justifiable claim to certain rights as well. Hungarians in Romania, Russians in the Baltic states, Turks in Bulgaria, Chinese in Malaysia and in Indonesia, Albanians in Kosovo, and Indians in East Africa may have been imposed on an earlier people by colonial authorities, but as long-term settlers they also have legitimate rights. Though an injustice may have been committed by the imperial power that once forced or induced them to migrate, the migrants and their descendants have done no wrong. To force them to "return home" would be to compound the injustice. A newly independent state may insist that the minority learn the majority language, that privileges in education or employment given by the imperial power to the minority be withdrawn, and that relatively recent illegal transfers of property be nullified. The state may insist that the migrant community opt for the citizenship of one country or another, rather than hold dual citizenship. The state may also promote the culture of the newly empowered majority and the education of a community that has been unequally treated in the past, but should it restrict the opportunities of members of the minority community or limit their efforts to maintain their own language and culture? These issues are bound to be fought out in the political arena, as each side asserts its own moral claims in a situation that is morally unclear. But the state ought not to expel people who have lived there for some time, even if demographically they threaten to become a majority. It is one thing for governments to limit the future immigration of people who may threaten to overwhelm the dominant culture but quite another for a state to engage in expulsions or discrimination to ensure that one group retains political dominance.

ILLEGALS: FOR WHOSE BENEFIT?

How a society treats its migrants becomes a moral issue when migrants are classified by the state as illegals. The public policy debate over illegals has centered on two issues: first, whether it is morally right for individuals to employ illegal migrants and, second, what rights, if any, are acquired by illegals merely by their presence in a country.

The issue of hiring illegals became a major issue in the United States in January 1993, when President Clinton's choice for attorney general, Zoë Baird, withdrew her candidacy following public uproar over her having hired an illegal migrant couple to work in her home as nanny and chauffeur. A 1986 law imposed penalties on employers who knowingly hire illegal immigrants. Baird paid a fine and made a public apology, but the public was unforgiving.

Opponents of employer sanctions, however, were more sympathetic. They consider the law that penalizes employers for hiring illegals both unenforceable and undesirable. Instead, they advocate turning a blind eye to the presence of illegals or, alternatively, expanding U.S. immigration quotas to admit people to work as household helpers or in other positions for which there is a large demand but few available workers in the United States.

While the media gave much attention to Baird, less was said about the Corderas, the Peruvians she employed, who, after being dismissed, disappeared into the labor force, presumably to find illegal employment with someone else.

"It's just a reality of life that without the illegal girls, there wouldn't be any nannies, and the mommies would have to stay home and mind their own kids," said the owner of a Manhattan agency who regularly places illegal migrants. "Illegal immigration provides us with an informal, widespread system of day care," added Professor Mitchell Moss, director of the Urban Research Center at New York University.[25] It does so, however, at a price. Illegal workers are paid less than legal residents, do not pay social security or income taxes for fear of leaving a paper trail, and are not free to work outside the underground economy. By keeping wages down, illegal workers displace some native workers, although the magnitude of the displacement is unclear. In the absence of illegals, wages would go up, and more legal workers would find employment, but then higher wages would also reduce the demand for household workers.

Beyond the economic arguments for and against illegals, many lawmakers and the public have supported penalizing employers on moral grounds: first, because people who want to enter and work in the United States should not be allowed to violate the law when others are in a legal queue waiting for their migration papers and, second, because workers in the underground economy are easily exploited and lack both the benefits and the protections ordinarily provided by the state.

Nevertheless, in the United States, employer sanctions are rarely enforced. Few INS officials (and no officials from the Labor Department) are assigned to the task, documents are easily forged, there are no enforcement provisions for employers of domestics, and there is no system to verify whether an individual is authorized to work. Most studies report, therefore, that individuals who illegally cross borders or who overstay their visas can readily slip into the labor market. In the absence of effective employer sanctions or, indeed, of any effective policy of expelling illegals, the United States continues to have an increasing number of illegal residents. Should these illegals be provided with medical care at state expense? Should their children be provided with free education? Should their children born in the country be granted automatic citizenship at birth? Each question is fraught with moral ambiguity precisely because society and government are ambivalent as to whether illegals should be regarded as individuals who have violated the law or whether it is their employers who should be regarded as lawbreakers. If government (and society) chooses to cast a blind eye on illegal immigrants, who are then, in effect, permitted to remain in the country, it is hard to argue that these individuals are not entitled to the same benefits given to permanent residents. The moral issue of entitlements, therefore, cannot be separated from the question of whether the state is able or willing to enforce entry and residence rules.

GUEST WORKERS AND CITIZENSHIP

The moral debate over guest workers centers on two issues—their right to remain and, if they do remain, their claims to citizenship. Guest worker programs, once thought of as beneficial to both the host countries and the foreigners they employed, are now subject to criticism on moral grounds. As discussed in an earlier chapter, guest worker or temporary migration programs have existed for decades in the United States, Western Europe, and the Persian Gulf. During the Second World War, the United States brought workers in from Mexico to fill a temporary labor shortage in agriculture created by the wartime draft. This program, known as the *bracero* program, was terminated in 1964, but similar programs continued to enable employers to bring in seasonal fruit pickers. In the 1960s, the countries of Western Europe imported workers to meet temporary labor shortages in the industrial and building sectors, and in the 1970s, the oil-rich, underpopulated Persian Gulf states promoted temporary worker migration when the rise in oil prices enabled them to build airports, roads, hotels, desalinization plants, hospitals, schools, and new factories.

It is important to distinguish two types of conditions under which these guest workers have been employed: to fill temporary needs in the labor force and to fill long-term jobs. Temporary employment may be needed in agriculture, where there are seasonal fluctuations in the demand for labor, and in the construction industry when there is a construction boom. Conversely, the "temporary" employment of migrants in permanent positions occurs where there is a high demand for labor that is not being met by the native workforce because the jobs are poorly paid or are considered undesirable. In the former instance, temporary workers are hired for temporary jobs; in the latter, temporary workers are hired to meet long-term demands for labor.[26] Each category raises its own moral problems.

If migrant workers are to be temporary, host governments may reasonably restrict their rights to change employment or limit their access to the social benefits given to citizens. In fact, it was in an effort to prevent temporary guest workers from entrenching themselves that the Persian Gulf states imposed such restrictions on their migrants. In particular, the Gulf states also excluded the family members of most guest workers, reasoning that if families were admitted and resided in the country for a period of time, they would in effect acquire membership in the community—especially if their children were born locally or had spent some years in the local schools and built a network of social ties. When individuals have been recruited for short-term employment and are not accompanied by their families, repatriation imposes far less of a burden on all parties. In contrast, Western European governments gave their migrants a broad range of rights, including the right to bring spouses and children. As a result, an estimated 12 million migrants and their families became permanent residents in Europe in the 1980s with little or no prospect of returning home. In contrast to the Gulf states, Europe's liberal democracies created a social contract that provided rights to migrant workers, including the right to remain.

The International Labor Organization advocates a position closer to that of the Europeans than that of the Gulf states. The ILO Covenant on the Rights of Migrant Workers specifies that governments should permit family unification and extend a full range of benefits to guest workers (including the right to stay) once they have worked in a country for two years. In effect, therefore, the guest worker

---

26. A demand for migrant labor does not necessarily mean that labor is not available locally, only that workers are not available at existing wages and benefits.

category would be limited only to short-term workers meeting temporary labor shortages, not to workers filling long-term jobs.[27]

No fundamental moral issue is at stake in a public policy that admits short-term migrant workers without their families, as long as the workers are provided with basic health and housing amenities and market wages. But once migrants have been allowed, for whatever reason, to remain in a country for an extended period of time, they and their families acquire membership in the community, which entitles them to the rights, benefits, and obligations accorded to citizens. Human rights are violated when some permanent residents of a country are given rights and others are not and when these distinctions are perpetuated from one generation to the next. Seen in this light, we can understand why the question of admitting temporary guest workers to Western Europe in the 1960s appeared to be a straightforward issue of public policy whereas in the 1980s and 1990s, the question of whether and how migrants and their children should be incorporated as citizens has become a moral issue.

MORAL CLAIMS FOR PROTECTION

Though few individuals would take issue with the moral argument that refugees are in need of protection, the question remains as to who is a refugee. According to the 1951 United Nations Refugee Convention and the 1967 Protocol Relating to the Status of Refugees, a refugee is "a person who has a well-founded fear of being persecuted for reasons of race, religion, nationality, membership in a particular social group, or political opinion" and "is outside the country of his nationality and is unable, or owing to such fear, is unwilling to avail himself of the protection of that country." The Organization of African Unity offers a broader definition:

> The term refugee should also apply to every person who, owing to external aggression, occupation, foreign domination or events seriously disturbing public order in either part or the whole of his country of origin or nationality, is compelled to leave his place of habitual residence in order to seek refuge in another place outside his country of origin or nationality.[28]

Although the United Nations Refugee Convention limits the notion of refugee to individuals who are persecuted or fear persecution and the OAU definition includes individuals who flee from generalized violence,[29] both definitions view refugees as individuals who lack the protection of their own government. Neither definition, moreover, applies to displaced persons within a country, irrespective of

27. None of the Gulf states has signed the ILO Covenant, clearly recognizing that they would then be replacing their temporary migration program with an immigration policy.

28. Organization of African Unity Convention Governing the Specific Aspects of Refugee Problems in Africa, adopted September 10, 1969.

29. A definition similar to that of the OAU was adopted by Mexico and several Central American states meeting in Colombia in November 1984. It provided that the concept of refugees in the region should include "persons who have fled their country because their lives, safety or freedom have been threatened by generalized violence, foreign aggression, internal conflicts, massive violations of human rights or other circumstances which have seriously disturbed public order."

whether there is persecution or violence, or to individuals fleeing from natural disasters such as floods, droughts, or earthquakes. And neither definition includes individuals who flee from a tyrannical regime unless they are personally persecuted or their society is torn by life-threatening violence.

Some human rights activists therefore consider both the UN and the OAU definitions too narrow. Andrew Shacknove, of Oxford University's Refugee Studies Programme, asserts that a moral claim to refugee status arises whenever a state fails to protect the basic needs of its citizens.[30] Consistent with such a broad moral definition, some human rights activists argue that liberal democratic countries ought to admit all individuals whose human rights are violated by their government. Hence a Saudi woman is justified in seeking asylum in Canada because of her views on the status of women. A woman from Mali may legitimately flee to France rather than undergo a clitoridectomy. A homosexual fearing persecution in his homeland, Brazil, because of his sexual orientation may claim asylum in Canada. A Chinese couple is justified in claiming asylum in the United States because they have had more children than are permitted by the Chinese government. A Gypsy may claim asylum in Germany because the Gypsy community suffers from discrimination in Romania. In each case, there is a plausible claim for asylum based on human rights violations.

There are, however, several legitimate objections to broadening the definition of refugees. If acts of discrimination short of persecution are the basis for claiming asylum, a large part of the world's population could do so. Asylum on the basis of discrimination could plausibly be claimed, for example, by over 100 million Indian Muslims whose mosque at Ayodhya was destroyed and who were fearful after many Muslims in Bombay and elsewhere were killed by Hindus. Millions of women around the world could similarly point to discriminatory restrictions imposed by their state or society as justification for seeking asylum. Moreover, a country that does not want its minorities could engage in systematic discrimination and impel countries that embrace a liberal conception of refugees to admit all whose human rights have been violated. The more liberal democratic states and international agencies become in granting asylum to persecuted minorities, the greater the inducement for a nationalist regime to engage in some form of "ethnic cleansing."

Thus a broader definition of refugees would, in effect, offer refugee status to entire populations in societies with civil conflicts, authoritarian regimes, or weak governments that fail to protect human rights. Refugee politics would move from a consideration of individual cases to an assessment of regimes. Given the number of countries that could be classified as violators of human rights, developed countries would have to open their borders to much of the world. This shift has moral implications both for sending countries, which might have incentives to increase injustices against their minority populations, and for receiving countries, which would face the dilemma of accommodating an increasing migrant population while responding to the needs of its own citizens.

30. Andrew Shacknove, "Who Is a Refugee?" *Ethics*, January 1985, pp. 274–284. Also see Andrew Shacknove, "American Duties to Refugees: Their Scope and Limits," in *Open Borders?* ed. Mark Gibney (Westport, Conn.: Greenwood Press), pp. 131–150.

Refugee status is, as one scholar put it, a scarce resource.[31] Individuals who have been granted refugee status are in a privileged category; it is an entitlement that allows one to move to a safe country for protection and assistance. Governments must decide to whom these entitlements should be given and how generous they should be. The broader the definition and the greater the entitlements, the more refugees will come. Citizens of a poor country with an authoritarian regime who have the option of moving permanently to a more prosperous democratic country will readily do so. Even the narrower definition of a refugee as having "a well-founded fear of persecution" has its problems by producing so many claimants that their claims cannot be properly evaluated. How can government adjudicators readily distinguish among those who are seeking better economic opportunities, who are fleeing from violence, or who have a personal well-founded fear of persecution? How might governments create enforceable criteria for admission that would be morally defensible?

No simple test can reveal who is at risk and who is not. We enter into the realm of intangibles: judgments about the motivations of claimants, problems of evidence when the burden is on claimants to demonstrate that they are at risk of persecution, and more general judgments about conditions in the home country that threaten the lives of individuals on account of their race, religion, ethnic identity, or political beliefs.

At times, the advocates and the policymakers shout at one another: Human rights activists accuse government officials of callousness and of failing to recognize their responsibility to people at risk; government officials, in turn, accuse human rights activists of insensitivity to the needs of home countries—particularly the needs of the poor and internal social and political stability—and to the impact that generous asylum and refugee policies can have on the behavior of countries eager to unburden themselves of their own poor and their minorities.

Facing the prospect of a large refugee influx, many governments have argued that refugees should remain in the country of first asylum. Several moral justifications are offered for such policies, including these: (1) The adjustment of refugees is likely to be easier when economic and social conditions are more similar, (2) the costs of maintaining refugees are lower if they remain in Third World countries than if they are settled in developed countries, and (3) refugees are more likely to repatriate voluntarily when conditions change at home if the country of asylum does not provide them with material advantages. When the first-asylum rule is put into effect, governments of refugee-receiving countries are often angry not only at the country that generates refugees but also at countries that are unwilling to share the refugee burden. Germany has been irritated by the refusal of other members of the European Union to admit Bosnians, Croatians, and Romanians; Thailand and Malaysia were insistent that they would accommodate refugees from Indochina only if the United States, France, and other countries took some of them; the United States tried, with very limited success, to persuade Caribbean countries to take in some of the Haitian refugees; and Japan annoyed many of its Asian neighbors by accepting only a handful of refugees from Indochina.

Whatever the criteria, there is the practical matter of determining who qualifies for asylum. The debate is between advocates of onshore reviews and those who

31. David Martin, "The Refugee Concept: On Definitions, Politics and the Careful Use of a Scarce Resource," in *Refugee Policy*, ed. Howard Adelman (Toronto: York Lane Press, 1991).

insist on offshore reviews. Offshore reviews require that asylum seekers first apply to embassies or to designated immigration officials in their home country. Airlines would be required to check the visas of individuals before transporting them from countries with significant numbers of asylum claimants. Ships at sea would be halted and forced to return home—possibly after some onboard asylum review process.

Human rights advocates have objected to all of these procedures, arguing instead that asylum seekers should be allowed to enter a country where their claims can receive a full and fair legal review under the guidance of legal counsel. Furthermore, pending the resolution of their claims, asylum seekers should not be detained and should be allowed to work or receive public benefits. Human rights advocates also insist that rejected claimants should have full rights of appeal and should not be sent home if they are at risk. Finally, they assert that the embassies of asylum countries proposing to return rejected claimants should monitor the human rights situation in the home countries and, in particular, the fate of people who were returned after their claim for asylum was rejected.

Yet even while taking the high moral ground, human rights groups create another moral conundrum. Liberal democratic states, in adopting the proposed protections, then become the ultimate guarantors of human rights: first, by admitting people whose rights have been violated by their home government and, second, by monitoring human rights conditions so as to determine whether it is safe for rejected asylum claimants to return home. The right of asylum is thus elevated to being the mechanism by which liberal democratic states guarantee human rights to all individuals in repressive societies, assuring individuals who can escape that the rights they seek can be obtained elsewhere if they cannot be obtained at home. Critics of this approach argue that it is beyond the capacity of liberal democratic states to provide such generous protection to all whose rights are violated and that the goal of these states must be the more modest one of providing protection to those whose rights and lives are the most egregiously threatened while deterring all others.

At the end of the day, we are left with a political judgment. How far is a country prepared to go in deciding not only what kinds of refugees should be admitted but also how many, for judgments about who is qualified are likely to be made within a context of numbers; the more there are, the narrower will be the criteria for admission.

HUMANE DETERRENCE

Given the problematic moral issues surrounding just the delimitation of the term *refugee,* it should come as no surprise that the treatment of refugees or asylum claimants raises moral questions as well. Facing an increasing number of claims, states and international agencies have devised strategies intended to reduce their number. Several countries already require that refugees obtain visas before coming and penalize airlines for carrying asylum seekers without visas. Under the Dublin Agreement signed by several European governments, asylum seekers will be returned to the country of first asylum, thereby forcing countries to scrutinize the claims of nonresidents who cross their borders. International agencies, meanwhile, have advocated the creation of "safe havens" and provided humanitarian assistance so that displaced persons need not leave their country. All of these policies have their critics, but perhaps the most acute debate centers around the policy known as humane deterrence.

Most Third World countries place refugee claimants in refugee camps, provide for their minimal basic needs, and restrict their access to the local labor market. This is a policy adopted in large measure out of necessity to minimize the damage to the local community and to enable international donors to provide assistance. But some countries have also placed their asylum seekers in detention camps as a strategy of deterrence. Australia's humane deterrence policy combines a system of tight border controls, offshore procedures for asylum claimants, and detention centers for those who claim asylum from within Australia. The policy has resulted in the growth of offshore claims and a corresponding decline in the number of onshore claims, with the exception of the large number of Chinese students in Australia at the time of Tiananmen Square. In general, by creating minimally acceptable conditions, governments reduce the entitlements associated with refugee status and, in theory, make immigration attractive only to people who are genuinely concerned for their safety. Furthermore, by attending primarily to the *security* needs of the refugees, governments make it unlikely that individuals will use the asylum claim to migrate for economic reasons. If, after a period of time, these refugees are unable to return home, the host society will have to face the issue of permanent settlement, but humane deterrence can discourage those who want to come for economic reasons. Humane deterrence, it is further argued, also reduces the danger that generous admission policies will induce individuals to risk their lives in risky journeys at sea.[32] Consequently, a policy of humane deterrence is said by advocates to serve the needs of sovereign states by enabling them to control migration and is a moral good because it prevents migrants from subjecting themselves to unnecessary hazards.

A humane deterrence strategy entails creating the following conditions for refugees: austere camp conditions, detention within the camps or in hostel facilities, and, often, a lengthy stay and review process before individuals can be relocated, resettled, or repatriated. Critics argue that such conditions may be below acceptable minimum standards established by the UN Refugee Convention for the treatment and protection of refugees and that detention, which restricts the movement of refugees within the camps or hostels and prohibits refugees from seeking employment, is a denial of rights.[33] Critics further argue that humane deterrence has been ineffective in slowing refugee flows.

---

32. Michael Teitelbaum characterizes the explicit or implicit promise of admission as a "moral hazard," a term to describe insurance that encourages risk-taking. Teitelbaum writes that President Carter's "open arms" policy unintentionally stimulated tens of thousands of Cubans to head for Mariel Harbor, while the failure to deal promptly and fairly with Haitian asylum claims induced many Haitians to head for boats that would bring them to Florida, where they could find high-wage jobs. "And who knows how many people died in the boats that headed out to sea as a result?" Michael S. Teitelbaum, "Tragic Choices in Refugee Policy," in *American Refugee Policy*, ed. Joseph M. Kitagawa (Minneapolis: Presiding Bishops Fund for World Relief/Winston Press, 1984), p. 34.

33. A particularly poignant criticism of humane deterrence came from Hannah Arendt, who wrote that "contemporary history has created a new kind of human being—the kind that are put in concentration camps by their foes and internment camps by their friends." Hannah Arendt, *The Jew as Pariah*, ed. Ron H. Feldman (New York: Grove Press, 1978), p. 56.

The question of fairness is legitimate because humane deterrence imposes austere conditions on individuals who are genuine refugees in order to screen out individuals motivated primarily by economic considerations. We deny or at least severely limit benefits to some people because we want to discourage others who do not deserve to be beneficiaries.[34] Advocates of humane deterrence argue that it is an effective screening device that protects the status of genuine refugees. The large-scale influx of unqualified claimants for asylum into Western Europe has strained the entire system for adjudicating claims, antagonized citizens who see unwarranted claimants supported by the state, and puts at risk the entire refugee system. It is therefore argued that only if the public is persuaded that the refugees are in fact genuine will it support their continued admission.

Critics argue that the harsh conditions in camps in Thailand and Hong Kong did not deter refugees from Vietnam;[35] but perhaps this demonstrates that people who are fearful of persecution or violence will flee even to unsatisfactory camps. An indirect method for assessing the efficacy of humane deterrence strategies is to consider what conditions might have induced refugees to repatriate rather than to remain in refugee camps. Fred Cuny and Barry Stein examined five cases—Ethiopia, Cambodia, Mozambique, Uganda, and El Salvador—in which large numbers of people voluntarily repatriated, all in 1987.[36] In each instance, they write, the hosts were hostile to the refugees, camp life was often regarded as unsatisfactory, and opportunities for resettlement were absent. They reported that many refugees returned home in large part because of the conditions under which they lived in their country of refuge, despite the fact that some violence persisted, economic conditions were poor, and authoritarian regimes remained in place. They concluded that the humane deterrence policies of the host country succeeded in inducing refugees to return home and, moreover, that only Thailand's forced return of the Cambodians appears not to have been in the refugees' best interests.

Although the UN Convention offers protection, it does not entitle refugees to go to the country of their choice; nor are refugees offered the same rights and benefits of citizens of the country that provides protection. Governments and international institutions can therefore offer protection in a variety of ways: "safe havens" within the country of origin with military protection from an outside force; temporary refugee camps on islands or even on ships at sea; or remote camps within a protecting host society. It is not a violation of the UN Convention, nor indeed is it immoral, for a government to rent space in another country for refugee camps to be placed under the jurisdiction of the UNHCR.

The moral efficacy of specific humane deterrence policies ultimately rests on two issues: whether the conditions of deterrence are indeed humane and whether

34. A similar logic is applied by many governments in determining the size of welfare benefits: If payments are too low, people will suffer, but the higher payments are, the more likely it is that people employed at low wages will drop out of the labor market and apply for welfare benefits.

35. See Dennis McNamara, "The Origins and Effects of 'Humane Deterrence' Policies in Southeast Asia," in *Refugees and International Relations,* ed. Gil Loescher and Laila Monahan (New York: Oxford University Press, 1989), pp. 123–134.

36. Fred Cuny and Barry Stein, "Prospects for and Promotion of Spontaneous Repatriation," in *Refugees,* ed. Loescher and Monahan, pp. 293–312. Other relatively successful cases of repatriation include refugees from Angola, Chad, Zaire, and Zimbabwe.

such policies will effectively deter people who are not fleeing persecution and violence while enabling genuine refugees to obtain protection.

INTEGRATION, TEMPORARY ASYLUM, OR REPATRIATION?

Under what circumstances should refugees be permanently integrated into the host country, provided temporary asylum, or repatriated? Once again, these questions pose a set of policy choices in which there is a moral dimension.

The UNHCR advocates temporary asylum for refugees, followed by repatriation when it is safe to return home. It calls for temporary asylum even for those who do not fit the Convention definition. The Council of Europe has accepted this view in its distinction between Convention refugees and de facto refugees. De facto refugees are persons not recognized as refugees within the meaning of the UN Conventions of 1951 and 1967 but "who are unable or, for reasons recognized as valid, unwilling to return to the country of their nationality or, if they have no nationality, to the country of their habitual residence." The Council of Europe classifies such de facto refugees as B-status refugees. The United States has a similar category of refugees, known as temporary protected status (TPS) beneficiaries or as individuals with extended voluntary departure (EVD) status. Under these various categories, asylum seekers who do not qualify under national laws may be permitted to remain temporarily on humanitarian grounds.

In many cases, however, refugees become permanent residents of their host countries. For example, most refugees admitted into the United States are given permanent residence and the right to seek naturalization. Only a small number are given temporary asylum, and most of these are usually able to arrange for a change in their status so that they can remain permanently. Though the criteria for admission are different for a refugee and for an immigrant, the outcome is usually the same: permanent residence followed by naturalization.

Nevertheless, in most countries, asylum is usually thought of as temporary, dependent on conditions in the home country. The presumption is that refugees are individuals who are in need of legal protection because their own government either is persecuting them or is unable to provide them with protection. Refugees are not immigrants, and hence it is expected that they will return home when conditions have changed so that they no longer need protection from a foreign government or an international agency. This view persists despite the fact that when a refugee exodus is under way, the prospects for change in the country producing the exodus are usually unclear, but the assumption is that conditions will in time change for the better. The civil war that led individuals to flee might end, the autocratic government might fall, and human rights might be restored. Consequently, temporary asylum, rather than local integration, is the first response of most governments—the American policy of providing permanent residence and citizenship to most refugees notwithstanding.

Under what circumstances, then, should individuals who have been granted temporary asylum or whose request for asylum has been rejected be repatriated? The internationally recognized principle of *non-refoulement* forbids states from forcibly returning asylum seekers to their home country when there is risk of serious human rights violations (Article 33 of the UN Convention on Refugees). There is obviously an anomaly in this principle, however, because people who flee from violent societies are not refugees under the UN Convention but are still protected from being sent home to a country torn by violence once they have crossed the border. Confronting suffering human beings who have entered the country, liberal governments are not inclined to insist that they leave. But they are prepared to reject as refugees sufferers in similar circumstances who make a claim from far away. In practice, there are thus different criteria for asylum seekers according to the circumstances of the asylum request: a more generous approach for those who successfully cross borders (who will not be repatriated if their country is violent) than for those who apply at embassies (who must prove a "well-founded fear of persecution").

Who should decide whether and when an individual should be repatriated? What if asylum seekers do not want to return even when the host government concludes that conditions in the country of origin have become safe? Is it acceptable to return shiploads of Chinese immigrants to Fujian province, where many will be placed in "reeducation camps"? Is it reasonable for the German government to repatriate thousands of Gypsies under an agreement with the government of Romania, or will their return lead to violent attacks in the Romanian villages and towns from which they initially departed? Was it safe to repatriate Vietnamese refugees from Hong Kong?

Human rights activists and international agencies have been unwilling to specify whether there are *any* conditions under which asylum seekers can be repatriated against their will. They have also been reluctant to agree that asylum countries rather than the migrants themselves should decide the time and conditions of repatriation because they do not believe that asylum countries can be trusted to do what is in the best interests of refugees. But asylum seekers may be unwilling to return home for many reasons, including a preference for living in the host society. If the host country does forcibly repatriate, it assumes the moral responsibility for the safety of the returnees. Governments may find it useful to seek an assessment from the UNHCR or Amnesty International, but they regard these institutions (as indeed, they regard themselves) as advocates. The conundrum thus remains unresolved: It seems necessary that states rather than asylum seekers should determine if and when repatriation is in order, but can these same states be relied on to make an impartial decision as to whether conditions for the returnees are safe? And if not states, who else can make the determination? Finally, are the criteria clear as to what constitutes safe conditions?

MORAL DILEMMAS: THREE FINAL EXAMPLES

We have argued that refugee and migration policies often pose moral dilemmas, choices between equally unsatisfactory alternatives. We shall draw from the foregoing discussion to identify three policy areas, each entailing unsatisfactory moral alternatives but in which choices are nonetheless both necessary and possible.

The first, as we have discussed earlier, is the question of whether all individuals whose human rights have been violated or who are confronted by violence should be granted asylum. To exclude entry to such persons is to deny them the freedom and safety that others have. The number of such persons is clearly enormous if one includes all who live under authoritarian regimes or in countries torn by ethnic or religious strife. But to broaden the definition of refugees in this fashion is to incorporate most of the world's population. If virtually everyone is entitled to be a refugee, then governments, dictated by their own notion of what is in their national interest and that of their citizens, will adopt measures to bar entry, for if everyone is a refugee, no one can be accepted as a refugee. For governments of advanced industrial societies to have a refugee and asylum policy, the criteria for admission must be narrowly defined so that the numbers who qualify are manageable.[37]

A second example of a moral dilemma involves the issue of forcible repatriation of individuals who do not qualify under the UN Convention but who do not wish to return home to an impoverished country or one with an authoritarian regime. Again, from a human rights point of view, it would be desirable that such individuals not be returned home against their will. But to permit such individuals to remain would be to induce people from impoverished and authoritarian regimes to emigrate in the hope that even if their asylum claim is rejected, they could remain nonetheless. As the number of such individuals increases, governments will invariably look for means to prevent new entries by interdicting boats at sea and preventing individuals from entering without legal entry documents. The latter option is opposed by human rights advocates because such policies prevent the entry of individuals who do qualify for asylum. Which policy, then, is morally more acceptable, a policy of forcible repatriation of people who do not qualify for asylum or a policy of interdiction? Which one is more likely to provide protection for those who are persecuted?

A third example can be drawn from the policy debate concerning illegal migrants. None of the policy choices for preventing the entry of large numbers of illegals is morally attractive.[38] Border controls may entail intensive military surveillance, barbed-wires fences, visa checks at border posts and by airlines, and other controls that can be personally irritating and humiliating as well as insulting to neighboring states with which one otherwise has friendly associations. The alternative may entail internal checks involving employer sanctions, identity cards for all citizens and legal residents, police raids on small businesses where illegals may be employed, and fines or prison sentences for illegals—policies that are intrusive for employers and for citizens and legal residents and may put at risk legal immigrants and people of the same ethnic background as those who are in the country illegally. Again, both choices are unattractive, but most governments (and their citizens)

---

37. The ultimate moral nightmare is that the number who do qualify under the existing UN Convention increases beyond the capacity and willingness of governments to provide protection; under such circumstances, the moral argument grows for some form of intervention in states that persecute their citizens.

38. Policy choices can be avoided if the number of illegal entries is small enough to be acceptable. Some analysts have suggested that the numbers of illegals can be reduced by establishing guest worker programs or by increasing the number of legal migrants, but this assumes that there is a finite number of people likely to seek entrance, legal or otherwise.

would clearly prefer border controls as these are the least intrusive for citizens and legal residents.

Notwithstanding the existence for nearly a century of international institutions to deal with refugees and countless international and regional agreements, many of the moral issues surrounding refugee flows remain unresolved. These include, as we have seen, the question of who is entitled to receive asylum, how the burden of accommodating refugees can be shared both among developed countries and between developing and developed countries, whether satisfactory offshore proce-dures for determining who is a refugee can be implemented when the number of potential claimants is very large, whether any reasonable system can be devised that deters people from using the refugee route for purposes of immigration, how best to halt the influx of illegal migrants, and what conditions in the home country would justify repatriating refugees or rejected asylum seekers against their will.

MORALITY AND PUBLIC OPINION

In dealing with these issues, individual governments must apply moral reasoning to balance the views of their citizens with the needs and interests of migrants and refugees. To what extent should a government base its immigration and refugee laws on public opinion? What if a substantial part of the electorate is xenophobic? For example, was it wrong for the U.S. Congress to impose national quotas on immigration after World War I because an anti-immigrant lobby sought to halt the influx of migrants from Eastern and Southern Europe? Was it wrong for the British government in the 1970s to pass restrictive immigration laws after Enoch Powell, a member of Parliament, warned of the dangers to Britain of migration? Was it wrong for French politicians to adopt a restrictive stance toward refugee admission and migration with the rise of popular support for Jean-Marie Le Pen's right-wing antimigrant party? Was it wrong for the German government to revise its generous asylum laws because of violent attacks against foreigners? Was it wrong when sev-eral governments of Southeast Asia refused to accept Vietnamese refugees because of local opposition? And was it wrong for the government of Pakistan to refuse to admit "stranded Pakistanis" (as they call themselves) left in Bangladesh after inde-pendence because local people in the Karachi region opposed the further influx of immigrants?

Government leaders often take the position that they must be responsive to public sentiments even if the public is irrationally xenophobic. Political leaders fear, moreover, that opposition politicians will use antimigrant sentiment to win electoral support. A somewhat more sophisticated version of this argument is that unless responsible policymakers take heed of deeply felt public sentiments, extreme right-wing parties will grow and threaten the democratic system. This fear has particular credibility in countries with authoritarian traditions and fragile democratic struc-tures.

Yet if the proposed policies are morally unjust, they should not be adopted, no matter how strong public sentiment may be, even in a democracy. Consequently, a complex balance must be struck between catering to the wishes of a citizenry and protecting the rights of migrants and refugees. Antimigrant, antirefugee sentiment may come from a relatively small, though vociferous, group of citizens. It is generally within the power of a government to seek public support for existing policies if it is clear that these policies are sensible ones. The Swiss government was able to resist a widespread popular demand that its guest worker population be expelled by demonstrating that workers were engaged in occupations for which Swiss workers were not available and that the country's economy would suffer if the guest workers were expelled. The Australian government has generally been ahead of Australian public opinion in its support for a nondiscriminatory immigrant admission policies. The French government has successfully resisted demands that locally born children of migrants not acquire citizenship. There are times, too, when a public has been willing to accept extraordinary large numbers of refugees, as was the case of the Pakistani willingness to accommodate millions of Afghans and the American and French willingness to take in many Indochinese. When there is public opposition, moreover, it may be for good reasons. The concerns expressed by many Americans and Europeans that their governments should take steps to halt illegal migration, establish more rigorous procedures to prevent foreigners from entering under false asylum claims, repatriate rejected asylum seekers, and reduce immigration during a period of recession should not be dismissed, no matter how unsavory some of the antimigrant rhetoric. For a country to have an acceptable immigration policy, it must be able to control illegal immigration. And for a country to have an acceptable refugee policy, it must be able to prevent large numbers of immigrants from entering under false asylum claims. The unwillingness of governments to take steps to halt an unwanted massive influx of foreigners can erode immigration and refugee policies, strengthen right-wing parties, and generate xenophobic fears that may put democratic societies at risk.

Policy choices are rarely clear, not simply because there can be a conflict between what is morally right and what is politically feasible but often because there are conflicting moral claims. Moral reasoning in migration policy must take into account many countervailing but equally legitimate concerns. It must also take into account the unintended moral consequences of policies, recognizing that moral intent in itself is a poor guide to public policy.

chapter 9

MEETING THE CRISIS

What can and ought to be done to meet the global migration crisis? What options are available to states confronting growing immigration pressures? There are three possibilities: accommodation, control, or intervention. This concluding chapter will examine each of these in both empirical and normative terms.

ACCOMMODATION

To consider the accommodation option, we must first ask whether the world economy and global communications are such powerful forces for international migration that states are essentially powerless to control who enters. We now have, some people assert, a global labor market that determines the flow of people so that attempts to restrict entry simply result in the growth of an illegal migrant population living without the benefit of any rights. Under these circumstances, it is further argued, it is best to allow the market to work and to reap its benefits and mitigate its costs.

The argument for this view is as follows: Developed countries find it difficult to prevent illegal migration because many employers want the low-skilled, low-wage workers that they are unable to find in the local labor market. A number of factors have contributed to this demand. In particular, employers can no longer recruit from the rural hinterland, now absent, or among the urban poor, who often reject low-wage employment if they can do better on welfare entitlements. Declining fertility and population aging in industrial societies may also lead to an increase in the demand for labor. Facing a tight labor market for low-wage labor, employers of labor, like users of capital, turn to the global market to meet their needs. U.S. employers have found low-wage workers in Mexico and the Caribbean; German employers have turned to Turkey, Yugoslavia, and Greece, and, more recently, to Eastern Europe; and French, Italian, and Spanish employers find their workers in North Africa. Even when employers can find workers on the local market, they often prefer foreign workers, who are pliable, unlikely to join unions, willing to work long hours, tolerant of conditions that local labor finds unacceptable, and readily dismissable when no longer needed.

The emergence of a global labor market has been made possible by advances in information technology and transportation. Mexicans, Turks, Chinese, Algerians, Filipinos, Jamaicans, Tunisians, Croatians, and Serbs are now familiar with the labor markets of Europe, the United States, and Canada. They have friends and relatives abroad who inform them of changing market conditions and of the opportunities for employment and housing. Moreover, transportation costs have declined, and brokers have now organized the international market in labor. Potential migrants have also learned entry regulations and how best to get around them, such as by entering a country as tourists and staying to find jobs. They also know that they can claim political asylum and, while their cases are reviewed, find work or live at government expense. Employment opportunities abound in the less regulated secondary labor market—restaurants, small businesses, domestic service. Forged documents are readily available for purchase. Meanwhile, circumstances in their home countries are often dire. In developing countries, an estimated 38 million people join the labor force every year, and as many as 700 million people are already unemployed or underemployed.[1] Consequently, the risks of illegal migration are relatively low and the rewards, in terms of finding employment and obtaining higher wages than at home, are high. Indeed, it is surprising that only a small fraction of employment-age individuals in developing countries have attempted to migrate.

It is further argued that because illegal migration and nonjustifiable claims for asylum are strongly employment- and employer-driven, policy instruments to reduce the flow significantly are not likely to work. Government penalties against employers who hire illegal migrants in the United States appear to have had only limited effects. Studies of the 1986 U.S. Immigration Reform and Control Act report that the legislation has not halted illegal migration and may have only marginally reduced the flow.[2] Western European guest worker programs, intended to rotate workers to discourage illegal migration and prevent permanent settlement, have also not had their intended effects. And Japan, in spite of imposing large fines on employers for the import of foreign workers and the employment of illegal aliens, has been unable to prevent the growth of an illegal labor force.[3]

Moreover, notwithstanding efforts by countries in the European Union to tighten their immigration and asylum policies, the annual flow of irregulars has been increasing since the mid-1980s. The number of annual asylum seekers (excluding displaced persons from former Yugoslavia) increased from 165,000 in 1985 to 314,000 in 1989 to 690,000 in 1992; in the same years, the estimated number of illegal immigrants increased from 50,000 to 150,000 to 370,000. The num-

1. United Nations Development Programme, *Human Development Report, 1992* (New York: Oxford University Press, 1992), p. 54.

2. Wayne Cornelius, "Impacts of the 1986 U.S. Immigration Law on Emigration from Rural Mexican Sending Communities," *Population and Development Review,* December 1989, pp. 689–705. See also Frank D. Bean, Barry Edmonston, and Jeffrey Passel (eds.), *Undocumented Migration to the United States* (Washington, D.C.: Urban Institute, 1990), especially the chapter by Karen Woodrow and Jeffrey Passel, "Post-IRCA Undocumented Immigration to the United States: An Assessment Based on the June 3, 1988, Current Population Survey," pp. 33–76.

3. Research project of the Center for U.S.-Mexican Studies University of California, San Diego, 1992. The project, spearheaded by Wayne Cornelius, set out to evaluate alternative theoretical models to explain the rising demand for low-skilled immigrant labor in advanced industrial societies. The results appear in Wayne Cornelius, Philip Martin, and James Hollifield (eds.), *Controlling Immigration* (Stanford, Calif.: Stanford University Press, 1995). For an analysis that argues for a linkage between capital flows and illegal migration, see Saskia Sassen, *The Mobility of Labor and Capital* (Cambridge: Cambridge University Press, 1988). Sassen subsequently applied this analysis to the Japanese case. See Saskia Sassen, *The Global City* (Princeton, N.J.: Princeton University Press, 1991).

ber of annual registered migrants to Western Europe also increased, from 650,000 in 1985 to 1,380,000 in 1993, partly the result of family reunion but also reflecting the growth in the number of asylum seekers in previous years who were subsequently granted residence permits. The total annual migration into Western Europe since 1990 has exceeded 2 million and in 1992 reached 2.9 million.[4] Though, as noted earlier, the worldwide total of migrants constitutes only a small percentage of the world's population, the number can be significant for receiving countries. In at least 43 countries the percentage of foreign born or nonnationals is over 5 percent. In 42 countries the percentage is either over 10 percent, or the number exceeds 1 million. In 29 countries the migrant population is at least 20 percent, or the number exceeds 3 million.

Liberal democratic political systems are particularly constrained from adopting policies to control immigration tightly—partly by their liberal ideology, which leads governments to provide entitlements to legal and illegal immigrants and claimants for asylum and prevents them from engaging in large-scale expulsions, and partly by the influence of lobbyists (businesses, ethnic groups, civil libertarians) on behalf of illegal migrants and asylum seekers.[5] The introduction of a counterfeit-proof identity card that would be required as a condition of employment, for example, is opposed by civil libertarians. Many members of the middle class, meanwhile, employ illegal domestic servants—a lifestyle on which the government is reluctant to intrude. Furthermore, many people in Western Europe and North America do not regard the overstay of a visa or illegal entry as a crime but rather as an understandable effort of a person attempting to improve his or her position at no cost to others.

Less developed countries also find it difficult to control unwanted entries. Market forces play a role here as well; migrants move from one Third World country to another when opportunities are available for employment or for gaining access to land. Border control is made more difficult by the arbitrariness of many postcolonial borders, which cut across ethnic communities and divide lands customarily used by cattle farmers and shifting cultivators. In addition to market forces, moreover, civil conflicts and natural disasters have led millions of people, especially in Africa, to move across international borders within the Third World. Finally, new states often lack the military and administrative capacity to halt movement across their borders and are therefore even less capable than industrial societies of imposing restrictions and penalties on employers for using illegal aliens.

Given these realities, are both market and political forces now so powerful that traditional conceptions of state sovereignty, which rest on notions of borders and state capacity to define membership, have become or are becoming anachronistic? If the answer is yes, states must develop new approaches in addressing migration issues. If states, especially advanced industrial democracies, cannot control who enters, should they now turn instead to the question of how best to deal with the consequences of uncontrolled entry?

Proponents of policy changes to address the consequences do not suggest that governments should announce that their borders are open but rather that they

4. International Centre for Migration Policy Development, *A Comparative Analysis of Entry and Asylum Politics in Selected Western Countries* (Vienna: International Center for Migration Policy Development, 1994).

5. For an analysis of how "embedded liberalism" constrains states, see James F. Hollifield, *Immigrants, Markets, and States* (Cambridge, Mass.: Harvard University Press, 1992).

Table 18   GLOBAL MIGRATION, 1990

Country	Population (millions)	Nonnational Population		Foreign-born Population	
Argentina	32.3			1,628,000	(5.0%)
Australia	17.1			4,000,000	(23.4%)
Austria	7.7	512,000	(6.6%)		
Azerbaijan	7.2	1,220,000	(17.4%)		
Bahrain	0.5			112,000	(32.0%)
Belarus	10.3	2,250,000	(22.2%)		
Belgium	9.9	900,000	(9.1%)		
Brunei	0.3	150,000	(50.0%)		
Canada	26.5			4,000,000	(15.1%)
Cameroon	11.8	250,000	(5.4%)°		
Estonia	1.6	600,000	(38.5%)		
France	56.4	3,600,000	(6.4%)		
Gabon	0.9	300,000	(25.0%)		
The Gambia	1.2	50,000	(16.7%)		
Georgia	5.5	1,600,000	(29.2%)		
Germany	63.2	5,000,000	(7.9%)		
Hong Kong	5.8			2,223,000	(37.7%)
Iraq	18.9	1,282,000	(6.8%)		
Italy	57.1	1,400,000	(2.5%)		
Japan	123.5	1,348,000	(1.1%)		
Kazakhstan	16.7	9,930,000	(60.3%)		
Kuwait	2.1	1,499,000	(71.4%)		
Kyrgystan	4.4	2,000,000	(47.7%)		

Note: As is reflected in this table adapted from a study prepared by three major international institutions dealing with population movements, there is no uniform worldwide system for reporting the number of migrants. Some countries report the number of foreign-born residents, inclusive of those who are citizens. Other countries report the number of nonnational residents, excluding foreign born who are citizens but including locally born noncitizens. The figures for several European countries, therefore, exclude immigrants who have become naturalized citizens. The figure for Germany excludes migrants of German origin from eastern Europe and the former Soviet Union since they become German citizens when they immigrate. Nonnationals in the former Soviet Union are reported here, though many migrated when the Soviet Union was a single country, and some of the nonnationals were born locally but are not citizens. The table does not, however, similarly list nonnationals in other countries that have

should expand the amount of legal migration and quietly accept "unauthorized" or "undocumented" migration. An analogy can be drawn with free international markets in goods and the globalization of capital markets. If the free market in trade and capital is beneficial to all countries, proponents of this approach assert, so is a free market in labor. Furthermore, just as it has become difficult, as well as undesirable, for countries to prevent the free movement of goods and capital (legally or through smuggling), so too is it difficult and undesirable to prevent the globalization of labor.

Country	Population (millions)	Nonnational Population		Foreign-born Population	
Latvia	2.7	1,280,000	(48.0%)		
Libya	4.5	250,000	(22.7%)°		
Lithuania	3.7	750,000	(20.4%)		
Luxembourg	0.4	117,000	(28.4%)		
Malaysia	17.9	1,000,000	(5.6%)		
Moldova	4.4	1,540,000	(35.6%)		
Netherlands	14.9	692,000	(4.6%)		
Oman	1.5	442,000	(70.0%)°		
Qatar	0.4	230,000	(92.0%)°		
Russia	148.3	27,200,000	(18.5%)		
Saudi Arabia	14.9	2,878,000	(60.0%)°		
Singapore	3.0			600,000	(20.0%)
South Africa	35.3	500,000	(4.9%)°		
Sweden	8.6			814,000	(9.5%)
Switzerland	6.7	1,200,000	(17.9%)		
Tajikistan	5.3	1,920,000	(37.8%)		
Turkmenistan	3.7	987,000	(28.1%)		
Ukraine	51.9	14,100,000	(27.4%)		
United Arab Emirates	1.6	805,000	(89.0%)°		
United Kingdom	57.2	1,894,000	(3.3%)		
United States	250.0			21,000,000	(8.4%)
Uzbekistan	20.5	5,685,000	28.7%)		
Venezuela	19.7			1,000,000	(5.1%)

been divided, such as India and Pakistan, Pakistan and Bangladesh, Singapore and Malaysia, Ethiopia and Eritrea, North and South Korea. Several countries, especially oil-producing countries of the Middle East, only report the number of nonnationals in their labor forces and exclude nonemployed family members. There are several other notable omissions from this table: Taiwan and Israel, both with large numbers of immigrants; refugees, except where they have been resettled; and illegal or irregular migrants. In the main, therefore, this table underreports the magnitude of global migration.

°Nonnationals in the labor force (with percent of labor force in brackets).

Source: Migrants, Refugees and International Cooperation. 1994 Geneva: International Labour Organization, International Organization for Migration, and United Nations High Commissioner for Refugees.

Such a policy conclusion draws on the views of neoclassical economists, who long ago demonstrated the economic benefits of the free movement of the factors of production. Everyone gains, they argue, if communities produce what they can make most efficiently and then trade their goods with others: Capital would move to where it could be used most efficiently (and most profitably), and every country would be better off if money and goods could move freely. Neoclassical economists have applied this same logic to the free movement of labor within a country: Individuals would move to where their labor was most needed, and the price paid would be the highest, making the country, as well as individuals, better off. Given this economic rationale, would it not be desirable to permit as much free movement of labor across international boundaries as is politically acceptable? Labor-exporting countries would presumably gain by earning remittances from their overseas workers, and receiving countries would gain by employing unskilled foreign workers in jobs that locals do not want and by making up for domestic labor shortages. "The absorptive capacity of Western European countries," wrote *The Economist,*

> though not as great as that of America or Australia, is still bigger than timid people think. European politicians who run scared of racist or anti-immigrant feeling will be doing their countries no favors. Their guiding principle as they map out Europe's immigration plans should not be "How few can we get away with letting in?" but rather, "How many can we possibly take without creating unbearable social strain?"[6]

The question of what drives migration flows and to what extent they are beneficial to receiving countries is, of course, central to any analysis of policy alternatives. It is first necessary to note that the consequences of the free movement of labor across international borders are not the same as the consequences of the free movement of capital and goods across these same borders. The logic of free trade between countries is that it finds its own equilibrium: A country that bought more than it sold would see the value of its currency decline, the cost of imports go up, and the price of its exports go down until a trade balance was established. No such simple mechanism operates with respect to the free movement of people across national boundaries. A world without borders might indeed be one in which the free movement of people and the free movement of capital and goods would benefit all; but in a world in which states and boundaries do exist, the free movement of people—unlike the free movement of capital and goods—would damage countries that chose to have unregulated borders. Indeed, much the same argument is used by advocates of some form of managed trade in conditions in which, they argue, there is no free movement of the factors of production because governments provide subsidies or impose costs on their own producers and place a variety of tariff and nontariff restrictions on imports.

Even a relatively free international labor market is not without its costs. Migrants do displace some local labor; a large-scale influx does put a burden on housing, education, and social services and depress wages; refugees can impose heavy costs on the government and on local people, push up food prices, crowd urban settlements, and damage the local ecology; some societies can be threatened by a large number of immigrants from another culture; and ethnic conflicts between migrants and locals, especially between migrants and indigenous minorities, and among different migrant communities can be politically destabilizing and violent. There are also hidden costs, or what economists call opportunity costs. In a tight labor market, employers have an incentive to seek ways to make labor more productive. Technological and managerial innovations are more likely to occur when labor costs go up. These costs vary; some are higher for developing countries,

---

6. *Economist,* August 4, 1990, p. 15. The article goes on to observe that for Western Europeans, it will be easier to absorb Eastern Europeans than North Africans.

some for developed countries. For these and other reasons, countries need to impose limits on how many migrants, if any, to admit and what kinds.

But do advanced industrial economies need migrants? Demographers have argued against a widely held view that declining fertility rates and aging population necessitate a need for importing labor. For one thing, fertility rates have not been declining in all advanced industrial countries; since the mid-1980s, fertility rates have risen in Germany, the United States, and Canada. More significant, unemployment rates are high—over 10 percent in Western Europe and above 6 percent in the United States. Workers have been losing jobs in Rust Belt industries, and in many sectors of the economy, the demand for low-skilled labor has declined. If there is an unmet demand for low-skilled workers in some sectors of the economy, it is because the welfare system removes some low-skilled workers from the labor force and many young people are unwilling to do manual work that is considered dirty, socially undesirable, and low-paying. It seems unlikely that the labor market, especially for low-skilled workers, will be tight during the next 10 or 20 years, given the growth of labor-displacing technologies, the movement of low-cost labor-intensive industries from developed to developing countries, the growing capacity of the service sector to transfer computer and telecommunication functions from high-wage to low-wage economies,[7] increased opportunities for female participation in the labor force, and the continued availability of young people in a labor force that has a persistent high level of unemployment.[8]

Particularly telling is the growth in movement to developed countries even in the midst of a recession, suggesting that either supply is creating its own demand or that ease of access rather than the structure of the labor market is shaping the flow. The very large increase in the number of migrants to Germany—the stock of foreigners increased from 4.5 million in 1988 to an estimated 6.5 million by 1994—had little to do with a growth in the demand for labor. During this same period, the United Kingdom experienced no increase in the size of its foreign population. The difference clearly had to do with ease of access. Britain's insular position at the edge of Western Europe and its greater capacity than Germany's for border control has kept down the flow of illegals, and it has also adopted a more restrictive asylum policy. Similarly, the presumed globalization of the labor market did not prevent Japan from choosing not to have a guest worker program when Western Europe did, nor has it prevented Japan from keeping down the number of asylum seekers and illegals by imposing tighter controls than most Western governments have implemented.

No country has given up control over entry, nor is there any reason to do so.

---

7. For example, one major American firm closed its accounting department in the United States, dismissed its staff of 50, and transferred the department to Bombay, where it hired 50 qualified individuals at significantly lower wages.

8. See David A. Coleman, "Does Europe Need Immigrants? Population and Work Force Projections," *International Migration Review*, Summer 1992, pp. 413–461. "It seems eccentric," writes Coleman, "to propose the resumption of immigration for low-grade labor when there are 15 million unemployed in Europe, most under age 25 and many themselves immigrants, especially since future demand for labor emphasizes high skills" (p. 413). The same argument holds for the United States, where there is a large underutilized low-skilled and young labor force.

CONTROL

Can countries slow the flow of illegal migration and the large-scale influx of asylum claimants who do not meet the legal criteria for entry by establishing more effective controls over entry? Control policies may include increasing the military and police presence at borders, punishing common carriers that permit travelers to enter without visas, running computer checks on all employees to ensure that they are citizens or have permission to work, enforcing employer sanctions, issuing national counterfeit-proof identity documents, expelling illegal aliens, insisting on offshore reviews of asylum seekers, detaining onshore asylum seekers pending their review, promptly repatriating asylum seekers whose claims have been rejected by adjudicating officers, and classifying most asylum seekers as temporary residents and requiring their repatriation when conditions permit. In liberal democratic regimes, such measures can work only if there is substantial public support. If a large part of the public regards illegal migration as a victimless crime, however, and remains sympathetic to illegals, few of these measures can be introduced or effectively implemented.

Once the premise is granted that states have the right to control entry, it is morally justifiable to pursue a variety of policies aimed at preventing illegal entries at borders, assessing penalties on employers, and expelling illegals. It then becomes necessary to decide whether controls should take the form of border or internal regulations; a corollary question is whether and when controls infringe on individual rights.

Border controls have become less and less efficacious. For many countries, the sheer volume of border traffic makes road checks for illegal entries time-consuming and obstructive. Passport control officers at airports have only seconds to check and detect false passports and visas. And as governments promote tourism and business travel, it becomes easier for would-be immigrants to enter a country with the intention of staying. Moreover, migrants, whether through the assistance of smuggling agents or on their own, have become more and more adept at finding new ways to get in. Still, it is not beyond the capacity of states to improve their control over entry if they are prepared to put more resources into border guards, post asylum officers in embassies, and establish more stringent policies toward asylum seekers.

An alternative to border control is internal control—a policy that makes civil libertarians uneasy. Tamper-proof electronic identity cards are possible but costly, for one must first determine who is entitled to such cards. A system to ensure that illegals are not employed in the underground economy or work as domestics is similarly costly and intrusive. A comprehensive national registration system (as exists in Sweden and as has been proposed by the U.S. Commission on Immigration Reform) is feasible as long as employers are required to check the central registry before employing anyone and are penalized for failing to do so. If the number of illegal entries to the United States, Canada, Japan, and Central and Southern Europe continues to increase, governments may be prepared to introduce more elaborate internal controls.

When the number of asylum seekers is low and the number of unwarranted claims relatively small, a case-by-case review onshore, with the right of appeal and without detention, is both feasible and desirable. But when the flows become heavy and the proportion of unwarranted claims rises, the costs—financial, political, social, economic, and administrative—go up, and governments and their citizens are more inclined to adopt sterner measures. As international market forces and domestic turmoil in population-exporting countries cause international migration to rise, more states will want to take more rigorous steps to control entry.

In some respects, this has become more of a problem for developed countries than for Third World countries because many of the latter, their limited administrative capacities notwithstanding, can expel large numbers of illegals, guest workers, and refugees. As discussed earlier, this instrument of control is not readily available to liberal democratic societies in the West, and many Western governments have even been reluctant to repatriate rejected asylum seekers or individuals given temporary asylum. Historically, although Third World countries have been more generous in admitting refugees and more tolerant of illegal migrants than many developed countries, they have also been more willing to force immigrants and refugees to return home. Many developing countries can engage in such practices because they are unencumbered by protests from human rights organizations in their own country and unrestrained by a liberal ideology. Nigeria, Saudi Arabia, and Kuwait have expelled migrant workers; India speedily cleared its camps of millions of Bangladeshi refugees after its war with Pakistan; and Thailand and Pakistan both cut supplies to camps to press their Cambodian and Afghan refugees to return home.

In the future, control policies are likely to become increasingly important in both developed and Third World countries. At present, many of Africa's 6 million refugees are in countries with regimes that are too weak either to halt the refugee flows or to force repatriation. But as some of these states and others in the Third World increase their administrative, financial, and military capabilities and as a sense of nationhood grows, they are likely to become less accommodating to refugees and illegal migrants. This, in turn, will have an impact on developed countries. As Third World countries become more effective at keeping out unwanted refugees and migrants, individuals who want to leave their own country will look beyond their near neighbors to countries with less restrictive control policies. Consequently, as exit barriers drop and the level of violence and insecurity in many countries increases, governments will have little choice but to look for more effective ways to control entry.

INTERVENTION

A third approach for addressing the global migration crisis is intervention, seeing that much migration is the result of political and economic conditions in sending countries. The foreign policy problem is how to halt the flow of refugees by changing the conditions in the sending country so that individuals will no longer find it necessary to flee. As the number of refugees has increased and as the pressure on receiving countries has grown, policymakers have been wrestling with two issues: (1) how to control their own borders to prevent illegal immigration and limit the admission of migrants and refugees to the ones they choose and (2) whether and how to intervene in the affairs of states whose treatment of their own citizens impels them to leave. Both issues raise practical and moral questions.

A discussion of intervention must begin with the question of why people move, the so-called root causes of these flows. "The only solution" to the refugee crisis, wrote Jean-Pierre Hocke when he was the United Nations High Commissioner for Refugees,

> lies in attending to the root cause, first to remove the reason for further flows where refugee movements appear likely to continue, and then to reverse the flow through the creation of appropriate conditions for the voluntary repatriation of those who have already left.[9]

Few would disagree with this assessment. But what constitutes the "root cause" or causes? Gil Loescher answers: "The underlying forces of nationalism, ethnic conflict, foreign intervention, arms sales, incompetent government, and widespread human rights violations overlap, and it is difficult if not impossible to determine the exact 'root causes' of different refugee outflows."[10] To this list of already unmanageable causes, moreover, Jonas Widgren adds population growth and the rapid increase of young people entering the labor force in developing countries, starvation resulting from crop failures, and "the overall economic imbalance between developed and developing countries."[11]

Given the difficulty of identifying specific causes, some proponents of intervention advocate rather broad policies. "Since refugees are a global problem, the search for solutions must also be global," writes Loescher.[12] For Loescher, Widgren, and many others, the root causes lie in global inequalities that must be remedied by attempts to achieve a greater distribution of the world's resources and wealth. Others assign heavy responsibility to the great powers and the cold war, pointing to the ways in which conflicts between the United States and the Soviet Union, or their surrogates, contributed to the refugee flows in Angola, Mozambique, Afghanistan, Somalia, Ethiopia, Nicaragua, and elsewhere.[13] Still others see United States support of regimes characterized by repressive conduct as

9. Jean-Pierre Hocke, "Beyond Humanitarianism: The Need for Political Will to Resolve Today's Refugee Problem," in *Refugees and International Relations*, ed. Gil Loescher and Laila Monahan (New York: Oxford University Press, 1989), p. 45.

10. Gil Loescher, "Introduction: Refugee Issues in International Relations," in ibid, p. 18.

11. Jonas Widgren, "Europe and International Migration in the Future," in ibid., p. 57. Widgren also writes: "The long-term solutions to the migration challenge are the same as those outlined for all the other burning global problems that we face: stabilizing world population at a reasonable level, reinstalling human rights, reinforcing democracy, peacefully settling regional conflicts, halting environmental degradation, allowing for continued economic growth, abolishing trade protectionism, alleviating poverty, relieving the debt burden, increasing sound development aid, strengthening UN cooperation—and in general maintaining peace, regionally and globally" ("International Migration and Regional Stability," *International Affairs*, October 1990, p. 766). To the extent that states regard migration and refugee flows as threats to their security, more direct and immediate measures are necessary.

12. Loescher, "Introduction," op cit., p. 2.

13. For a statement of this position, see Charles S. Milligan, "Ethical Aspects of Refugee Issues and U.S. Policy," in *Refugee Law and Policy*, ed. Ved P. Nanda (Westport, Conn.: Greenwood Press, 1989), pp. 165–184.

the cause of a population flight from Haiti, Chile, and El Salvador.[14] One political philosopher, a disciple of Rawls, argues that

> as citizens of the developed nations, we have created and are perpetuating by use of our economic and military power a global institutional order under which tens of millions avoidably cannot meet their most fundamental needs for food and physical security.[15]

According to this view, ordinary citizens in the West are not responsible for the human misery that exists in the Third World, but their societies or governments are in part responsible for the misery in that they collaborated in the perpetuation of an unjust global order. A more complex variant of this view is that foreign capital investment in low-income countries induces emigration by promoting export agriculture, which pushes farmers off the land; introducing labor-displacing agricultural technologies; and creating female-intensive employment in electronics, which promotes male emigration.[16]

The attempt to identify root causes is only partly intended to suggest what might be done to reduce refugee flows. Often its purpose is to assign blame and thereby to impose a moral obligation on the parties in the West who are presumed to be responsible for the flow. If the flow is the result of an unjust distribution of the world's wealth, then, to quote Widgren, "what the world needs is a kind of new Marshall Plan—a massive transfer of resources from the North to the South."[17] If intervention by the United States is a major factor, the United States has incurred a moral obligation to bear the costs of admitting and settling refugees. "To the extent," writes Charles Milligan, "that the United States has contributed to causes for the flow of refugees, whether directly or by proxy, there is a special responsibility to grant safe refuge."[18] An alternative view of blame is offered by Gervase Coles, who writes that

> the modern refugee problems is, basically, that of the adverse conditions within the country of origin which are forcing people to flee. If the refugee problem is to be solved the solution must basically be sought among those adverse conditions.[19]

14. Peter Koehn, "Persistent Problems and Political Issues in U.S. Immigration Law and Policy," in ibid., pp. 67–87. Koehn writes: "The United States has an obligation to bear a major share of the costs associated with assisting the victims of brutal regimes it has supported and of economies its firms have exploited," and again, "the principle of giving preference to persons of 'special humanitarian concern' to the United States should be interpreted to encompass those who are in danger because of the overseas actions of this country's government agencies or corporations" (p. 79).

15. Thomas W. Pogge, *Realizing Rawls* (Ithaca, N.Y.: Cornell University Press, 1989), p. 238.

16. See Wayne Cornelius, "Mexican Immigration: Causes and Consequences for Mexico," in *Sourcebook on the New Immigration,* ed. Roy Bryce-Laporte (New Brunswick, N.J.: Transaction Books, 1980), p. 778, and Saskia Sassen-Koob, "Direct Foreign Investment: A Migration Push-Factor?" *Environment and Planning C: Government and Policy,* 2, 1984, pp. 399–416.

17. Widgren, "Europe and International Migration," p. 58.

18. Milligan, "Ethical Aspects," p. 172. Critics of U.S. policies justified providing sanctuary to Central American refugees who slipped across the U.S. borders on the grounds that the U.S. was morally responsible for the war. See Todd Howland and Richard Garcia, "The Refugee Crisis and the Law: The 'City Sanctuary' Response," in *Refugee Law and Policy,* ed. Nanda, pp. 185–199.

19. Gervase Coles, "Approaching the Refugee Problem Today," in *Refugees and International Relations,* ed. Loescher and Monahan, p. 387.

Ultimately, how we identify the determinants of unwanted international migration and refugee flows shapes our view both of what should be done to reduce these flows and what our obligations are with respect to admissions and settlement. Theorists who blame the international system or the behavior of the great powers want a more generous distribution of resources and more generous admission and settlement policies by the industrial states. Those who point to the internal conditions of countries that produce refugees and to the behavior of their governments are more likely to consider steps to force states to respect the rights of minorities, end their civil conflicts, and cease behaving in ways that force people to flee. In this case, emphasis shifts from the question of how to resettle refugees to the question of what steps can be taken to prevent a refugee flow and to enable repatriation to take place.

Several kinds of interventions might change internal conditions that produce refugees. Ironically, one of the most effective ways to induce political change may be to refuse to admit an authoritarian country's refugees. A refugee policy to admit political dissenters may actually reinforce authoritarian regimes. It has been argued, for example, that U.S. immigration law, which treated all Cuban refugees as political refugees, has been an inducement for opponents of the Cuban regime to leave.[20] To date, U.S. policy has enabled more than half a million Cubans to depart, many of whom, had they remained, would have constituted an important political force for change. So while other Communist systems have been overthrown from within, the Cuban regime has persisted in part because U.S. immigration policy unintentionally strengthened the regime. In contrast, in the mid- and late 1980s, the United States government urged members of Poland's Solidarity movement not to leave the country but to participate in the struggle for political reform; the resultant absence of flight is believed by many observers to have contributed to Solidarity's success in overthrowing the Communist regime.

The theoretical case for considering the relationship between emigration and political reform has been put forth by Albert Hirschman in his classic study *Exit, Voice, and Loyalty* and his subsequent examination of the fall of the German Democratic Republic.[21] Hirschman writes:

> Exit and voice were defined in my book as two contrasting responses of consumers or members of organizations to what they sense as deterioration in the quality of the goods they buy or the services and benefits they receive. Exit is the act of simply leaving, generally because a better good or service or benefit is believed to be provided by another firm or organization. Indirectly and unintentionally exit can cause the deteriorating organization to improve its performance. Voice is the act of complaining or of organizing to complain or to protest, with the intent of achieving directly a recuperation of the

20. Under the Cuban Adjustment Act, which remains in force, Cubans are classified as refugees without having to demonstrate that they have been persecuted. The difference in policies toward Haitians and Cubans is often pointed to as an indication of American racial views when in fact they are a reflection of the American view that anyone who leaves a Communist country is, by definition, a refugee fleeing an oppressive regime. In August 1994 the United States changed its policy by diverting rafters leaving Cuba to the U.S. Naval Base at Guantanamo as the United States had similarly diverted Haitian Vessels.

21. Albert O. Hirschman, *Exit, Voice, and Loyalty* (Cambridge, Mass.: Harvard University Press, 1970), and "Exit, Voice, and the Fate of the GDR: An Essay in Conceptual History," *World Politics,* January 1993, pp. 173–202.

quality that has been impaired. Much of my book and of my subsequent writings on this subject deal with the conditions under which exit or voice or both are activated.[22]

As applied to the fall of the German Democratic Republic, Hirschman argues that the opportunity for exit is what fundamentally distinguished East Germany from Poland, Czechoslovakia, and Hungary. In other words, the lack of exit opportunities led to the 1956 revolt in Budapest, the Prague Spring of 1968, and the emergence of Solidarity in Poland in 1980.

Conversely, the GDR policy of pushing out well-known dissident intellectuals beheaded opposition groups, thereby reducing the government's need for repression. The Berlin Wall halted the mass hemorrhage that was undermining the economy, but the government continued to permit some departures and forced out other citizens as part of a strategy to undermine protest movements. Hirschman asserts that the reason the GDR pursued such policies was that government officials "realized that they could weaken internal opposition by a selective policy of either permitting certain people to exit or outright expelling critical voices considered to be dangerous or obnoxious."[23]

According to the Hirschman analysis, a generous asylum and refugee policy may therefore abet authoritarian regimes. If the disaffected can readily leave, reformers and opponents of the regime may lose potential supporters. Furthermore, if large numbers of workers can find employment abroad, the home government may be relieved of the pressures for economic reforms that would increase economic growth and employment.

The empirical evidence does not provide us with a straightforward confirmation of this view. It may be true that the exit of dissenters is a benefit to authoritarian regimes, but dissidents abroad can also play an active role in rallying international opposition to a regime and in filtering information back to people at home. For example, Chinese dissidents in Australia, France, Canada, and the United States have contributed to keeping alive the movement for human rights. Would they be more effective if they returned home to an environment in which they would be silenced?

Thus even though the exodus of a small number of key dissidents *can* undermine efforts to build an opposition, the degree to which the opposition is damaged clearly depends on how much freedom is given to advocates of political reform. A system that is already divided and somewhat open, as was the case of Poland, or has an evident potential for political transformation, as in the case of Cuba, needs opponents to support the demand for change. Conversely, a ruthless leadership that incarcerates and kills its opponents is one in which dissidents can make little difference. Flight in such circumstances may in fact make some contribution to undermining the regime. Countries facing an influx of refugees and asylum seekers therefore need to make a difficult political judgment as to whether a generous admission policy is essential to protect people at risk or whether dissenting individuals and social classes should be persuaded or induced to remain at home to participate in the struggle for political change.

22. Hirschman, "Exit, Voice, and Fate," pp. 175–176.
23. Ibid., p. 184.

Much the same argument can be applied to the question of whether admitting immigrants relieves the economic burden on poor countries that face an unfavorable balance of payments. Remittance flows are a major component of the balance of payments of many Third World countries, yet it is not always clear whether these remittances increase or decrease the possibilities for economic reform. Again, there is no simple answer. A balance-of-payments crisis has sometimes forced inward-looking regimes to liberalize their trade policies, devalue their currencies, and pursue a set of policies aimed at expanding exports. Remittances, by relieving the balance-of-payments crisis, may therefore reduce the pressure for reform. In other situations, remittances have been part of a reform package providing governments with the foreign exchange they need to expand capital imports for their export industries. One wonders, consequently, what the political consequences would have been for countries like Mexico, Algeria, Turkey, Greece, India, and Pakistan had they not been able to export their labor to Western Europe or the Middle East. If their balance of payments had been worse and their unemployment rates higher, would major political changes have taken place, and would these have strengthened or destabilized the country and improved or worsened the human rights situation? These questions highlight the difficulties faced by population-receiving countries in making decisions about the admission of migrants and refugees; it is extremely difficult to discern what is most likely to bring about political or economic reforms that would reduce future pressures for emigration from sending countries.

Leaving aside the option of refusing refugees, a number of other interventions may be employed to address the causes of the migration crisis. Any analysis of what kinds of interventions might reduce illegal migrations and refugee flows must first consider the varied reasons for these flows. Acknowledging the difficulties discussed earlier of identifying causes, a partial list would certainly include the following:

- The persistent large differentials between countries in wages and employment opportunities
- A global information technology that enables people to become aware of opportunities for employment and for migration
- A global transportation system that makes it increasingly easy and less costly for people to migrate
- High rates of population growth that have made it difficult for developing countries to provide employment for young entrants into the labor force
- Low population growth rates in some developed countries where demand for labor periodically increases
- The changing structure of labor markets in advanced industrial countries, which results in an increased demand for low-wage labor in service sectors of the economy not met, for a variety of reasons, by local labor
- Land scarcity in many high-density agrarian societies, which induces peasants to migrate across international borders for grazing and agricultural lands or for urban employment
- Environmental degradation, droughts, floods, and famines that compel people to flee within or across international borders

- A boom in oil prices, which in the past resulted in large-scale investments in construction in regions with small populations and low labor force participation rates
- Ethnic conflicts, "ethnic cleansing," and discriminatory policies in newly independent states, which have caused minorities to flee
- Civil conflicts, including struggles among warlords and wars of secession, which have generated a refugee exodus
- Wars between states that threaten civilian populations
- The forced flight of political dissidents, including entire social classes, from authoritarian regimes
- The pull that migrants create for friends and relatives in their country of origin

These conditions induce people to move—through legal means when possible, through illegal means when necessary.

Which of these conditions can be changed through intervention? Turning first to the economic dimensions of international migration, could employment and income conditions in sending countries be significantly improved by an increase in economic assistance? Would a globally more open trade regime allow developing countries to expand their exports and enhance their employment? Similarly, would more international investment in job-producing industries aid developing countries enough to stem migration flows?

Most economists agree that economic policies that reduce differentials in wages and employment between migrant-producing and migrant-receiving countries would, in the long run, lower the incentives for international migration. Countries with similar wages and employment conditions—Canada and the United States, Germany and Denmark, for example—do not experience a significant flow of economic migrants across their common borders. Flows among the members of the European Union have remained small in spite of the absence of barriers to movement. The short-term effects of a reduction in differentials, however, might very well be an increase in the propensity to migrate, primarily because of rising expectations, the increase in resources necessary to migrate, and growing disparities *in the migrant-producing country.* Moreover, the historical evidence on the relationship between economic growth and emigration does not support arguments that programs to accelerate growth and an expansion of employment will necessarily reduce the pressures for emigration. The nineteenth century, for example, was an era of rapid industrial growth and urbanization in Europe; it was also an era that produced a large-scale exodus of Europeans to North and South America and to Australia. Similarly, the countries that have in the past sent the largest numbers of guest workers to Europe or migrants to the United States and Canada were among the most rapidly expanding economies in the Third World: South Korea, Taiwan, Singapore, Hong Kong, Algeria, Turkey, Mexico. Today the coastal regions of China are areas of high economic growth, expanding employment, and increasing wages, yet they are also the regions producing the largest number of migrants from China to the United States and Taiwan. Consequently, in the short term, trade and foreign investment, rather than serving as a substitute for labor migration, may actually induce it by creating new networks, expanding channels of communication, and increasing expectations. Only after an extended period of economic growth and a significant rise in wages is there likely to be a substantial reduction in pressures for emigration.[24]

Economic aid, however, may be intended not to remedy a country's high unemployment or low economic growth rate but rather as payment to a government to halt a refugee flow. To put it bluntly, governments may pay to avoid what they do not want. In the 1970s, U.S. economic assistance to Haiti halted a growing refugee flow (although it resumed again in early 1992, following a coup); similarly, the flow of Sri Lankan refugees to West Germany from East Germany was reduced when the Federal Republic of Germany agreed to provide credits to the German Democratic Republic. In the Haitian case, government-to-government aid was intended by the donor country to persuade the recipient country to halt the exodus; in the German case, the aid was intended to persuade the recipient country to stop providing transit to unwanted refugees.

Assistance can also be used by governments to persuade other governments to retain refugees. Hence the United States and France were willing to provide economic assistance to Thailand on the condition that the Thais would hold Vietnamese refugees rather than permit these refugees to seek entrance into the United States and France.[25] The UNHCR and other international agencies, financed largely by the West and Japan, provide resources to refugee-receiving countries—especially in Africa—not only as an expression of humanitarian concerns but also as a means of enabling refugees to remain in the country of first asylum rather than attempting to move elsewhere, as to advanced industrial countries.[26]

International financial support has also been important in inducing refugees to return home when a conflict subsides. Funds for transportation, resettlement, and mine clearance are often critical for a successful speedy repatriation process.

Another form of economic assistance has made a substantial and immediate difference in the magnitude of emigration: aid to disaster-afflicted areas from which people have fled. International aid, including food, medical supplies, blankets, and shelter, has been both a practical and a humanitarian means of discouraging the internally displaced from fleeing across international borders. Such sup-

24. For an attempt to deal with the relationship of migration, investment, and trade, see U.S. Commission for the Study of International Migration and Cooperative Economic Development, *Unauthorized Migration* (Washington, D.C.: Government Printing Office, 1990). The bipartisan commission, created by Congress in the Immigration Reform and Control Act of 1986, concluded that "any serious cooperative effort to reduce migratory pressures at their source must be pursued over decades, even in the face of intermediate contrary results" (p. xvi).

25. John R. Rogge, "Thailand's Refugee Policy: Some Thoughts on Its Origin and Future Direction," in *Refuge or Asylum*, ed. Howard Adelman and C. Michael Lanphier (Toronto: York Lane Press, 1990), pp. 150–171. Rogge describes how the Thais came to regard the influx from Vietnam as a security threat (pp. 162–163).

26. In 1991 and 1992, the United States sought to use its financial leverage to induce the government of Israel not to settle Soviet Jews on the West Bank, arguing that the settlement policy was damaging to the peace negotiations between Israel, the Palestinians, and Israel's neighboring Arab states. The Israeli Labour Party's opposition to settlements and the implication that the suspension of settlements would lead the United States to provide guarantees for $10 billion in bank loans may have been a factor in the Labour victory. See David Bar-Illan, "Why Likud Lost—and Who Won," *Commentary*, August 1992, p. 28.

port is generally limited, however, to crises that local people regard as temporary—a flood, an earthquake, a drought, a hurricane—so they are not inclined to flee if relief can be provided. Often, even in the midst of civil conflicts, many displaced persons prefer to remain in their country if the conflict is believed to be temporary and some form of assistance is forthcoming. The potential impact of assistance in many of these circumstances should not be underestimated. There are more people in the world who are internally displaced than there are refugees. The case for international assistance to the internally displaced could not be stronger—both on humanitarian grounds and as a means of reducing international refugee flows. Yet international agencies have often found it easier to raise resources for refugees than for the internally displaced. The United Nations High Commissioner for Refugees, moreover, does not have a mandate to work with internally displaced persons, although in fact it often does. In the future, to address the global migration crisis adequately, ameliorating the conditions that give rise to internally displaced persons must be high on the list of international interventions aimed at reducing refugee flows.

If a state is forcing its citizens to leave, the intervention options are somewhat more complex. When a state so mistreats its citizens that large numbers are compelled to flee, are other states morally obliged to take in their refugees, or alternatively, do they acquire a morally justifiable right to compel the state to stop persecuting its citizens?[27] This question requires an examination of what constitutes morally justifiable grounds for intervention, what the risks are to the parties who intervene, whether intervention is sanctioned by international institutions, whether and when interventions should be collective or unilateral, whether interventions would create more human losses than doing nothing, and above all, how to withdraw responsibly.

Interventions can take four forms: conditionality, sanctions, coercive diplomacy, and armed intervention.

- Conditionality refers to the use of economic assistance, loans, most-favored-nation trade arrangements, the sale of arms and of high technology, and other positive incentives to induce states to treat their citizens in accordance with international human rights norms.
- Sanctions involve the withholding of trade and investment against states that persecute minorities or political dissidents. Sanctions can also include the impounding of overseas bank accounts of individuals or governments, halting air and sea traffic, the breaking of diplomatic relations, and expulsion from international institutions. An important distinction is whether sanctions are directed at the entire economy of a country or are targeted toward specific individuals and social classes that can be held accountable for the behavior.
- Coercive diplomacy involves the plausible threat of sanctions and the use of force if the unacceptable behavior is not ended.

27. Some human rights advocates are concerned lest intervention become an alternative to providing asylum. See Andrew Shacknove, "From Asylum to Containment," *International Journal of Refugee Law,* 1993, pp. 516–533.

- Armed intervention can take the form of providing arms to the people under attack within the country, arming refugees, engaging in air or sea strikes, and military invasion.

The strategic analyst Thomas Schelling identified two analytically distinct strategies for affecting the behavior of states: compellent strategies and deterrence strategies.[28] The former involve policies to force changes in behavior; the latter are intended to prevent states from engaging in behavior that they might otherwise attempt. The two strategies can be in contradistinction to each other, as when the United States sought to compel North Korea to halt its nuclear development program without provoking the North into attacking South Korea. In this instance, a compellence strategy threatened to undermine a deterrence strategy. Both strategies are classically used to affect how states act toward one another, but they can also be invoked to influence how states treat their own citizens. Compellent strategies can, for example, be used to force a state to *cease* violating the human rights of its citizens. A deterrent strategy is useful to *prevent* a state from violating the human rights of its citizens. Ordinarily, in dealing with a recalcitrant state, a deterrence policy is more effective than a compellence strategy, for the latter is more likely to induce an intense and negative nationalist response, whereas the former policy allows the government greater maneuverability. Hence the earlier steps are taken to induce countries not to violate the human rights of their population, the more likely they are to be effective. The efforts of several Scandinavian countries to work with the Baltic states to reconcile their nationalist tendencies with the need to provide protection for their Russian minorities is a good example of the use of incentives as a form of deterrence.

Once a massive exodus has begun, however, the emphasis shifts to compellence strategies. Note that interventions usually impose costs for the country that employs them as well as for the target country. For example, cutting off the sale of technology has a negative impact on exports, and military intervention can mean a loss of life for members of the armed forces. Countries will bear lower costs for humanitarian reasons, but higher costs usually require that a government and its citizens believe that their national interests are jeopardized.

Much of the discussion of intervention assumes that one country has the economic and military power to apply leverage on another, but it is well to remember that the country producing the refugees also has leverage against the county that is receiving them. As discussed in Chapter 6, countries can, for example, threaten to produce refugees or to repatriate guest workers unless other countries bow to their will by providing loans or financial aid or by calling a halt to a human rights campaign. Intervention is a two-way street.

The most problematic situation is one in which a refugee-producing state is incapable of taking action to halt the flow, usually because the country is torn by civil conflict and the government itself is unable to establish internal order. This "failed state" phenomenon is widespread within the Third World: examples include Somalia, Liberia, Afghanistan, Angola, Cambodia, Mozambique, and, until recent-

28. Thomas C. Schelling, *The Strategy of Conflict* (Cambridge, Mass.: Harvard University Press, 1960), p. 195.

ly, Lebanon. Should or can such states, once independent, be placed under an international mandate, as some people have suggested? Internationally supervised elections have been proposed as a mechanism for the establishment of governmental authority. International mediating teams can attempt to negotiate among warring factions. Donors can provide support to local nongovernmental organizations in an effort to create the civil society that is necessary to underpin democratic institutions. The United Nations and its members have had a growing number of experiences—we might call them experiments—with intervention: Cambodia, which was placed under UN administration pending elections and the restoration of a government; Somalia, where U.S. and other forces entered to provide humanitarian relief and to deal with warlords; northern Iraq, where internationally protected "safe havens" were established for the Kurds; Bosnia, where NATO has provided protection to some communities and where international mediating teams have sought to facilitate a negotiated settlement; Rwanda, where French forces have endeavored to provide humanitarian assistance in the midst of an armed conflict between rebel forces and the government; and Haiti, where U.S.-threatened military intervention forced the government to step down. It is not clear yet as to what kinds of interventions can change the conditions in countries producing a population outflow. What is clear, however, is that the international community is proceeding in an ad hoc fashion, without any systematic strategies, policies, or institutions, to deal with repressive authoritarian regimes and failed states whose actions or inability to take action is resulting in the loss of life and liberty that impels people to flee. Consequently, new strategies for intervention must be explored if the global migration crisis is to be confronted

SOME MORAL GUIDELINES

It is not immoral for people to want to leave their country for another, nor is it immoral for states to try to prevent people from entering. In thinking about the development of migration and refugee policies, is it possible to reconcile these opposing positions? Where do human rights and the interests of states intersect?

States will and, in the main, should decide what people to admit, how many of them, and for how long, based on what they and their citizens regard as their own best interests. Some states will generously admit migrants; others will not. Some states will open their doors to people who flee from violence; others will admit only refugees who fear persecution. We can applaud the generosity of some countries, but that does not necessarily make others immoral. A lack of generosity is not the same as immorality. There is no moral requirement that all states must admit migrants, as distinct from refugees. As we have often noted, there are many reasons why governments may consider it desirable to have migrants—to fill needs in the labor market, to reunite families, to provide cultural diversity, or to incorporate members of one ethnic and religious communities living elsewhere. But governments and their citizens are also free to decide that they prefer to remain culturally homogeneous, do not want the short-term dislocations that ordinarily accompany immigration, and are concerned over increased population densities or environmental consequences. It is not immoral not to admit immigrants.

Does this mean that there can be no international norms to guide how states ought to behave toward migrants and asylum claimants? Are there any principles that will satisfy the national interests of states as well as the concerns of human rights advocates for moral justice? We will explore principles that might serve as guideposts in a battleground where the interests of people who wish to leave their countries often collide with the people and the governments of the countries to which they wish to go.

First, states may choose not to admit immigrants, but if they do, their migration policies ought to be nondiscriminatory. They may give preference to people who fit the requirements of their labor market, are relatives of individuals already living in the country, or share the language and culture of their citizens, but states ought not to bar individuals because they belong to a particular race, religion, or ethnic group—that is, because they belong to a group with largely immutable characteristics. The moral line between preferences and exclusion is clearly a thin one, but there is a line. Whites only and Asian exclusion policies clearly fall on the wrong side of the line.

A second guiding principle for state policies is that foreigners who are admitted into a country's labor force and permitted to stay for an extended period should be entitled to become naturalized citizens. Their locally born children should also be admitted into citizenship, as should genuine refugees with no realistic prospects of returning home. Similarly, illegals who remain in a country for an extended period because the state has been lax in its enforcement, acquire a de facto right to remain and to become citizens. A state has no obligations to individuals who have evaded detection because it lacks the administrative capacity to detect and expel illegal residents, but if a state tacitly admits individuals by choosing to look the other way, an obligation is created by the fact that the illegal residents have become, in effect, members of the community. States that deny citizenship rights to long-term residents of a country undermine the central principle of a modern state, which is that those who live and work within its boundaries and have become part of the community should be given equal rights under the law. To create a permanent distinction between citizens and long-term resident aliens is to deny rights to a class of people who participate in the economy and social order. States need not, however, be precluded from having a temporary work program that enables workers to join the labor force for a brief period to fill a temporary labor need, as long as the need is short-term and the workers receive much the same benefits and protection provided to the local labor force. Whether it is possible or economically desirable to have a temporary work program in a democratic society is an empirical issue; it becomes a moral question only when workers and their families are permitted to remain for an extended period but are denied the political rights of citizenship.

A third guiding principle is that countries that already have large migrant populations whose cultural traditions and religious practices differ from those of the host population ought to allow their migrants to maintain their beliefs and practices as long as these do not impair the civil order. In fact, the countries of Western Europe, with a large and growing migrant population, cannot escape coming to grips with the growing diversity of their own societies. Older notions equating nationality, culture, and citizenship are no longer appropriate. Europeans will need to learn to accommodate the presence of Muslims, Hindus, and Buddhists and to address the implications of this religious diversity for their educational systems and church-state relations; in turn, the need will arise for dialogue with members of these communities about those beliefs and practices that are at variance with the values of the larger community.

A fourth principle is that guest workers worldwide are in need of protection. There are no international norms that provide for their protection, no international agencies with the authority to intervene on their behalf. Countries that export labor are often more concerned with the remittances that workers send home than with protecting their nationals from abuses by employers. As a result, in some countries, workers are paid wages below what contracts provide and are abused without any mechanism for dealing with their grievances. The International Labor Organization has drafted conventions on the treatment of migrant workers, but these agreements have not been ratified by the Gulf states, where large numbers of guest workers reside. Furthermore, the ILO, perhaps because of its tripartite role representing governments, employers, and workers, does not have the authority or the administrative machinery to create an international migration regime comparable to that of the UNHCR. One is sorely needed.

A fifth principle is that states have a moral obligation to provide asylum and to assist outsiders who are persecuted or at risk of being killed. The ghosts of shiploads of Jewish refugees who were turned back to Nazi Germany, where they were then slain, should haunt policymakers. The definition of refugees, however, need not be expanded to include all whose human rights are violated or who are in economic distress, for that would result in a massive increase in claimants beyond what states can reasonably be expected to accept and hence would undermine the asylum and refugee regime. Distinguishing between people who qualify as refugees under international norms and illegitimate asylum seekers could in part be dealt with as an administrative problem, not a moral one. Accelerated asylum review procedures and information programs might deter individuals from falsely seeking asylum and using the refugee route to become migrants. Nonetheless, states will not escape from the moral conundrum of devising ways of deterring false claimants without deterring genuine refugees. As we have noted earlier, the higher the number of false claims for asylum, the greater becomes the justification for developing systems of deterrence. Finally, it should be added, though bona fide refugees are in need of protection, they have no claim to go to the country of their choice.

A sixth principle is that no single country should be asked to provide protection and bear all the costs for caring for individuals who are persecuted or are at risk of being killed. Any country that opens its borders to people who are desperate is certainly worthy of praise; however, generosity is costly, and these costs must be shared. The policy of confining asylum seekers to the country of first asylum increases the burdens on countries with generous refugee policies and invariably taxes the patience of their citizens. It is no surprise that Germany, which once had some of the most liberal asylum laws in the world, decided to tighten its entry regulations when other countries of Europe were unwilling to admit refugees who had ever entered Germany. Burden-sharing of refugees is a morally attractive idea, which might alleviate disparities in the impact of refugees on receiving states; however, there are at present no international or regional agreements as to what form burden-sharing should take. For example, it is unclear how far away refugees should be transported from their home countries and whether financial contributions to countries that host refugees constitute an adequate form of burden-sharing.

There is a presumption that each region or cultural zone should care for its own refugees: Eastern European and Soviet refugees have a place in the United States and Western Europe, Central Americans and Caribbeans go to the United States or stay within the region, Tamil and Afghan refugees remain in South Asia, Latin Americans stay in the western hemisphere (or Iberia), and people in flight from African countries find refuge on their own continent. Furthermore, although the United States and Western European states do admit refugees from the Third World, the overwhelming majority of these refugees stay within their own region despite the fact that Third World governments are often financially and politically too weak to cope with a large refugee influx. Given these patterns of refugee distribution, how can burdens be shared? If some countries are prepared to accept refugees and others are not, should the latter be asked to bear a substantial portion of the costs? How does one develop a more equitable international regime for sharing the costs of accommodating refugees and refugee resettlement? There are no easy answers to these questions. What is clear is that the present system of financing international institutions that assist in the protection of refugees, their repatriation, and their resettlement is unsatisfactory, dependent as it is on ad hoc voluntary contributions.

A seventh principle is that the repatriation of refugees to their home country should remain the first objective of refugee and asylum policies. Asylum should ordinarily be regarded as temporary, and the decision as to when conditions have changed enough to enable refugees to return home cannot be left entirely in the hands of those who have been granted asylum, preferable as the notion of voluntary repatriation is. There are times when governments and international agencies must make that decision, keeping in mind the moral obligation not to send individuals and communities back to life-threatening situations. It may be necessary, for example, to close refugee camps and force refugees to return home because the camps have become military bases, camp resources are being skimmed by local leaders, and refugees are being terrorized. Forced repatriation is not necessarily morally objectionable.

The eighth and final guiding principle is that there are circumstances when intervention, including military intervention, in the internal affairs of another country is morally justified. States that engage in genocidal behavior, failed states that cannot bring an end to civil conflict, and states that deliberately force people to become refugees cannot be allowed to retreat behind the principles of sovereignty and nonintervention. In such cases, other countries are morally justified in intervening. There is, however, a distinction between being morally justified and being morally obligated. This distinction is ordinarily made on the basis not of the magnitude of the crime being committed but on the cost of intervention. We are morally justified in breaking up a gang war in which people are killing one another, but we are not obliged to do so if we put our own lives—or those of our soldiers—at risk, unless the magnitude of the crime being committed is so great that it would be immoral not to intervene. Beyond some threshold, in other words, countries cannot morally ignore atrocities perpetrated by a state against its own citizens. There are no clear rules to tell us what this threshold is. The higher the costs of intervention, moreover, the greater the need for public support for intervention. Nevertheless, there are instance when a state's treatment of its own citizens is so heinous that intervention, including armed intervention, is justified or even obligated.

Force may be used for a variety of objectives: to keep combatants apart; to separate an ethnically divided people (rarely to bring them together!); to carry out a peaceful transfer of populations following a redrawing of borders; to restore an overthrown elected government; to remove a genocidal regime; to create a militarily secure safe zone for noncombatants; to prevent belligerents from using artillery, helicopter gunships, and bombers against civilians; to disarm warring groups, including the military; or to enable the formation of a new government (perhaps legitimized through elections). The exercises of military power (or a credible threat) may be part of a panoply of instruments for inducing the state or conflicting groups to change their behavior; there are circumstances when behavior cannot be changed without a credible threat that external force will be employed.

For military intervention in the internal affairs of another country to be justifiable, a government must persuade the international community (usually international or regional organizations) that the intervention is for humanitarian purposes, that it is likely to do more good than harm, and that it is not simply serving its own narrow interests.

The global migration crisis will not disappear. There is every reason to expect that, paradoxically, even in an era of nationalism, more and more people will want to leave their home country. The international flow of information will continue to be a major determinant of these flows and perhaps will become more significant as satellite television spans the globe. More than ever before, individuals have become aware of the opportunities for employment and income in other countries. A worldwide reduction in income disparities and employment opportunities is unlikely to compensate for this greater awareness of disparities. The declining cost of travel, moreover, is making it easier for migrants and refugees to go longer distances. The price of a ticket from Sri Lanka to Berlin, Trivandrum to Kuwait, Manila to Canberra, Hong Kong to Vancouver, and Amritsar to Brighton is now only a discounted airfare often paid for by previous migrants or by borrowing against future income. A global network of agents can arrange air and sea voyages from one part of the world to another at a price that people are prepared to pay. Violence and repression, always factors in international population movements, are everywhere greater now than in the nineteenth century, when the imperial powers imposed peace on much of the world. Postcolonial societies, often torn by ethnic and religious conflicts, governed by repressive elites, or not governed at all, are producing refugees on an unprecedented scale.

All these factors will exacerbate the global migration crisis. Facing growing numbers of migrants and refugees, governments are confronting increasingly uncomfortable choices, some of which require the balancing of potentially high economic, political, and moral costs and uncertain benefits. The challenge to governments is to create policies based on humanitarian considerations that are consistent with a country's national interest. On matters of migration and refugees, governments will also be moved by both the generosity and the visceral anxieties of their citizens. But at the end of the day, states will not and cannot allow others to decide who will permanently live and work in their own societies.

BIBLIOGRAPHY

Adelman, Howard (ed.). 1991. *Refugee Policy: Canada and the United States.* Toronto: York Lane Press.

Adelman, Howard, and C. Michael Lanphier. 1990. *Refuge or Asylum: A Choice for Canada.* Toronto: York Lane Press.

Adler, Stephen. 1977. *International Migration and Dependence.* Farnborough, England: Gower Publishing House.

Alonso, William (ed.). 1987. *Population in an Interacting World.* Cambridge, Mass.: Harvard University Press.

Alvarez, Robert R. 1987, Summer. A Profile of the Citizenship Process Among Hispanics in the United States. *International Migration Review, 21*(2): 327–351.

Amjad, Rashid (ed.). 1989. *To the Gulf and Back: Studies on the Economic Impact of Asian Labour Migration.* New Delhi: International Labour Organisation, Asian Employment Program.

Amnesty International. 1991. *Europe: Human Rights and the Need for a Fair Asylum Policy.* London: Amnesty International.

Appleyard, Reginald (ed.). 1989. *The Impact of International Migration on Developing Countries.* Paris: Development Center for the Organization for Economic Cooperation and Development.

Arendt, Hannah. 1978. *The Jew as Pariah: Jewish Identity and Politics in the Modern Age,* ed. Ron H. Feldman. New York: Grove Press.

Arnold, Fred, and Nasra M. Shah (eds.). 1986. *Asian Labor Migration: Pipeline to the Middle East.* Boulder, Colo.: Westview Press.

Ash, Timothy Garton. 1989, December 21. The German Revolution. *New York Review of Books, 36*(20): 14–18.

Avineri, Shlomo, and Avner de-Shalit (eds.). 1992. *Communitarianism and Individualism.* Oxford: Oxford University Press.

Bach, Robert L. 1987. The Cuban Exodus: Political and Economic Motivations. In *The Caribbean Exodus,* ed. Barry B. Levine (pp. 106–130). New York: Praeger.

Bade, Klaus J. 1994. Immigration and Social Peace in United Germany. *Daedalus, 123*(1): 85–106.

Baron, Dennis E. 1990. *The English-Only Question: An Official Language for Americans?* New Haven, Conn.: Yale University Press.

Barry, Brian. 1973. The Liberal Theory of Justice: A Critical Examination of the Principal Doctrines. In *A Theory of Justice* by John Rawls. Oxford: Clarendon Press.

Barth, Fredrik (ed.). 1969. *Ethnic Groups and Boundaries*. Boston: Little, Brown.

Bean, Frank D., Barry Edmonston, and Jeffrey Passel (eds.). 1990. *Undocumented Migration to the United States: IRCA and the Experience of the 1980s*. Washington, D.C.: Urban Institute.

Bean, Frank D., Georges Vernez, and Charles B. Keely. 1989. *Opening and Closing the Doors: Evaluating Immigration Reform and Control*. Washington, D.C.: Urban Institute.

Beitz, Charles R. 1979. *Political Theory and International Relations*. Princeton, N.J.: Princeton University Press.

Bennett, Douglas C. 1986, August. Immigration, Work, and Citizenship in the American Welfare State. Paper presented at the annual meeting of the American Political Science Association, Washington, D.C.

Bennigsen, Alexandre A., and S. Enders Wimbush. 1978. Migration and Political Control: Soviet Europeans in Soviet Central Asia. In *Human Migration: Patterns and Policies*, ed. William H. McNeill and Ruth S. Adams (pp. 173–187). Bloomington: Indiana University Press.

Betts, Katharine. 1988. *Ideology and Immigration: Australia, 1976 to 1987*. Carlton, Victoria: Melbourne University Press.

Birks, J. S., I. J. Seccombe, and C. A. Sinclair. 1986, Winter. Migrant Workers in the Arab Gulf: The Impact of Declining Oil Revenues. *International Migration Review*, 20(4): 799–814.

Birrell, Robert, Douglas Hill, and Jon Nevill (eds.). 1984. *Populate and Perish? The Stresses of Population Growth in Australia*. Sydney: Fontana/Australian Conservation Foundation.

Böhning, W. R. 1972. *The Migration of Workers in the United Kingdom and the European Community*. London: Oxford University Press.

Böhning, W. R. 1974, Summer. Immigration Policies of Western European Countries. *International Migration Review*, 8(2): 155–164.

Böhning, W. R. 1981. Elements of a Theory of International Economic Migration to Industrial Nation-States. In *Global Trends in Migration: Theory and Research on International Population Movements*, ed. Mary M. Kritz, Charles B. Keely, and Silvano M. Tomasi (pp. 28–43). New York: Center for Migration Studies.

Böhning, W. R. 1984. *Studies in International Labour Migration*. London: Macmillan.

Borjas, George J. 1987, April. Immigrants, Minorities, and Labor Market Competition. *Industrial and Labor Relations Review*, 40(3): 382–392.

Borjas, George J. 1990. *Friends or Strangers: The Impact of Immigrants on the U.S. Economy*. New York: Basic Books.

Bouvier, Leon F. 1992. *Peaceful Invasions: Immigration and Changing America*. Lanham, Md.: University Press of America.

Brown, Colin. 1983. Ethnic Pluralism in Britain: The Demographic and Legal Background. In *Ethnic Pluralism and Public Policy: Achieving Equality in the United States and Britain*, ed. Nathan Glazer and Ken Young (pp. 32–53). Lexington, Mass.: Lexington Books/Heath.

Brown, Michael E. (ed.). 1993. *Ethnic Conflict and International Security*. Princeton, N.J.: Princeton University Press.

Brubaker, William Rogers (ed.). 1989. *Immigration and the Politics of Citizenship in Europe and North America*. Lanham, Md.: University Press of America.

Brubaker, William Rogers. 1989. *Immigration and the Politics of Citizenship in Late Nineteenth Century France.* Cambridge, Mass.: Society of Fellows, Harvard University.

Buchanan, Allen. 1991. *Secession: The Morality of Political Divorce, from Fort Sumter to Lithuania and Quebec.* Boulder, Colo.: Westview Press.

Bulatao, Rodolfo A., Eduard Bos, Patience W. Stephens, and My T. Vu. 1990. *World Population Projections 1989–90 Edition: Short- and Long-Term Estimates.* Baltimore: Johns Hopkins University Press, published for the World Bank.

Busey, Samuel C. 1969. *Immigration: Its Evils and Consequences.* New York: Arno Press. (Originally published 1856.)

Carens, Joseph H. 1987, Spring. Aliens and Citizens: The Case for Open Borders. *Review of Politics, 49*(2): 251–273.

Carens, Joseph H. 1987, Who Belongs? Theoretical and Legal Questions About Birthright Citizenship in the United States. *University of Toronto Law Journal, 37* (4): 413–443.

Carens, Joseph H. 1988. Immigration and the Welfare State. In *Democracy and the Welfare State,* ed. Amy Gutmann (pp. 207–230). Princeton, N.J.: Princeton University Press.

Carens, Joseph H. 1988. Nationalism and the Exclusion of Immigrants: Lessons from Australian Immigration Policy. In *Open Borders? Closed Societies? The Ethical and Political Issues,* ed. Mark Gibney (pp. 41–60). Westport, Conn.: Greenwood Press.

Carens, Joseph H. 1989. Membership and Morality: Admission to Citizenship in Liberal Democratic States. In *Immigration and the Politics of Citizenship in Europe and North America,* ed. William Rogers Brubaker (pp. 31–49). Lanham, Md.: University Press of America.

Carens, Joseph H. 1991. States and Refugees: A Normative Analysis. In *Refugee Policy: Canada and the United States,* ed. Howard Adelman (pp. 18–29). Toronto: York Lane Press.

Carens, Joseph H. 1992. Migration and Morality: A Liberal Egalitarian Perspective. In *Free Movement: Ethical Issues in the Transnational Migration of People and Money,* ed. Brian Barry and Robert Goodin (pp. 25–47). London: Harvest Wheatsheaf.

Carens, Joseph H. 1992, January. Refugees and the Limits of Obligation. *Public Affairs Quarterly, 6*(1): 31–44.

Carr-Saunders, A. M. 1964. *World Population: Past Growth and Present Trends.* London: Frank Cass.

Carrothers, William Alexander. 1965. *Emigration from the British Isles: With Special Reference to the Development of the Overseas Dominions.* London: Cass.

Castles, Stephen. 1986, Winter. The Guest-Worker in Western Europe: An Obituary. *International Migration Review, 20*(4): 761–778.

Castles, Stephen, and Godula Kosack. 1973. *Immigrant Workers and Class Structure in Western Europe.* London: Oxford University Press.

Chakravarti, N. R. 1971. *The Indian Minority in Burma: The Rise and Decline of an Immigrant Community.* Oxford: Oxford University Press.

Chaliand, Gérard (ed.). 1980. *People Without a Country: The Kurds and Kurdistan.* London: Zed Press.

Chaliand, Gérard, and Jean-Pierre Rageau. 1991. *Atlas des Diasporas.* Paris: Odile Jacob.

Cheng, Lucie, and Edna Bonacich (eds.). 1984. *Labor Immigration Under Capitalism: Asian Workers in the United States Before World War II.* Berkeley: University of Californa Press.

Choucri, Nazli. 1977, Winter. The New Migration in the Middle East: A Problem for Whom? *International Migration Review, 11*(4): 421–443.

Choucri, Nazli. 1986, April. Asians in the Arab World: Labor Migration and Public Policy. *Middle Eastern Studies, 22*(2): 253–273.

Clad, James, and Robert Keith-Reid. 1990, June 28. Harvest of Unrest: Racial Tensions Stirred as Foreign Criticism Wavers. *Far Eastern Economic Review, 146*(26): 15.

Coleman, David A. 1992, Summer. Does Europe Need Immigrants? Population and Work Force Projections. *International Migration Review, 26*(2): 413–461.

Coleman, David, and John Salt. 1992. *The British Population: Patterns, Trends, and Processes.* Oxford: Oxford University Press.

Cornelius, Wayne. 1978. *Mexican Migration to the United States: Causes, Consequences, and U.S. Response.* Cambridge, Mass.: Migration and Development Study Group, Center of International Studies, Massachusetts Institute of Technology.

Cornelius, Wayne. 1980. Mexican Immigration: Causes and Consequences for Mexico. In *Sourcebook on the New Immigration: Implications for the United States and the International Community,* ed. Roy Bryce-Laporte (pp. 69–84). New Brunswick, N.J.: Transaction Books.

Cornelius, Wayne. 1989, December. Impacts of the 1986 U.S. Immigration Law on Emigration from Rural Mexican Sending Communities. *Population and Development Review, 15*(4): 689–705.

Crewe, Ivor. 1983. Representation and the Ethnic Minorities in Britain. In *Ethnic Pluralism and Public Policy: Achieving Equality in the United States and Britain,* ed. Nathan Glazer and Ken Young (pp. 258–300). Lexington, Mass.: Lexington Books/Heath.

Crystal, Jill. 1991. *Kuwait: The Transformation of an Oil State.* Boulder, Colo.: Westview Press.

Cuny, Fred, and Barry Stein. 1989. Prospects for and Promotion of Spontaneous Repatriation. In *Refugees and International Relations,* ed. Gil Loescher and Laila Monahan (pp. 293–312). New York: Oxford University Press.

Curtin, Philip D. 1969. *The Atlantic Slave Trade: A Census.* Madison: University of Wisconsin Press.

Curtin, Philip D. 1989. *Death by Migration: Europe's Encounter with the Tropical World in the Nineteenth Century.* Cambridge: Cambridge University Press.

Daniels, Roger. 1988. *Asian America: Chinese and Japanese in the United States Since 1850.* Seattle: University of Washington Press.

Davies, Julian. (compiler). 1990. *Displaced Peoples and Refugee Studies: A Resource Guide.* London: Zell.

De Sipio, Louis. 1987, Summer. Social Science Literature and the Naturalization Process. *International Migration Review, 21*(2): 390–405.

De Vos, George A., and William O. Wetherall. 1983. *Japan's Minorities.* London: Minority Rights Group.

Dib, George. 1979, June. Migration and Naturalization Laws in Egypt, Lebanon, Syria, Jordan, Kuwait and the United Arab Emirates, Part 2: Naturalization Laws. *Population Bulletin of the United Nations Economic Commission for Western Asia,* June 1979, pp. 3–18.

Dominguez, Jorge I. 1990. Immigration as Foreign Policy in U.S.-Latin American Relations. In *Immigration and U.S. Foreign Policy,* ed. Robert W. Tucker, Charles B. Keely, and Linda Wrigley (pp. 150–166). Boulder, Colo.: Westview Press.

Dominguez, Jorge I. 1992. Cooperating with the Enemy? U.S. Immigration Policies Toward Cuba. In *Western Hemisphere Immigration and United States Foreign Policy,* ed. Christopher Mitchell. University Park: Pennsylvania State University Press.

Dowty, Alan. 1987. *Closed Borders: The Contemporary Assault on Freedom of Movement.* New Haven, Conn.: Yale University Press.

Druke, Luise. 1989. *Preventive Action for Refugee-producing Situations.* Frankfurt: Peter Lang.

Dummett, Ann, and Andrew Nicol. 1990. *Subjects, Citizens, Aliens and Others: Nationality and Immigration Law.* London: Weidenfeld & Nicolson.

Easterlin, Richard A., David Ward, William S. Bernard, and Reed Ueda. 1982. Naturalization and Citizenship. In *Immigration.* Cambridge, Mass.: Harvard University Press.

Esman, Milton J. 1986. Diasporas and International Relations. In *Modern Diasporas in International Politics,* ed. Gabriel Sheffer (pp. 333–349). London: Croom Helm.

Evans, M. D. R. 1988, Summer. Choosing to Be a Citizen: The Time-Path of Citizenship in Australia. *International Migration Review,* 22(2): 243–264.

Fawcett, James T., and Benjamin V. Carino (eds.). 1987. *Pacific Bridges: The New Immigration from Asia and the Pacific Islands.* New York: Center for Migration Studies.

Fawcett, James T., Benjamin V. Carino, and Fred Arnold. 1985. *Asian-Pacific Immigration to the United States.* Honolulu: East-West Population Institute.

Fitzgerald, Stephen. 1972. *China and the Overseas Chinese: A Study of Peking's Changing Policy, 1949–1970.* Cambridge: Cambridge University Press.

Fix, Michael, and Jeffrey S. Passel. 1994. *Immigration and Immigrants: Setting the Record Straight.* Washington, D.C.: Urban Institute.

Fleming, Donald, and Bernard Bailyn (eds.). 1969. *The Intellectual Migration: Europe and America, 1930–1960.* Cambridge, Mass.: Harvard University Press.

Freeman, Gary P. 1979. *Immigrant Labor and Racial Conflict in Industrial Societies: The French and British Experience, 1945–1975.* Princeton, N.J.: Princeton University Press.

Freeman, Gary P., and James Jupp (eds.). 1992. *Nations of Immigrants: Australia, the United States and International Migration.* Melbourne: Oxford University Press.

Fries, Yvonne, and Thomas Bibin. 1984. *The Undesirables.* Calcutta: Bagchi.

Fuchs, Lawrence H. 1990. *The American Kaleidoscope: Race, Ethnicity, and the Civic Culture.* Middletown, Conn.: Wesleyan University Press.

Fuchs, Lawrence H. 1990. The Reactions of Black Americans to Immigration. In *Immigration Reconsidered: History, Sociology and Politics,* ed. Virginia Yans-McLaughlin (pp. 293–314). New York: Oxford University Press.

Garrard, John A. 1971. *The English and Immigration: A Comparative Study of the Jewish Influx, 1880–1910.* London: Oxford University Press.

Gellner, Ernest. 1983. *Nations and Nationalism.* Ithaca, N.Y.: Cornell University Press.

George, Alexander L. 1991. *Forceful Persuasion.* Washington, D.C.: United States Institute of Peace Press.

Gibney, Mark (ed.). 1988. *Open Borders? Closed Societies? The Ethical and Political Issues.* Westport, Conn.: Greenwood Press.

Glazer, Nathan (ed.). 1985. *Clamor at the Gates: The New American Immigration.* San Francisco: Institute for Contemporary Studies.

Glazer, Nathan, and Ken Young (eds.). 1983. *Ethnic Pluralism and Public Policy: Achieving Equality in the United States and Britain.* Lexington, Mass.: Lexington Books.

Glenny, Misha. 1992, August 13. Yugoslavia: The Revenger's Tragedy. *New York Review of Books*, 34(14): 37–43.

Glenny, Misha. 1992. *The Fall of Yugoslavia: The Third Balkan War.* New York: Penguin.

Goodwin-Gill, Guy S. 1978. *International Law and the Movement of Persons Between States.* Oxford: Clarendon Press.

Gordenker, Leon. 1987. *Refugees in International Politics.* New York: Columbia University Press.

Gordon, Linda W. 1990. Asian Immigration Since World War II. In *Immigration and U.S. Foreign Policy,* ed. Robert W. Tucker, Charles B. Keely, and Linda Wrigley (pp. 169–191). Boulder, Colo.: Westview Press.

Gunatilleke, Godfrey (ed.). 1986. *Migration of Asian Workers to the Arab World.* Tokyo: United Nations University.

Gurr, Ted Robert. 1993. *Minorities at Risk.* Washington, D.C.: United States Institute of Peace Press.

Hailbronner, Kay. 1989. Citizenship and Nationhood in Germany. In *Immigration and the Politics of Citizenship in Europe and North America,* ed. William Rogers Brubaker (pp. 67–79). Lanham, Md.: University Press of America.

Hammar, Tomas. 1985. Citizenship, Aliens' Political Rights, and Politicians' Concern for Migrants: The Case of Sweden. In *Guests Come to Stay: The Effects of European Labor Migration on Sending and Receiving Countries,* ed. Rosemarie Rogers (pp. 85–107). Boulder, Colo.: Westview Press.

Hammar, Tomas (ed.). 1985. *European Immigration Policy: A Comparative Study.* Cambridge: Cambridge University Press.

Hammar, Tomas. 1989. State, Nation, and Dual Citizenship. In *Immigration and the Politics of Citizenship in Europe and North America,* ed. William Rogers Brubaker (pp. 81–95). Lanham, Md.: University Press of America.

Hanami, Tadashi. 1991, August. Discrimination in the U.S. and Japan from a Legal Viewpoint. *Journal of American and Canadian Studies,* pp. 1–31.

Hannum, Hurst. 1987. *The Right to Leave and Return in International Law and Practice.* London: Nijhoff.

Harrell-Bond, Barbara E. 1986. *Imposing Aid: Emergency Assistance to Refugees.* Oxford: Oxford University Press.

Hartz, Louis. (ed.). 1964. *The Founding of New Societies: Studies in the History of the United States, Latin America, South Africa, Canada, and Australia.* New York: Harcourt, Brace & World.

Hawthorne, Lesleyanne. 1982. *Refugee: The Vietnamese Experience.* London: Oxford University Press.

Heisler, Martin O., and Barbara Schmitter Heisler (eds.). 1986, May. From Foreign Workers to Settlers? Transnational Migration and the Emergence of New Minorities [special issue]. *Annals of the American Academy of Political and Social Science, 485.*

Higham, John. 1963. *Strangers in the Land: Patterns of American Nativism, 1860–1925.* New York: Atheneum.

Higham, John. 1984. *Send These to Me: Immigrants in Urban America.* Baltimore: Johns Hopkins Press.

Hirschman, Albert O. 1970. *Exit, Voice, and Loyalty: Responses to Decline in Firms, Organizations, and States.* Cambridge, Mass.: Harvard University Press.

Hirschman, Albert O. 1993, January. Exit, Voice, and the Fate of the German Democratic Republic: An Essay in Conceptual History. *World Politics*, 45(2): 173–202.

Hobsbawm, E. J. 1990. *Nations and Nationalism Since 1780: Programme, Myth, Reality.* Cambridge: Cambridge University Press.

Hocke, Jean-Pierre. 1989. Beyond Humanitarianism: The Need for Political Will to Resolve Today's Refugee Problem. In *Refugees and International Relations,* ed. Gil Loescher and Laila Monahan (pp. 37–48). New York: Oxford University Press.

Hoffmann-Nowotny, Hans Joachim. 1985. Switzerland. In *European Immigration Policy: A Comparative Study,* ed. Tomas Hammar (pp. 206–235). Cambridge: Cambridge University Press.

Hollifield, James F. 1992. *Immigrants, Markets, and States: The Political Economy of Immigration in Postwar Europe.* Cambridge, Mass.: Harvard University Press.

Horowitz, Donald L. 1985. *Ethnic Groups in Conflict.* Berkeley: University of California Press.

Horowitz, Donald L. 1989. Europe and America: A Comparative Analysis of Ethnicity. *Revue Européene des Migrations Internationales,* 5(1): 47–59.

Horowitz, Donald L., and Gerard Noiriel (eds.). 1992. *Immigrants in Two Democracies: French and American Experience.* New York: New York University Press.

Howland, Todd, and Richard Garcia. 1989. The Refugee Crisis and the Law: The "City Sanctuary" Response. In *Refugee Law and Policy: International and U.S. Responses,* ed. Ved P. Nanda (pp. 185–199). Westport, Conn.: Greenwood Press.

Hughes, Robert. 1987. *The Fatal Shore.* New York: Knopf.

Intergovernmental Consultations on Asylum, Refugee and Migration Policies in Europe, North America and Australia. 1992, June. The Country Assessment Approach and Beyond. Geneva: Intergovernment Consultations.

Intergovernmental Consultations on Asylum, Refugee and Migration Policies in Europe, North America and Australia. 1992, February. Toward International Recognition of the Need for Consistent Removal Policies with Respect to Rejected Asylum-Seekers. Geneva: Intergovernmental Consultations.

International Center for Migration Policy Development. 1994. *A Comparative Analysis of Entry and Asylum Policies in Selected Western Countries.* Vienna: International Center for Migration Policy Development.

International Organization for Migration. 1992, November 3. Policies and Practices with Respect to Rejected Asylum Seekers. Geneva: International Organization for Migration.

Jacobson, Jodi L. 1988. *Environmental Refugees: A Yardstick of Habitability.* Washington, D.C.: Worldwatch Institute.

Jenkins, Shirley (ed.). 1988. *Ethnic Associations and the Welfare State: Services to Immigrants in Five Countries.* New York: Columbia University Press.

Jensen, Joan M. 1988. *Passage from India: Asian Indian Immigrants in North America.* New Haven, Conn.: Yale University Press.

Jervis, Robert. 1976. *Perception and Misperception in International Politics.* Princeton, N.J.: Princeton University Press.

Johnston, H. J. M. 1972. *British Emigration Policy, 1815–1830: Shovelling Out Paupers.* Oxford: Clarendon Press.

Joly, Danièle. 1992. *Refugees: Asylum in Europe?* London: Minority Rights Publications.

Jupp, James. 1991. *Immigration.* Sydney: Sydney University Press.

Keely, Charles B. 1981. *Global Refugee Policy: The Case for a Development-oriented Strategy.* New York: Population Council.

Keely, Charles B., and Sharon Stanton Russell. 1994. Responses of Industrial Countries to Asylum-Seekers, Refugees, and Migrants. *Journal of International Affairs, 47*(2): 399–417.

Keohane, Robert O. 1984. *After Hegemony: Cooperation and Discord in the World Political Economy.* Princeton, N.J.: Princeton University Press.

Kindleberger, Charles Poor. 1967. *Europe's Postwar Growth: The Role of Labor Supply.* Cambridge, Mass.: Harvard University Press.

King, Timothy. 1983, April. Immigration from Developing Countries: Some Philosophical Issues. *Ethics, 93*(3): 525–536.

Klein, Sidney (ed.). 1987. *The Economics of Mass Migration in the Twentieth Century.* New York: Paragon House.

Koehn, Peter H. 1989. Persistent Problems and Political Issues in U.S. Immigration Law and Policy. In *Refugee Law and Policy: International and U.S. Responses,* ed. Ved P. Nanda (pp. 67–87). Westport, Conn.: Greenwood Press.

Koehn, Peter H. 1991. *Refugees from Revolution: U.S. Policy and Third-World Migration.* Boulder, Colo.: Westview Press.

Koizumi, Koichi. 1992. Refugee Policy Formation in Japan: Developments and Implications. *Journal of Refugee Studies, 2:* pp. 123–135.

Korte, Hermann. 1985. Labor Migration and the Employment of Foreigners in the Federal Republic of Germany Since 1950. In *Guests Come to Stay,* ed. Rosemarie Rogers (pp. 29–49). Boulder, Colo.: Westview Press.

Kramer, Jane. 1972. *Unsettling Europe.* New York: Random House.

Krasner, Stephen D. (ed.). 1983. *International Regimes.* Ithaca, N.Y.: Cornell University Press.

Kritz, Mary M. (ed.). 1983. *United States Immigration and Refugee Policy: Global and Domestic Issues.* Lexington, Mass.: Lexington Books.

Kritz, Mary M., Charles B. Keely, and Silvano M. Tomasi (eds.). 1981. *Global Trends in Migration: Theory and Research on International Population Movements.* New York: Center for Migration Studies.

Kritz, Mary M., Lin Lean Lim, and Hania Zlotnik (eds.). 1992. *International Migration Systems: A Global Approach.* Oxford: Clarendon Press.

Kubat, Daniel (ed.). 1984. *The Politics of Return: International Return Migration in Europe.* New York: Center for Migration Studies.

Kulischer, Eugene M. 1948. *Europe on the Move: War and Population Changes, 1917–47.* New York: Columbia University Press.

Kurian, George, and Ram P. Srivastava (eds.). 1983. *Overseas Indians: A Study in Adaptation.* Bombay: Vikas.

Kymlicka, Will. 1989. *Liberalism, Community and Culture.* Oxford: Clarendon Press.

Larrabee, F. Stephen. 1992, Spring. Down and Out in Warsaw and Budapest: Eastern Europe and East-West Migration. *International Security, 16*(4): 5–33.

Layton-Henry, Zig. 1985. Great Britain. In *European Immigration Policy: A Comparative Study,* ed. Thomas Hammar (pp. 89–126). Cambridge: Cambridge University Press.

Leveau, Remy, and Gilles Kepel. 1988. *Les Musulmans dans la société française.* Paris: Presses de la Foundation Nationale des Sciences Politiques.

Light, Ivan, and Edna Bonachich. 1988. *Immigrant Entrepreneurs: Koreans in Los Angeles, 1965–1982*. Berkeley: University of California Press.

Loescher, Gil. 1992. *Refugee Movements and International Security*, Adelphi Paper 268. London: Brassey's, for the IISS.

Loescher, Gil. 1993. *Beyond Charity: International Cooperation and the Global Refugee Crisis*. New York: Oxford University Press.

Loescher, Gil, and John A. Scanlan. 1983, May. U.S. Foreign Policy, 1959–1980: Impact on Refugee Flow from Cuba. *Annals of the American Academy of Political and Social Science, 467*: 116–137.

Loescher, Gil, and John A. Scanlan. 1986. *Calculated Kindness: Refugees and America's Half-open Door, 1945 to the Present*. New York: Free Press.

Loescher, Gil, and Laila Monahan (eds.). 1989. *Refugees and International Relations*. New York: Oxford University Press.

Mamdani, M. 1973. *From Citizen to Refugee: Ugandan Asians Come to Britain*. London: Pinter.

Marrus, Michael R. 1985. *The Unwanted: European Refugees in the Twentieth Century*. New York: Oxford University Press.

Martin, David. 1991. The Refugee Concept: On Definitions, Politics and the Careful Use of a Scarce Resource. In *Refugee Policy: Canada and the United States*, ed. Howard Adelman (30–51). Toronto: York Lane Press.

Martin, Philip L. 1991. *The Unfinished Story: Turkish Labour Migration to Western Europe, with Special Reference to the Federal Republic of Germany*. Geneva: International Labor Organization.

Martin, Philip L. 1993. Germany: Reluctant Land of Immigration. Paper prepared for the Controlling Illegal Immigration Conference, University of California, San Diego.

Martin, Philip L. 1994. Migration and Trade: Challenges for the 1990s. Discussion paper prepared for the World Bank, Washington, D.C.

Masud-Piloto, Felix. 1988. *With Open Arms: Cuban Migration to the United States*. Totowa, N.J.: Rowman & Littlefield.

Matras, Judah. 1973. *Populations and Societies*. Englewood Cliffs, N.J.: Prentice-Hall.

Mayo-Smith, Richmond. 1968. *Emigration and Immigration: A Study in Social Science*. New York: Johnson. (Originally published 1890.)

McDonald, Hamish. 1987, June 4. Rabuka Rides High: Fijians Head for Political Dominance After Coup Leader Backed. *Far Eastern Economic Review, 136*(23): 40–41.

McNamara, Dennis. 1989. The Origins and Effects of "Humane Deterrence" Policies in Southeast Asia. In *Refugees and International Relations*, ed. Gil Loescher and Laila Monahan (pp. 123–134). New York: Oxford University Press.

McNeill, William H., and Ruth S. Adams (eds.). 1978. *Human Migration: Patterns and Policies*. Bloomington: Indiana University Press.

Migrants, Refugees and International Cooperation. 1994. Geneva: International Labour Organization, International Organization for Migration, and United Nations High Commissioner for Refugees.

Miller, David. 1990. *Market, State and Community*. Oxford: Clarendon Press.

Miller, Mark J. 1979, Fall-Winter. Reluctant Partnership: Foreign Workers in Franco-Algerian Relations, 1962–1979. *Journal of International Affairs, 33*(2): 219–237.

Miller, Mark J. 1989, Winter. Dual Citizenship: A European Norm? *International Migration Review*, 23(4): 945–950.

Miller, Mark J., and Demetrios G. Papademetriou. 1983. Treating the Causes: Illegal Immigration and U.S. Foreign Economic Policy. In *The Unavoidable Issue: U.S. Immigration Policy in the 1980s*, ed. Demetrios G. Papademetriou and Mark J. Miller (pp. 185–214). Philadelphia: Institute for the Study of Human Issues.

Milligan, Charles S. 1989. Ethical Aspects of Refugee Issues and U.S. Policy. In *Refugee Law and Policy: International and U.S. Responses*, ed. Ved P. Nanda (pp. 165–184). Westport, Conn.: Greenwood Press.

Mitchell, Christopher (ed.). 1992. *Western Hemisphere Immigration and United States Foreign Policy*. University Park: Pennsylvania State University Press.

Morris, Benny. 1987. *The Birth of the Palestinian Refugee Problem, 1947–1949*. Cambridge: Cambridge University Press.

Nanda, Ved P. (ed.). 1989. *Refugee Law and Policy: International and U.S. Responses*. Westport, Conn.: Greenwood Press.

Nichols, J. Bruce. 1988. *The Uneasy Alliance: Religion, Refugee Work, and U.S. Foreign Policy*. New York: Oxford University Press.

Noiriel, Gérard. 1992. Difficulties in French Historical Research on Immigration. In *Immigrants in Two Democracies: French and American Experience*, ed. Donald L. Horowitz and Gérard Noiriel (pp. 66–79). New York: New York University Press.

North, David S. 1987, Summer. The Long Gray Welcome: A Study of the American Naturalization Program. *International Migration Review*, 21(2): 311–326.

Offen, Elizabeth N. 1992, June. The Persian Gulf War of 1990–91: Its Impact on Migration and the Security of States. Master's thesis, Department of Political Science, Massachusetts Institute of Technology.

Pachon, Harry P. 1987, Summer. Naturalization: Determinants and Process in the Hispanic Community—An Overview of Citizenship in the Hispanic Community. *International Migration Review*, 21(2): 299–310.

Paine, Suzanne. 1974. *Exporting Workers: The Turkish Case*. Cambridge: Cambridge University Press.

Papademetriou, Demetrios. 1979. Greece. In *International Labor Migration in Europe*, ed. Ronald E. Krane (pp. 187–200). New York: Praeger.

Pastor, Robert A. (ed.). 1985. *Migration and Development in the Caribbean: The Unexplored Connection*. Boulder, Colo.: Westview Press.

Peck, Jeffrey M. 1992. Refugees as Foreigners: The Problem of Becoming German and Finding a Home. Dissertation, United Nations University.

Pinkus, Benjamin. 1988. *The Jews of the Soviet Union: The History of a National Minority*. Cambridge: Cambridge University Press.

Piore, Michael J. 1979. *Birds of Passage: Migrant Labor and Industrial Societies*. Cambridge: Cambridge University Press.

Plender, Richard. 1972. *International Migration Law*. Leiden, Netherlands: Sijthoff.

Pogge, Thomas W. 1989. *Realizing Rawls*. Ithaca, N.Y.: Cornell University Press.

The Politics of Exile [special issue]. 1987, January. *Third World Quarterly*, 9(1).

Portes, Alejandro, and John W. Curtis. 1987, Summer. Changing Flags: Naturalization and Its Determinants Among Mexican Immigrants. *International Migration Review*, 21(2): 352–371.

Portes, Alejandro, and Ruben G. Rumbaut. 1990. *Immigrant America: A Portrait.* Berkeley: University of California Press.

Portes, Alejandro, and John Walton. 1981. *Labor, Class, and the International System.* New York: Academic Press.

Portes, Alejandro. 1978. Migration and Underdevelopment. *Politics and Society, 8*(1): 1–48.

Portes, Alejandro. 1979, April. Illegal Immigration and the International System: Lessons from Recent Legal Mexican Immigrants to the United States. *Social Problems, 26*(4): 425–438.

Posen, Barry R. 1993. The Security Dilemma and Ethnic Conflict. In *Ethnic Conflict and International Security,* ed. Michael E. Brown (pp. 103–124). Princeton, N.J.: Princeton University Press.

Poulton, Hugh. 1989. *Minorities in the Balkans.* London: Minority Rights Group.

Prasai, Surya B. 1990. *Third World Priorities for the 90s.* Chicago: University of Chicago Press.

Price, Charles. 1973. Australia. In *The Politics of Migration Policies: The First World in the 1970s,* ed. Daniel Kubat (pp. 3–18). New York: Basic Books.

Pronk, Johannes P. 1993, June. Migration: The Nomad in Each of Us. *Population and Development Review, 19*(2): 323–327.

Rawls, John. 1971. *A Theory of Justice.* Cambridge, Mass.: Harvard University Press.

Refugee Studies Programme, Oxford University (ed.). 1990. *Displaced Peoples and Refugee Studies: A Resource Guide.* London: Zell.

Reimers, David M. 1985. *Still the Golden Door: The Third World Comes to America.* New York: Columbia University Press.

Ricca, Sergio. 1989. *International Migration in Africa: Legal and Administrative Aspects.* Geneva: International Labor Organization.

Rist, Ray C. 1978. *Guestworkers in Germany: The Prospects for Pluralism.* New York: Praeger.

Rist, Ray C. 1979, Fall-Winter. The European Economic Community and Manpower Migrations: Policies and Prospects. *Journal of International Affairs, 33*(2): 201–218.

Rogers, Rosemarie (ed.). 1985. *Guests Come to Stay: The Effects of European Labor Migration on Sending and Receiving Countries.* Boulder, Colo.: Westview Press.

Rogge, John R. 1990. Thailand's Refugee Policy: Some Thoughts on Its Origin and Future Direction. In *Refuge or Asylum: A Choice for Canada,* ed. Howard Adelman and C. Michael Lanphier (pp. 150–171). Toronto: York Lane Press.

Russell, Sharon Stanton. 1986, June. Remittances from International Migration: A Review in Perspective. *World Development 14*(6): 677–696.

Russell, Sharon Stanton. 1993. *International Migration in North America, Europe, Central Asia, the Middle East, and North Africa.* Geneva: Economic Commission for Europe.

Russell, Sharon Stanton, and Michael S. Teitelbaum. 1992. *International Migration and International Trade.* Washington, D.C.: World Bank.

Safe, Helen I., and Brian M. Du Toit (eds.). 1975. *Migration and Development: Implications for Ethnic Identity and Political Conflict.* The Hague: Mouton.

Saha, Panchanan. 1970. *Emigration of Indian Labour, 1834–1900.* New Delhi: People's Publishing House.

Salt, John. 1989, Fall. A Comparative Overview of International Trends and Types, 1950–80. *International Migration Review, 23*(3): 431–456.

Salt, John. 1992, Winter. The Future of International Labor Migration. *International Migration Review, 26*(4): 1077–1111.

Sassen, Saskia. 1988. *The Mobility of Labor and Capital: A Study in International Investment and Labor Flow.* Cambridge: Cambridge University Press.

Sassen, Saskia. 1991. *The Global City: New York, Tokyo.* Princeton, N.J.: Princeton University Press.

Sassen-Koob, Saskia. 1978, October. The International Circulation of Resources and Development: The Case of Migrant Labor. *Development and Change, 9*(4): 509–545.

Sassen-Koob, Saskia. 1984. Direct Foreign Investment: A Migration-Push Factor? *Environment and Planning C: Government and Policy, 2:* 399–416.

Scanlan, John A., and O. T. Kent. 1988. The Force of Moral Arguments for a Just Immigration Policy in a Hobbesian Universe: The Contemporary American Example. In *Open Borders? Closed Societies? The Ethical and Political Issues,* ed. Mark Gibney (pp. 61–107). Westport, Conn.: Greenwood Press.

Schelling, Thomas C. 1960. *The Strategy of Conflict.* Cambridge, Mass.: Harvard University Press.

Schuck, Peter H. 1985. Immigration Law and the Problem of Community. In *Clamor at the Gates: The New American Immigration,* ed. Nathan Glazer (pp. 285–307). San Francisco: Institute for Contemporary Studies.

Schuck, Peter H. 1989. Membership in the Liberal Polity: The Devaluation of American Citizenship. In *Immigration and the Politics of Citizenship in Europe and North America,* ed. William Rogers Brubaker (pp. 51–65). Lanham, Md.: University Press of America.

Schuck, Peter H., and Rogers M. Smith. 1985. *Citizenship Without Consent: Illegal Aliens in the American Polity.* New Haven, Conn.: Yale University Press.

Schultz, Theodore W. 1978. Migration: An Economist's View. In *Human Migration: Patterns and Policies,* ed. William H. McNeill and Ruth S. Adams (pp. 377–386). Bloomington: Indiana University Press.

Sekine, Masami. 1992–1993, Winter. Guest Worker Policies in Japan. *Migration, 9*(Berlin): 44–69.

Shacknove, Andrew. 1985, January. Who Is a Refugee? *Ethics, 95*(2): 274–284.

Shacknove, Andrew. 1988. American Duties to Refugees: Their Scope and Limits. In *Open Borders? Closed Societies? The Ethical and Political Issues,* ed. Mark Gibney (pp. 131–150). Westport, Conn.: Greenwood Press.

Shacknove, Andrew. 1992. *From Asylum to Containment: Refugee Policy and Interests of State in the Post–Cold War Era.* Oxford: Refugee Studies Programme, Oxford University.

Shacknove, Andrew. 1993. From Asylum to Containment. *International Journal of Refugee Law,* pp. 516–533.

Shah, Nasra M. 1986, Winter. Foreign Workers in Kuwait: Implications for the Kuwaiti Labor Force. *International Migration Review, 20*(4): 815–832.

Shain, Yossi. 1989. *The Frontier of Loyalty: Political Exiles in the Age of the Nation-State.* Middletown, Conn.: Wesleyan University Press.

Shain, Yossi (ed.). 1991. *Governments-in-Exile in Contemporary World Politics.* New York: Routledge.

Sheffer, Gabriel (ed.). 1986. *Modern Diasporas in International Politics.* London: Croom Helm.

Shils, Edward. 1978. Roots—the Sense of Place and Past: The Cultural Gains and Losses of Migration. In *Human Migration: Patterns and Policies,* ed. William H. McNeill and Ruth S. Adams (pp. 404–426). Bloomington: Indiana University Press.

Shimada, Haruo. 1990. A Possible Solution to the Problem of Foreign Labor. *Japan Review of International Affairs,* 4(1): 66–90.

Shimada, Haruo. 1994. *Japan's "Guest Workers": Issues and Public Policies.* Tokyo: University of Tokyo Press.

Shklar, Judith N. 1990. *The Faces of Injustice.* New Haven, Conn.: Yale University Press.

Shue, Henry. 1980. *Basic Rights: Subsistence, Affluence, and U.S. Foreign Policy.* Princeton, N.J.: Princeton University Press.

Sidgwick, Henry. 1891. *The Elements of Politics.* London: Macmillan.

Simon, Julian L. 1981. *The Ultimate Resource.* Princeton, N.J.: Princeton University Press.

Simon, Julian L. 1989. *The Economic Consequences of Immigration.* New York: Blackwell.

Singer, Peter. 1979. *Practical Ethics.* Cambridge: Cambridge University Press.

Singer, Peter, and Renata Singer. 1988. The Ethics of Refugee Policy. In *Open Borders? Closed Societies? The Ethical and Political Issues,* ed. Mark Gibney (pp. 111–130). Westport, Conn.: Greenwood Press.

Singh, I. J. Bahardur (ed.). 1984. *Indians in South Asia.* New Delhi: Sterling.

Smith, Anthony D. 1981. *The Ethnic Revival in the Modern World.* Cambridge: Cambridge University Press.

Smith, Anthony D. 1991. *National Identity.* New York: Penguin.

Smyser, W. R. 1985, Fall. Refugees: A Never-ending Story. *Foreign Affairs,* 64(1): 154–168.

Sohn, Louis B., and Thomas Buergenthal (eds.). 1992. *The Movement of Persons Across Borders.* Washington, D.C.: American Society of International Law.

SOPEMI. 1992. *Trends in International Migration: Continuous Reporting System on Migration.* Paris: Organization for Economic Cooperation and Development.

Stahl, Charles W. 1982, Winter. Labor Emigration and Economic Development. *International Migration Review,* 16(4): 869–899.

Swanson, Jon C. 1979. *Emigration and Economic Development: The Case of the Yemen Arab Republic.* Boulder, Colo.: Westview Press.

Tambiah, Stanley J. 1986. *Sri Lanka: Ethnic Fratricide and the Dismantling of Democracy.* Chicago: University of Chicago Press.

Tambiah, Stanley J. 1992. *Buddhism Betrayed? Religion, Politics, and Violence in Sri Lanka.* Chicago: University of Chicago Press.

Teitelbaum, Michael S. 1980, Fall. Right Versus Right: Immigration and Refugee Policy in the United States. *Foreign Affairs,* 59(1): 21–59.

Teitelbaum, Michael S. 1984, Summer. Immigration, Refugees, and Foreign Policy. *International Organization,* 38(3): 429–450.

Teitelbaum, Michael S. 1984, Summer. Political Asylum in Theory and Practice. *Public Interest,* 76: 74–86.

Teitelbaum, Michael S. 1984. Tragic Choices in Refugee Policy. In *American Refugee Policy: Ethical and Religious Reflections,* ed. Joseph M. Kitagawa (pp. 32–36). Minneapolis: Presiding Bishops Fund for World Relief/Winston Press.

Teitelbaum, Michael S. 1985. Forced Migration: The Tragedy of Mass Expulsions. In *Clamor at the Gates: The New American Migration,* ed. Nathan Glazer (pp. 261–283). San Francisco: Institute for Contemporary Studies.

Teitelbaum, Michael S. 1985. *Latin Migration North: The Problem for U.S. Foreign Policy.* New York: Council on Foreign Relations.

Thistlethwaite, Frank. 1991. Migration, Ethnicity, and the Rise of an Atlantic Economy. In *A Century of European Migrations: 1830–1930,* ed. Rudolph J. Vecoli and Suzanne M. Sinke (pp. 17–57). Urbana: University of Illinois Press.

Thomas, Brinley. 1973. *Migration and Economic Growth: A Study of Great Britain and the Atlantic Economy.* Cambridge: Cambridge University Press.

Thomas, Eric-Jean (ed.). 1982. *Immigrant Workers in Europe: Their Legal Status.* Paris: UNESCO Press.

Tinker, Hugh. 1974. *A New System of Slavery: The Export of Indian Labour Overseas, 1830–1920.* London: Oxford University Press.

Tinker, Hugh. 1977. *The Banyan Tree: Overseas Emigrants from India, Pakistan, and Bangladesh.* Oxford: Oxford University Press.

Torres, Raidza. 1991, Winter. The Rights of Indigenous Populations: The Emerging International Norm. *Yale Journal of International Law, 16*(1): 127–175.

Tucker, Robert W., Charles B. Keely, and Linda Wrigley (eds.). 1990. *Immigration and U.S. Foreign Policy.* Boulder, Colo.: Westview Press.

United Nations. 1982. *International Migration, Policies and Programmes: A World Survey.* New York: United Nations.

United Nations. 1985. Expert Group on Population Distribution, Migration and Development. *Population Distribution, Migration and Development.* New York: United Nations.

United Nations Development Programme. 1994. *Human Development Report, 1994.* New York: Oxford University Press.

United Nations High Commissioner for Refugees. 1979. *Collection of International Instruments Concerning Refugees* (2d ed.). Geneva: Office of the United Nations High Commissioner for Refugees.

United Nations High Commissioner for Refugees. 1994. *The State of the World's Refugees: The Challenge of Protection.* New York: Penguin.

United Nations Population Fund. 1993. *The 1993 State of the World Population Report.* New York: United Nations.

United Nations Subcommission on Prevention of Discrimination and Protection of Minorities. 1987. *Study of the Problem of Discrimination Against Indigenous Populations.* New York: United Nations.

Unna, Warren. 1985. *Sikhs Abroad.* Calcutta: Stateman.

U.S. Commission for the Study of International Migration and Cooperative Economic Development. 1990. *Unauthorized Migration: An Economic Development Response.* Washington, D.C.: Government Printing Office.

U.S. Department of State. 1987, December. *Afghanistan: Eight Years of Soviet Occupation.* Washington, D.C.: Government Printing Office.

Vatikiotis, Michael. 1992, August 6. Malaysia: Worrisome Influx, Foreign Workers Raise Social, Security Fears. *Far Eastern Economic Review, 155*(31): 21.

Vecoli, Rudolph J., and Suzanne M. Sinke (eds.). 1991. *A Century of European Migrations, 1830–1930.* Urbana: University of Illinois Press.

Vincent, R. J. 1986. *Human Rights and International Relations.* Cambridge: Cambridge University Press.

Walker, Mack. 1964. *Germany and the Emigration, 1816–1885.* Cambridge, Mass.: Harvard University Press.

Walzer, Michael. 1983. *Spheres of Justice: A Defense of Pluralism and Equality.* New York: Basic Books.

Wattenberg, Ben J., and Karl Zinsmeister. 1990, April. The Case for More Immigration. *Commentary, 89*(4): 19–25.

Weil, Patrick. 1991. *La France et ses étrangers: L'aventure d'une politique de l'immigration, 1938–1991.* Paris: Calmann-Levy.

Weiner, Michael A. 1994. *Race and Migration in Imperial Japan: The Limits of Assimilation.* London: Routledge.

Weiner, Myron. 1971. Population Demography: An Inquiry into the Political Consequences of Population Change. In *Rapid Population Growth: Consequences and Policy Implications,* ed. National Academy of Sciences (vol. 2, pp. 567–617). Baltimore: Johns Hopkins University Press.

Weiner, Myron. 1978. *Sons of the Soil: Migration and Ethnic Conflict in India.* Princeton, N.J.: Princeton University Press.

Weiner, Myron. 1982, March. International Migration and Development: Indians in the Persian Gulf. *Population and Development Review, 8*(1): 1–36.

Weiner, Myron. 1983, June. The Political Demography of Assam's Anti-immigrant Movement. *Population and Development Review, 9*(2): 279–292.

Weiner, Myron. 1985, September. On International Migration and International Relations. *Population and Development Review, 11*(3): 441–455.

Weiner, Myron. 1985. Transborder Peoples. In *Mexican Americans in Comparative Perspective,* ed. Walker Connor (pp. 130–158). Washington, D.C.: Urban Institute.

Weiner, Myron. 1986. Labor Migrations as Incipient Diasporas. In *Modern Diasporas in International Politics,* ed. Gabriel Sheffer (pp. 47–74). London: Croom Helm.

Weiner, Myron. 1987. International Emigration and the Third World. In *Population in an Interacting World,* ed. William Alonso (pp. 173–200). Cambridge, Mass.: Harvard University Press.

Weiner, Myron. 1989. Asian Americans and American Foreign Policy. *Revue européenne des migrations internationales, 5*(1): 97–109.

Weiner, Myron. 1990, January. Immigration: Perspectives from Receiving Countries. *Third World Quarterly, 12*(1): 140–165.

Weiner, Myron. 1990. Asian Immigrants and U.S. Foreign Policy. In *Immigration and U.S. Foreign Policy,* ed. Robert W. Tucker, Charles B. Keely, and Linda Wrigley (pp. 192–213). Boulder, Colo.: Westview Press.

Weiner, Myron. 1990. The Indian Presence in America: What Difference Will It Make? In *Conflicting Images: India and the United States,* ed. Sulochana R. Glazer and Nathan Glazer (pp. 241–256). Glen Dale, Md.: Riverdale.

Weiner, Myron. 1992. Citizenship and Migration: Implications for Liberal Democracies. In *Civility and Citizenship in Liberal Democratic Societies,* ed. Edward Banfield (pp. 129–151). New York: Paragon House.

Weiner, Myron. 1992. International Population Movements: Implications for Foreign Policies and Migration Policies. In *Immigrants in Two Democracies: French and*

American Experience, ed. Donald L. Horowitz and Gerard Noiriel (pp. 439–461). New York: New York University Press.

Weiner, Myron. 1992. Peoples and States in a New Ethnic Order? *Third World Quarterly,* 13(2): 317–333.

Weiner, Myron (ed.). 1993. *International Migration and Security.* Boulder, Colo.: Westview Press.

Whelan, Frederick G. 1981, September. Citizenship and the Right to Leave. *American Political Science Review,* 75(3): 636–653.

Whelan, Frederick G. 1988. Citizenship and Freedom of Movement: An Open Admission Policy? In *Open Borders? Closed Societies? The Ethical and Political Issues,* ed. Mark Gibney (pp. 3–39). Westport, Conn.: Greenwood Press.

Widgren, Jonas. 1987. International Migration: New Challenges to Europe. *Migration News,* 2: 23–35.

Widgren, Jonas. 1989. Europe and International Migration in the Future. In *Refugees and International Relations,* ed. Gil Loescher and Laila Monahan (pp. 49–62). New York: Oxford University Press.

Widgren, Jonas. 1990, October. International Migration and Regional Stability. *International Affairs,* 66(4): 749–766.

Widgren, Jonas. 1992. *The Informal Consultations, 1985–1992.* Geneva: Intergovernmental Consultations.

Widgren, Jonas. 1992, March. The Need to Improve Coordination of European Asylum and Migration Policies. Address to the Conference of the Trier Academy of European Law, Trier, Germany.

Williams, Raymond Brady. 1988. *Religions of Immigrants from India and Pakistan: New Threads in the American Tapestry.* Cambridge: Cambridge University Press.

World Development Report, 1982. 1982. New York: Oxford University Press, published for the World Bank.

Yans-McLaughlin, Virginia (ed.). 1990. *Immigration Reconsidered: History, Sociology and Politics.* New York: Oxford University Press.

Zolberg, Aristide R. 1981. International Migrations in Political Perspective. In *Global Trends in Migration: Theory and Research on International Population Movements,* ed. Mary M. Kritz, Charles B. Keely, and Silvano M. Tomasi (pp. 3–27). New York: Center for Migration Studies.

Zolberg, Aristide R. 1987. Keeping Them Out: Ethical Dilemmas of Immigration Policy. In *International Ethics in the Nuclear Age,* ed. Robert J. Myers (pp. 261–298). Lanham, Md.: University Press of America.

Zolberg, Aristide R., and Astri Suhrke. 1984. Social Conflict and Refugees in the Third World: The Cases of Ethiopia and Afghanistan. Paper presented at the annual meeting of the American Political Science Association, Washington, D.C.

Zolberg, Aristide R., Astri Suhrke, and Sergio Aguayo. 1986, Summer. International Factors in the Formation of Refugee Movements. *International Migration Review,* 20(2): 151–169.

Zolberg, Aristide R., Astri Suhrke, and Sergio Aguayo. 1989. *Escape from Violence: Conflict and the Refugee Crisis in the Developing World.* Oxford: Oxford University Press.

Zucker, Norman L., and Naomi Flink Zucker. 1987. *The Guarded Gate: The Reality of American Refugee Policy.* San Diego: Harcourt Brace.

INDEX

THE GLOBAL MIGRATION CRISIS

Challenge to States and to Human Rights

MYRON WEINER

THE GLOBAL MIGRATION CRISIS examines the turbulence that has been caused by the worldwide increase of migration across national boundaries. Through its global perspective, the book considers the consequences of international migration and refugee flows for both developed and developing countries, focusing on how governments and their citizens define the problems posed by international migrations, including security issues and ethnic conflict. At the same time, the book also seriously evaluates the concerns of human rights advocates searching for greater global social justice and protecting those who flee persecution, violence, and poverty. Finally, THE GLOBAL MIGRATION CRISIS considers the ways in which movement of people across international boundaries is changing our understanding of the meaning of sovereignty.

ISBN 0-06-500232-6

90000

9 780065 002324